# A GOOD & FAITHFUL SERVANT

The life and times of
## Prof. John C. Whitcomb, Th.D.

by David C. Whitcomb, M.D., Ph.D.

First printing: April 2022

Master Books®, P.O. Box 726, Green Forest, AR 72638
Master Books® is a division of the New Leaf Publishing Group, Inc.

ISBN: 978-1-68344-264-6
Digital ISBN: 978-1-61458-804-7
Library of Congress Number: 2021952512

Cover by Diana Bogardus

Please consider requesting that a copy of this volume be purchased by your local library system.

**Printed in the United States of America**

Please visit our website for other great titles:
www.masterbooks.com

For information regarding author interviews,
please contact the publicity department at (870) 438-5288.

Master
Books®
A Division of New Leaf Publishing Group

# Contents

# Introduction

Baby boomers generally recognize that their fathers fought the Axis powers in the 1940s but seldom know the details. The Greatest Generation was also the Silent Generation.

My daughter Laura, while in junior high school, interviewed her grandfather about his WWII experiences as one of her class assignments. For the first time, I learned many fascinating details of my father's tour of duty as a soldier in Germany, including fighting in the Battle of the Bulge.

Beginning with a "fight to the death" stand in Marche, Belgium — just west of Bastogne — I began working with my father to document and describe the events of his life. As word of this effort leaked out to friends and family, we discovered great interest in his life and times *outside* of Germany — information that gave insights into how he became a world-changing teacher, theologian, and author. He was clearly an inspiration and role model to thousands and thousands of Christians throughout the world, and his life story is worth telling.

This volume covers the first half of his life, culminating in the publication of *The Genesis Flood* in 1961. Fortunately, I was able to work with my dad on every chapter — typically beginning with a 12–15 page draft that was returned with innumerable edits and comments to be corrected before addressing the content. He also called me every Sunday afternoon, asking briefly how my wife, Chris, and I were doing followed by "I hate to ask, but how is the biography coming?" He became increasingly excited about the project as it took shape. He did not want it to focus on him, but rather what God did for him and through him.

This volume was completed while my father was alive, so the text reflects his state at the time. On January 18, 2020, I drove from Pittsburgh, Pennsylvania, to Indianapolis, Indiana, to the house of my brother Don and his wife, Kim, who were caring for my dad and his wife, Norma. The reason was to hand him a completed copy of the manuscript. He was overwhelmed. In contrast, I was just thankful for the rich experience of getting to know my dad better.

Dad immediately began editing the final chapters. At 10:00 p.m. on February 4, 2020, my brother heard him working and entered his living area to see why he was awake so much later than usual. Dad turned to him, handed him an edited chapter, and said, "Here, I am now finished!" He then went to bed and awoke in heaven.

I have been a successful physician, scientist, professor, and entrepreneur, a career for which I thank God. But, from my perspective, generating this biography is the most rewarding, fulfilling, and important achievement of my life. I learned that I am not my father, nor is anyone else. However, the life story and example of this man of God will be of great interest to those who knew him personally and will be a great inspiration to those who never met him.

# Section 1

# Life and Legacy

# Chapter 1

# The Man

"A Good and Faithful Servant"
June 22, 1924, to the present

I have known my father for 60 years, but I never knew him until I carefully studied his life and the world in which he lived. This is a story that must be told.

Growing up as an undifferentiated kid, I often heard the comment, "Do you know who your father is?" Of course, I would always say, "Yes!" But this one-word answer only related to my limited perspective as his child. The rest of the story, told below, is amazing.

My father became internationally known after co-authoring *The Genesis Flood* with Henry Morris, Ph.D. After reading and reviewing it several times, it continues to impress me as a remarkable and powerful book — one that very few other people could have written. And I wondered how he did it.

The story of Professor Whitcomb's life begins in Chapter 4. But before diving into the times and circumstances of his life, it is important to provide insights into who he is as a man, the impact of *The Genesis Flood* book on Christian thought, and his legacy as a theologian and teacher.

## Personal Observations

It is a strange task to write a biography on one's own father. The account must be complete and accurate, critically analyzing the characteristics and responses to challenges that contributed to making him a man greatly used by God. But it must be accurate and real, balancing the positives and negatives so that the story is true. The work must also provide insights into his person and personality, which stands in contrast to other people, including me. I begin the story talking about my father as "dad" or "father." Later, however, I refer to him by his given name, or nicknames, to help maintain objectivity.

I will be the first to admit that I am very different from my father in personality, temperament, and abilities. One major difference is that I am dyslexic; I struggle to read, am unable to spell simple words, and am continually grappling with illegible handwriting. This made written communication with my father challenging, since he is an exceptional writer and editor. He would return my handwritten documents of thoughtful expressions covered with red pencil markings, including lines to the margins to correct misspelled words or grammatical errors in gorgeous handwriting.

Another difference between my father and me is in organization and attention to detail. He kept a diary almost every day of his life since age 11 years (~30,000 pages). Furthermore, he saved every letter that he received and filed them carefully for future reference. His desk always appeared cluttered with stacks of papers — giving the appearance of total chaos; but unlike my cluttered desk, he could immediately find any item he needed within seconds, whether on his desk or carefully tucked away in a filing cabinet for safekeeping. He continually organized and checked his things.

Dad loves people. This fascinated me for several reasons. First, he expresses interest in everyone, not just the Very Important People (VIPs). This interest is genuine and attested to by all who know him. Second, he cared about people and would give someone his bus money and walk home if he saw that it would meet a real need. Third, his relationships with people were natural. His graciousness and gentleness and compassion were from his heart and soul. He had no prejudices or malice, but he was not a fool either — knowing the nature of fallen man's heart, the difference between right and wrong, and the schemes of the enemy. But he had very few close friends, people that he relied on, confided in, and with whom he spent his free time.

I talked to him from time to time about his broad (international) circle of friends and acquaintances. Being dyslexic, language and communication can be challenging and stressful, and I tended to be more comfortable as a loner. So I asked him why he is continually reaching out to friends and strangers, and especially Christian believers. His response was that he cares about people because God loves them. Jesus Christ Himself showed His love for people while walking on the earth, and He died on the Cross for people who did not know Him and hated Him. Jesus demonstrated how to love people. And God's program today is about people and about the truth.

Physically, my dad displays unusual strength and endurance, excellent physical health, and an ability to focus on complex problems while ignoring distractions — characteristics that I did inherit. So, in those ways I can relate to him. But these features are not the essence of a man, nor can they explain his life and accomplishments.

My father is a man of deep conviction, a characteristic I believe that I share — although I do not communicate my convictions with the grace and thoughtfulness with which my father is naturally blessed. Although he never wavers on the fundamental principles that he tightly holds, he hates controversy and avoids confrontations unless forced into it by duty or circumstances. This is not to say that he is totally passive. But his preferred way is to wait for the right moment and then provide a well-timed and targeted comment that perfectly captures the situation and exposes the problems and errors — delivered as inoffensively and constructively as possible. When he speaks, he is correct in the facts, accurate in his assessment, and insightful in his perspectives. This skill reveals the fact that his convictions are based on diligent study guided by a brilliant mind and total commitment to the service of his Lord.

Dad never aspired to leadership positions. In fact, he often confided that he felt inadequate and unqualified for leadership positions because he was not raised in a Christian home and was missing some critical components that leaders required. Nobody that knew him agreed, but that was his view. Nevertheless, he continually demonstrated biblical leadership as described by our Lord Jesus Christ in Matthew 20:25–28:

> ". . . you know that the rulers of the Gentiles lord it over them, and their great men exercise authority over them. It is not this way among you, but whoever wishes to become great among you shall be your servant, and whoever wishes to be first among you shall be your slave; just as the Son of Man did not come to be served, but to serve. . ." (NASB 1995).

The aversion to positions of administrative leadership might also reflect another facet of his personality. While confident in the things that he thoroughly studied, he appeared uncomfortable speaking or taking action in areas that he had not yet mastered. Administrative leaders cannot know all of the details of all areas of their responsibilities. At times they need to take decisive action based on the best available evidence and instinct. They also must fire incompetent or disruptive people, or terminate good people because of organizational or budgetary reasons — an action that may be devastating for the individual being fired. My perception is that emotionally, my dad's compassion for people conflicted with administrative responsibilities, and that while he supported decisive actions based on administrative principles, he could not pull the trigger.

When conflicts or controversies arose in areas that were outside of his area of expertise, he preferred to defer to others that he believed were "experts." He avoided taking on new responsibilities or becoming entangled in these situations.

He preferred to keep is eyes focused on the divine rather than the mundane. He did not want to be distracted by petty arguments, employment contracts, maintenance issues of the physical buildings and campus, finances, fund raising, etc.

At other times, I believe, my father fell into the dilemma articulated by Plato, "One of the penalties for refusing to participate in politics is that you end up being governed by your inferiors."[1] But he often accepted a lesser role so that the precious moments of his life could fully focus on much higher, eternal goals.

## A Man with Four Fathers

Great leaders fascinate my father. He loves history. He met many great men that *made* history! And he respected men with great leadership skills. He also valued the time and effort of the great men that taught him personally and guided him — especially through dedicated father-son type relationships.

Four men fulfilled the role of "father" in my dad's life: a biological father, a spiritual father, a theological father, and a scientific father. A

---

1. Plato (c. 428–347 B.C.), *Republic*, Book 1, 347c. An alternate translation is "The punishment which the wise suffer who refuse to take part in the government is to live under the government of worse men." From https://wist.info/plato/3168/, accessed August 21, 2012.

brief introduction to these four great men will serve as a backdrop to the development of Professor Whitcomb in all key areas of his life.

## 1. Biological Father

Professor Whitcomb grew up in a godless home that focused on the advancement of his own father to a high office in the U.S. Army. Moving constantly with new assignments precluded the opportunity to develop hometown roots and lifelong friends. He spent much time alone — exploring the world in books and magazines. By nature and personality, Professor Whitcomb was always a "book person." His father, on the other hand, was a "man's man" who loved competition and the outdoors where a real man could battle the elements. He loved competitive sports, prize fighting, and the Army. Although my father and grandfather were, by personality, like oil and water, they learned to love and respect each other for who they were. My father recalls:

> As I look back over ninety years in God's world, I am amazed and humbled to think of all the men He has used to prepare me for Christian ministry. Although he was not a believer during my early years, my biological father, Col. John C. Whitcomb (a West Point graduate and Chief of Staff, 90th Division, under Gen. George Patton in Europe, 1944–1945), taught me discipline, respect for those in authority, and comprehension of the world outside of the USA — especially China, Europe, and Latin America.[2]

My grandfather rescued my dad from a failing high school in rural Georgia and sent him to McCallie Military Academy in Chattanooga, Tennessee, for his junior and senior years. This proved to be a turning point in his life academically, resulting in acceptance into Princeton University, where he graduated with honors. The U.S. Government interrupted his college education to fight against the Nazis in WWII, including deploying him to face German Tiger Tanks in the Battle of the Bulge. But while at Princeton, he met his spiritual father, Donald B. Fullerton.

## 2. Spiritual Father

A remarkable man, Donald Fullerton led my father to the Lord during his freshman year at Princeton on February 13, 1942. He continued

---

2. Written by John C. Whitcomb for the biography on June 3, 2016.

to disciple my father after the war. His impact on the life of my father cannot be overestimated, as he mentored and guided him as a student leader of the Princeton Evangelical Fellowship, and on to seminary. Dad recalls the impact of Dr. Fullerton:

> In God's marvelous providence, Dr. Donald Fullerton, a Princeton University graduate, class of 1913, and a veteran missionary (India, Pakistan, and Afghanistan), was permitted to teach the Bible on Sunday afternoons at Murray-Dodge Hall. During my first year at the university (1942–43), he led me to a saving knowledge of our Lord Jesus Christ. Thus, he became my spiritual "father." He wrote to me on July 8, 1970, "Dear Jack, my 'beloved son,' " following the example of the Apostle Paul who referred to Timothy as his "true son in the faith" (1 Tim. 1:2).[3]

## 3. Theological Father

After Princeton my father entered Grace Theological Seminary in Winona Lake, Indiana. He dedicated himself to mastering the Bible and theology in order to be equipped to be a missionary in China. But the door to China closed to all Western missionaries. However, the Founder and President of Grace Theological Seminary, Alva J. McClain Th.D., recognized the heart and mind of my father and urged him to stay on as faculty. The time and mentoring of Professor McClain as a scholar and theologian served as a model that my father sought to emulate.

> After graduating from Princeton University (1948), I was carefully and systematically taught Christian theology and Bible prophecy by Dr. Alva J. McClain, President of Grace Theological Seminary, Winona Lake, Indiana. To this extent, at least, I consider him to have been my "theological father." During my senior year he assisted me in preparing a 120-page book, *The History of Grace Theological Seminary*, 1931–1951, which included a very valuable thirty-page analysis of "The Background and Origin of Grace Theological Seminary.[4]

---

3. Written by John C. Whitcomb for the biography on June 3, 2016.
4. Ibid.

The time spent with Dr. McClain learning the inside details about battles for the faith and taking a stand on biblical principles, while abounding in grace, became invaluable lessons for Professor Whitcomb. Another great man, Cornelius Van Til, Th.D., whom my father came to know during a two-week summer course, helped him develop a presuppositional approach to apologetics (see Chapter 17), which was critical to the writing of *The Genesis Flood*, and beyond. Perhaps Van Til could be considered my father's "theological uncle."

## 4. Scientific Father

My father also had the highest regard for his dear friend and colleague, Henry Morris, Ph.D. Morris gave a guest lecture at Grace Theological Seminary in September 1953, arguing that the geological landscape reflected a universal Flood, and that such an event is described in Genesis. This provided a better framework for understanding everything that we see on earth today. My father agreed with this perspective, especially after carefully examining the whole of Scriptures and finding the Bible to be absolutely consistent with six literal days for the world's creation, and later global destruction with a Flood. This became his Th.D. thesis. Although my dad reached out to a number of Christian leaders for help in articulating the scientific arguments, it was Henry Morris who responded and offered essential assistance. While the training of Whitcomb and Morris was vastly different as a theologian and a scientist, their convictions were aligned. A joint effort which addressed the issues of the Bible and evolutionary science became *The Genesis Flood*. Dad recalls:

> During my first two years as a professor at Grace Seminary (1951–1953), I had wrestled with the popular "gap theory" of Genesis 1:1–2, which postulated a global flood and total darkness because of the fall of Satan before the six days of creation.[5] But Dr. Morris pointed out very clearly that the trillions of plants and animals we find in horizontal layers around the world were formed during the year-long, mountain-covering Flood of Noah's day. It was the enormous hydrodynamic work of this deluge (see Matthew 24:37–39

5. Cf. J.C. Whitcomb, *The Early Earth* (Winona Lake, IN: BMH Books, 2010), 113–130.

and 2 Peter 3:6) that wiped out millions of years of earth history which the "gap theory" assumed. I was profoundly impacted by the biblical and geological perspectives of this "father" whom God brought into my life and ministry.[6]

The respect and honor that my father gave to these men was genuine. He never aspired to leadership positions, positions of power, or positions of great influence. He preferred to identify extraordinary men of purpose and virtue and follow in their shadows.

As time passes, great men pass away. When he himself was recruited to replace Dr. McClain as President of Grace Seminary, he declined. He never considered himself an organizational leader, but rather a teacher, a preacher, an analyst, an advisor, and a servant.

## Happy Thoughts!

Dad, on a few occasions, quoted the following verse to me, and I believe this is a verse he lived by, "Finally, brethren, whatsoever things are true, whatsoever things are honest, whatsoever things are just, whatsoever things are pure, whatsoever things are lovely, whatsoever things are of good report; if there be any virtue, and if there be any praise, think on these things" (Philippians 4:8; KJV).

Knowing God; knowing that you are called by Him to His service; being filled with faith and hope; and abiding on the things that are true, honest, pure, and lovely leads to being a happy man! And, I admit, Dad is among the happiest men I've ever known.

Two visions dominate my memory. The first is his sense of humor, and the second is seeing him break out into songs of joy — played by whistling through his hands. But his humor stands out as the greater measure of his life.

Those who know my father recognize his great sense of humor. My grandfather, John C. Whitcomb Sr., likely influenced my father's appreciation for specific types of humor, since John Whitcomb Sr.'s nickname was "Whit," reflecting his quick wit. My dad loves plays on words, clever puns, hyperbole, understatement, paradox, and irony. These "gems" filtered into his writing, teaching, and preaching, and I believe that he thoroughly enjoyed all of them despite having many clever quips sail over the heads of his audience.

---

6. Written by John C. Whitcomb for the biography on June 3, 2016.

# The Man

Before we met, my wife Chris visited some friends who were attending Grace Seminary and took the opportunity to sit in on one of my father's lectures. She really enjoyed the Bible teaching but came away with two stark impressions. First, she thought that Professor Whitcomb was hilarious, but the class showed almost no reaction as they diligently scribed his statements as notes in their syllabus. Second, she kept wondering if the professor had a son, and what he might be like. I hope she was not disappointed.

As a child, I remember times at the supper table laughing and laughing when interesting topics came under the scrutiny of various family members who began popping comments known as "Whitcomb humor." Guests, at times, sat bewildered, not understanding the barrage of ambiguous comments or enjoying the nuances of clever puns. Dad loved it!

My sister Connie recalls the first night that her future husband joined the Whitcomb family for dinner.[7] "When Mark [Rosendahl] first joined our family dinner discussions, he found it challenging to join the developing conversations. Mark decided to just sit back and enjoy it all. I especially found it remarkable because [Dad's] humor was always immediate, appropriate, and never at anyone else's expense. Being such a distinguished dignitary, he used his humor to set his guests at ease. I always found that to be one of his hallmarks of humility."

Connie also remembers a day when Dad was being shown some new property purchased by his sister-in-law Willie and her husband Sib (Chapter 13). Noting a freshly planted flower bed, he turned to Sib and remarked, "I see the ground is producing flowers *by the sweat of your Frau*."[8]

Connie noted that his joy was linked to his faith in a sovereign God. She noted, "I believe his humor represented a deep reliance on the grace and providence of God. His life was not without sorrows and disappointments, but he was able to trust God, transcend the darkness, enjoy the beauty and wonder of Creation, and share that joy with others."[9]

---

7. The story was sent by email to the author on May 2, 2016.
8. Dr. Whitcomb was alluding to Genesis 3:17–19: "Cursed is the ground because of you; through painful toil you will eat food from it all the days of your life. It will produce thorns and thistles for you, and you will eat the plants of the field. *By the sweat of your brow* you will eat your food until you return to the ground" (NIV; emphasis added). The word *Frau* is German for a married woman or wife — teasing that he had his wife do the work rather than him.
9. Constance Salome Whitcomb [Rosendahl], the third of four children, and the only girl of Professor Whitcomb, was born on October 14, 1958. She lives in Moscow, Idaho, with her husband, Mark. They have five children.

The youngest of the Whitcomb children, Bob, who performs juggling and speaks at youth retreats and prison ministries and other events, also learned from Dad's example. "Growing up and seeing Dad speaking in front of groups with such comfort and speaking with such a kind, friendly manner with humor mixed with truth is what inspired me [for these ministries]."[10]

Another example of "Whitcomb humor" comes from my own experience. During an interview of a young woman for inclusion or exclusion in a research study, I asked what her occupation was. She stated, "I am a student at the Pittsburgh Institute of Culinary Arts." I jotted down "P.I.C.A." Tapping my finger on the initials, I said, "PICA, I bet they make a mean mud pie!" — and I broke out in a big grin since *pica* is the medical term for "eating dirt." The girl replied, "You must like chocolate desserts," since there is a dessert called a mud pie. I nodded yes because it was true. The joke was a pun. The girl, not being a medical person, only recognized the statement as a compliment. I believe my father would note that even alluding to the second option would be "distasteful."

Dad often used jokes to make his points while teaching or preaching. In thinking through the dilemma of how Noah and his family could manage all of the animals in the Ark for a year during the Flood of Genesis chapters 6–9, dad hypothesized that they went into hibernation. The evidence he gave is that "the animals went into the Ark two-by-two, and a year later came out two-by-two, *including the rabbits!*" To me, this is his signature joke.

## Jack is Kind, Patient, and Forgiving

Professor Whitcomb's wife and old friends call him by his boyhood nickname, Jack. A few of them provided some observations about him. The greatest insights come from his wife, Norma.

Norma is his second wife, as Edisene, who was my mother and his first wife, died in 1969 of primary biliary cirrhosis (Chapter 16). Norma became a widow in 1968 after her husband, a doctoral student at Grace Seminary, died of a heart attack at age 40, leaving her with two children. On January 1, 1971, Jack and Norma married and have been together for nearly 50 years.

---

10. Robert Edward Whitcomb (Bob) was born on August 24, 1960, in Warsaw, Indiana. He lives in Orlando, Florida.

Norma related a story that remains precious to her because it indicated the kind of man her new husband would be.

> One week after our marriage, we flew to Arizona for a week of meetings. I packed the suitcases, as I had done when Robert (my first husband) and I traveled. What a surprise when I opened the suit bag at the motel. The jackets were on the hangers, but no trousers. Robert always put jacket and trousers on the same hanger. Jack hung them separately. Of course, I was horrified to have to tell my new husband what happened. It was then that I found out what a kind, patient, and forgiving husband God had given me. His response was, "That's alright. We will buy some trousers."[11]

This memory of Norma seems like a small thing to me but, according to my wife, is very meaningful to a woman, and especially a new wife.

I also asked Norma to write a list of words that summarize Dad's personality and characteristics — a "word cloud." There were many. "Unassuming, mild, compassionate, kind-hearted, forgiving, gracious, gentle, lenient, charitable, human, spiritual, pleasant, obliging, yielding, pleasing, brilliant, certain, honest, reserved, mellow, dependable, backer, bright, merciful, unintentional, peacemaker, different, retiring, modest, compliant, submissive, courteous, agreeable, amenable, quiet, peaceful, harmonious, genial, sacrificing, disorganized, clutterer, calm, composed, pacifying, reputable, temperate, delightful."

My sister Connie listed only a few, but with significant overlap with Norma: "Personable, gospel-oriented, intelligent, wise, thoughtful, humble, caring, selfless, gracious, God-fearing."

## A Man of Faith

One example of my father's faith stands with vivid clarity in my childhood memories. My mother suffered from a rare autoimmune disease called primary biliary cirrhosis, although the diagnosis was never made in her lifetime. Every effort was made to find a doctor who could make a diagnosis and offer a cure. During these difficult years he never wavered from his complete trust in God's sovereignty and goodness.

One day, in the mid 1960s, as my mother's health spiraled downward while in a hospital, and as the limited family resources dwindled,

---

11. Email to the author on March 16, 2016.

my father called his children together and told us that he was out of money and he needed $155 to pay on a debt that day. He asked us all to pray with him to the Lord.

In the early afternoon the U.S. Post Office driver on rural route #8 swung by our house and dropped the mail into the mailbox. I ran to retrieve the letters and to bring them to my dad. As he began opening them his eyebrows raised, and he said something like, "God has answered our prayers!"

Among the letters was a personal note from an old student. The letter stated that Dad had lent him some money, but he never repaid it. The man remembered the debt, wrote a short note, and stuffed it into an envelope along with a personal check. The check was for exactly the amount needed to pay the debt. Happily, we got into the old Ford station wagon and went to the bank with my dad to deposit the check and pay the debt in full.

Dad never mentioned this again, but I never forgot his faith, and God's answer to prayer — to the penny.

## Others' Perspectives

Great men and Christian leaders who knew Professor Whitcomb at various times of his life have valuable perspectives that are presented here.

### Judge Paul Pressler

Judge Paul Pressler, a graduate of Princeton University like my father, became a freshman and a member of Princeton Evangelical Fellowship (PEF) the fall following my father's graduation in 1948. In a letter to me about some details of PEF, Judge Pressler noted,

> With regard to your father, I did not know him well, but I stood in awe of him, his intellectuality, and his faithful testimony for our Lord Jesus Christ. I did not get to Princeton until 1948 and so your father was long gone by the time I arrived on the scene. Everything I heard about your father was wonderful. Mr. Fullerton[12] admired him as he admired few people. He never had anything but good things to say about

---

12. Donald B. Fullerton was the founder and leader of the Princeton Evangelical Fellowship and the man who led John Whitcomb to Christ. See Chapter 11, "Mr. F."

your father and he is one of only a few people like that. All of the attendees at the PEF considered your father a tremendous leader and we were in awe when his name was spoken. I always felt that he was both quiet and outgoing. He was a leader.[13]

## A Connecticut Pastor

George Zeller arrived at Grace Seminary in 1972. He came to Grace Seminary primarily because of Dad, having heard some cassette tapes of him speaking, and being familiar with *The Genesis Flood*. He completed his doctoral work with Dad and then became pastor of Middletown Bible Church in Middletown, Connecticut. A close friendship developed, and Dad made annual trips to teach at their Bible conferences from 1974 to 2010. There were multiple attributes that greatly impressed George Zeller, with two highlighted here, beginning with his teaching abilities.

> Dr. Whitcomb was a remarkable teacher. He taught much like he preaches. He was always well prepared. His course on apologetics was so helpful to many. He was a great theology teacher. He was a worthy successor to Alva Mc-Clain [teaching on the kingdom and on eschatology]. I tried to take every "Whitcomb course" possible, and most of my friends did the same.[14]

A second attribute is his continuous passion for reaching the lost. Zeller recalls that Winona Lake, Indiana, where Grace Theological Seminary was located, did not have a commercial airport. The closest airport was in Fort Wayne, Indiana, about 30 miles east. So various students and volunteers would often shuttle people back and forth from the airport. Zeller, and others, took advantage of this situation, since it provided an hour of "captive" time with busy professors, such as John Whitcomb. At least one recurring event sticks in his mind. Zeller

---

13. Paul Pressler was a prominent Texas lawyer, legislator, and judge, becoming Justice of the 14th Court of Appeals. Pressler, as a strong, Bible-believing conservative Christian and member of the Southern Baptist Convention, helped reverse a trend toward liberal theology, back to the Bible-believing basics. His account is documented in the book, *A Hill on Which to Die: One Southern Baptist's Journey*, (Nashville, TN: Broadman & Holman Publishers, 1999).
14. Email from Dr. George Zeller to the author on October 24, 2015.

writes, "I'd pick him up from the airport and as we would go through the gate to pay for parking, he would always have a tract handy and say, 'Here George, give him (or her) this tract.' "[15]

This practice of reaching out to the lost by giving tracts to everyone continues today. In his late eighties Dad bought a hat that says, "WWII Veteran." He always puts it on when going to the store or a restaurant, and inevitably people come up to him and say, "Thank you for your service." He would smile and say, "I have something for you!" and he would give them a tract with the words "You are Special" on the front.

During December 2014, Dad came to Pittsburgh to celebrate Christmas with our family. Since he loves Chinese food, we took him out to dinner. Afterward he asked the waitress if he could meet her colleagues and the cooks. He greeted them, noting that he grew up in China, and gave them his favorite tracts. They thanked him and said, "We remember you! You gave us some nice tracts when we worked in Indianapolis!"

*A Chance Encounter*

My wife, Chris, and I had the privilege of visiting Jerusalem, Israel, on several occasions. We made a special effort to visit the Garden Tomb where many believe Jesus was buried and rose again. On one occasion, as we approached the open door, a figure emerged from the darkness into the bright sunlight, filling the narrow entrance. The man was dressed in white, with snow-white hair. His face emanated a warm familiarity. As his eyes turned toward us, he called out, "Dave and Chris Whitcomb!"

It was John Willett, our former pastor from Columbus, Ohio, and a graduate of Grace Theological Seminary. More than 30 years had passed since we last talked. But on that day, John led a church group from Greenville, North Carolina, to the Holy Land, and to the tomb.

After a moment he continued, "How is your dad?"

"He is doing well," I responded. "He is still writing and doing radio broadcast at age 89."

"Did you know," John continued, "that I think of him every day. The example of his life is written on my heart and soul."

John Willett came to Christ as a Naval Officer in 1967. He left the Navy to study at Grace Theological Seminary from 1969 to 1972. As a

---

15. Ibid.

new Christian he appreciated the excellent teaching of the professors but noted that one stood out profoundly — Dr. Whitcomb. He specifically recalled:

> His knowledge of the history of the total world situation as the Bible unfolds was extraordinary! His teaching style was totally engaging — he made the Bible live in a way that pierced your heart! I feel that for my 45 years in ministry my style is very much like his! His fingerprints are all over me!! I took every course that he taught. I even said, "If he taught a course in nursery rhymes, I'd take it!" He was that profound![16]

John Willett went on to full-time Christian work as a pastor, a teacher, and staff member of SEARCH Ministries.[17] He sought to follow Christ, by following the example of his beloved seminary professor, John Whitcomb.

## Peter Masters

On July 30, 2013, I had the privilege of meeting with Dr. Masters in his office in London, England, at the Metropolitan Tabernacle, a legacy of Charles Haddon Spurgeon. He reflected on the many years that they had corresponded, times that Professor Whitcomb traveled to London to teach in the School of Theology, and theological issues that they addressed together.

Dr. Masters noted he and Professor Whitcomb had an unlikely relationship, based on different doctrinal positions on eschatology. Professor Whitcomb is a strong pretribulation, premillennialist, while Dr. Master's position is clearly amillennial. Dr. Masters noted that Professor Whitcomb was always gracious and avoided making any differences on issues during his lectures in England, as they were united on so many fundamental doctrines. Professor Whitcomb, on the other hand, remembers a private conversation with Dr. Masters in which he noted that, indeed, Spurgeon himself was a premillennial dispensationalist. "Yes," Dr. Masters acknowledged, "even the great Charles Spurgeon had temporary lapses in logic."

Dr. Masters first contacted Professor Whitcomb in 1979 at the urging of Henry Morris, Ph.D, while teaching at the School of Theology.

---

16. John Willett, email to the author on September 29, 2016.
17. Greensboro, NC. http://www.searchministries.org/searchgreensboro/.

Dr. Morris's endorsement was that there was no one better equipped and knowledgeable on both the scientific and biblical issues surrounding Genesis than Professor Whitcomb. So contact was made, and the relationship began.

Dr. Masters noted that, while Dr. Whitcomb provided outstanding teaching on Genesis and presuppositional approaches with Scripture over secondary evidences, the greatest contribution to the work at the Metropolitan Tabernacle came from discussions on biblical separation. The concept was well illustrated with a diagram of fellowship within circles of truth. The example was a systematic and insightful evaluation of the case of Fuller Seminary, leading to sub-biblical thinking. The case was documented in a carefully prepared syllabus that was filled with valuable insights that presented a compelling case. What was more remarkable was that the tone of the writing was without rancor or malaise. It was a document to provide understanding and to teach truth, without attacks on people or personalities. This, Dr. Masters concluded, was one of the most important contributions to the leaders of the Metropolitan Tabernacle as they worked their way through some perilous times.

Beyond the technical theological details, Dr. Masters was impressed by several characteristics that have been highlighted by others: Prof. Whitcomb was unfailingly affable and friendly to everyone. He was never self-conscious, self-serving, or self-promoting. But he revealed his nature of paying careful attention to detail by filling his teachings with insightful, memorable, and often humorous facts that typically were not noticed by others. He revealed profound knowledge of the subject matter. In addition, the staff at Metropolitan Tabernacle appreciated the precision of his presentations such that a direct transcription of his lectures resulted in text that was nearly ready for publication as a manuscript or book.

## Character

The few snapshots of John Whitcomb's personality and character fail to tell the full story. They are intended to provide a backdrop for other stories of struggles, hardships, and successes. In short, it is the story of a unique man that God raised up and molded into a good and faithful servant to stay true to his convictions and forever change the Christian world.

# Chapter 2

# Impact of *The Genesis Flood*

A Watershed
1961 to the Present

It is amazing how a singular event can symbolize a person's life and legacy. Martin Luther nailed "95 Theses" to the door of the Wittenberg Castle church on October 31, 1517. Thomas Edison lit the first light bulb on October 22, 1879. Albert Einstein published the equation $E=mc^2$ on September 27, 1905. Neil Armstrong set his left boot on the surface of the moon on July 21, 1969. These acts and events, in themselves, such as posting an announcement on a door, turning on a light, publishing a scientific paper, and stepping on the ground, are common in human history. But the historical context and the implications of the specific act of these extraordinary individuals elevated a "common event" into an historic one, recognized as a watershed[1] event that divides history into times "before" and "after." Great men become recognized through both the content and context of their actions. They accomplished something that subsequently became recognized as a solution to a fundamental problem or served as a catalyst to change the world.

John C. Whitcomb Jr. and Henry M. Morris, with their publication of *The Genesis Flood* in 1961, defined their legacy in history. This book became a watershed in both theology and science for a number of important reasons, including changing the worldview of millions of

---

1. A watershed is a line along a ridge of a mountain where a drop of water will flow in one of two opposite directions and ending in two different oceans, depending on which side of the ridge it falls. It can also refer to a historic event that changes thinking or practices from before to after the event.

25

people. But before exploring the life and times of John C. Whitcomb Jr., it is useful to put the book's impact into perspective — not focusing on the arguments and hypotheses, but rather on how it changed the entire fields of theology and science.

## The Book

*The Genesis Flood* is a 518-page analysis of the biblical and scientific evidence for the divine creation of the world and a global Flood from the perspective of a literal reading of the Bible.[2] The first edition was published in 1961 by John C. Whitcomb Jr., Th.D., and Henry Morris, Ph.D., as a follow-up of Dr. Whitcomb's Th.D. thesis entitled, *"The Genesis Flood: An investigation of its geographical extent, geological effects and chronological settings."*[3] *The Genesis Flood* also included multiple chapters on flood geology and scientific evidences revised and expanded from draft chapters of a future book being written by Dr. Morris. (This book was never published but mostly folded into *The Genesis Flood.*)

Major Christian publishing companies rejected the original manuscript, in part because of its length and highly technical content, and in part because of concerns that it would be highly controversial. Indeed, the central thesis and arguments stood in sharp opposition to both the secular theory of evolution, and the prevailing Christian concept of the gap theory, an attempt to fit the theory of evolution into the supposed "gap" between Genesis 1:1 and Genesis 1:2. Charles Craig, president of the small Presbyterian and Reformed Publishing Company in New

---

2. **Hermeneutics** is the branch of theology that deals with the methodological principles of interpretation of Scripture. **Exegesis** is focused on the text only, whereas hermeneutics includes contextual information. The *historical-grammatical method*, used in *The Genesis Flood*, seeks to understand the author's original meaning — based on the premise that the original Scriptures are directly communicated from God and, in the original text, are both authoritative (i.e., God says) and inerrant. In contrast, the *historical-critical method* of hermeneutics (i.e., higher criticism) is philosophical interpretation based on what the interpreter believed the author was thinking based on the author's historical setting, cultural influences, and political intent — and therefore is not inerrant or ultimately authoritative. The *allegorical method* seeks to find a spiritual meaning behind an illustrative (but non-historical) Bible story, so the Bible, from this perspective, does not mean what it says.

3. John C. Whitcomb Jr., "The Genesis Flood: An Investigation of Its Geographical Extent, Geological Effects and Chronological Settings." Submitted in partial fulfillment of the requirements for Doctor of Theology, Grace Theological Seminary, May 1957, 452 pages.

Jersey, finally published the book in 1961. From a humble beginning, *The Genesis Flood* grew in reputation and effects, becoming the catalyst of the modern Creation Movement and forcing major changes in the theory of evolution.

*The Genesis Flood* became one of the most important Christian books of the 20th century.[4] Despite a slow start, it went through nearly 40 reprints and sales approaching half a million copies. Over the past 50+ years, many book reviews critically evaluated the arguments set forth in *The Genesis Flood*, including a Master of Theology thesis that reviewed the reviews![5]

The authors' premise was that God created the heavens and earth in six days, as literally stated in Genesis chapters 1–3 and that He destroyed the world through a global Flood, except for people and animals in Noah's Ark, as described in detail in Genesis chapters 8–11. They argued that this literal interpretation was consistently carried throughout the entire Scripture, including the teachings of Jesus, and that no other interpretation was ever considered by the authors of the 66 books of the Bible. Secondly, they argued that the appearance and state of the physical universe, and especially the earth, are consistent with the creation/deluge history in Genesis, as demonstrated by principles of physics, especially hydrodynamics, geology, and global geography.

A literal interpretation of Genesis as the premise of *The Genesis Flood* did not originate with Whitcomb. Likewise, the geological arguments for a global Flood, such as fossils on top of mountains, began long before Morris. However, the confident, unapologetic approach and careful, detailed content of *The Genesis Flood* sparked intense responses in the hearts and minds of laymen, clergy, and scientists, both in support and rejection of the thesis and evidences. Whitcomb's approach was to avoid any arguments based on his own expert opinion as an academic theologian and instead to use his technical skills to determine exactly what *God said*, based on careful exegesis of the Hebrew and Greek text within the context of the entire Scriptures from Genesis to Revelation. Nothing more — nothing less. His demonstration of how to use *inductive* reasoning based on Scripture alone, rather than *deductive* reasoning

---

4. William J. Peterson and Randy Peterson, *100 Christian Books That Changed the Century*, Revell (October 1, 2000), 224 pages.
5. Charles Clough, "A Calm Appraisal of THE GENESIS FLOOD," Th.M. Thesis, Dallas Theological Seminary, 1968, 196 pages.

based on extrabiblical evidences proved to be both the correct approach and compelling — setting the standard for Christian Bible study and apologetics for the future. Without doubt, the arguments forced the reshaping of the worldview of millions of Christians.

Before discussing the impact of *The Genesis Flood* on Christian doctrine and the theory of natural evolution, it is necessary to define the context. Specifically, to whom was the book written and from what perspective did the various responses arise?

## Jesus and the Sadducees

Consider the confrontation between Jesus and the Sadducees in Matthew 22:23–33. The Sadducees and Pharisees were the two leading religious political parties of Jesus' time. The Sadducees were politically and theologically liberal, i.e., the Scriptures *could* mean *anything,* and it has no divine authority. The Pharisees were politically and theologically conservative, i.e., the Scriptures came directly from God and are to be obeyed to the letter.

Although the Sadducees did not believe in the resurrection of the dead (Matthew 22:23), they posed a trap question to Jesus to highlight what they believed proved the absurdity of the idea of a resurrection. The question centered on a story about a woman who married a man who then died. Jewish law required that the man's brother marry the widow to provide children for his dead brother and continue his legacy. In the story, seven brothers sequentially married the same woman and died. Then the woman died. Their question was, "In the resurrection, therefore, whose wife of the seven will she be? For they all had married her" (verse 28; NASB 1995).

Jesus answered them in the following way,

> "You are mistaken, not understanding the Scriptures nor the power of God. For in the resurrection they neither marry nor are given in marriage but are like angels in heaven. But regarding the resurrection of the dead, have you not read what was spoken to you by God: 'I AM THE GOD OF ABRAHAM, AND THE GOD OF ISAAC, AND THE GOD OF JACOB'? He is not the God of the dead but of the living." When the crowds heard *this,* they were astonished at His teaching" (Matthew 22:29–33; NASB 1995).

This answer is instructive on at least three levels. First, He pointed out the Sadducees' fundamental problem, "You are mistaken, not understanding the Scriptures nor the power of God." Second, He solved their riddle by *correctly* using the Scriptures to demonstrate life after death. Third, He was not intending to convince the *Sadducees* with His answer — but *the crowds*! Jesus' answer was irrelevant to the Sadducees since they did not really care about the details of who was married to whom at the resurrection since they were unbelievers and rejected a literal interpretation of the Scriptures. However, Jesus' answer *was* important to the crowds, many of whom were, or would become, believers in Jesus the Christ.

The premise of *The Genesis Flood* was that the only *authoritative* source of truth resides within the Scriptures. Insightful and correct answers to questions of origins and flood geology in response to atheistic evolutionists will not convince the unbeliever — but can be of great help to crowds of believers and future believers. With clear biblical teaching and personal study, Bible-believing Christians can recognize the correct interpretation of Scriptures and its implications.

## Starting with Scripture

*The Genesis Flood* began by laying down the foundation for all subsequent arguments by demonstrating that the biblical record consistently and unequivocally presents the Genesis Flood as a *historic* event. Specifically, the book demonstrated that a literal six-day creation, followed later by a global Flood that destroyed the world, represented the one and only account of the world's creation and destruction presented in the Bible. The arguments followed a careful, *historical-grammatical hermeneutic* assuming an inerrant and authoritative text (see footnote 2). Specifically, the textual, linguistic, historical, and theological evidences were meticulously articulated by an outstanding young academic scholar with impeccable scholastic training (Princeton University) and theological training (Grace Theological Seminary).

Within the framework of Scriptures, the authors used *scientific methods* to test the hydrodynamic models to determine the conditions necessary to generate the geographical features seen in the world today. Detailed information about global topography, geological strata, and their contents were addressed with observable and measurable *evidences,* topic by topic. The mechanisms, evidences, and logic were meticulously presented by an outstanding academic scholar with impeccable secular training (University of Minnesota) and accomplishments (Chairman, Civil Engineering Department, Virginia Polytechnic Institute and State University, i.e., Virginia Tech).

These two perspectives (creation and creationism)[6] proved to be internally consistent and complementary approaches. Furthermore, the comprehensive nature of the book and effective critique of alternative arguments precluded the objections that the authors "cherry-picked" a few obscure Bible verses or geographical landmarks to build an argument while ignoring the broader weight of evidence.

The undeniable implication of a literal interpretation of Scriptures is that the all-powerful and all-knowing God of the Bible created the world, then destroyed it with a global Flood as a punishment for human sins. The theological arguments of the literal, historical interpretation divided the visible Christian world[7] while the careful scientific, mechanistic arguments and supporting evidence convinced and satisfied Christian scientists and engineers. It also forced changes in the theory of evolution — despite strong secular condemnation of the book's premise, by proving that the original theory of evolution hypothesizing that the present conditions were the key to the past was wrong — there *MUST* have been a worldwide catastrophe.

## Impact of *The Genesis Flood* on Personal Lives of Scientists and Engineers Who were Bible-believing Christians

The purpose of *The Genesis Flood* was not to convince unbelievers to accept a divine Creator but to enlighten the minds of Bible-believing Christians using Scripture. Furthermore, the book did not oppose science, but exposed the erroneous application of scientific data using hypothetical models and timelines to support the atheistic theory of evolution, even though scientific testing of the models demonstrates the impossibility of the evolutionary models (e.g., artificial life, evolutionary genetics, and extreme complexity of the simplest forms of

---

6. Some argue that creation is a doctrine, while creationism is an apologetic. Creation is held as true; creationism is a dynamic process of studying hypotheses and scientific evidences.

7. The visible Christian world includes everyone who claims to be a Christian, or comes from a Christian tradition or cult, regardless of their understanding of the Bible or acceptance of Jesus Christ as their personal Savior. See 1 Corinthians 11:19.

life).[8] The same scientific data, when analyzed using sound scientific principles and the correct model, accurately predicts and explains the observed phenomenon.

For Christians with training and careers in various fields of science and engineering, *The Genesis Flood* provided answers to vexing, unanswered questions about the veracity of the Bible and a rational direction into the future. Christians from non-scientific backgrounds, and especially those from more fundamental perspectives, also found the arguments to be refreshing and compelling, strengthening their faith and deepening their appreciation of the greatness of God. Two life-changing testimonies illustrate this effect.

Ken Ham, president of Answers in Genesis, in an interview with the *New York Times*, recalls picking up a copy of *The Genesis Flood* in Brisbane, Australia, while a graduate student in 1974. "It was a groundbreaking work," Ham stated, "in that [they] basically, in this culture, in this day and age, showed that there were scientific answers to be able to defend the Christian faith and uphold the Bible's account."[9] Ken Ham has dedicated his life and career to furthering these ideals by first working with Prof. Henry Morris and later founding Answers in Genesis.

Andrew Snelling, BSc (Applied Geology), Ph.D. (Geochemical Geology), also of Answers in Genesis, relates a similar story of how *The Genesis Flood* impacted his life.

> I read this book as a young Christian in my teenage years when I was already a budding geologist, and it totally

---

8. *Artificial life* is a computer experiment using a self-replicating computer program with random "mutations" altering the code to understand how simple things could become more complex by random changes (i.e., an evolving computer program). *Tierra* was among the first of >20 "artificial life" programs that ran on high performance computers for decades — ending in complete failure to demonstrate any improvement. *Evolutionary genetics* seeks to track genetic variants between living species to recapitulate the phylogenetic tree (Darwin's "Tree of Life"). However, the variants in DNA code *do not* coincide with the theory of evolution — even at the branch and twig level! Instead, the DNA sequences across species tend to correlate with function, suggesting intentional design to accomplish special purposes. *Complexity* reflects the problem of biological research that demonstrates the extreme complexity of the biological systems in living organisms that are all necessary for controlling normal function, survival, and reproduction, even in the simplest forms of life — noting that new technologies reveal to physicians and scientists that we are only scratching the surface of incredible design.

9. Jodi Rudoren, "Henry M. Morris, 87, a Theorist of Creationism, Dies," *New York Times* (March 4, 2006), http://www.nytimes.com/2006/03/04/national/04morris.html?_r=0, accessed January 2, 2016.

resolved my ongoing struggle to reconcile the geology I was learning in the secular textbooks with the true account of earth's history in God's Word. Not only did this book convince me that God's Word provides the only reliable basis for understanding geology, but it was foundational in igniting my passion for and calling into full-time creation ministry to uphold the truth of God's Word and defend it from compromise, beginning at the very first verse.[10]

During a personal interview with Andrew Snelling, Ph.D., I asked him what part of *The Genesis Flood* convinced him and his scientist colleagues to become dedicated creationists and flood geologists. Was it the biblical arguments or the scientific arguments? He chuckled and said,

> We are scientists with advanced degrees and real-world experience. We know how science works. What was convincing was the argument that the creation-flood account was the correct and the only interpretation of the Bible. Once that was settled, we became 6-day creationists who accepted a global flood as outlined in Genesis. We then continued doing science.[11]

Shortly after the publication of *The Genesis Flood*, the many Christian engineers and scientists with responses similar to Ham and Snelling began meeting together to discuss the Bible, flood geology, biology, evolution, missing links, astronomy, and related issues. In 1963, Henry Morris helped start the Creation Research Society, which grew into the *Institute for Creation Research*. Dozens and dozens of other local young-earth creation societies sprang up around the world, and many churches held Bible-science classes and creation conferences. Although most of the new "young earth creationists" continued in their existing careers, the impact of their new zeal and enthusiasm triggered ripple effects that continue to this day.

## Impact of *The Genesis Flood* on "Christian Doctrine"

Seldom does a book cause the religious world to reconsider its beliefs and "officially" change a position that was considered "false" to now be accepted as "true." The principles and processes for how this type of transformation

---

10. 50th Anniversary edition of *The Genesis Flood*, cover.
11. Interviewed in Pittsburgh, PA, July 31, 2018.

occurs within Christianity is briefly outlined to better understand the process by which *The Genesis Flood* changed Christian doctrine.

The word *doctrine* means "teachings," specifically the articulation of principles or positions in a branch of knowledge or system of belief.[12] Doctrine also implies teaching specific information from a position of authority, where an authoritative body determines the consequences for acceptance or rejection of the teachings.

In the case of *The Genesis Flood*, the authors appealed to the Scripture as coming directly from God and without error,[13] and then articulated what they understood was the correct interpretation of key passages in Genesis in light of the entire Scriptures. The questions then became, "Is the biblical interpretation and the inductive and deductive logic of Whitcomb and Morris true (orthodox[14]) or false (heretical[15])?" If true, "should it be accepted as church doctrine, with opposing teaching deemed false?"

## *False Doctrine*

Church leaders and laymen are repeatedly warned to avoid false doctrine because of the devastating effects of false doctrines on people's lives (e.g., 1 Timothy 1:18–19, 4:1; 2 Peter 2:1, 3:14–16; Jude 1:10–11). Protection from false doctrine comes from knowing *and applying* the Scriptures to one's life (e.g., Matthew 7:24–29; John 7:17). Unfortunately,

---

12. See "Doctrine," https://www.merriam-webster.com/dictionary/doctrine and http://www.biblestudytools.com/dictionary/doctrine/.

13. See *The Chicago Statement on Biblical Inerrancy*, Short Statement 2 and 4. "2. Holy Scripture, being God's own Word, written by men prepared and superintended by His Spirit, is of infallible divine authority in all matters upon which it touches: it is to be believed, as God's instruction, in all that it affirms: obeyed, as God's command, in all that it requires; embraced, as God's pledge, in all that it promises." "4. Being wholly and verbally God-given, Scripture is without error or fault in all its teaching, no less in what it states about God's acts in creation, about the events of world history, and about its own literary origins under God, than in its witness to God's saving grace in individual lives," http://www.bible-researcher.com/chicago1.html.

14. The word *orthodox* is from the Greek word *orthodoxia*, which means "right opinion" or "right belief." Although there is general agreement on most doctrines, various organized church groups such as the Roman Catholic Church, the Eastern Orthodox Church, protestant denominations, various Christian organizations, fellowships, and the cults disagree on which doctrines are orthodox.

15. The word *heretical* is the adjective form of the noun *heretic*, which comes from the Greek word *hairetikos*, meaning "able to choose." It came to mean an opinion or belief that differs or is against what is considered orthodox or correct. A person holding a heretical position is called a *heretic*.

there are consequences for ignorance of the Scripture — just as in the legal system where "Ignorance of the law excuses no one."[16]

Providentially, God gives new and mature believers resources and assistance in avoiding major errors. The first is the Scripture itself, which is the final source of truth and which must be studied (Acts 17:11; 2 Timothy 3:14–17; Hebrews 4:12–13; Revelation 1:2–3). Second, the Holy Spirit works within the heart and mind of true believers (e.g., John 16:13). In addition, there are the positive examples and teachings of godly leaders, the progressive maturity and discernment of believers who learn to study the Bible and who are determined to obey the Scriptures, and the biblical mandate to run from teachings that even "sound like" error.[17] The Scriptures also provide strong warnings to anyone who *teaches* false doctrine either intentionally or out of ignorance,[18] compelling the conscientious teacher to study carefully and teach respectfully in submission to God and His Word. However, the final responsibility of understanding and responding appropriately to truth and error rests on the individual Christian who will give an account of what they did with the light given to them.

*Growing List of Orthodox Doctrines*

Over the course of church history, the number of doctrinal statements continues to increase. This phenomenon highlights the fact that True Doctrine typically arises as a *refutation of false doctrine*. Thus, early creeds and confessions failed to include important doctrines that were articulated later, in response to heresies or false teachings that emerged in subsequent times.

*How* The Genesis Flood *Led to Orthodox Doctrine*

The first chapters of Genesis were generally considered by Christians to be historical accounts throughout early church history, up until the 1860s. The most effective challenge to the biblical account came with the publication of *The Origin of Species* by Charles Darwin in 1859.

---

16. This is a fundamental legal principle that holds that a person who is unaware of a law may not escape liability for violating that law merely because he or she is unaware of its content.

17. See John 14:16–17, 26, 16:13; Romans 18:14; John 7:16–17, 10:4–5, 17:17; 2 Timothy 2:15; 2 Peter 3:14–18.

18. E.g., James 3:1, "Let not many of you become teachers, my brethren, knowing that as such we will incur a stricter judgment" (NASB 1995).

This became the rallying point for unbelievers who found that this new model of origins solved the greatest problem of all, the need for a Creator and the authority of a judge. With no creator and no sovereign and righteous judge, there was no accountability and no fear of judgment (cf. 2 Peter 3:3–7).

The battle lines between the traditional view of a six-day creation within the past 10,000 years followed by a global Flood and the theory of evolution were drawn by *supposedly* pitting the Bible against science (see Chapter 7). Christian leaders capitulated to the pressure of secular scientists during the next 50 years by trying to fit evolution (directed by God?) into a supposed gap between Genesis 1:1 and Genesis 1:2 (the gap theory).

A series of compelling hermeneutical arguments against the gap theory arose in conservative Christian circles in the 1950s. John Whitcomb, a young professor at Grace Theological Seminary in Winona Lake, Indiana, began teaching seminary students literal creation in six days and a literal global Flood that formed present-day geography. Whitcomb's reason was that a thorough study of the Scriptures using careful exegesis and hermeneutical principles and the context of every reference and every verse in the entire Bible gave a single, consistent narrative; God created the world in six literal days, and God destroyed the world by a global Flood as a punishment for sin. There was no other narrative or explanation supported by Scripture. This inductive reasoning, using the entire Bible as evidence, was therefore taught without apology or compromise.

Whitcomb's view of a young earth and opposition to the gap theory was brought to the attention of the President of Grace Theological Seminary, the internationally acclaimed theologian, Alva J. McClain, Th.D. (see Chapter 12). The other faculty, who were teaching the gap theory, asked McClain to help determine whether or not the interpretation of Whitcomb was orthodox. McClain studied the materials and came to a historic conclusion. At one point he stood up, leaned forward, twisted the end of his mustache, and remarked, "You know, I think that young whippersnapper Whitcomb is right!"

With McClain's endorsement and the subsequent approval of the faculty, Grace Theological Seminary began teaching a literal interpretation of Genesis as historically accurate and orthodox Christian doctrine.

This action by the president and faculty of Grace challenged other conservative colleges and seminaries to seriously consider the exegesis and evidences, with a growing recognition that a literal interpretation of the text and inductive reasoning was indeed warranted and therefore the theory of evolution and any compromise of the Scriptures to support evolution must be false.

Publication of *The Genesis Flood* in 1961 placed the arguments in the hands of everyone interested in the debate, and the inductive approach and tools to study the issues for themselves. Whitcomb anticipated the impact of this careful, comprehensive, and hermeneutically sound approach to the Bible. "It can no longer be a matter of Genesis *and* uniformitarian geology; it is now a question of Genesis *or* uniformitarian geology."[19]

## Impact on the Christian Academic World

Henry Morris, Ph.D. (Chapter 18), in his memoirs on the history of the Creation Movement,[20] noted the stark differences in reception of *The Genesis Flood* at different colleges and seminaries. In general, most conservative Bible colleges and seminaries enthusiastically embraced the thesis and arguments of the book. In contrast, theologically liberal schools rejected the book. The issue boiled down to the authority of Scripture over the opinion of atheists who demanded the theory of evolution as an alternative to the Creator.

## International Council on Biblical Inerrancy

The *International Council on Biblical Inerrancy* represented the effort of conservative scholars to articulate the principles and doctrines related to biblical inerrancy, biblical hermeneutics, and application of biblical principles. The council called for a workshop in Chicago, Illinois, near the O'Hare International Airport in 1978. The result was *The Chicago*

---

19. John C. Whitcomb Jr., "The Genesis Flood: An Investigation of Its Geographical Extent, Geological Effects and Chronological Settings," 283. Submitted in partial fulfillment of the requirements for Doctor of Theology, Grace Theological Seminary, May 1957. Uniformitarianism is the premise behind the theory of evolution in 1960 and is further described later in this chapter. See footnote 22
20. Henry M. Morris, *A History of Modern Creationism* (Green Forest, AR: Master Books, 1984).

*Statement,*[21] signed by nearly 300 noted evangelical scholars, including James Boice, Norman L. Geisler, Carl F.H. Henry, Harold Lindsell, J.I. Packer, Francis Schaeffer, R.C. Sproul, Henry Morris, and John Whitcomb. During the workshop, Dr. Whitcomb stood and requested inclusion of statements on the issues of creation and the Flood. The committee reviewed and endorsed the following statements.

> Article XII.
>
> WE AFFIRM that Scripture in its entirety is inerrant, being free from all falsehood, fraud, or deceit.
>
> WE DENY that Biblical infallibility and inerrancy are limited to spiritual, religious, or redemptive themes, exclusive of assertions in the fields of history and science. **We further deny that scientific hypotheses about earth history may properly be used to overturn the teaching of Scripture on creation and the flood.**

This statement affirmed the truth of divine creation, without articulating the details of creationism — while denying that any scientific hypothesis could legitimately refute this truth.

While *The Genesis Flood* did not convince all Christians of literal history of Genesis 1–11, it certainly had a major, lasting impact. Following *The Chicago Statement*, many churches and denominations included similar statements on the origin of the universe and a global Flood of Genesis as part of their official church doctrine.

## Impact of *The Genesis Flood* on the Theory of Evolution

Darwin's theory of the origin of species, built on Charles Lyell's model of uniformitarian geology,[22] served as the framework for the secular theory of natural evolution. *The Genesis Flood* brought international attention to critical flaws in these theories. The arguments in *The Genesis Flood* caused the collapse of the original theory of evolution, necessitating the development of *new* theories that included catastrophism. Furthermore, *The Genesis Flood* highlighted the fact to the scientific

---

21. The full statement can be found at http://www.bible-researcher.com/chicago1.html.
22. Uniformitarianism, as applied to geology, is the idea that the present, observable conditions are the key to the past, and that the geology of the earth reflects current processes extended backward over millions and billions of years. The opposing view is catastrophism, arguing that massive disasters are needed to explain observed geology.

community (believers and non-believers) that there is no known *scientific mechanism*[23] to explain naturalistic evolution — it is a theory *without* a plausible scientific mechanism to support it.

At the same time the six-day creation and the global deluge interpretation of Scripture was adopted into orthodox Christian doctrine by believers, new doctrines of evolution were being developed and pushed into the mainstream by atheistic evolutionists. The response of evolutionists to *The Genesis Flood* is summarized into phases of: (1) ignoring creationism, (2) refuting creation science, and (3) ridiculing and silencing creation advocates. In addition, there are continued efforts to (4) find *any* scientific mechanisms that plausibly explain macroevolution — which continues to fail.

*The Scientific Framework for Scientific Knowledge*

The word *science* comes from a Latin word that means "knowledge." It is defined as "a systematic enterprise that builds and organizes knowledge in the form of testable explanations and predictions about the universe."[24]

Science is not truth. It is a method to systematically explain things in the physical world that are observed. The explanation is a logical one *based on a premise* (set of assumptions) such that *if* the premise is true, *if* the experiments are well designed and without bias, and *if* the interpretation is valid, *then* the conclusions are assumed to be true.[25]

Thomas Kuhn, a 20th-century physicist and science historian, provided clarity as to the nature and progression of scientific thought in

---

23. A *scientific mechanism* describes how the pieces of a thing that are linked together respond to an outside action, resulting in a characteristic reaction. The thing is often reduced to structured models that attempt to explain what the parts are, what they do, and how they interact. Scientists use hypotheses to design experiments to test their model (based on principles of mathematics, physics, etc.) and record the outcome to see if the model produces the expected outcome or not. Rigorous and unbiased testing of models that reproduce the anticipated outcome establish the model as a simplified example of the more complex mechanism causing the observed reaction or phenomenon. The theory of evolution describes a phenomenon (i.e., people are living on the earth) without any *scientific mechanisms* that predict their creation by natural causes and that stand up to rigorous testing (see Chapters 18–20).

24. https://en.wikipedia.org/wiki/Science, accessed March 11, 2017.

25. A paradigm, as used in science, is "a philosophical and theoretical framework of a scientific school or discipline within which theories, laws, and generalizations and the experiments performed in support of them are formulated," accessed March 11, 2017.

his famous book, *The Structure of Scientific Revolutions.*[26] He defined the idea of "normal science" developing within a paradigm that continues to organize knowledge in a systematic way until so many anomalies to the predictions of the paradigm emerge that a crisis develops. A new paradigm must be constructed that explains both the previous observations and the anomalies. A "paradigm shift" occurs when an old paradigm is rejected, and a new paradigm is accepted.

So scientific knowledge accumulated within a specific framework is relative, and therefore is not "true truth." Thus, in light of the previous discussions, "scientific truth" is *doctrine.* It may include a concise articulation of the essence of a thing, its characteristics or how it works, and may also represent the consensus of authoritative leaders in the field as a current best *understanding* of truth. Indeed, scientific knowledge is limited to observable phenomenon within a defined context. Scripture, which conveys Divine Truth, supersedes all observable and unobservable domains in the past, present, and future.

*Origins: The Key to Purpose and Destiny*

The battle ignited in scientific circles by *The Genesis Flood* was not about science. It was about the origin of man.

When considering complex and functional things, the issue of origins becomes critical because it touches on design, purpose, and uses. So it is with the wonderful and complex things of nature, including human beings themselves. The size, complexity, and amazing functionality of the things within the universe came from *somewhere*, and begs the questions, "Who, When, Where, and Why?"

The hermeneutical and exegetical[27] examination of the Bible articulated in *The Genesis Flood* answered these questions from the greatest source of the ultimate and unchanging truth that is available to man — the Scriptures. And the answer is clear: The Most High God created the universe, including man, in six days. The Scriptures also define the *purpose* and *destiny* of mankind — to glorify God and enjoy Him forever. Furthermore, the Bible details the destruction of the world by a *Flood* for the *punishment* of unrepentant sin, with the salvation of only

---

26. T.S. Kuhn, *The Structure of Scientific Revolutions* (Chicago, IL: University of Chicago Press, 1962).
27. See footnote 2.

Noah and his family. It also teaches of additional personal and global judgments, which are yet to come, and how to be saved from God's judgment through the work of Jesus Christ.

The Bible teaches the fact that most people will reject God. Furthermore, it teaches that there is a spiritual battle between God and the forces of evil, led by Satan. The methods of Satan and his followers is not to kill people, but to deceive them into disobeying God and His moral standards, leading to their own destruction. It is a strategy of lies, deceit, disinformation, false doctrines (religious realm), and false paradigms (scientific realm). So, **the battle lines are not between theologians and scientists**, they are between theologians and scientists *who know and follow God* (believers) and theologians and scientists *who oppose Him* (unbelievers).

The information in the Bible about the origin, purpose, and destiny of man, including judgment for sin or salvation from judgment through the work of Jesus the Christ, is very clear. *The Genesis Flood* not only clarified the orthodox teachings of Scripture on creation and the Flood, but also demonstrated that scientific evidence supported the Creation/Deluge Paradigm and refuted the Natural Evolution Paradigm as mechanistically impossible and devoid of hard supporting evidence. Sixty years later, the Creation/Deluge Paradigm remains intact while the Natural Evolution Paradigm has been forced to undergo major revisions and is still a scientific failure (see Chapters 19 and 20). The attraction of the Natural Evolution Paradigm is *not science!* Rather, it is a justification to reject God and His Word. Thus, the mantra of the unbelieving theologians and scientists is to *claim* that scientific evidence supports their paradigm and to ridicule, exclude, and silence anyone who disagrees.

*A Brief History of Global Flood Geology and Fossils*

Debate on the historicity of a global Flood has continued for millennia. About A.D. 200 , for example, Tertullian, an early Christian author, included a fascinating comment in *De Pallio*, a treatise on morality:

> (2.3) There even was a time that the whole earth changed and was covered by all the water that exists. Even today

shell-fish and circular shells from the sea stay abroad in the mountains, craving to prove to Plato that even the steeper parts were flooded. But by swimming out the earth changed and took on shape again, the same but different.[28]

As the scientific revolution advanced in astronomy, a number of prominent academics began addressing issues of geology and biology. Georges Cuvier (1769–1832),[29] the great French paleontologist who developed comparative biology and founded vertebrate paleontology as a scientific discipline, demonstrated from fossil evidence that some types of animals became extinct. He believed that "revolutions" or catastrophes affecting the entire earth must be considered as the primary explanation for the disappearance of some extinct creatures, although he did evoke the Flood of Genesis. In contrast, James Hutton (1726–1797) began arguing that the world's geologic features can be explained by observable processes that are in operation today, given that they extend over extremely long periods of time. This theory came to be known as uniformitarianism.

## Uniformitarianism and the Theory of Evolution

**Sir Charles Lyell** (1797–1875)[30] was a British lawyer and geologist who wrote *Principles of Geology*. This work was popularized through James Hutton's concepts of *uniformitarianism*. Lyell was one of the first geologists to effectively argue to the scientific community that the world is older than 300 million years since, under current processes, it would take that long to accumulate the large changes seen in the geological strata.

Lyell befriended a young scientist named **Charles Darwin**. Lyell urged Darwin to look for evidence that supported the theory of uniformitarian geology during Darwin's voyage on the HMS *Beagle*. Upon the return of Darwin to England in 1858, Lyell helped to arrange the publication of Darwin's papers on natural selection as *Origin of the Species*. The power of Darwin's theory of evolution was that it

---

28. From Vincent Hunink, Tertullian: *De Pallio* (2005), English translation, http://www.tertullian.org/articles/hunink_de_pallio.htm.
29. For a brief history of Georges Cuvier (1769–1832), see http://www.ucmp.berkeley.edu/history/cuvier.html. He famously used the comparative anatomy of African and Indian elephants, and fossil mammoths of Europe and Siberia to demonstrate that each was a distinct species.
30. Charles Lyell, see online reference: https://en.wikipedia.org/wiki/Charles_Lyell.

proposed a *scientific hypothesis* through which complex species might have evolved from simpler species *without* God as the Creator. The hypothesis seemed plausible, but it was untested.

*Demise in Popularity of the Biblical Creation Story*

The atheist scientists and theologians especially loved the hypothesis that the world was millions of years old and that fossils represented living creatures from another age. In response to the ridicule of atheist scientists, many Christian leaders abandoned the literal creation/deluge account of Genesis and tried to harmonize Genesis with the theory of evolution, eventually settling on the "gap theory" (see Chapters 15 and 19). Whitcomb himself was taught the gap theory and initially accepted it until he began critically studying the Book of Genesis, and especially considering the Hebrew language.

By 1917, even the influential Scofield Reference Bible and commentary[31] included the following notes on Genesis 1:1, "In the beginning God created the heaven and earth." Scofield suggested that Genesis 1:1 "refers to the dateless past, and gives scope for all the geologic ages." He went on to state that the phrase "without form and void" in Genesis 1:2 "clearly indicates that the earth had undergone a cataclysmic change as the result of divine judgment. The face of the earth bears everywhere the marks of such a catastrophe." He did not attribute the "cataclysmic changes" to the Flood of Genesis 6–8.

Unfortunately, nearly all Christian leaders and laymen succumbed to the pressure of atheistic scientists culminating in the 1925 "Scopes Monkey Trial" in Dayton, Tennessee, that focused on education in public schools. During the trial, William Jennings Bryan, a famous politician and orator who was a lifelong Baptist (but not a theologian, despite being recognized *by the court* as an expert on the Bible), conceded that the universe *could be* millions of years old and that all life forms, including humans, *could have* been created by God far more than a few thousand years ago. Indeed, Bryan, and most conservative Christians at the time, believed in "theistic" evolution, justified through the gap theory. This was considered the "death blow" of the literal interpretation of Genesis.

---

31. *The Scofield Bible Commentary,* by Cyrus Ingerson Scofield, 1917, online version at http://www.sacred-texts.com/bib/cmt/sco/gen001.htm.

## Voices for a Six-day Creation and Global Flood in the Early 20th Century

There were a few voices that continued to call for a literal interpretation of Genesis 1–11, including six days of creation and a global Flood. In the early 20th century, a professor and prolific author, George McCready Price, championed an opposition to the evolutionary theory and uniformitarian geology of Sir Charles Lyell. Although well-educated and brilliant, he received continuous criticism from evolutionists for not earning an advanced degree in geology in a secular university. Raised as a Seventh Day Adventist (SDA),[32] Price was taught that the Bible gave a literal and historically accurate account of creation (literally seven days) and a global Flood as God's judgment. While Price argued against uniformitarianism and for catastrophism through a global Flood described in Genesis, he did so with limited hermeneutical rigor and without the tools of scientists trained in mechanistic models, mathematics, statistics, and hypothesis testing. Other Christians, such as Harry Rimmer and some Lutherans, also continued to argue for a literal interpretation of Genesis, a recent earth, and global Flood (see Chapter 19). However, these voices were generally dismissed or ignored altogether.

## The Genesis Flood, Geology, and the Resurrection of Creationism

In *The Genesis Flood*, Henry Morris utilized rigorous scientific principles of hydrodynamics and flood geology to address plausible *mechanisms* leading to the appearance of the earth's surface, fossils, strata, and other features visible today (see Chapter 18). Importantly, Morris demonstrated that the effects of a universal flood, as described in Genesis would never produce small, temporary effects, as seen in a local flood, but

---

32. The Seventh Day Adventists (SDA) are considered by many Christians to be a cult since they follow the teaching of the 19th-century self-proclaimed prophet Ellen White as being equal in authority to the Scriptures. Ron Graybill, an SDA apologist states, "Since we believe that Mrs. White received revelations equal in quality to those received by Bible writers, though different in purpose and function, we bring her counsel and witness to bear on all stages of the doctrine-forming process — not as a final authority, but as a source of influence and insight" (*Ministry* magazine, October 1981, https://www.ministrymagazine.org/archive/1981/10/ellen-whites-role-in-doctrine-formation). The issue is not that SDA is wrong on everything, or that there are no strong Bible-believing Christians among their church members, but rather as to where the authority to interpret the Scriptures lies on issues such as on which day of the week believers should gather together to worship.

instead would cause catastrophic changes to the face of the earth, sufficient to produce *all* of the strata, fossils, coal, and other geological features throughout the world. Previous Christian apologists grossly underestimated the destructive power of the Genesis Flood. There was no need for the gap theory to explain buried fossils or other features of the world's crust. Furthermore, the arguments in the book adequately refuted the uniformitarian theories of Charles Lyell, demonstrating that it does not take millions of years to form sediment, and that the objective evidences throughout the earth point to global catastrophe, *not* slow, gradual, uniformitarian processes as seen today (see Chapter 18).

In the 60 years following the publication of *The Genesis Flood*, numerous updates and more sophisticated mechanistic approaches continue to emerge from scientists working within the Creation/Deluge Paradigm. New discoveries, for example the movement of tectonic plates, must be considered from a creationism perspective since this phenomenon was not appreciated in 1961. Complementary scientific fields such as genetics, cell biology, computational biology, and omics technologies further challenge evolutionary theories. Advances in scientific knowledge generally molds and refines the arguments *within* the Creation/Deluge Paradigm, without diminishing the validity of premise.[33]

## Conclusions

History demonstrated the impact of *The Genesis Flood* in the realms of personal lives of Christian men and women, Christian doctrines on the creation of the world and divine judgment by a global Flood, and on Darwin's theory of evolution.

The careful, scientific arguments for a global Flood articulated in *The Genesis Flood* changed the argument about origins from "religion

---

33. Many have noted that some young-earth creationism apologists contradict each other and/or propose theories that are untenable. This is also true for all areas of science. Theories are proposed to provide structure for critical testing of mechanistic relationship through experimentation. Hypotheses are then generated to help develop experiments to test the predictions of the theories. If the analysis of the experimental data suggests that the hypotheses and theory are wrong, then the hypothesis is rejected and modified, or new theories with new hypotheses are developed to explain the mechanism underlying the observed phenomenon, and the process is repeated. The theories themselves are framed within a *premise*, which are assumptions about what is true. Thus, creationists start with the premise that all things were created by God and destroyed by the Flood. Within this framework there is debate as to how and why specific things appear as they do today.

vs. science" to the scientific evidence *within* the Creation/Deluge Paradigm or the Natural Evolution Paradigm. The book forced major changes in the theory of evolution, which previously faced minimal scientific challenges. It also invigorated a new breed of scientific creationists who continue to contribute new insights into the nature of our universe and challenge the proposed evidences of the evolutionary theory. Although the Natural Evolution Paradigm has been exposed as a theory *without any plausible scientific mechanisms for its core tenants,* it remains the *politically correct* anti-religion mantra of unbelievers while continuing to struggle for *any* scientific validation.

This vigorous rejection of the Creation/Deluge Paradigm is not based on science at all. It is exactly what the Bible prophesizes:

> Know this first of all, that in the last days mockers will come with their mocking, following after their own lusts, and saying, "Where is the promise of His coming? For ever since the fathers fell asleep, **all continues just as it was from the beginning of creation.**" For when they maintain this, it escapes their notice that by the word of God the heavens existed long ago and the earth was formed out of water and by water, through which **the world at that time was destroyed, being flooded with water.** But by His word **the present heavens and earth are being reserved for fire,** kept for **the day of judgment and destruction of ungodly men** (2 Peter 3:3–7; NASB 1995; emphasis added).

Science is *not* the problem. The problem is that if the Creation/Deluge Paradigm is true, with the rest of Scripture, then a day is coming when God will judge all men, both the living and the dead at the resurrection.

The impact of *The Genesis Flood* was so great that by the 1980s, half of Americans believed that God created man and destroyed the world as stated in Genesis. By 2005, nearly two thirds of American adults still believed human beings were created by God. As of 2017, only 19% of Americans believe that humans evolved without God having any role.[34]

---

34. See A.D. Attie, E. Sober, R.L. Numbers, R.M. Amasino, B. Cox, T. Berceau, et al., "Defending Science Education Against Intelligent Design: A Call to Action," *Journal of Clinical Investigation,* 2006, quoting references 2 and 3. See also Gallop pole, "Evolution, Creationism, Intelligent Design," http://www.gallup.com/poll/21814/Evolution-Creationism-Intelligent-Design.aspx, accessed March 19, 2019.

## A Good and Faithful Servant

The 1961 publication of *The Genesis Flood* in many ways defined the lives and legacies of John Whitcomb and Henry Morris. They quickly moved from the solitude found between the bookshelves in obscure libraries into the spotlight, being asked to lecture, speak, preach, teach, and write about the Flood and its implications to a worldwide audience.[35] The correspondence, interviews, travel, celebrations, condemnations, attacks, alliances, follow-up books, new organizations, allied ministries, and other opportunities followed them for the rest of their lives.

Although this monumental work brought international attention to Whitcomb and Morris and proved to be a pivot point in their public careers, it did not change the essence of their persons, motivations, or priorities in life. While the current chapter highlights the impact of *The Genesis Flood* on science, Christian doctrine, and personal lives, it was not a "one-hit wonder"[36] for the authors. Indeed, the legacy of both Whitcomb and Morris reflects an enormous body of work, molded and defined by who they were as men of God.

Professor Whitcomb continued to participate in the creation/ Flood debate through additional books, lectures, and discussions. His focus differed from many of his Christian colleagues, however, in that he focused on *biblical* creationism rather than *scientific* creationism or intelligent design, since the problem of unbelievers is in the heart rather than in the head. Therefore, he poured his time and talent into the personal biblical training of over 1,000 men of God (Chapter 3) who sustain the legacy and continue to impact the entire world.

---

35. See Professor Whitcomb's summary of the "History and Impact of the Book, *The Genesis Flood*" at the Answers in Genesis Mega-Conference, July 18, 2005, published in Impact #395, May 2006.
36. A one-hit wonder is any entity, such as a musical band, that achieves mainstream popularity and success exactly once, and becomes known among the general public solely for that momentary success (modified from https://en.wikipedia.org/wiki/One-hit_wonder, accessed December 25, 2016).

# Chapter 3

# 1,000 Men

"... entrust these things to faithful men ..."
1946 to 2020

Most people who have heard of Dr. Whitcomb primarily associate him with Henry Morris as coauthors of *The Genesis Flood* and founders of the modern creation movement. However, this is not how he thinks of himself, nor how those who know him view him. Instead, they know him as a devoted teacher of God's Word, a theology teacher, and a servant of the Lord.

His methods of teaching include formal teaching in a classroom, preaching in churches, writing books, developing systematic syllabi, producing lecture series via audio recordings and video, personal mentoring and, most importantly, by personal example. This chapter highlights the impact of his teaching.

Many Bible teachers, preachers, and Christians choose a "life verse." Dr. Whitcomb chose 2 Timothy 2:2:

> The things which you have heard from me in the presence of many witnesses, entrust these to faithful men who will be able to teach others also (NASB 1995).

In 1 Corinthians 1:26, Paul notes, "For consider your calling, brethren, that there were not many wise according to the flesh, not many mighty, not many noble. . . ." The Greek word for *wise* can be interpreted as a person who is cultivated, learned, skilled as an orator, teacher, writer, or philosopher, showing originality, distinction, and sustained achievement. It is used of distinguished Greek philosophers, Jewish theologians, and some Christian teachers. It is also used of individuals who can form the best plans and use the best means for their execution. Although there are "not many wise according to the flesh" who are devoted disciples of Christ, there are some.

The Apostle Paul also tells us in Ephesians that, upon His Resurrection, the Lord Jesus Christ gave special gifts to men to build and strengthen the church. Paul writes:

> But to each one of us grace was given according to the measure of Christ's gift. ... And He gave some as apostles, and some as prophets, and some as evangelists, and some as pastors and teachers, for the equipping of the saints for the work of service, to the building up of the body of Christ; until we all attain to the unity of the faith, and of the knowledge of the Son of God, to a mature man, to the measure of the stature which belongs to the fullness of Christ (Ephesians 4:7, 11–13).

It is unquestioned that Dr. Whitcomb was uniquely gifted as a *teacher*. While he reached out to the lost in evangelistic talks and meetings, and served for a short time as a pastor, he was not unusually gifted in these areas either by personality or effectiveness. However, he is an extraordinary communicator, teacher, and preacher, and by extension, author. The ability to communicate complicated information in clear, simple terms is a gift. The ability to communicate God's truths in a way that rings *true* in the mind and heart of willing believers is a spiritual gift working in harmony with the effects of the Holy Spirit.[1]

Dr. Whitcomb's life's mission was to reach as many people as possible with the Gospel and teach believers to become disciples of Christ. His passion was to serve God through teaching and ministering to His people. His approach was to advance the Great Commission with true doctrines and defend against false teachings through biblical apologetics.

Dr. Whitcomb also had the gift of targeting his teaching to the level of his audience. Truth was presented clearly so that each person could learn and benefit from God's Word and ways. Each believer was viewed as one of God's chosen people and he respected and treated them all from this perspective, regardless of race, country of origin, occupation, or social status. And he cared that they heard the "whole counsel of God,"

---

1. See John 7:17, 8:31–32, and 14:16–17.

that his students and listeners knew how to apply it *and* defend it, and that they were equipped to pass these things on to the next generation.

God, in His divine plan, brought more than a thousand men *and women* to study directly under Professor Whitcomb. Through these individuals, complemented by books, charts, outlines, and recordings, he succeeded in entrusting God's divine truths to many future generations of students throughout the United States and to the ends of the earth.

Dr. Whitcomb primarily provided systematic teaching within an academic framework at Grace Theological Seminary, at Word of Life Bible Institute, and through the Christian Workman School of Theology. Through these teaching vehicles, he impacted the world through "1,000 men" who became equipped to go on to teach others. The additional people who were taught through his books, recorded messages, videos, and other media, plus the ripple effect of the teaching of the "1,000 men," are innumerable.

To better understand the impact of his teaching, the testimonies of a few of the "1,000 men" who studied directly under his mentorship and learned from him personally are presented in their own words.

## Men of Grace

Dr. Whitcomb began his teaching at Grace Theological Seminary in 1951. His academic background was at Princeton University, where he excelled as an undergraduate and graduated with honors. He expected the same high academic standards held in the Ivy League from students at Grace and was considered to be one of the toughest teachers in the seminary, especially by those who came from less prestigious and demanding academic backgrounds. With time, experience, and mentoring by more senior professors and pastors, he blossomed into one of the most effective teachers who maintained the highest academic standards while encouraging and assisting struggling students. Many of his earlier students have now served the Lord for many years before passing away from sickness and old age. However, some of the students from the 1950s still remember the early days. The following sampling of student testimonies covers six decades.

## Pastors

*Michael (Mick) Funderburg Sr.*, now a retired pastor after over 45 years of active ministry as pastor of four Grace Brethren churches, attended

Grace College and Seminary from 1956 to 1962 when Dr. Whitcomb was a young teacher and was writing *The Genesis Flood*.

> I was privileged to sit under the teaching of five highly respected warriors for the faith: Dr. John Whitcomb, Dr. Alva McClain, Dr. Herman Hoyt, Dr. James Boyer, and Dr. Homer Kent Jr. Dr. Whitcomb was always approachable and thorough. It was not always easy to balance [secular] work time and study time, but I always knew that if I was properly prepared for an exam in Dr. Whitcomb's classes I would do well, and if I was not well prepared it would also be reflected in the grade I received. . . . Through the years [as a pastor] my wife, Nancy and I have had the privilege of being friends with Dr. and Mrs. Whitcomb and have admired them as godly examples of walking with Christ. When we have talked on the phone, Dr. Whitcomb has often offered a prayer to God for the topic we have talked about. When he has eaten at a restaurant, he is quick to share a testimony and a tract with a waitress. He and Norma have continually displayed a gracious and compassionate spirit.[2]

*Larry R. Weigle* attended Grace College from 1964 to 1968 and Grace Theological Seminary from 1968 to 1971, where he studied under Dr. Whitcomb for all of his theology courses. He then went on to pastor the Reading Grace Brethren Church in Storystown, Pennsylvania, for over 45 years. He recalls:

> Dr. Whitcomb was a positive influence in my life and gave me a greater desire to study and search the Scriptures. He truly cared about his students. His teaching of the Bible and Theology has been a great help to me in my ministry. And, his Practorium Tapes[3] have been a great "refresher course." Dr. Whitcomb has also been a great "Prayer Warrior." I know he prays for all of us pastors. He has been an inspiration to me,

---

2. Email from Michael Funderburg to the author for this biography, July 6, 2018; used with permission.
3. The *Practorium* is a program under the Christian Workman Schools of Theology to bring seminary level teaching and credits within the local church where the trainees can receive teaching and mentoring as they develop their spiritual gifts. Dr. Whitcomb is one of several seminary professors who developed detailed syllabi and videotaped their lectures to be used within this teaching program. See more details later in this chapter.

and I am eternally grateful for all he has taught me. He is one of my "Heroes of the Faith."[4]

*Dr. Russ Simpson* entered Grace Seminary in 1974. He went on to become the senior pastor at Lakeland Grace Brethren Church, an educator through founding Lakeland Christian Academy, a leader of the Conservative Grace Brethren Churches International and a Practorium director. He recalls being especially impressed by Dr. Whitcomb while at seminary because he knew the Bible *very* well, and that he was totally dedicated to following God's Word without compromise. Dr. Simpson summarized the most important lesson learned from Dr. Whitcomb as, "Lift up Christ, it isn't about me."

Ronald Welsh studied under Dr. Whitcomb between 1976 and 1982 in preparation to become a pastor. Pastor Welsh noted, "He was a great intellect, at the same time he never came across as a 'know it all,' but was always very gracious."

*Dave Jodry* serves as the senior pastor of the Peru Grace Brethren Church in Peru, Indiana, where Dr. Whitcomb was a regular *Bible and Science Conference* speaker. Pastor Jodry notes that few men impacted his life, the lives of his fellow students, and the people of the church to the degree that God used Dr. John Whitcomb to impart "the precious and timeless truths of the *Word of God.*" Pastor Jodry recalls,

> Dr. John Whitcomb was used by God to impact my life in so many ways before I graduated from Grace Seminary. Ironically, I had never heard of him until my first year in Grace College, arriving as a transfer student in the Fall of 1976. His son, David, was supposed to be my roommate, but God moved him to Manchester College instead to prepare for life in the world of medicine. Some of the other guys in the dorm were telling me, "Hey…your roommate is Dr. Whitcomb's son." But I didn't have a clue who they were talking about…but it wasn't long until I came to know about this Seminary professor, whose books I would soon read for some of the college courses that I took.
>
> When I entered Grace Seminary, I walked into his *God and Revelation* class and met the man for the first time in

---

4. Written by Larry Weigle for this biography, received and approved October 6, 2018.

1980. We've had a growing friendship ever since. My two favorite "Whitcomb Golden Nuggets" which were gleaned in
his classes were: 1) The Bible: It's the only Book God ever
wrote…and 2) His explanation (with dramatic gestures and
self-generated sound effects) of how the Pre-Incarnate Christ
created everything, as the holy angels watched with amazement and applauded at every turn. The man knew how to
work humor into his teaching and I'll never forget his broad
smile and unique laughter in that teaching.[5]

*David Troxel* studied under Dr. Whitcomb between 1978 and 1982 in
preparation to be a pastor. After his graduation, Dr. Whitcomb visited
two of the churches that he pastored and spoke at each of them on
several occasions. Pastor Troxel recalled that Dr. Whitcomb's knowledge of science and theology was truly astounding. But that is not the
picture that he holds of Dr. Whitcomb in his mind.

> The most impressive aspect of Dr. Whitcomb is how Dr.
> Whitcomb the professor is also always Dr. Whitcomb the man.
> In spite of the tremendous schedule he continues to keep, he
> still calls me at church just to find out what is happening, and
> how the church is doing, and asks how my wife is doing, then
> prays for us. He always remembers her name, and the names
> of our children. To this day, my daughter remembers how he
> would play his hands like a flute, and how it made her dog react.
>
> His sense of humor, subtle though it is, comes through
> in his lectures and his conversations alike. I'll never forget
> his humorous way of slipping sarcasm into his comments in
> class as he describes the narrow-minded thinking of evolu-
> tionists. He was once describing how scientists said that the
> Coelacanth was extinct for thousands of years, having adapt-
> ed to the land, and evolving into a mammal. Then a news
> story told of how some fishermen had caught one out in the
> ocean, and the story came complete with a picture of the fish-
> ermen holding up the "extinct" fish [in front of him]. And
> then Dr. Whitcomb said, "…and here in the photo! As you
> can see, the beast has developed nice, long, lovely legs at last!"

5. Written by David Jodry for this biography, received and approved October 6, 2018.

This humor, honest love of God and man, and his unstoppable quest that the world know the truth has inspired me in my own ministry for 35 years. The world needs more Dr. Whitcombs to be able to see for themselves how truth can be taught both in the classroom, and in life, and with consistent love of each.[6]

*Scott Libby* serves as the pastor of the Grace Brethren Church of Irasburg, Vermont. After coming to know Christ as his Savior, he completely changed his life's direction to serve God in full time ministry. He writes,

I met Dr. Whitcomb in the fall of 1983 in my first class at Grace Theological Seminary. I was only one year and four months old in the Lord and Dr. Whitcomb's course *God and Revelation* had a profound impact on me. His teaching laid the foundation for everything else I received during my training. Through all his courses and the other times that I've had the privilege to sit under his teaching, he has definitely left his "fingerprint of discipleship" upon me. I only hope to carry on Dr. Whitcomb's legacy of standing on the truth of God's Word at any cost, and exulting the name of Jesus Christ above all.[7]

## Missionaries

While Dr. Whitcomb's passion was to train pastors, he also trained missionaries who went throughout the world.

*Bob Provost* studied under Dr. Whitcomb at Grace Theological Seminary before serving as a missionary to Russian-speaking people and as president of the Slavic Gospel Association for nearly 25 years. He encouraged the translation of Dr. Whitcomb's materials into Russian and notes that they have been a great blessing to countless Russian pastors, strengthening their commitment to God's Word and making them more effective pastors and teachers. While it is clear that the Russian government is still trying to rid the country of all evangelicals, the Slavic Gospel Association continues to stand in the gap for the believers.

---

6. Email from Davy Troxel for this biography, received and accepted on July 7–9, 2018.
7. Email from Scott Libby, July 7, 2018.

# A Good and Faithful Servant

In September 2016, Robert Robertovich (his Russian name), while recovering from a major arterial bypass surgery at Mayo Clinic, reflected on his life and career and then penned the following letter to Dr. Whitcomb.

Dr. Whitcomb, second only to my salvation, was the impact of your life and ministry upon my life that God blessed to set me apart for a lifetime of service to Christ. I can never thank you enough!

More than 40 years ago you came for a weekend of preaching at The Chapel in Akron, Ohio. My wife and I were new believers. I had been serving as the human resources director for an engineering "think tank" called Design and Development, Inc., a technical subsidiary of the prestigious consulting firm, Booz-Allen and Hamilton.

I was so very impressed with your unique combination of scientific knowledge and Biblical authority. I purchased *The Genesis Flood*, read it from cover to cover, and said to my wife, "If I ever go to seminary I want to go where Dr. Whitcomb teaches." I knew nothing else about *Grace Theological Seminary*, only that you were a professor there. On this basis, never having even seen a catalogue, I resigned from my position on August 6th. We moved over Labor Day Weekend. The dean, Dr. Kent allowed me to begin my studies on a provisional basis and 3-4 weeks into the semester I breathed a sigh of relief when I was formally accepted.

Now, by God's grace it is 45 years later, I am 79, but by His grace keep pressing on. In God's preparation, before salvation, I had served in Air Force Intelligence, intercepting Soviet Air Force communications. This served to help equip me to serve these past 29 years in 13 Russian-speaking countries including Israel for the past nearly five years. Our first priority has been training pastors and the total trained so far, by God's grace, now exceeds 10,000 servants of Christ with 1,300+ current students. At one of our seminaries in Russia we are very near to the launching of the first Ph.D. program for training seminary professors. And, we are currently in the process of expanding our certificate program in Israel to a BA level.

From time to time, we need to drive through Indianapolis. With some advance notice we would love to have you and Norma join us for lunch at your favorite restaurant. Please advise if this might be a possibility.

In the meantime, we shall keep you in our prayers.

In His love, Bob Provost[8]

The work of Bob Provost [Robertovich] in the Soviet Union is remarkable. The fall of the Berlin Wall in 1989 opened the Soviet Union to the West, but the cause for celebration also sent a cold chill to many of the leaders of the Soviet Baptist churches. For 72 years their members had been totally denied university-level education. Also illegal was Christian education at any level, Christian books, and Christian media, except for SGA's short-wave programming, which saturated the country nearly 24-7. In God's wonderful providence, limiting these Christians to the study of the Bible had served to keep their doctrine undisturbed and thoroughly biblical throughout the Communist era.

Bob Provost was in Kiev with the highly respected Baptist theological leader of the USSR, Pastor Yakov Kuzmich Dukhonchenko (who had been sentenced to 10 years in Soviet prisons for his faith), when the news of the Berlin wall collapse spread throughout the Soviet Union. He said, "Brother Robert, we think this could lead to a freedom that will bring a flood of false teachers to destroy our precious churches." Provost responded, "I am sorry to have to tell you that the threat is even worse than you may know. There are over 500 evangelical seminaries and Bible colleges in America and only five or six of them hold to a literal six-day creation view." Pastor Dukhonchenko said, "The English version must be different than the Russian text." Verse by verse the two of them compared the six-day narrative and found the Russian and English texts to be identical. Then Pastor Dukhonchenko concluded, "Brother Robert, if they don't believe the first page what do they do with the rest of the book?" "Robert Robertovich" knew what he must do.

He returned to Los Angeles and resigned from his position as executive vice president of The Master's University and Seminary. In January 1990, Grace Community Church dispatched him and Louetta as missionaries to the Soviet Union. Pastor Dukhonchenko then asked him to help develop the first theological seminary. In February 1991,

8. Letter used with permission from Robert Provost via email to the author, October 9, 2018.

with the help of the faculty of The Master's Seminary, the Irpen Biblical Seminary (IBS) was launched.

To date, more than 2,000 servants of Christ have been trained, and their impact has changed Ukraine. The Baptist commitment to a literal six-day creation has never wavered. In time, the Ministry of Education asked IBS to train men and women to teach the Bible in the public schools all over Ukraine, and a public school ministry major was added. Over the years, many faithful Baptists have been elected to public office, including an excellent preacher, who for several months served as the acting president and has continued as a parliament leader and as the director of national security and defense.

The impact of the biblically faithful Baptists has helped Ukraine to become the leading evangelical Christian nation in all of Europe. In 2016, the 1,000+ pastors who attended the Baptist Congress in Moscow each received a Russian version of Dr. Whitcomb's Answers in Genesis article affirming the critical importance of all pastors embracing the authenticity of the literal six-day creation account. Bob Provost concluded, "I have no doubt that Dr. Whitcomb's relentless stand on the authenticity of Genesis Chapter One has been his pre-eminent contribution in the Russian-speaking lands, and it has influenced all of this glorious progress for Christ."

*Ike Graham* studied under Dr. Whitcomb in the late 1970s, graduating from Grace Theological Seminary with a Th.M. in 1981 before going to Japan as a missionary. Graham recalls the great impact that Dr. Whitcomb had not only in the classroom but in his response to being viciously attacked by others.

> I did not grow up in a Christian home, but God in His infinite mercy reached me through His inerrant word when I was a senior in high school. He opened my heart to believe in December of 1970. Eight months later, I attended a college where my faith was challenged by professors who did not believe the Bible. I became so nauseated with their errors that I went to Grace Theological Seminary in the fall of 1975. There, I met Dr. John Whitcomb. He brought such spiritual refreshment to my heart through the Word of God and the work of the Spirit of God through him that it was difficult to take notes through the tears.

I have been instructed deeply by Dr. Whitcomb's response to mockers and even Christians who have treated him with disrespect. His graciousness was so evident in many situations where even pastors were unkind to him. I wanted to punch them (in Christian love of course), but Dr. Whitcomb was so gracious as 1 Peter 2:19; 4:14 instructs us. He not only taught the word of God; he lived the word of God.

I really find it difficult to put into words the impact that Dr. Whitcomb has had on my life. His faithful insistence on the authority and inerrancy of the Bible has molded my heart, by the work of the Holy Spirit through his instruction to the word of God. This has carried me through many storms of life both in my ministry in Japan and here in the U.S.; and now also in the ministry we have in India and Myanmar. I remember a particular time in Japan when I was very discouraged. I was sitting at my desk pouring out my heart to God and the telephone rang. It was Dr. Whitcomb calling to see how I was doing! As I explained my predicament, he said: "God specializes in the impossible!" Then, he prayed for me. He was like a spiritual father to me. How do I thank a man who was far more than a professor to me? He is my teacher; my discipler; and my faithful brother in Christ.[9]

## Princeton Connection

Dr. Whitcomb was not the only scholar who graduated from Princeton University and went on to Grace Theological Seminary for Bible training. There was a "pipeline" of students to Grace, sent by Dr. Donald Fullerton of Princeton (Chapters 7, 11, 14), who founded the Princeton Evangelical Fellowship, did the work of an evangelist, and helped numerous young students discover the purpose and meaning of life.

*Ron Furst* was a Princeton graduate who studied at Grace under Dr. Whitcomb from 1963 to 1966. After graduation he went on to serve the Lord as a missionary church-planter in Germany and Luxembourg (1997–2003) with Biblical Ministries Worldwide. Pastor Furst recalls,

I experienced Dr. Whitcomb as a professor of the Book of Daniel, Theology I (Inspiration) and Theology II (the Person

---

9. Email letter from Isaac Graham to the author for this biography, October 6, 2018.

of Christ), the Pentateuch, Apologetics and the prophetic books of Isaiah, Jeremiah, and Ezekiel. Two characteristics marked his teaching.

He was exacting. If he wrote parallel references in his notebooks, the student was expected to reflect that reference in the final test. When he gave a due date for a 5,000 word paper (20 pages), he expected it to be handed in on that date, not later! Otherwise, it would be marked down in grade. It was a good disciplining process for future servants of the Lord.

He was encyclopedic in his knowledge. If a student tendered a question, Dr. Whitcomb did not satisfy the student with a superficial answer. He usually drew from all the sources of knowledge at his disposal and gave a comprehensive answer. He took time to answer the question thoroughly and never looked at his watch. As students, we always knew that Dr. Whitcomb came to each class prepared for any contingency or question that might arise.

For me there was one defining experience. In the school year of 1986-87, Hildegard and I resided in Winona Lake, so that I might complete my Master of Theology degree in missiology. One evening in February of 1987 we invited him and Norma to dinner in our rented quarters in [sic] Maple Street. During the meal I complemented [sic] him on the calm manner in which he answered students who were stubbornly addicted to post-tribulationism or other theological aberrations. I recall that he turned to me and exclaimed, *"But, oh Ron, I praise God for my students and their questions down through the years."* No question was a nuisance or a source for impatience for Dr. Whitcomb!

Admittedly Dr. Whitcomb is difficult to capture on paper! He cultivated a sense of humor! I once told him in 1967 that both my parents had earned their Ph.D's in 1967 at the age of 55. Without hesitation he turned to me and said, *"Ron, you have a real paradox (play on words = pair of docs) on your hands!"* He and Norma were very hospitable. In the summer of 1987, while they were in the Philippines, the Whitcombs permitted us to dwell in their house. Dr. Whitcomb was missions-minded. He visited us in Germany in 1990, and gave lectures on creationism. A 30-year old housewife attended and received the Lord. Later her two children received the Lord. In Luxembourg he taught Apologetics and Genesis to an international audience.

For us Princeton students who attended Grace Theological Seminary, Dr. Whitcomb served as an indispensable liaison person. He knew how a saved Princeton man *"ticked."* For those who had difficulties in their transition from secular to theological studies, he served as a real mentor, helping us over the *"humps."*[10]

*Paul Apple* graduated from Princeton University along with his wife, Karen *(Kisling Apple)*, with the class of 1975 and was an active member of PEF. He attended Grace Theological Seminary where he received his M. Div. in 1979 and was awarded the Alva J. McClain Award in Systematic Theology. He worked in Marketing and Business Management for the next 28 years with a Caterpillar (heavy equipment) dealership in Baltimore, Maryland, and 9 years with Johnson & Towers Inc. as Director of Business Development. With this background in Bible and business, Paul and Karen have served the Lord in multiple ways.

They worked from their home to provide tools for students of the Bible through producing pdf versions of Bible commentaries that are distributed for free via the internet (www.BibleOutlines.com and www.solidrockmd.org). Karen helped to found and lead the Christian homeschooling movement in the state of Maryland under the organizational name of CHEN (Christian Home Educators Network). As one of the regional pioneers in the homeschooling movement, Karen also mentored many moms who chose homeschool over a secular education for their children. Paul focused on developing and mentoring in the Christian Athletic Association, a local sports ministry for children that is a Christian alternative to the Recreation Council leagues. His church ministries focused on teaching and promoting a biblical form of church government that includes a plurality of qualified elders and New Testament polity. They are currently working with the Freedom Church in Baltimore, planting a new work on the west side of the city.

---

10. Written by Ron Furst for this biography, received and approved October 10, 2018.

## A Good and Faithful Servant

Paul first met Dr. Whitcomb during his college years at Princeton (1972–1975), as he would return for special conferences and speak especially on creationism and topics related to science and the Bible. This was his first real exposure to any in-depth teaching on those subjects. He recalls:

> I had grown up in a Christian family but always assumed that some sort of progressive creationism that allowed for vast amounts of time was the way to reconcile evolution and the Bible. Dr. Whitcomb made the case for the Early Earth very clear and compelling. He was one of the main factors that influenced me to attend Grace Seminary. Karen remembers the story of how he called us up to congratulate me for receiving the theology award upon graduation. When Karen answered the phone, he asked her: "How does it feel to be married to a theologian?" She says that after many decades of taking stands for God's truth that have not always been well received in our local Christian circles, she now has a better frame of reference to answer that question. He was a true friend to Karen and me while at the seminary.
>
> I was always struck with his graciousness and his sense of humor. He had a unique gift in teaching OT character studies to make the people of the Bible come alive. He impacted us to always take a very high view of Scripture; I loved his emphasis on 2 Tim. 2:2 -- you need to communicate the entire body of truth to faithful men who will pass it on -- not some watered down or minimalistic version.
>
> I loved the fact that he was a man of conviction and integrity. Those are two qualities that I have always tried to emulate. He was greatly criticized as being overly harsh in some of the stands he took against other Christian leaders who were compromising the truth in some area. I remember an incident after we had just moved back to the Baltimore area and were trying to fit into a new church start-up. I was playing basketball with a couple of the leaders. [One of them] asked me specifically about whether I knew Dr. Whitcomb from my days at seminary. As I responded with my words of clear admiration, I could tell that he pegged me as someone who [would take an

uncompromising stand] along the lines of how he viewed Dr. Whitcomb. But what a testimony that such a brilliant scholar could remain so kind and gentle and gracious while still taking very hard-line stands on the truth of Scripture.[11]

*Michael O'Connor* is another Princeton University graduate who attended Grace Theological Seminary and studied under Dr. Whitcomb. He remembers the way that Dr. Whitcomb mentored him through a challenging time when he needed both discipline and mercy in the context of final exams. He recalls:

> Perhaps his biggest case of mercy that I remember from seminary was December 1985, a Friday, the last day of the semester. I had to write a book review for *Kingdom & the Church*. But for some reason, I didn't. Maybe I was concentrating on other courses? Other papers? I may have thought, "if I didn't turn it in, I'd get an F". That, averaging in with the rest of the course, would give me a passing grade.
>
> Dr. Whitcomb called me at home. "Mike, you have to turn in that book review. You won't get an F if you don't do it, you'll get a zero! And that, averaging in with other courses matters, WOULD lead to an F!" The clock was ticking. I was going to give someone a ride to Chicago, and leaving late that afternoon. I sat down with Earl Radmacher's *What the Church Is All About*, and hand-wrote a two-page book review, front & back. (I did fortunately read it!) I handed it in, got a D, averaging with other parts of the course maybe giving me a C, & drove to Chicago. He could've flunked me. But he cared enough about me, being a kindred spirit with PEF, to seek me out, warn me of what was happening, and basically rescue me from a failing grade. Who knows, maybe I still have that book review in my files!
>
> When I think of [Dr. Whitcomb's] kindness & mercy, that event looms exceedingly large in my mind. . . . And, it wasn't the only incident. He usually really liked my book reviews, giving high grades & margining off paragraphs with a "+" sign, like he was saying, "Great point, Mike!" When

---

11. Written by Paul Apple for this biography, received and accepted, October 11, 2018.

Pastor French was going through frequent changes in his eyeglasses (because of heightening diabetes), I remember his caringly talking with Pastor French about it in the Student Lounge. He sought me out with the news that the Lord had taken Dr. Fullerton home.

My father did not know the Lord, until perhaps the end of his life. God gave me substitute fathers wherever I have gone. Dr. Whitcomb was such a father-figure at Grace. I guess, if there's any one person I would wish to grow up & be like, it would be John Whitcomb. At age 62 . . . I guess I'm still working on growing up![12]

## Word of Life (WOL) Bible Institute

John "Jack" Whitcomb met John "Jack" Wyrtzen,[13] the founder and director of Word of Life Bible Institute, while Dr. Whitcomb was an undergraduate student at Princeton University. The two "Jacks" became life-long friends and partners in teaching God's Word.

Jack Wyrtzen was an evangelist, radio host, and founder of Word of Life ministries and founding member of Youth for Christ International. In 1946, he purchased a resort island on Schroon Lake, New York, and transformed it as an evangelistic summer youth camp, which has hosted over 300,000 kids.[14] Jack Wyrtzen loved the Lord and was an incredibly talented and gifted preacher and organizer. He never had formal theological training, although he recognized the critical importance of rightly dividing the Word of Truth. He did have unusually keen insights into sound Bible teaching and surrounded himself with godly and theologically sound advisors. Jack Wyrtzen recognized the talent and character of Dr. Whitcomb and relied on him throughout the next 50 years as a friend, consultant, and teacher.

In 1970, Jack Wyrtzen and Harry Bollback opened the first American version of the WOL Bible Institute at Schroon Lake, New York, that utilized the facilities for the entire year. The model for the Bible institutes included structured discipleship, world class Bible teachers, and practical ministry training for the young students. Wyrtzen insisted that Dr. Whitcomb serve as one of the primary faculty, giving

---

12. Emails from Michael O'Connor to the author for this biography, October 9–10, 2016.
13. John Von Casper Wyrtzen, (April 22, 1913–April 17, 1996).
14. https://www.wol.org/about/history/.

a block of lectures each autumn. The formula was a success for WOL and a great joy for Dr. Whitcomb. The Word of Life Bible Institute model was replicated in Florida, and in 14 countries around the world. Dr. Whitcomb graciously supported several of these schools through the years with lecture series in WOL Florida near Tampa, WOL Canada in Owen Sound, Ontario, WOL Argentina, and WOL Brazil.

Dr. Whitcomb continues to be a strong believer and supporter of the WOL Bible for the half-century since its inception. He modified his teaching materials for the kids who were often just out of high school and who had minimal academic backgrounds. The illustrations were simplified and the assignments minimized, but the content was delivered without compromise. He also recognized that these kids would fan out from these locations to the rest of the world, and that this was a tremendous opportunity to impact a new generation.

Laura Edisene Whitcomb, now Laura E. Graf, is the granddaughter of Dr. Whitcomb. She studied under his teaching at WOL Bible Institute at Schroon Lake, New York during the 1999–2000 academic year. She remembers him well, highlighting two memories.

> He was calm and kind. And he was like a kid in the candy store at every meal because they had a dessert table and grandma wasn't there to tell him no.
>
> I remember a friend telling me that at first she was confused because, during the middle of his lectures, he would just start praying and she never knew if she should close her eyes or not. He would be going over something and then just say "and thank you Jesus for this gift, and help us not to waste it" and then go right back to his lecture. But then she said she realized that it was because he truly was praying without ceasing and he was so comfortable talking to God that it just came out!

My wife and I are also enthusiastic about structured Bible institutes for Christian men and women, especially between high school and college when they leave the supervision of their parents and begin forming enduring friendships and life-long habits. All four of our children attended the WOL Bible Institute in Schroon Lake, New York, between high school and college. We did not force our children to go but offered them four years of full college tuition plus support for living expenses if (a) they attended the WOL Bible Institute for one year (successfully), and (b) they maintained a B grade point average in the college of their choice. It worked out very well!

## Church Bible Conferences

Dr. Whitcomb loved church-sponsored Bible conferences that would typically begin on a Friday night, have several sessions on Saturday, then conclude with an adult Sunday school class and Sunday morning worship. There were many churches that he visited multiple times and a few that he would visit annually. One example is visits to Middletown Bible Church that he visited annually for seventeen years.

George Zeller was a seminary student of Dr. Whitcomb from 1972–1975. He has served as elder and assistant pastor of the Middletown Bible Church in Middletown, Connecticut, from the time he graduated from Grace Theological Seminary in 1975 through 2021 (more than 46 years). Pastor Zeller was instrumental in starting regional and national Bible conferences for pastors with a shared passion for teaching and following God's Word. He recalls:

> We decided to have a National Bible Conference especially for men all over the country who were dissatisfied with the compromises of [their denominations]. So we would meet the last week of every April for a four day conference and our mailing list included men from all over the country. Our attendance reached as high as 425. Then we also had a two-day conference in the Fall which was not national in scope but more for the men in our part of the country (New England, New York, Pennsylvania, New Jersey, Ohio, etc.).

> Dr. Whitcomb first spoke in April of 1994, and every April after that until his last conference in 2010. He loved our conference but at that point he felt, due to age, that he would not continue. That was seventeen straight years we had him at our four day Bible Conference in April. He would usually speak 5 or 6 times at each conference. The men who shared the platform with him were Robert Lightner, Robert Delnay, Renald Showers, Paul Van Gorder, John Hartog II, missionary Richard Mercado, Myron Houghton, Wayne Van Gelderen Jr., and my pastor, George Parsons. Many of the topics he spoke on later became cassette albums or CD albums: Daniel, Zechariah, Malachi, Isaiah 53, God's Truth

Circles, Old Testament Prophets and Christian Preachers, Jonah, Apologetics, and his final series was 35 messages on the book of Acts which took place over the course of about 6 or 7 conferences. I'm now taking this material and seeking to write a commentary on Acts based on his messages and adding additional material of my own.

He was known for his kind heart, being willing to talk to anyone who came up to him no matter who they were. He was known for his great sense of humor, both from the pulpit and in private conversations. He was always a delight to be with and we miss him greatly.[15]

## Perpetual Teaching through Christian Workman Schools of Theology

After leaving Grace Theological Seminary, Dr. Whitcomb helped establish a program of local church "Practoriums." The idea was to follow the pattern of the Apostle Paul in Acts 19: 7–10:

> There were in all about twelve men. And he entered the synagogue and continued speaking out boldly for three months, reasoning and persuading them about the kingdom of God. But when some were becoming hardened and disobedient, speaking evil of the Way before the people, he withdrew from them and took away the disciples, reasoning daily in the school of Tyrannus. This took place for two years, so that all who lived in Asia heard the word of the Lord, both Jews and Greeks.

The Practorium functions as a Bible school linked to a local church where men and women can study the Scriptures at a seminary level, while developing their ministries under the guidance of elders and observation of the congregation. Dr. Whitcomb and other former Grace Theological Seminary professors taught their seminary courses at sponsoring churches. The lectures were recorded and made available to other churches to use, and also syllabi for a program of intense training that could be used indefinitely. Churches throughout the United States currently offer these courses, as well as churches in

---

15. Written by George Zeller for use in this biography, received and accepted on October 29, 2020.

Canada, Brazil, Argentina, England, France, Italy, Spain, Switzerland, Philippines, Singapore, Cameroon, Central African Republic, Democratic Republic of Congo, Uganda, Kenya, Tanzania, and Rwanda!

*Dave Blevins* is the pastor of the Grace Brethren Church in Limestone, Tennessee. Pastor Blevins was in the very first Grace Brethren Practorium class in Mansfield, Ohio. He was also in the first graduating class and has pastored churches ever since. He met Dr. Whitcomb in 1981 when he came as a guest lecturer, while still teaching at Grace Theological Seminary. Pastor Blevins was elected President of the Conservative Grace Brethren Churches, International for the 2017–2018 term. During the meeting he highlighted the continuing effects of Dr. Whitcomb's ministries spanning multiple generations.

> At the 25th Anniversary of the CGBCI (June 29-July 4, 2018) I had the privilege of seeing one of the young men that I trained through the Practorium be examined for Ordination. He not only passed his exam, but he passed with "flying colors." His handling of God's Word is a lasting tribute to the ongoing success of the Practorium approach to training men for the ministry. Through the video courses used in the Practoriums, Dr. Whitcomb will continue to have an impact on training men long after the Lord calls him home. I praise the Lord for Dr. Whitcomb's faithfulness to our Lord and Savior Jesus Christ.[16]

*William (Billy) Anderson*, Ph.D., is a chemist from Knoxville, Tennessee, who works as a chemical consultant for incineration stack emissions testing. Billy's story highlights another side of Dr. Whitcomb's tireless efforts to serve the Lord. Billy wrote:

> I grew up in one of America's liberal church denominations, and as a result, I never got saved, didn't know the gospel, and led a very troubled life for many years. After going through a debilitating divorce, I made an attempt at personal reform by going back to my church and getting into Bible studies at the old liberal institution. After about eight years of self-help attempts, the Lord finally intervened in mercy, and I was saved at the age of 45. I was alone in my truck at

---

16. Email letter from David Blevins to the author for this biography, October 6, 2018; used with permission.

the time and on my way to work. I got saved while listening to Moody Church's "Running to Win." I took Jesus Christ as my personal Savior while alone in my vehicle.

In the moments immediately following having been born again the thought occurred to me that five minutes earlier I was not saved and would have gone to Hell had I died. I resolved to "study to show myself approved" from that time on. I had been deceived for 45 years and it was up to me to know the Truth. So I began reading books by men like Dr. Harry Ironside and tuning into the Bible Broadcasting Network (BBN) to listen to conservative preaching by various Bible teachers. And that is when it happened.

One night I was listening to BBN radio and a gentleman came on that was teaching on the Sovereignty of God and man's free will; man's responsibility and God's elect. This speaker explained that both doctrines were true and referred to this issue as an antinomy. That is, two things that are apparently contradictory, but not solvable by the human mind. Only an infinite, Holy God could set up such an arrangement, and only a keen-minded Spirit-taught Bible teacher could present such Biblical truth in lucid terms. The speaker was Dr. John Whitcomb and I knew that I had to acquire more of his insightful teaching. I wrote to BBN and requested copies of all of Dr. Whitcomb's lectures for that week. Sometime later my wife and I travelled to Winona Lake, Indiana, to try and find this fine teacher at Grace Seminary.

We learned that he hadn't been there for several years, but that he had recorded Bible classes that were available to churches to equip the saints in instruction of the Word of God. I was encouraged to contact Dr. Whitcomb to find out more. I wrote him a letter requesting information and received an immediate phone call at our home to tell me about **Christian Workman School of Theology**. Dr. Whitcomb explained that the video classes were intended to be administered by local churches for the formal instruction in Biblical Theology. I tried to get a church to sponsor this program and offered to pay all of the expenses. The churches in

Knoxville that I knew were not interested in these classes, and I continued to dialogue with Dr. Whitcomb regarding the negative responses I had received from area pastors. Finally, he consented to let me use his fine teaching materials for conducting Bible classes in our home which we immediately set up. He outlined for us the preferred order of study material and continued to coach us throughout the various series. That was 13 years ago, and we are still using Dr. Whitcomb's friendship, encouragement, materials, and prayers to study the Word of God on Saturday mornings.

I have learned from Dr. Whitcomb that everything we know has to be put through the grid of Bible knowledge. He taught me that an understanding of systematic Biblical theology is necessary if I am to perform the Lord's will and do good deeds in the Lord's Name. Bible Study done properly requires hard work, discipline, and dedication. Dr. Whitcomb was the model teacher, and he has continued to help and encourage us to this day. I hope to be able to carry his torch forward and honor the Lord the way he taught me by teaching others to do the same. I believe that Dr. Whitcomb taught us by example the definition of Biblical love. It is doing what is best for a person in light of eternity no matter what the cost is to me personally. I love Dr. Whitcomb and Mrs. Norma. He is a true Warrior for the Gospel![17]

*Steve Craig* works as the Ark Volunteer Coordinator at Ark Encounter[18] in Williamstown, Kentucky, an attraction of Answers in Genesis (AIG). He shared the impact of Dr. Whitcomb as a layman.

As a baby boomer, I, along with the rest of America, grew up just accepting what our secular public-school teachers taught. And, although my parents took me to church every Sunday, I don't remember ever being taught in Sunday school, or hearing the preacher preach anything different. I believe that I was saved (ironically) in 1961. I earned my "God and Country" Boy Scouts of America merit badge

---

17. Letter to the author received August 2, 2018; used with permission.
18. Answers in Genesis' Ark Encounter is in Williamstown, Kentucky, about 40 miles south of Cincinnati, Ohio.

and was a member of the "Fellowship of Christian Athletes" in high school. My college years were unfortunately ". . . two steps back." After college I worked in property management for a state park with a uniformitarian evolutionist message.

In 1984, beginning to think about my own young family and their spiritual health, "somehow" we were led to a Bible teaching church. The pastor invited me to the donut shop on a Tuesday morning. We met together for years. The pastor's sister and my best friend were commuting to Grace Seminary, about 40 miles from my home. I thought I'd tag along. I was not interested in an advanced degree, just biblical truth.

I audited 18 hours at Grace in 88-89 and 89-90 and was privileged to sit under Dr. Whitcomb's teaching. *The Genesis Flood* was the first book I read on creation apologetics, but it was certainly not the last. On page 137 of my copy of *The Genesis Flood* I circled the statement, "Uniformitarianism, in other words, has simply been assumed, not proved. Catastrophism has simply been denied, not refuted." These words have stuck with me and lead me to seek more information on Creation and the Flood, and then to teach at my own church. My wife and I began to volunteer at AiG in 2008 and the Ark Encounter since 2016 where we serve as Volunteer Coordinators.

I [continue] to thank [Dr. Whitcomb] for his influence in my life. And I also thank my Father in Heaven for him as well.[19]

*Salomon Zambo* is a French speaking, self-described "Evangelist for the Lord" from Cameroon, Africa. He describes the impact that Dr. Whitcomb, his students, and his teaching materials had on him and many others who are ministering for the Lord in Central Africa.

I am Pastor Zambobene Salomon Gerard. I came to Christ in 1993 in my homeland of Cameroon, Africa. The Lord's agenda since then came clearly in my life. I felt the desire to proclaim Jesus who saved me, everywhere. Being a student in Yaounde University, I had no peace or joy to continue my economy studies. I had one goal: preach Jesus! I became a student of the written Word on my own. I left the

---

19. Letter received July 13, 2018; used with permission.

University and went back to my liberal Presbyterian church. I became a catechist. The church intended to send me to the liberal Protestant University of Yaounde. But God worked in a marvelous way! Instead I decided to attend the Cameroon Biblical Seminary and in my first academic year was introduced to Dr. Whitcomb and Dr. McClain through the courses taught in the Seminary.

For somebody who came from such a liberal church, you can imagine my surprise when I began to study the Bible as God's inerrant Word during Dr. Whitcomb's courses such as *God and Revelation, Biblical Fundamentalism, Daniel, Biblical Eschatology*. I had never been nourished in the Word like that before. It was 19 years since I believed. I asked myself, "where have these people been, with all these truths, that I never heard before?" Dr. Whitcomb's defense of 6 literal days of creation versus the evolution gave me great respect for this person. I learned that as long as we remain in the truth, the Bible, the whole Bible and nothing but the Bible, we will have God's approval, which is better than man's approval.

Paul urged Timothy to preach the Word (2 Timothy 4:2). He wrote to him as well, that the things which he had heard from him in the presence of many witnesses, to entrust them to faithful men, who would be able to teach others also (2 Timothy 2:2). This verse, which has been so dear to Dr. Whitcomb, has become the motto of our Seminary and our Practoriums.

I also felt the burden to go out and establish local churches, where the things I have heard could be taught to faithful men. I had a burden to establish Bible institutes, which we call "Practorium." My first missionary field was Oku, in the NW of Cameroon. We started with 8 men. I was assisted once in a while by men from the seminary, then joined by Pastor Raymond, an African pastor. It was such a tremendous experience!

We received several of Dr. Whitcomb's video classes. I have been using the DVDs he has been sending us to continue the training of the 19 men in our Yaounde Bible Institute. We trained the first generation of 8 men in Oku. They are now training their third generation with all the syllabi Dr. Whitcomb wrote. I put them on a thumb drive and shared them with the director of the training program of the NW region of Cameroon. In the East of Cameroon, in Abong-Mbang, Pastor Raymond Olinga received the DVD and the same thumb drives with all the revised syllabi that Dr. Whitcomb wrote. He is on his third generation of students. Over the past 18 years we trained 41 leaders among who are evangelists, pastors, and teachers.

The Lord has been so faithful to us. One of us, Pastor Roger, went to Uganda to start the ministry there, and today 23 men from the Democratic Republic of Congo, Uganda, Kenya, Tanzania and Rwanda are serving the Lord. All of them use the same studies that Dr. Whitcomb passed on with a thumb drive and installed on our computers. What a privilege for us to be able now to translate these syllabi into French.

Words cannot express, my gratitude to the Living God, who worked out all things for my good. He brought me from darkness to the light and from ignorance to the saving knowledge of His Word. What a privilege to have the excellent teachings of Dr. Whitcomb. The materials he made available for our ministry here in Africa are the keys of our ministry. Our prayer requests are to see this spread all over Africa, that many will come to be saved and come to a knowledge of the truth. A lot is still to be done to translate his syllabi into French, Swahili, Spanish, and Arabic. May the Lord of the harvest keep us safe and bless the tremendous work of the Gospel He called us to do in Africa! May all the needs be provided in order to see each day the fulfillment of 2 Timothy 2:2 with Dr. Whitcomb's teaching material! Our gratitude to him and all that were under him, who also came and taught us. As I personally have been telling him and his students who taught us, our payment is to remain faithful to the Lord and grounded in the truth of His Word! He is more than able to do it! To Him alone be the glory![20]

---

20. Written by Solomon Zambo (Zambobene Salomon Gerard) for this biography, received and accepted July 25, 2018. Several spelling and grammatical errors were corrected.

## Teaching by Example

The process of " . . . entrust[ing] these things to faithful men . . ." is a multifaceted command of Paul to Timothy. Entrusting "these things" certainly involves teaching the Bible, but it also includes demonstrating how to apply God's truths to everyday life. Paul makes this distinction in 1 Corinthians 4:15–17 as he distinguishes teaching as a tutor in contrast to teaching as a good father would his child.

> For if you were to have countless tutors in Christ, yet you would not have many fathers, for in Christ Jesus I became your father through the gospel. Therefore I exhort you, be imitators of me. For this reason I have sent to you Timothy, who is my beloved and faithful child in the Lord, and he will remind you of my ways which are in Christ, just as I teach everywhere in every church.

The true impact of a great teacher is not the immediate awe of his or her listeners to a great lecture or speech. Rather, it is the long-lasting effects of the teacher on the lives of their students. The lifetime impact of a few of the "1,000 men" whom Professor Whitcomb personally taught and mentored highlight this important aspect of his legacy over multiple generations.

Pastor Mick Funderburg captured the essence of Dr. Whitcomb's life as he reflected on 1 Corinthians 11:1.

> The Apostle Paul said "Imitate me, just as I also imitate Christ." Dr. Whitcomb is one of the few men who could also say these words. But because he is a very humble man, he would simply say, "Follow Christ!"[21]

---

21. Email from Michael Funderburg to the author for this biography, July 6, 2018; used with permission.

**1.1** John C. Whitcomb Jr. was born on June 22, 1924. He is being held by his father, John C. Whitcomb Sr. He was 2 months, 15 days old.

**1.2** Buster Whitcomb posing with mother, Salome, and sporting a gun belt and gun. He was to be a "Defender of the Nation." Taken in Harrington Park, NJ, in June 1925 at age 1 year.

**1.3** Buster, a nickname for little John Whitcomb, with a new scooter, age 2.

**1.4** By age 3, he got his first car.

**1.5** Buster Whitcomb (left) with a friend taking a slow boat to China.

**1.6** A view of a room in the Whitcombs' new home in Tientsin, China. The three-member family was aided by multiple servants and other helpers.

**1.7** Buster with his nanny, Pung.

**1.8** Junior officer training (China).

**1.9** A picture of Buster with Pung in China, circa 1928.

**1.10** John Whitcomb and his dad in China, 1928, age 4.

**1.11** Sunshine Kindergarten in Tientsin. Buster Whitcomb is front and center.

**1.12** Fort Leavenworth, Kansas. The "Beehive" with officers lined up outside. Buster lived in a 3rd floor apartment.

**1.13** Whitcomb family, 1930.

## Transition to Seattle, WA

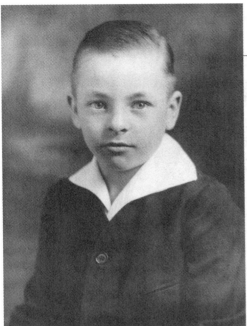

**1.14** Young Buster Whitcomb, now called "Jack," loved Seattle, Washington, where he spent much of his childhood. His kind personality and gentle nature are already evident in this 1933 portrait, age 9 years.

**1.15** The Whitcomb family at their new home in Seattle, Washington, 1933.

**1.16** Jack Whitcomb boating on Limekiln Lake, New York. This was the Whitcomb family summer retreat and sanctuary. Jack is taking his dog Lupe for a ride on a nice summer evening.

**1.17** Jack as a boy scout, 1933, 1934, and 1936, respectively.

**1.18** Camp San Juan near Seattle, WA, 1933.

**1.19** Jack Whitcomb (second from left) with boyhood buddies.

**1.20** Leaving Camp Parsons, July 17, 1937, with a broken arm.

**1.21** Salome, Jack's mother, Seattle, WA, 1935. During Jack's childhood, he wondered about his mother's love, since she was continually involved in social activities and travel, often leaving him in the care of others.

**1.22** Jack viewing Mt. Rainier, WA, August 24, 1935.

**1.23** Golfing at the University golf course, Seattle WA, 1938. Jack finally found an activity loved by his dad, mom, and himself.

**1.24** Jack Whitcomb approaching his 14th birthday, June 9, 1938.

**1.25** Swimming in Limekiln Lake, NY, age 15 years.

## Leaving Seattle, entering Fort Benning, Georgia.

**1.26** Sightseeing on a car trip leaving Seattle, WA, behind and heading to Limekiln Lake, NY, 1939.

**1.27** Cousin Sally, General Patton's flower garden helper.

**1.29** Jack Whitcomb becomes a cadet at McCallie Military Academy in September 1940.

**1.28** Personal golf ball and tees of General Omar Bradley. Jack would often play with various generals to complete a foursome.

81

## Jack Whitcomb's Drawings

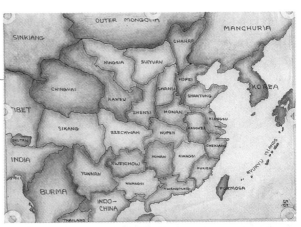

**1.30** Maps of China (top) and Germany (bottom) 1940.

**1.31** Drawing of British Field Marshall Earl Wavell of the Middle East, drawn by Jack Whitcomb from the cover of a magazine while at McCallie School.

**1.32** Newspaper clipping of Jack Whitcomb (third from left) with his golf team.

**1.33** Cadet Jack Whitcomb at graduation with Adele Von Bergman Miller, "Auntie," who raised Jack's mother and was like a grandmother to him.

# Section 2

# Childhood

# Chapter 4

# Buster

"My Amah Pung"
June 1924 to May 1933

Buster is a nickname that might be given to a little boy who is a rascal. It could also apply to an inquisitive or very active tot that gets into everything or a busy little fellow who breaks things. For reasons that are lost to history forever, the parents and family friends of the future Professor Whitcomb called him "Buster."

Sally Salvador, Dr. Whitcomb's second cousin and 13 years his junior, remembers the professor when he was a young man. "He was the pride of the family," she recalls. Sally, as an only child who lived with Dr. Whitcomb's parents from time to time, viewed him as her big brother. But she adds with a twinkle in her eye, "To me, he was a prankster and a tease."

John Clement Whitcomb Jr. was born in Washington, D.C., on June 22, 1924, at the U.S. Army's Walter Reed Hospital. Born into a career military family, he would be the only child of John C. Whitcomb Sr. and Salome Josephine (Von Bergman) Whitcomb.

Buster's father, John Whitcomb Sr. was a brilliant military strategist with a photographic memory. He had a great sense of humor and a quick wit, leading to his life-long nickname of "Whit." Whit had a fascinating childhood as the only son of an accomplished military surgeon, Colonel Clement Colfax Whitcomb, MD, who won the Medal of the French Legion of Honor for his efforts in World War I. Highlights of Whit's childhood included time in Cuba following the Spanish-American War where he learned to speak perfect Spanish, and an assignment at Fort Apache, Arizona, where he learned to ride horses bareback in the wild with American Indian boys on ponies. Whit went on to become a cadet at West Point, fought in World War I in the 7th Infantry Division, and in World War II. As a Colonel in the U.S. Army, he commanded the 331st Regiment, 83rd Infantry Division at Omaha Beach, Normandy, France, in June 1944 before a promotion to Chief of Staff for the 90th Infantry Division in Patton's 3rd Army. He loved the military and had similar ambitions for his own son.

Buster's mother, Salome, was born on March 5, 1897. Orphaned at age 12, she was raised in Harrington Park, New Jersey, by her aunt and uncle, Adele (Auntie) and Clyde Woodward (Woodie) Miller. Salome was trained as a typist and commuted about 13 miles to work in New York City, which was just across the Hudson River from Harrington Park. She had an attractive personality, a great sense of humor, and was quite the debutant. Harrington Park was also a few miles south of the United States Military Academy at West Point, providing ample opportunities for young women to meet young cadets or junior faculty. Salome met Whit, who became a Spanish instructor at West Point after WWI, and the two were married on May 19, 1923. They attended various Episcopal churches, but neither Whit, nor his wife, Salome, were Bible-believing Christians. According to their son, they lived in deep spiritual darkness. To them, success in life meant climbing the social ladder, enjoying the benefits of a high-profile job, and having close and influential friends — typical goals of many Americans today.

Throughout their lives, Whit and Salome demonstrated a strong marriage and love for each other. Salome was fully committed in her support of Whit. She admired him as a man, as a leader, and as an example to follow. This admiration and respect of Buster's mother for his father provided an important foundation for his view of early life.

On July 24, 1924, when Buster was one month old, his parents and their son moved — a pattern that typifies a military family. Transfer orders directed his father to move from Washington, D.C., to West Point, New York, for one month, then to Fort Benning, Georgia. On May 8, 1925, they returned to Salome's hometown of Harrington Park, New Jersey, to spend time with the in-laws then moved a few miles to their own place on Governors Island, New York, just south of Manhattan, where they remained for two years. But the next move would have profound effects on the life and international perspective of the future Professor Whitcomb.

## China 1927–1930 (age 3–6)

Buster, age 3 years, scurried up the gangplank in New York City Harbor to board the *U.S.A.T. Thomas*,[1] a U.S. Army transport ship heading west. On August 12, 1927, close friends and family wished the trio a *bon voyage*, and the ship headed to sea on its way to China. The ship steamed around the Florida Keys, through the Panama Canal, and north to San Francisco. After an exchange of people and cargo, the ship continued to Honolulu, Guam, Manila, and finally to Qinhuangdao, China, on September 2, 1927. The family continued to Tientsin (Tianjin), China, by train. Tientsin rested on the Hai Ho River about 65 miles southeast of Peking (Beijing). This would be the Whitcombs' home for nearly three years.

*The Boxers*

China was recovering from the Boxer Rebellion of 1899–1901. "Boxers" was the name given by Westerners to a secret society called "the Righteous and Harmonious Fists." Members believed that through martial arts and ritual boxing they would become impervious to bullets. The society began in rural areas of northern China and became more and more popular as a reaction against abuses of foreign nations in trade, opium importation, and colonial expansion — including carving Korea and Formosa (Taiwan) away from the Chinese empire to become European colonies. The Boxers also rebelled against abuses of Christian organizations, such as the Catholic Church, that acquired vast tracks of land following the Peking Convention of 1860. The Peking Convention also gave foreigners and missionaries special privileges and rights over the Chinese.[2] Many of the missionaries were astoundingly insensitive to Chinese customs and culture and lived along the coast in comfort while their converts lived in abject poverty. Some missionaries also perverted justice by pressuring local officials to side with Christian converts — often from the lower classes of Chinese society

---

1. http://en.wikipedia.org/wiki/USAT_Thomas.
2. http://www.omf.org/omf/us/resources__1/omf_archives/china_inland_mission_stories/death_to_the_foreigner.

— in local lawsuits and property disputes.[3] Furthermore, the growing influence of higher criticism and allegorizing of the Scripture, which theologians at Princeton University of the late 1800s were struggling to oppose, were taking their toll among Chinese Christians, as the clarity and authority of the Bible was undermined, and the faith of many was to be shaken by uncertainty and confusion.

The colonialist typically focused on personal status and comfort, including some highly visible missionaries. But these people represented the exception rather than the rule as the devotion, zeal, and good works of the majority of Christian missionaries continued to receive wide recognition by the common Chinese people. However, the presence of true Christian missionaries was considered by other Chinese as a standing insult, "for does it not tell the Chinese their conduct is bad and requires change, their culture inadequate and wants addition, their gods despicable and to be cast into the gutter, their forefathers lost and themselves only to be saved by accepting the missionary's teaching?"[4] Thus, disdain for all foreigners continued to pervade the perspective of a majority of the native people.

As anti-foreign sentiment swept China, the Boxers, who initially wanted to destroy the Ch'ing dynasty (which had ruled China for over 250 years) as well as all foreign influences, became increasingly popular.[5] The Empress Dowager, who previously supported many positive Western ideas and reforms, suddenly reversed herself, and backed the Boxers. Emboldened, the Boxers focused their attention on eliminating foreigners. By 1899, bands of Boxers were indiscriminately massacring Christians. On June 18, 1900, the Empress further empowered the Boxers by ordering all foreigners to be killed. The deaths were horrific.[6] Missionaries and Chinese Christians were beaten and burned to death — some were tortured and beheaded. Others were shot, stabbed, cut into pieces, stoned, run over by carts, or strangled. Chen Xikong, for example, had his heart cut out and displayed on a stone. Many missionaries died kneeling in prayer. Over 30,000 Chinese Roman Catholics,

---

3. http://www.britannica.com/EBchecked/topic/76364/Boxer-Rebellion.
4. Alfred E. Cornebise, *The United States 15th Infantry Regiment in China, 1912–1938* (Jefferson, NC: McFarland & Company, 2004), p. 24.
5. http://history1900s.about.com/od/1900s/qt/boxer.htm.
6. http://www.omf.org/omf/us/resources__1/omf_archives/china_inland_mission_stories/death_to_the_foreigner.

47 Roman Catholic priest and nuns, 2,000 Chinese Protestants, 35 Protestant missionaries, plus 53 of their children were martyred. But this persecution clarified the passion of real Christians, who, knowing their God, willingly died for their faith out of love for the Chinese and a burden for their souls.

By July 1900, numerous foreigners and missionaries had fled to Peking (Beijing) and barricaded themselves into fortified buildings. In the meantime, an eight-nation army, including elements from the United States, assembled on the coast and fought their way to Beijing. On August 14, 1900, the international coalition rescued the surviving missionaries, who had less than a week's food left, and drove the Boxers from Beijing. The foreign army looted the city and burned down imperial palaces and temples. The Boxer Rebellion was finally quenched. Then the international coalition began peace negotiations. And on September 7, 1901, a peace treaty was finally signed.

Hudson Taylor, founder of the China Inland Mission, refused to accept payment for the loss of property or life, to show the "meekness and gentleness of Christ." In contrast to many foreign missionaries who maintained their western culture and lifestyle, Hudson Taylor dressed and lived as the people he loved and longed to reach for Christ. His response was crucial to re-opening the hearts of the Chinese to the Gospel and resulted in the commitment of hundreds of new missionaries who poured into China with the purpose of developing Chinese pastors and teachers equipped and capable of carrying out the Great Commission independent of foreign support.

The United States, as well as other governments, established a number of military garrisons in China that were maintained for decades. Hong Kong, for example, remained under British control until July 1, 1997. The garrison in Tientsin was a magnificent facility that was built by the Germans but was conceded to the Americans after the Germans lost WWI. The U.S. Army now held this garrison with the help of a young officer, John "Whit" Whitcomb, and his family.

Whit was assigned to the 15th Infantry Regiment of the U.S. Army in Tientsin. The 15th Regiment originally participated in the relief expedition to rescue Americans under siege in Peking in August 1900, and continued as the American military representatives in China until

1938.[7] After WWI the unit was stationed in Tientsin, China, which became their primary base of operations in China.

Tientsin was a port city, filled with laborers carrying huge boxes, and dirty streets filled with humanity and rickshaws. The soldiers described the population as "masses of dirty, crippled, stinking, terrible-looking beings."[8] Most of the Chinese people lived in deep poverty. However, little Buster, who had no comparisons or prejudices, learned to know and love these people. The soldiers' contempt for the Chinese people stood in stark contrast to most missionaries whose hearts were filled with compassion. Hudson Taylor, for example, penned this perspective; "Oh, for eloquence to plead the cause of China, for a pencil dipped in fire to paint the condition of this people."[9]

The Americans, in contrast to the Chinese, lived in an isolated military compound within the city. The compound, the size of a city block, included three rows of large, four-story gray barracks. One visitor described the compound as "majestic," with an academic air, a dining facility reminiscent of a hotel,[10] and even a hospital. The garrison generally accommodated about 50 officers and 800 soldiers. The 15th Infantry Regiment was famous for high-caliber soldiers and officers (with a large number of West Point graduates), who were all meticulously dressed and destined for greatness. The commanding officer at the time was George Marshall Jr., who would later be Chief of Staff of the U.S. Army in World War II, Secretary of Defense, Secretary of State, and a Nobel Laureate for the "Marshall Plan" following World War II. Marshall left the 15th Infantry Regiment as Whit, Salome, and Buster arrived. George and Whit would meet again, with significant effects for both of their careers.

*Living in China*

In contrast to the United States, the cost of labor in China during the 1920s was low, and the availability of cheap help was high. American military officers enjoyed apartments or homes filled with servants and

---

7. The history of the 15th Regiment is from Alfred E. Cornebise, *The United States 15th Infantry Regiment in China, 1912–1938* (Jefferson, NC: McFarland & Company 2004).
8. Ibid., 10.
9. Hudson Taylor, *China's Spiritual Need and Claims*, 1865. Cited in https://en.wikipedia.org/wiki/Hudson_Taylor, accessed February 7, 2016.
10. Ibid., 12.

other helpers. The Whitcombs hired a butler and gardener, who would bring in additional help as needed. On one occasion, the young Whitcomb family returned from a short trip and, to their surprise, found 30 sub-servants huddled in their basement, attesting to the plight of many of the Chinese people. Of all the servants the Whitcombs employed, the most special was the woman hired to care for Buster.

Buster was assigned to the care of Pung, an "amah" employed as a maid and nanny. Her job consisted of looking after young Whitcomb while his parents were busy with grown-up things. Although Buster did attend a school for American children, most of his education came from Pung — in Chinese. In fact, Mandarin would become the first of several languages that Professor Whitcomb would learn. Pung came to love Buster as her own son. Buster also loved Pung as a caring, affectionate mother figure.

By the time the Whitcombs left China in 1930, Pung and Buster were inseparable. Pung accompanied the family to the train station to say good-bye. As a special gift, she slipped a bright red apple to six-year-old Buster and gave him a final hug. It was a major gift from a poor Chinese woman. As the train pulled out, Pung fully realized that she was losing this beautiful child forever. She began running beside the train — screaming and crying for Buster. The train soon outran her.[11]

Buster pulled the apple out of his pocket and showed it to his mom. "From Pung!" he exclaimed. As he was about to take a bite, his father grabbed it from his little hands and threw it out of a window of the train. "Poison!" he announced. The explanation given to Buster's mother was that these apples were shiny red because they were painted with colored shellac to make them look delicious. However, the shellac was toxic, especially for a child. Buster, of course, did not understand. It was a special gift from Pung.

*Returning to the USA*

On March 17, 1930, the young family boarded another ship for the long trip back to their homeland. Buster found a friend on board named Bobo Smith, who taught him the new skill of making paper airplanes.

---

11. The Chinese amahs were apparently forbidden from going to the port with the children they cared for because of the fear that they would grab the children and jump into the ocean and commit suicide rather than lose them.

The game was to make the best possible planes with available materials and to launch them out of the porthole windows to see whose airplane could stay aloft the longest or fly the farthest. This game, and others, occupied the long days as the ship sequentially docked at Nagasaki, Japan; Honolulu, Hawaii; San Francisco, California; back through the Panama Canal; and to New York City where the 6-week journey ended on April 29, 1930.

Unbeknownst to Buster, certain papers have greater value to older people than aeronautical potential enjoyed by kids. Some of the projectiles were carefully crafted from official military documents, immigration papers, and passports needed to re-enter the United States. Buster remembers a spanking — the only one of his life. He also remembers seeing the land but not being able to disembark for a number of days until verification of citizenship and replacement documents could be obtained.

## Transition to Life in the United States

Initially, life in the United States seemed foreign and stressful for Buster. Nobody else could speak Mandarin Chinese, and Buster could barely speak English! The other school children were amused at the big, blond-haired, blue-eyed boy who would ask, "How many clock say?" A quick study, Buster soon mastered English and promptly forgot Chinese. What haunted him, however, was the feeling that Pung loved spending time with him to a level that was much greater than that of his own mother.

It was clear that Salome loved and treasured her own family. In later years, she developed a positive relationship with her son, extended for many years after Jack left home as documented by their frequent letters and visits.

However, Buster's early life experiences, and that of his mother, combined in a perfect storm. This resulted in this only son having a life-long sense that his mother did not enjoy spending time to the degree he expected from his mom. While Salome likely retained some trust and attachment limitations from her early childhood, Buster's early formative years centered on his relationship with his Chinese amah, Pung. The continuous love, affection, and attention given to him by Pung provided all the nurture that a child could want, but the Chinese tradition of not disciplining young children, especially boys, conflicted with Northern European traditions in child rearing — perhaps making Buster's parents appear harsh. The emotional closeness and time investment between Buster and his mother compared to Buster and Pung may be reflected by the fact that Professor Whitcomb learned Mandarin Chinese as a first language rather than English.

As he grew older, Buster also wondered why his small, middle-class family needed maids and butlers to help care for him at all. In other homes, it appeared that the mother's job, 24 hours a day, 7 days a week, was to care for the kids. These factors, plus the constant moving from Army base to Army base during the formative years may have contributed to a real or perceived deficit in the mother-son and other relationships.

## The Rest of the World

October 29, 1929, remembered as Black Tuesday, marked the day that 16 million shares on the New York Stock Exchange were lost, leading to the loss of billions of dollars and countless jobs. As a military officer, Whit had job security. This was important to the young Whitcomb family as the United States plunged into the Great Depression. After China, Whit reported to a new assignment in Washington, D.C.

## Limekiln Lake, New York

Prior to the 1960s, most residential homes did not have air conditioning. Summers in polluted cities during the hot, humid days of July and "dog days" of August were nearly intolerable — especially for the weak, elderly, sickly, children, and the wealthy. Thus, during the first half of the 20th century, there was an annual migration of millions of Americans from Eastern cities to vacation homes in New England and upstate New York. In the summer of 1930, the Whitcomb family joined the migration and made the first of many trips with Buster to Limekiln Lake, a beautiful glacial lake in central New York State.

Limekiln Lake rests about 300 miles north of New York City in the Adirondack Mountains. The lake remained the favorite site on earth for Buster's mother, who had been visiting the site since age 12. Like many glacial lakes stretching across the northern United States from the Ice Age following the Flood, Limekiln Lake had clear water, an irregular shoreline, and a panoramic view of deciduous and pine forest. The surroundings offered fresh cool air and peace and quiet, except for the cries of the loons in the morning and the occasional splash of a jumping fish or clang of a paddle on the side a canoe.

The family had a favorite cabin that Uncle Woodie began leasing as a hunting lodge before he and Adele were married. The site became even more sentimental when Woodie took Adele to the cabin for their honeymoon and taught her to cook. Sally Salvador remembers the little cabin as being very "rustic" without running water or electricity. There was an outhouse "with a beautiful view," a pump for spring water, a tin-lined hole in the ground in which residents put large blocks of ice for food storage, and wood burning stoves for heating and cooking. For light they used kerosene lamps and used a wind-up Victrola phonograph for evening entertainment. Fishing was always part of the vacation, and Whit triangulated the perfect location for dropping hooked worms to entice and catch bullhead catfish. It was a place that the family would return to over and over, through the years. When September arrived, the family packed their summer gear and headed to their new home in Fort Leavenworth, Kansas.

## Kansas 1930–1933 (age 6–9)

Fort Leavenworth was a major advancement in the career pathway for Whit, but not so fun for Salome and Buster. Fort Leavenworth served as home for the U.S. Army Command and General Staff College. Whit joined an elite group of future leaders as they developed new approaches to war to avoid the stalemate and carnage of WWI. Among Whit's colleagues at the College were some West Point colleagues including Dwight D. Eisenhower, Omar N. Bradley, and George S. Patton.

The college specialized in general staff procedures, hands-on experience with various combined arms, and handling large military formations in combat.Officers graduating from the College were recognized for demonstrating leadership skills, superior decision-making skills in major conflicts, and both flexibility and innovation on the battlefield.

As a place to live, Fort Leavenworth, Kansas, has never reached a "Top 10" ranking in the United States. Officers and their families lived in a rickety military barracks on the base called the Beehive. One would surmise that there were few children of Buster's age, and as an only child, he often had to entertain himself.

96

## Buster

Professor Whitcomb remembers one great toy, the "hootenanny." This was a mechanical device for drawing circular designs (hypotrochoids), much like a Spirograph.[12] This type of toy appeared to fascinate and stimulate his organized and detail-oriented mind. He also began collecting and organizing stamps, coins, and magazines.

From July to September 1931, the family had a short reprieve from life in the Beehive. They journeyed back to their favorite refuge at Limekiln Lake, New York, for summer vacation — relaxing and eating catfish. Then back to Kansas.

Kansas nearly became the final resting place for young John Whitcomb's body. Buster caught a cold, which progressed to pneumonia. The pneumonia became life threatening, with survival from minute to minute remaining tenuous. By the grace of God, the illness was not fatal, and Buster made a full recovery.

As Buster grew, his original nickname no longer seemed to apply. Instead, John Whitcomb Jr. became "Jack," a nickname that stuck for the rest of his life.

On May 23, 1933, Whit departed Fort Leavenworth for a new assignment near Seattle, Washington. Mother and son headed east, leaving Kansas for good. The summer of 1933 was spent visiting Jack's mother's family in New Jersey and his father's family in St. Petersburg, Florida. Then they headed north to enjoy the waning days of summer at Limekiln Lake. In September the family would be reunited in Seattle to begin the next phase of life in the Great Northwest.

In summary, Professor Whitcomb's early life consisted of times of stability and times of stark transition. The early years in China became a highpoint of love and undivided attention by a loving caretaker named Pung. Leaving China suddenly (to Buster), losing Pung, and adapting to a strange new country would be stressful and confusing for any young boy. And Buster's mother may have lacked some of the warmth and attention that Pung delivered. The constant moving, changing homes, different people, new surroundings, and a limited number of children and friends his own age resulted in personal characteristics of flexibility and adaptability, but strained other characteristics such as developing close attachment to people, places, and things.

---

12. Hootenanny was the common name for "Mystic Designer." See http://www.retrowow.co.uk/retro_collectibles/60s/spirograph.php. A demonstration of the apparatus can be seen on YouTube: https://www.youtube.com/watch?v=_KrL9ia-R2Y.

## A Good and Faithful Servant

In some ways, Jack likely felt somewhat distant from his parents, in that the next part of his life's journey in Seattle, Washington, focused on trying to please his parents and gain their approval. Other children might have responded differently to the circumstances under which Jack lived and developed. But in retrospect, the circumstances were perfect, in God's sovereign plan, in developing and molding Jack for his providential mission.

# Chapter 5

# Jack

"I wanted to be like [Abraham] Lincoln and be very honest."
May 1933 to August 1939 (age 9 to 15 years)

## Seattle, Washington

Seattle, Washington, is the location that Professor John C. Whitcomb Jr. connects with his childhood. Many important events in his life began here, leading him into his later teenage years and adulthood.

Living conditions in Seattle were a step up from the Beehive in Kansas. The family rented a house just north of downtown Seattle on Capitol Hill. Though it was a 45-mile commute, Whit traveled to Fort Lewis each day, where new opportunities awaited him.

The Capitol Hill district of Seattle was a more suburban area of small houses that offered a great panoramic view of Lake Union and had many majestic mountains in the background. It was so beautiful compared to the New Jersey suburbs of New York City that when Salome's family visited, Adele (who raised Salome as her own daughter) wanted her husband Woody to move the family west. But this never happened.

The Seattle area provided a great location for families with kids. Multiple city parks and playgrounds dotted the city map.[1] Roanoke Park, for example, was a grassy space located on north Capitol Hill where Jack learned to play football with the neighborhood kids. Rodgers playground offered tennis courts, two baseball fields, a water fountain, swings, and slides. Nearby Loyal field became the chosen site for Jack to play baseball. And of course, the Greater Seattle region provided the perfect landscape for hiking and camping.

---

1. http://www.seattle.gov/parks/park_detail.asp?ID=380.

Whit, with an eye on Jack as a future military leader, encouraged his son to join the Boy Scouts of America. The "Scout's Oath" appeared to encompass the values that a future leader would embrace:

> On my honor I will do my best to do my duty to God and my country and to obey the Scout Law; to help other people at all times; to keep myself physically strong, mentally awake, and morally straight.

Whit also loved the motto, "Be prepared!" Jack became a Scout while in Seattle, to please his father.

Very little information about the Whitcomb family remains from their arrival to Seattle in May 1933 until January 1935. Jack went to school, played with friends, did things with his family, read, and listened to the radio. A prominent local artist painted his portrait at about age 10, which captured his appearance as something of a quiet, subdued personality. Perhaps the sad appearance reflected the fact that he missed playing outside with friends — being forced to sit for hours in a studio. Or maybe, Jack felt a vacuum in his life that only the Lord could fill.

## Diary

On January 11, 1936, eleven-and-a-half-year-old Jack began a lifelong routine of keeping a diary. The inaugural entry read, *"I saw my first Robot (Alpha) in existence, at Fredrick-Nelson's store. Bought my first bond. (U.S. Postal #37:50)."* Not one of many words, Jack's journal reflected his to-the-point style. He decided not to use the diary as a means of expression, but rather a record of the activities and events of his daily life.

January 15, 1936: *"Collected papers and went to Cubs. Den 1 won the 'inter Den Contest,' we played several games."*

January 16, 1936: *"I saw Admiral Byrd and his pictures of his second trip to the South Pole. I went with Wheaton and Martin."*

January 18, 1936: *"Went to the Seattle Symphony with Wheaton Blanchard. Then I collected papers with Martin."*

January 19, 1936: *"Went to Sunday School. Walked down to see 7 keys to Baldests[2] and King of Burlesque with Mother and Daddy."*

---

2. Probably the 1935 film *Seven Keys to Baldpate.*

# Jack

January 21, 1936: *"Martin and I collected papers and tied them up into bundles. We had 378 lbs."*

As the days and months went by, typical entries looked more like this one from October 25, 1938: *"I went to high school. In the afternoon I played. In the evening I did my homework. I heard the radio."*

## Daily Life

Jack attended Broadway High School, which was so named because it was on Broadway Street. The school building was initially opened in 1902 as the first dedicated high school in the Seattle area.[3] In addition to being the building for elementary, junior high, and high school classes, the "high school" was used as a self-help center for unemployed workers struggling to learn new skills to capture a job during the Great Depression. According to his diary, Jack's performance in Seattle Public schools from 1935–36 was average. He received B's and C's in all his classes, except for geography, where he unsurprisingly earned an A.

Home life centered around going out to double feature movies with his mother on Sundays after attending the Episcopal Cathedral, attending the Boy Scouts meetings, occasional outings with his father, playing Monopoly with friends and family (the favorite game during the Great Depression since it allowed players to vicariously hold large amounts of money), and listening to the radio.

Whit and Salome were outgoing people. In addition to their U.S. Army friends, they took advantage of the greater sports, cultural, and outdoor opportunities in Seattle. To the Whitcombs' delight, there was much more to do in Washington than there had been in Fort Leavenworth, Kansas. Jack traveled with is dad to Silver Lake, Washington, to fish for bass and to Puget Sound to fish for salmon. The family saw the Seattle Mariners major league baseball team play visiting opponents, and they watched prize fights, including the Joe Lewis vs. Max Schmelling fight. They also attended educational and cultural events in Seattle, such as a travel log with Admiral Byrd or the symphony.

During the Great Depression, employment as an officer in the military provided job security and disposable income. The Whitcombs continued their practice from China in hiring maids and others to

---

3. http://www.historylink.org/index.cfm?DisplayPage=output.cfm&file_id=3204.

help with daily chores, including watching their son. Their domestic help included a Mrs. Brosman, who primarily helped with the cleaning, shopping, and Jack.

Household pets were another constant in the Whitcomb household. Salome preferred cats over dogs. While in Seattle they cared for at least two cats, "Sargent" and "Ra-de-kitten-aw-three."[4]

Jack's daily routine started before school with an inspection of the neighborhood as part of a morning patrol (likely linked to the Boy Scouts). In addition to school and Scouts, he attended glee club. He also made friends with kids in the neighborhood including Jim Taylor, Wheaton Blanchard, Martin Miller, John Myers, Jack Ervine, and Bret Carson. He sometimes went to their houses to play, but, judging from his diaries, he seldom invited anyone over to his house.

His parents loved entertaining their many friends, including high-ranking military officers. During these parties, Jack was tucked away in his room to do his homework, read books and magazines, draw pictures, and/or listen to the radio. His exclusion from these "family events" and the conduct of people who ingested too much alcohol, resulted in an aversion to these types of events and a longing for a different and more godly home.

The radio provided both education and entertainment to Jack, with access to world news, baseball games, and radio dramas. His favorite radio drama was *Gang Busters*.[5] This famous radio series, beginning in July 1935, was an exciting law-and-order series that celebrated good over evil, with gangsters and master criminals falling to the persistent hard work of American law enforcement officers. The sound of sirens, machine guns, and explosions at the beginning is the origin of the phrase, "came on like *Gang Busters*." Criminals included "Baby-Face"

---

4. Author note: I asked my dad about this name years ago. He had no idea where it came from or what it means.

5. *Gang Busters* was one of the most popular radio shows of the mid-20th century. It later became a movie series (1940s) and a TV series (1950s). Many of the radio episodes are preserved in the National Archives online: https://archive.org/details/Gangbusters-Otr. For example, Gang Busters, episode date August 8, 1935, http://www.myoldradio.com/include/popup.php?id=20272, and episode date 10-13-1937, http://www.myoldradio.com/old-radio-episodes/gang-busters-safe-crackers-and-vault-makers/5. TV episodes available on YouTube, https://www.youtube.com/watch?v=HpY5yR1aiJc&ebc=ANyPx-Kpy1Q5hCFIbtEjiDmo_q1-9lQXdr1o8duAKwV2mNeEQytJ5y2f6OnVmSJDCeKniS-LYa8B-IcLkG2MyjMvah9Kgn8r5MNg.

Nelson, Ma Barker and her boys, John Dillinger, and Willie "The Actor" Sutton — and none of them escaped justice. The series was hosted by famous law men, including Colonel H. Norman Schwarzkopf (father of the Gulf-War Col. Schwarzkopf) and Lewis J. Valentine, the New York City Police Commissioner credited for cleaning up the corruption in the Big Apple. Jack would not miss a single episode unless it was absolutely unavoidable.

Drawing also became a favorite activity of Jack's. Rather than drawing landscapes, animals, people, cars, or machines, Jack drew maps of various countries around the globe. This activity either spawned an interest in world cultures or reflected a deeper appreciation of places he already lived and the interesting people he knew, including China and Pung.

## Mother and Son

As an adolescent, one of Jack's regular sources of pleasure was going to movies and events with his mother. Salome was a warm, funny, and engaging lady who cared deeply for family and friends. She demonstrated unusual care for maids and hired help, providing in both material ways and personal guidance.

Jack's mother would fix his breakfast before school each day and pack him a lunch. She would also take him to the movie theater for a double feature on weekends, and sometimes during the week.

Salome, Jack's mother, suffered a stressful childhood. Her mother, Salome Juliet "Julia" Von Bergman, was largely forced, at the age of 20, into a secret marriage with an associate of her grandfather, resulting in the birth of Salome. Julia's husband disappeared from the family before Salome's birth, either through death or a secret divorce. Regardless, no future contact occurred. On July 5, 1900, when Salome was 3 years old, her mother Julia married a man named Arnold Green Verrinder. Julia was 25, while Arnold was 47. Jack's relatives remember Arnold as being "no good." Julia conceived a second child with Arnold, but the delivery went horribly wrong, and both the mother and daughter died. Thus, her life ended on August 29, 1906, at the age of 31. On her deathbed, she asked her sister Adele to take Salome as her own daughter and not to allow her child to be raised by Arnold.

Salome became the object of a major custody battle. In the end, Adele and her husband, Woodie, gained custody of Julia's child, and

Arnold left with all of the Von Bergman's family assets. Salome's rocky life then stabilized, with a loving aunt who treated her as a daughter and a cousin who treated her as a sister. However, children who go through such early life experiences often suffer residual effects in areas of trust and close attachment to others in core relationships.

## Church

Jack's diary records his going to Sunday school nearly every Sunday. His parents, however, did not appear to attend church very often. On April 25, 1937, Jack was confirmed at St. Mark's Church. On June 13, 1937, Jack was given a New Testament by his Sunday school teacher, which he kept for his entire life. But by the spring of 1938, attending church was not as much of a priority. He began doing other things on Sunday morning, namely enjoying the funny papers.

## The Clarks

While his son settled into a normal, rather unexciting routine, Whit excelled at Fort Lewis and made some strategic friends. One lifelong friend he got reacquainted with at the fort was Mark Clark,[6] who later became the youngest general in the United States Army during World War II. Mark was a cadet at West Point in the same class as Whit, graduating with him in 1917 along with many of the great future leaders of World War II. Mark Clark was an outstanding teacher and strategist, and he served at the Army War College in Carlisle, Pennsylvania, just before an assignment at Fort Lewis, Washington.

Upon Clark's arrival at Fort Lewis, Whit immediately renewed their friendship. Mark Clark and his wife, Maurine, had two children, a son named Billy, who played with Jack, and a daughter named Patricia Ann. The Clarks lived at Fort Lewis, which was a 45-minute drive from the Whitcombs, so getting together as young families took some effort. Jack's diary records multiple weekend rendezvous and special events that the families enjoyed together in 1937 and 1938.

The Clarks stayed at Fort Lewis until 1940 when Mark was appointed to teach at the Army War College. Clark worked with General Leslie McNair to refine and implement the new ideas and perspectives developed in Fort Leavenworth and other sites. The military leaders needed to train a new, modern army to fight against Panzer tanks rather than

6. Mark W. Clark; see http://en.wikipedia.org/wiki/Mark_W._Clark.

a cavalry charge. Furthermore, military strategists recognized that the ebb and flow of battle could spell victory or defeat as opportunities and dangers develop. In WWI, opportunities were lost when the commanders sat miles behind the battle in plush headquarters. In the new American Army, the commanders would be moved to within eyeshot of the front line. This was predicted to provide critical advantages to the front-line soldiers and to revolutionize the outcome of battles. Clark received the opportunity to pull these ideas together into a new, cohesive, strategic approach.

One of the most important parts of military readiness is the military exercise, known as "war games." Planning a major, coordinated attack or defense is incredibly complex and requires precise logistics, a sustained supply chain, command-control structures, and so forth. War games allow the entire military group to "practice" — to try new tactics and to discover who the best commanders are under dynamic circumstances.

War games were conducted in the northwestern United States throughout the 1930s. George Marshall, who was promoted to brigadier general in October 1936, was sent to command the Vancouver Barracks in Vancouver, Washington, from 1936 to 1938. His army group competed in war games with the army group at Fort Lewis, Washington. According to Whit, the commander at Fort Lewis suddenly became unavailable, resulting in the transfer of command to the next in line — John C. Whitcomb Sr. Apparently, Marshall's group was outmaneuvered and badly beaten by Whitcomb. The consequence was that Marshall was never given a field command. He held a grudge against Whit for the rest of his life. Marshall's career path changed to capture his skills as a capable organizer, but not as a fighter. In July 1938, Marshall was assigned to the War Plans Division in Washington, D.C. He continued to be promoted, becoming Chief of Staff of the U.S. Army on September 1, 1939, the day Germany invaded Poland and started WWII. Marshall was also trusted by President Roosevelt and others, picking outstanding candidates for major leadership positions. Marshall either picked or recommended Dwight D. Eisenhower, George S. Patton, Leslie McNair, Mark Wayne Clark, and Omar Bradley to command the new Army. But Marshall also kept a little "black book" with names of people that he opposed. Marshall never led troops into battle, and Whit was continually blocked from becoming a general, even with the repeated recommendations and requests of Mark Clark and George Patton.

Clark, however, later designed military exercises to test the new American Army doctrines of war on a massive scale. The new training ground would be located in a large, sparsely populated area in the southeastern United States, and the project was dubbed the Louisiana Maneuvers. These war games proved to be critical to the success of the Army in World War II. The exercises identified future battlefield leaders such as George Patton and Dwight Eisenhower. Later, Whit (as a colonel) would lead a similar series of war games in Tennessee, where the mountainous terrain mirrored that of Germany.

In 1943, Mark Clark was given command of the Fifth U.S. Army to liberate Italy. Although he had many successes, he was heavily criticized for ignoring the orders of his superior officer, General Alexander, in the rush to be the first Ally to enter Rome, and thereby missing an opportunity to surround and destroy the German 10th Army. He was also blamed for a disastrous plan to cross the River Rapido that may have unnecessarily cost many American lives. These criticisms were unjust, Whit argued until his dying days in 1974, based on numerous facts that stood independent of the life-long friendship between Whit and Mark.

## Camping

As Jack entered his teenage years, his father became more involved in his life, focusing on watching competitive sports events, fishing, hiking, and camping, with a focus on wilderness survival. When Whit was not available, Jack was sent to participate in these activities through the Boy Scouts or other organizations.

Washington State is a great place for hiking, fishing, camping, and other outdoor activities when it is not raining. According to his journal, Jack had two camping events at ages 12 and 13 that stand out among his experiences.

The San Juan International Camp for Boys,[7] founded in 1935 on San Juan Island's Westcott Bay, near Roche Harbor, Washington, became Jack's first major excursion away from home. The new camp offered very few facilities, and the campers lived in tepees. (It could

---

7. The camp is now called "Nor'wester." See http://norwester.org/about/history-1935.html.

euphemistically be called "primitive," especially to those individuals living in the wild without modern camping gear.) The camp attracted 30 boys for the summer of 1936, including one named Jack Whitcomb. He, however, was not a happy camper!

On August 1, 1936, Jack wrote: *"I am going to be in camp for 5 weeks."*

He was not enthusiastic about being sent to camp without prior warning and despite his protests. On most days while he was in camp, he just noted in his diary that he was *"in camp,"* a clear indication of his excitement level.

On August 30, his misery came to an end when he noted that he was finally *"picked up."*

The following summer's camping experience started better but ended even worse! On June 25, 1937, Jack Whitcomb boarded a truck in Seattle with other Boy Scouts and headed to Camp Parsons, located on the eastern border of Olympic National Forest. Camp Parsons, in contrast to San Juan International Camp for Boys, was well established (founded in 1919) and represents one of the oldest and best-run Boy Scout camps in America to this day.[8]

The initial program was to build teams and prepare for a hiking trip, culminating with an ascent to Mount Olympus' towering top. Jack began with a survey of the facilities.

*"I arranged my things in my cabin. I looked around the camp. In the eve, we had a large campfire."*

The following day they hiked up an Olympia National Forest trail, stopped to climb Mount Anderson (3,364 feet) and then camped along the Dosewallips River.

On the fourth day Jack wrote, *"Reached the peak (of Mount Olympus) at 7,900 ft. Glissaded[9] down the mountain."*

The adventure continued on July 1:

*"Reached the top of Duckabush valley, glissaded down through the snow till we reached camp."*

The trouble began on July 2 with the note *"sprained wrist."* This was later discovered to be a misdiagnosis because his left arm was actually

---

8. http://home.comcast.net/~kevinrudesill/camp_parsons_history_continued.htm.

9. *Glissading* is a method of descending a steep, snow-covered slope via a controlled slide on one's feet or buttocks. It may be used to expedite a descent, or simply for the thrill. From http://en.wikipedia.org/wiki/Glissade_(climbing).

broken. In spite of the pain, Jack pushed through the remainder of camp with a sore arm. After two weeks, his father finally picked him up.

Ironically, years later, in rural Indiana, Jack's own children would grow to love backpacking and outdoor camping. However, they would do so alone. The reason that Jack would offer for avoiding all camping events centered around an even worse outdoor experience than anything endured during childhood. It was called "bivouacking" during World War II with the U.S. Army during the bitter winter of 1944–1945 in Belgium and Northern Germany. While at these summer camps, Jack had no idea of the misery that he would experience in a mere five or six years.

## A Broken Left Arm

Upon arriving at Camp Parsons, Whit immediately recognized the seriousness of the injury to Jack's wrist. Whit took Jack to Seattle for x-rays, where the break was finally diagnosed. The next day, July 17, Jack was admitted to the hospital where *Dr. Buckner operated on my arm.* However, Whit became aware that the break was more serious than initially anticipated, and a referral was in order.

Whit's own father, Colonel Clement Colfax "C.C." Whitcomb, M.D., an Army Surgeon, was living in San Francisco, and he recommended that Jack see one of the Army's top orthopedic specialists. Thus, Whit would need to leave work at a critical time and drive the family south. However, an unanticipated delay in the trip occurred because *Louie,* the family car, was stolen the night before departure.

The police recovered Louie the following day in Kent, Washington. After retrieving the car and sending it to the mechanics for inspection, the family packed up their things for the journey. The drive to San Francisco took two days, and they finally connected with Jack's grandparents, "Grampy" and "Nana," in the Presidio region of the City by the Bay. The bright spot along the trip was that Jack got to see the Redwood Forest and the Golden Gate Bridge. However, Jack voiced disappointment with the bridge when he noted that *"it is actually orange!"*

X-rays were taken of the arm at Letterman Hospital on July 27, resulting in orders for Jack's admission for further surgery. This occurred the following day under the direction of Colonel Kerk. After two days of recovery, the patient was discharged, and the family began the trek back to Seattle, Washington, arriving on August 1 after brief stops in Ashland and Portland, Oregon. Therapy continued at Dr. Buchner's Seattle office with dressing changes every few days.

My dad's recollection of the broken arm incident centered around "my dad was very upset with me"! From my perspective, as a dad and physician, this was a remarkable 13-year-old kid to struggle through two weeks of camp with a seriously broken arm, then to have his whole summer ruined with surgeries and therapies. No complaints logged, just a matter-of-fact acceptance of the circumstances and a sense of disappointing his father, whom Jack must have believed had different visions and expectations for his son.

In spite of a broken arm, the plans for the Whitcombs and Clarks to get together as families proceeded on schedule. The Clarks came to visit the Whitcombs mid-August, and on August 28, 1937, the Whitcombs drove to Fort Lewis to stay with the Clarks and visit Mount Rainier. However, as is typical of Seattle weather, it rained their whole stay.

The whole ordeal of the broken arm ended just before reentering school, as noted by the August 31, 1937, diary entry, *"In the afternoon I had my bandage taken off for good!"*

With a now healed arm, Jack and the two families returned to Mount Rainier two weeks later for some hiking. As Jack and Bill went up the hill, Jack's mother, Salome, slipped and sprained her ankle. Having just recovered physically from breaking his own arm, Jack was still dealing with the emotions of feeling like he had disappointed his father by coming home from camp early. So perhaps his mother's accident provided Jack with some personal solace as yet another illustration to his father that unfortunate things happen to careful people in spite of best intentions. Regardless, that trip ended early, as they had to take Salome back down the mountain.

## Jack as a Young Teenager

The life of a teenager during the nine months between each September and June centers around school. On school nights Jack worked on his homework and began systematically drawing maps of various countries and took to reading books for fun. The small family also enjoyed game nights, Monopoly proving to be a favorite game.

Occasionally, Whit would plan something for father and son. On October 27, 1937, Jack got up at 3:30 in the morning to go pheasant hunting with his dad. However, they bagged nothing. They also took some fishing trips, even though Jack hated fishing. Ever ingrained in Jack's memory was one trip when Jack hooked his father's ear on a cast. Needless to say, Whit was rather upset by that experience.

Independent of his parents, some events that might have excited other children failed to appeal to Jack. On October 30, Jack recorded, *"In the evening I went around to houses and said, 'Trick or Treat.'"* There was no mention of his costume or of the booty he collected, just a matter-of-fact record of events.

As Christmas approached, father and son ventured into the wilderness to cut down their own Christmas tree. In spite of a dislike of the cold wilderness, the event was both successful and fun. On Christmas Day, Jack received his own radio, which became one of his favorite belongings. He listened to this radio in his room almost every day for the rest of his stay in Seattle.

The spring semester proceeded with predictable regularity. Jack went to school; played ping-pong, baseball, and football; and rode his bike with friends Wheaton Blanchard and John Myers. He participated in scouting meetings, went camping, and practiced throwing knives. He also spent time working on his coin collection, listening to the radio, reading books, and doing homework. A few times a week he went to a movie with his mother, and on Sundays, he religiously read the funny papers.

## The Summer of 1938

The summer of 1938 was an important time for Jack, as it marked a turning point in his relationship with his dad for the better.

On June 15, Jack's "Nana" and "Grampy" (C.C. Whitcomb) arrived in Seattle by train from St. Petersburg, Florida, where they had moved for retirement. Two days later, the family celebrated Jack's 14th birthday, five days before his actual birthday. His gifts included a golf bag and new shoes.

The following day, Jack said goodbye to his mother, who boarded a train for Harrington Park, New Jersey, to join Adele and Woody, the beloved aunt and uncle who raised her from childhood, for a four-month trip to Europe. Salome would witness the beauty and history of Europe herself, less than a year before the start of World War II. She saw the power and pride of Nazi Germany during the peak of its rise from the financial ashes of World War I. Little did she realize that her husband and son would follow her to Europe in only a few years as part of an unstoppable war machine of the Allies that would finally crush the Nazi regime — at the cost of unthinkable destruction and the overall loss of tens of millions of human lives.

With the departure of his mother, Jack came under the direct care of his father, with the help of Whit's aging parents, who would stay until Salome returned. On June 19, Whit took Jack to a golf course and dropped him off so that he could try out his new golf bag. On June 21 he penned, *"I played golf by myself. I made 63 and 71. I came home on the street car."* On June 22, 1938, Jack turned 14 years of age.

**Father and Son**

Jack and Whit were quite different in personality, interests, and temperament. When Jack entered new surroundings, he would walk around the facility and "check it out," then go to his place of lodging and straighten up his stuff. He did not go out of the way to meet new kids or adults. During his camping experience, he never recorded the names of any other campers, where they were from, or anything else about them.

Whit was an outgoing "people person" with many friends and relationships. His niece, Sally Salvador, remembers to this day that he always stressed the importance of fostering human relationships. Whit often said, "There is nothing more interesting than people." Whit and Salome continually entertained guest at their home or ventured out for events and dinner with friends.

Jack was more reserved than his parents. He had a few friends in Seattle, such as Wheaton Blanchard. He appeared equally content to spend time alone working on maps, reading, and listening to the radio.

Whit loved the outdoors — camping, hunting, and fishing — roughing it under harsh conditions. Whit loved adventure; competition; and battling against the elements, the wilderness, and the German army in WWI.

Jack accepted but did not choose many of the hobbies of his father, but he participated in these activities to have time with his family. He was more of a "book person," preferring quiet, clean, and organized surroundings.

Whit loved military events, prizefights, competitive sports, administrative order, and efficiency.

Jack was fascinated with history, countries, geography, cultures, and languages. His favorite magazines became *Time Life* and *National Geographic*. He enjoyed the funny paper but not the sports section.

Whit was quick to speak, direct, emotionally strong, and confrontational with strong leadership characteristics. Whit knew military protocols, respect, and performance.

Jack was more quiet, emotionally sensitive, and non-confrontational. He enjoyed reading, organizing things, learning, and doing activities alone.

Whit and Jack did have in common that they were both the only child of a military officer who was constantly transferring between countries and assignments. Therefore, they both may not have known how to relate to regular kids. Whit obviously cared deeply for Jack and wanted to raise him to be a great military man. But Whit did not understand his son. And while Jack cared deeply about his father's opinions and approval, he did not know how to connect with Whit.

## Boy Scouts

Primarily to please his dad, Jack was very active in the Boy Scouts. The Boy Scouts were akin to the Army in many ways, and Jack wanted to make his father proud by earning merit badges and service recognition. He earned various merit badges, and on April 19, 1938, received a "star" at a special meeting of the Court of Honor. His journal reflects his excitement at seeing his father there, as he simply wrote, *"Daddy went too!"*

Indeed, he continued to attend and excel. He proudly noted in his diary of September 8, 1937, *"I am a Lieutenant on Patrol now."* He remained heavily involved for the next year, often going on "patrol" before and/or after school and participating in meetings and activities. Jack did not abandon the Boy Scouts until well into high school. He also continued to enjoy the great outdoors with friends and family. Old pictures show Jack with Col. C.C. Whitcomb, M.D. (Grampy), overlooking the stunning natural scenery from the top of a mountain cliff.

## "Bring Your Son to Work"

As a special treat and opportunity for father and son bonding, Whit decided to bring Jack with him to the Camp Bonneville Military Reservation Site for two weeks. Camp Bonneville was located in the southwestern corner of Washington State, about 15 miles northeast of

Portland, Oregon. The camp was used for ammunitions storage and testing. Prior to World War II, the facility tested artillery, mortars, bombs, land mines, practice grenades, and small arms ammunition.[10] Later the site was used to test air-launched rockets, shoulder-fired rockets, guided missiles, and other explosives. It was closed in 1995 and remains closed for fear that live explosives remain hidden under the surface of the grounds.

Whit and Jack headed for camp on July 9, 1938. They arrived at 3:30 p.m., set up army tents, and unpacked. The tent was to be shared with some of the officers. The next day's agenda included learning to pace off a mile, filling in a mapping table, and learning to map a camp. On July 15, Jack watched soldiers on the firing range shooting machine guns. The next day Jack fired the machine gun himself. What an experience for a 14-year-old boy! But spraying hot lead at targets was not a highlight of the excursion for Jack.

Jack learned from some of the officers that excellent golf courses surrounded the camp. The brass began taking Jack out for a few rounds. Later, Whit joined them. Whit discovered that Jack had become a pretty good golfer. Whit actually liked golf, and the father and son finally "connected" on the golf course. They had finally found something that they both enjoyed, and enjoyed doing together. Father and son golfed together frequently for the remaining time in Seattle.

Seventy-seven years later, on his 90th birthday, Jack Whitcomb was asked if he remembered living in Seattle, and if his memories of the experience were positive or negative. He responded without hesitation, "It was very good. I golfed with my dad."

**New Skills and Challenges**

The excursion to Camp Bonneville resulted in some great times of fun and maturation. But as all good things do, the adventure came to an end, and father and son returned to Seattle.

After discovering their mutual love of golf, Jack enjoyed the development of several other hobbies with his father. These included stamp collecting, coin collecting, and photography. Of the three, photography became the hobby that lasted, with father and son taking pictures and developing them together through Jack's college years.

10. https://fortress.wa.gov/ecy/gsp/Sitepage.aspx?csid=11670.

Jack would continue to love photography for the rest of his life, taking literally thousands of pictures of people and places throughout the world. Everyone he met and every event he attended, it seemed to his children, got captured on film. Over the years, Professor Whitcomb's children groaned while sitting on the floor of their home, watching slideshows of hundreds of people who were important or interesting to the shutterbug, but whom the kids never met and who looked strikingly like everyone else.

With Whit returning to his work routine upon arriving home from Camp Bonneville, Jack began developing some new skills that would serve his future professional career. On August 1, Jack gained access to a typewriter and began teaching himself to type. This turned out to be one of the most valuable skills he ever developed.

Seattle also marks the place where Jack began learning new foreign languages! His memory of Mandarin, it seems, was a fading ember that would never rekindle. In contrast, Whit, who grew up in Cuba, learned to speak perfect Spanish as a child and continued to practice and teach this language. Whit worked with Jack to speak and read Spanish like a Spaniard, or more accurately, like a Cuban! Jack also began learning French using phonographic records. Unlike his own children, who all hated foreign languages, this activity became a lifelong passion and a valuable tool. His grades in the public school also began to improve. On November 16, 1938, Jack wrote, *"I got my report card (A-B-B-C)."*

Sadly, Jack recognized he was having more and more difficulty reading. On October 23, 1938, he finally had his eyes examined. This may be the only exam in his life that he failed. On November 2, he got his first pair of glasses. However, his eyesight became a growing problem, with slow deterioration and progressively stronger glasses despite religiously doing eye exercises. Poor eyesight played a major role in determining his future training and job opportunities, a disability that proved to be providential. The problem was finally corrected in the 1980s, when he was nearly blind. Cataract surgery proved to be a near miracle.

## Jack's Autobiography

Among the many old dusty papers in Professor Whitcomb's piles, a yellowed and crumpled piece of notebook paper appeared that was written by Jack Whitcomb in Seattle, likely in 7th or 8th grade. The heading was "My Autobiography," and it provides profound insights into Jack's personality, ethics, and view of leadership and service.

## My Autobiography

I was born on June 22, 1924 in Washington DC. We lived there for a while and moved as we have usually been doing. We lived in China for a few years and then moved to Fort Leavenworth Kansas. Well while I was there, I think I learned several of the traits which I now hold. When we were first there I was only about 6 or 7 so it was my beginning in trying to develop myself to hold some of the traits that are found in famous people. As I grew older I begin to read about Lincoln and how honest he was. Of course I wanted to be like Lincoln and be very honest so I tried that trait. I think that that was very good habit to get into because I think that I have kept it up pretty well. Then when I began to go to school, I soon found out that the only way to get good grades and to be a success is to work hard and do my homework well. That is another habit that I have got into that I think I have kept up well. After being in Kansas for three years or more, and living on an army post, I soon found out that leadership plays a big part in army life. Even though I tried it a few times I have not been so successful, but I expect to attain my leadership in the Army through service, and education.

We then moved to Seattle where I started in the fourth grade. There too I learned many valuable traits. One trait that I learned was concentration. During our class time we were given books to read while the teacher was out. Against the noise and talking in the room I soon found myself absorbed completely in my book. I have done that several times since, so I think that I have in a way mastered that trait. Coming into high school has been my biggest step, and I don't doubt that I shall learn some more good traits and perhaps get rid of some of my poor traits.

## Changing Landscape

Internationally, the thunderclouds of war emerged on the horizon. To their west, the Empire of Japan already invaded China, and the

Sino-Japanese war raged. What happened to Pung and their Chinese friends? No one is really sure. To the east, news reports also began documenting growing trouble in Europe. Jack wondered about his mother, who was on vacation in the center of growing tension. Communication remained challenging, so day-to-day communication was impossible. The travelers never encountered serious danger, but it would not be until October 28, 1938, that Jack's mother would return to Seattle and the safety of the United States.

The spring of 1939 unfolded with activities similar to the previous year, with most diary entries beginning with, *"I went to high school."* After-school activities included playing baseball, football, or ping-pong with his friends, then doing homework. Evening activities still included some Boy Scouts, listening to the radio, or reading books. Occasionally, sporting events or movies filled the free time. As the weather improved, Jack spent more and more time on the golf course alone; with friends; or, whenever possible, with his "daddy."

**Leaving Seattle**

As the summer of 1939 approached, Whit was ordered to Fort Benning, Georgia, to serve in the Infantry School. So the family packed their belongings and said "goodbye" to their home in Seattle. Jack, now almost 15 years of age, headed east toward Limekiln Lake to spend time with his mother, Auntie (Adele) and Woodie, Juliette and Clint, and the newest member of the extended family, Sally. The cross-country drive included sightseeing stops at key locations along the way, such as Yellowstone National Park. Jack, who loved maps and borders, located the invisible line that separated Montana from Wyoming and took a picture of the dirt.

**Conclusions**

The childhood events of Professor Whitcomb provide insights into the nature and nurture of a little boy who, in God's perfect design, began developing into a young man on track for a great mission. Some innate characteristics that emerge from his history include a sensitive yet resilient spirit, broad interest with great attention to detail, curiosity, and a desire to be appreciated and embraced by his parents.

Jack's mother exhibited some evidence of nurturing, care, and gentleness. She frequently attended double-feature movies with her son or played board games with him while Whit was away at work. However, Jack always wondered if she really *enjoyed* her time with him.

Jack's father instilled characteristics of honor, loyalty, and the importance of achievement. But children of highly successful fathers often find it difficult to feel capable and adequate in comparison to their parental role model. To his delight, however, father and son connected on the golf course. Indeed, Professor Whitcomb's fondest memory of his childhood was "playing golf with my dad in Seattle."

Jack developed a number of friends with neighborhood boys but also spent time alone. Jack's diaries reflected a matter-of-fact chronicling of life events but also a detached dissatisfaction with many things and, at times, a sense of sadness. Such should be the case of all bright and insightful adolescents who do not know the Lord.

# Chapter 6

# McCallie

"A Challenge"
September 1939 to May 1942

On September 1, 1939, the world changed forever as Hitler launched *blitzkrieg* against Poland, plunging Europe into World War II. Like dominoes, England and France declared war on Germany, with nation after nation following them by declaring war on one another until the entire world was engulfed a spiral of killing and mass destruction.

Jack Whitcomb, now 15 years of age, was just wrapping up a summer vacation at his family's favorite cottage on Limekiln Lake in New York. One day, Jack rowed his dad from their cabin to town to mail some packages, get a haircut, and get the news. The news was not good. Jack relayed the essence of the situation to his daily diary, *"We heard that a **European War** had started."* In just a few short years, both Jack and Whit would fight in this war on the side of the Allies as soldiers in the U.S. Army.

The Whitcomb family packed their belongings over the next three days, cleaned out the cabin and headed for Salome's family's home in Harrington Park, New Jersey, just across the Hudson River from New York City. After arriving, the in-laws, including Auntie, Woody, Clint, and Julie, huddled around the radio, absorbing reports on the worsening situation in Europe. Jack had a much better comprehension of the events than most kids his age, since he had drawn detailed maps of the key countries and studied their history. But the ladies had a more personal perspective, having just returned from these lands within the past year.

## NYC and the 1939 World's Fair

The proximity of Harrington Park to New York City allowed Jack to further his education and expand his worldview. He spent much of the 11-day family visit touring the Big Apple with his mother, father, and other members of the family. The first day began with shopping in Manhattan and enjoying an aerial overview of the city following an elevator ride to the top of the Empire State Building — which cost $3.00. Jack then made a voice recording and rode a double-decker bus to Central Park. The next day he returned to the city to explore the American Museum of Natural History, Haden's Planetarium (featuring a show called "A Trip to the Moon"), the Rockefeller Center for lunch, Radio City Music Hall to see Ginger Rogers in *5th Ave Girl* (which Jack described in his diary *"a beautiful theater"*), and finished the day at Jack Dempsey's Restaurant for supper before returning to New Jersey.

That same summer was the fabulous 1939 New York World's Fair. Everyone wanted to witness the unlimited possibilities of man, in contrast to the destructive inventions being developed and deployed in Europe. The League of Nations, a predecessor to the United Nations, was organized to prevent wars following WWI. The exhibit seemed strange, since major wars in Europe and Asia proved that it was rather impotent.

Jack waited in line for an hour to see the General Motors exhibit, "Railroads on Parade." He then went to the Chrysler Motors exhibition where he saw a "depth movie" with polarized goggles. Next on the list was the Firestone exhibit to witness the making of tires, and then he saw his first television at the Westinghouse exhibit. He also visited the House of Magic at the General Electric exhibit to see his first *"light running engine, or sun-motor."* Each exhibit was carefully recorded in Jack's diary, including the route to and from New York City, any subway or bus that was taken, the stations of entry and exit, and the time when each event occurred.

One day was not enough for a world's fair. Jack returned several times with various family members to experience all of the exhibits, to see a giant panda, and to make a parachute jump. He also impressed the women in his family with his sports skills — *"I won a little dog for throwing a baseball at milk bottles."* They ate dinner at the Schaefer Center, which featured two circular arenas, a restaurant, and an exhibit

119

area covered with air-filled plastic disks that looked like huge pillows. They returned home via subway, where he talked with a chef from the Schaefer Center, and completed the trip home by bus.

Back in Harrington Park, Jack's time was spent developing photographs in the basement. Meanwhile, his dad and mom entertained a continual stream of visitors from West Point, New York, as Whit jockeyed for new opportunities within the military hierarchy. Although the war was at the forefront of his father's mind, Whit also became more engaged in the rearing and education of young Jack, joining him from time to time in the basement to develop film and print pictures, all the while highlighting important places and things in New York City.

*The Trip to Georgia*

On September 14, 1939, Jack helped pack the car to drive south to their new home. *"Mother, Auntie and Julie cried, so we said goodbye to them and left in the car for Georgia."* A list of every major town was recorded as they circled through Pennsylvania to visit Gettysburg, where Whit gave a military history lesson. After spending a night in the Barbara Fritchie[1] cabin camp in Fredrick, Maryland, they continued in Washington, D.C., where Whit made key contacts and attended some meetings. The family visited the Capitol, the Washington Monument, and the Lincoln Memorial. They ate lunch at Child's, went to the Bureau of Printing and Engraving *"where we saw paper money being printed,"* stopped by the Smithsonian Institution, and ended the day at the Post Office Building where *"we saw stamps."* Late in the day, they returned to their car and viewed Washington, D.C., in the rear-view mirror and continued southwest for Charlottesville, Virginia. They enjoyed dinner at the Southern Restaurant, and they slept at the Monticello Hotel.

Cross-country travel through the southern USA in the late 1930s was either an adventure or torture, depending on your goals and perspective. The next morning started with Whit giving Jack his first facial shave. Then off they went to North Carolina. Whit, who loved the outdoors, decided to take advantage of the "cabin camps." The cabin camps were wood, stone, or mixed material structures that were built

---

1. Barbara Fritchie was the heroine of John Greenleaf Whittier's poem from the Civil War. " 'Shoot, if you must, this old gray head, but spare your country's flag,' she said" while leaning out an upstairs window.

in national parks' camping areas as a public work effort during the Great Depression.

After a day of navigating the state and local roads that crisscrossed Virginia and North Carolina, the family finally arrived at their targeted cabin camp. However, there were no bathing facilities, so they drove on. The second cabin camp not only had no bath, but they also had never changed the beds' sheets from the previous night, so the Whticombs walked out and continued their drive south. The third stop featured "King Tut's Cabins," which were *awful*. The family located a local gas station to obtain recommendations for a place to stay. The attendant recommended "King Tut's Cabins," which were "the pride of the county." To Jack and Salome's relief, Whit gave up on the "cabin camp" adventure.

The next stop was an ocean cottage on Sea Island near Brunswick, Georgia. As they neared Sea Island, they stopped at the "Mighty Fine Grocery" to locate a maid to serve them during their stay at an ocean cottage. They secured a recommendation from the grocer — a woman of African ancestry who lived somewhere off the beaten trail. A negro boy (the politically correct term at the time) offered to guide them to the maid's home through the poorly marked and potentially treacherous parts of town riding on the car's running board. Upon finally securing a maid, they retreated to the seaside cabin, only to be met by a major storm.

The three-day ocean vacation included reading *Captains Courageous*, playing Chinese checkers and Russian Bank with his dad, and watching the rain. The incoming storm strengthened in intensity through the second night. In spite of the squall, Whit and Salome left Jack with the maid to have dinner at The Cloister, a famous Spanish-style resort hotel with a low, red-tile roof; grand lounge with high, beamed ceiling; clerestory windows; and an outstanding restaurant. The storm buffeted the seaside cottage with gale-force winds, shaking the cottage and generating terrifying noises. Frightened, the maid abandoned Jack, who was left to hold the fort alone until his parents returned. That was the last time Jack was left with a maid as a babysitter!

By the next day, the storm subsided. Jack read *The Man Who Would Be King* by Kipling as he waited for the rain to stop. Finally, the family put on bathing suits and marched to the beach. The waves from the storm *"splashed over us, and we had a lot of fun fighting the undertow."*

On September 20, 1939, four months after leaving Seattle, Washington, the family completed the final leg of the journey to their new home in Fort Benning, Georgia. Upon their arrival, the Whitcombs' new home was not quite ready for occupancy. Major Marberry, a friend of Whit's who was also stationed at Benning, welcomed the Whitcombs into his own home for a few days. At long last, Whit was ready to report for duty.

## Ft. Benning, Georgia

Fort Benning, Georgia, was the home to the United States Army Infantry School. The purpose of the Infantry School was to "transform civilians into disciplined INFANTRYMEN that possess the Army Values, fundamental Soldier skills, physical fitness, character, confidence, commitment, and the Warrior Ethos to become adaptive and flexible Infantrymen ready to accomplish the mission of the Infantry."[2]

In 1939, the Infantry School headquarters took on an extremely important and exciting role. The school was practicing the new military doctrines and methods in order to defeat the technically superior Nazi army and their revolutionary tactics such as *blitzkrieg*. After seeing the Polish cavalry annihilated in minutes by the Germans, the American warhorses were put to pasture or killed. New war machines and tactics were developed and tested. The organization and methods for front-line combat underwent transformation. Whit's new assignment included developing and teaching new tactics, and he would witness the importance and consequence of these new doctrines on the beaches of Normandy, the plains of France, and the forest of Germany.

The officer's section of Fort Benning witnessed a revolving door of the future leaders and heroes of the U.S. Army in World War II. The Whitcombs were assigned a house on Baltzell Avenue, immediately across the street from the Fort Benning golf course, and a few houses down from Brigadier General George Patton, commander of the 2nd Armored Division. Patton just reached military stardom for his bold, aggressive tactics in the Louisiana exercises. But it was at Fort Benning that the 2nd Armored Division under Patton's command became known as

---

2. https://www.benning.army.mil/infantry/198th/2-19/index.html?_=11.

"Hell on Wheels." Although Patton would later leave the 2nd Armored Division through promotions, this daring Division, fighting within the 1st, 7th, and 9th Army, retained its reputation. A few years later, it would fight next to Jack's infantry division in the Battle of the Bulge.

Jack never met Patton, but he remembers seeing him in his backyard, ivory-handled Colt 45 pistols drawn, twisting and darting in an imaginary battle where he fearlessly fired away, killing imaginary German soldiers. Three-year-old Sally, who later came with her mother to stay with the Whitcomb family at Fort Benning, used the coy tactics of a little girl to endear herself to General "blood and guts." Patton was more of a gardener than a golfer, and the blond-haired, blue-eyed Sally would skip over to help him trim and weed his yard. Patton gave her a special commission of caring for his garden, including a white helmet to protect Sally's head from the sun.

Whit also knew Patton well, harkening back to West Point and Fort Leavenworth days. Later Whit would play a major role in Patton's Third Army fighting through France, Belgium, and Germany in an unrelenting push toward total victory. Patton summarized his approach well, "We shall attack and attack until we are exhausted, and then we shall attack again." Whit embraced this approach and proved himself worthy in the 90th Infantry Division of Patton's 3rd Army in Europe during WWII.

## Public High School in Georgia

Jack was about to enter his sophomore year of high school. The day after arriving at Fort Benning, Whit took Jack to Columbus, Georgia, for enrollment in the local public school. The Columbus High School was founded in 1890 and developed slowly. The building that Jack attended was built in 1926 and located in the Wildwood Park area of Columbus. There was no air conditioning or other conveniences, and the quality of the education was mediocre at best. Years later, on June 12, 1981, the old building was ravaged by fire. The community then dedicated itself to rebuilding the school and making it a model of success. The efforts paid off by 2005, as the school began receiving honors as a top school in Georgia and then one of the top schools in the United States as ranked by *U.S. News & World Report*. But this was about 70 years too late for Jack.

# A Good and Faithful Servant

The best part of the trip to Columbus was a detour to Sears and Roebuck, where Jack got a new bicycle. This transportation machine was used constantly, as Jack would ride around Fort Benning and surrounding areas with "no hands." Use of the handlebars, it seems, interrupted one of Jack's greatest skills — the "fist whistle." The trick was to cup the hands to make a narrow opening between the thumbs, which resulted in a harmonic whistle when air was blown into the opening. By manipulating the size of the vestibule, the pitch of the whistle could be changed, allowing for tunes and songs to be played. Jack mastered the fist whistle, entertaining family, friends, and astonished onlookers for the next 80 years. So, it is obvious why Jack could not hold the handlebars while riding his bicycle and listening to himself play his favorite tunes.

Back at Fort Benning, there were other kids that Jack knew and new kids to meet. Homer Mayberry was the 10-year-old son of Major Mayberry. Upon moving into the Whitcombs' own house, Jack found that they were living next to Harry Henderson (age 16), whom he knew from Tientsin, China. Although Jack and Harry were about the same age, Jack appeared to dislike Harry, initially choosing to play with Homer. Jack recorded an accident involving a boy and a car, in which the boy *"cut his arm, bruised his chest." "The driver,"* he wrote as if a deep secret was being revealed, *"was Harry Henderson."* Over time, however, Homer became annoying, and finally Jack had no alternative but to lock him in a closet.

Shortly after arriving at Fort Benning, Whit and Salome found a nice man named Mayfield to serve as a butler and to watch Jack. The good news for a 15-year-old boy was that there was someone to make breakfast, help with chores, and drive him around as needed. The bad news was that there was constant adult supervision by an employee rather than loving parents, who seemed to be continuously preoccupied with social events and things other than with their son. The happy days in Seattle were over.

Seventy-five years later, I asked my dad about the continuous series of maids, butlers, and servants. He responded that it was very discouraging because he wanted the time and attention of his parents. His diary reflected his home life with a typical entry penned on October 17, 1939:

## McCallie

*I came home — Some people were there when I arrived, so I went upstairs to study. After a while they left. I went downstairs and we had dinner. Mother and Dad went calling. I spend the evening arranging my desk. Later I took a bath and went to bed.*

Jack made friends with a couple of other boys his age: Alfred McKenney and Joe Warren. Alfred's dad was the Boy Scout troop leader, so Jack joined the outfit and was elected treasurer. He participated in the events but more for something to do with his time. He never really liked scouting. The highlight of the group was the chance to play ping-pong.

Jack's Boy Scout troop participated in some group projects. This culminated on March 29, 1940, as the scouts boarded several trucks that transported them to Columbus for a festival. The troop marched into town, went to the field, and made human pyramids. Jack summarized this experience in three words, *"It was awful."*

Alfred loved to play football, so Jack joined the Fort Benning football club. Jack played left tackle, but he was second or third string. When the weather was bad and very few kids showed up, Jack would get some practice time on the field with the team. Finally, on Sunday, December 3, he got into a real game during a 27-6 beating. However, he wrote, *"I did not play except for 3 minutes."* After that, any interest in pursuing organized football appeared to be lost (although he later enjoyed pick-up games in seminary!).

Joe Warren was Jack's other friend. They spent time together playing golf, bowling (scores typically ranged from 102–118), and going to movies with Joe's little sister, Helen, as a tag-along. Joe was a year older than Jack; Helen was a year younger. The Warrens had a piano, and on multiple occasions, Jack noted that he played while at their home. During the year, Joe developed interest in girls, and Jack became a third wheel on several outings. Jack did have at least one date of his own that year. On New Year's Eve, Jack went to the Polo Hunt Club with friends, including his date, Jean McCloughan. *"We danced and had Coca Cola and cookies."* That event fulfilled his dating obligations for the year.

When school was finally out for summer, Jack, Alfred, Joe, and another boy named Paul Fowler built a campsite about three miles away from home. The chosen location was in a wooded area by a stream. They dug and filled in a "beach," made steps, cleared a campsite, constructed a latrine, and then went swimming. Then they built lean-tos and covered them with leaves. It began to rain. After a two-hour downpour, the rain stopped, and they started a fire to try to dry their clothes. Without much luck, they decided to go home for the night. The next day they returned to build a dam and embellish the site with more steps and improved pathways. After a day of work and play, they made a fire and cooked corn, meat, and pineapple for supper. They tried to sleep, but the mosquitoes kept them up most of the night. At 4:30 a.m., they finally got up, made a fire, and had grapefruit juice for breakfast. By 5:00 a.m., Jack had had enough. He got on his bicycle and rode home. He showered, went to bed, slept until noon, and never went back to the campsite.

While Jack displayed average abilities in sports, he proved to be an avid reader and excellent student. His favorite reading materials continued to be *Life* magazine, *Time* magazine, *National Geographic* magazine, the *New York Times*, and the funny papers on Sunday mornings. In addition to his magazines, he read many classic novels and biographies.

His thirst for knowledge also spilled over to excellence in school. On November 22, 1939, he entered a typical note in his diary about his classes and academic achievements, *"We had a test in history. I was the only one that got 100%."* While he was a straight "A" student, school seemed boring and much time was spent in study hall, reading.

Throughout that fall, Jack's parents were continually active in social activities. His mother vacationed in both Florida and Georgia for a few weeks, leaving Jack home with Whit and Mayfield. In December, Jack accompanied his parents to St. Petersburg, Florida, to visit Whit's parents. However, Christmas was not celebrated by the family that year because C.C. Whitcomb (Jack's grandfather) was a militant atheist and decided that year to make a statement, of sorts.

In the spring, Juliette (Jack's aunt), who was now separated from her husband, came to live with the family. She and Jack's mother kept busy with social events and trips to various places. This allowed for Jack to spend more time with his father golfing, playing table games, and speaking Spanish. From time to time, they would have deeper talks on various topics, including "socialism," "religion and its effects on humanity," and politics.

Whit continued to hope that his only son would have a great military or government career. Jack was not interested in the military but did consider a future in government. Georgetown University School of Foreign Service was an option, but Whit was concerned that the Columbus High School was not a great college prep school. In fact, it was terrible.

In March 1940, a Captain Wedemeyer visited Whit and Jack with his boy Albert to talk about McCallie Military Academy in Chattanooga, Tennessee. Whit was sold on the idea, believing that a military academy would whip Jack into top shape and improve his chances of getting into a top-tier college such as West Point, or as a second choice, Princeton.

As the possibility of Jack going to McCallie Military Academy came into focus, the war in Europe was growing in intensity to the concern of all Americans. During these weeks, Jack kept an ear close to the radio. Besides the trivial events of the day, Jack recorded news highlights from abroad in his diary. *"Another British battleship was sunk"*; *"The British bombed a German naval base"*; *"Premier Édouard Daladier[3] and his cabinet resigned"*; *"Belgium Invaded"*; *"Italy declared war on the allies"*; *"Germans 35 miles from Paris"*; *"I heard Roosevelt on the radio."*

By the end of the school year, Jack was approaching his 16th birthday. Whit, delegating fatherly responsibilities, arranged driving lessons for Jack with a tank commander from the "Hell on Wheels" armored division. Three days after Jack turned 16, France surrendered to the Germans. A few weeks later, Whit was promoted to Lt. Colonel.

## McCallie Military Academy (September 1940–June 1942)

McCallie Military Academy (now McCallie School) was founded in 1905 by two brothers, James Park McCallie and Spencer J. McCallie.[4]

---

3. Premier Édouard Daladier was a French politician and Prime Minister from 1938–1940 who continually warned the world of Hitler's intentions but was forced into policies of appeasement by Neville Chamberlain from England during the Munich Agreement in 1938 where England and France agreed to allow Hitler to annex parts of Czechoslovakia in exchange for peace. Upon his return to France from the conference, he was cheered by crowds in Paris, to which he commented to his aids, "Ah, the fools!" After the fall of France to Germany, he was captured, tried for treason by the Vichy government, and sent to prison for several years.

4. McCallie School, http://www.mccallie.org/podium/default.aspx?t=103728, www.mccallie.org, en.wikipedia.org/wiki/The_McCallie_School.

# A Good and Faithful Servant

They were the sons of the Rev. T.H. McCallie, a Presbyterian minister who offered his sons $2,000 and 40 acres of the family farm to build a high school near Chattanooga with a specific purpose. "Our aim," he wrote to his boys in a note accompanying the gift, "is not wealth, or even having the family together, as desirable as this is, but the glory of God in Christ." The two well-educated sons, graduates of the University of Virginia and the University of Chicago, built McCallie School with a strong academic foundation designed for college preparation. But near to the core of their education philosophy was the belief that moral and physical education should accompany academics.

A rigorous academic curriculum served as the central mission of the school. The McCallies also instituted an honor code that all students had to copy and sign with the completion of each assignment and examination that read, "I have neither given nor received any aid on this examination." "Honor," according to the headmaster, "is not something you are born with; it is something you are taught." In 1918, McCallie School adopted a military training program, as did many private schools in the World War I era. Students were required to wear uniforms, to learn marksmanship, and to march in formation in the afternoon. The two McCallie men, who served as headmasters until 1947, were devout Christians. Their leadership and passion for the development of young men and boys was inspiring.

The school proved to be the perfect platform for Jack to learn to study and to develop critical thinking skills. Jack arrived at McCallie with his parents on September 9, 1940, and met his roommates — Hugh Wilson and Jimmy Pate. He was fitted for his school uniforms and started the new routine. His assignment for the year was to raise the school flag each morning and to carry the school flag during marching drills. Each night he was also assigned to clean all of the chalkboards, for which he was paid $1.75 per week. He slowly acclimated to this new environment, but eventually embraced it and rose to the top of his class.

Jack had a few friends but was content to be alone in his room reading or studying. On Friday, October 18, 1940, for example, school was dismissed early.

*After lunch we had no school, so most of the boys went to the Barnum & Bailey Circus or the football game. I went to my room to study Trig for the final test we will have tomorrow. . . I listened to 'Gang Busters.' I went to supper. I studied for a while after dinner and played chess with Orr . . . to bed at 11:00.*

On Saturday, October 19, he took the algebra examination from 8 a.m. until noon.

*After lunch most of the boys went down to the show. I stayed in my room and studied my Spanish. I borrowed Bob Smart's copy of Life and read it. I took a little nap, and then did some English homework. I listened to the radio for a while. Took a shower and dressed for supper. We didn't get much to eat. I bought a candy bar and went to my room to study for the evening. Went to bed at 10:00.*

This was typical of his diary entries during the fall semester, 1940.

As a Christian-based private school, the students were required to go to chapel daily, take a Bible class each semester, and to go to church twice on Sunday. Jack studied most of the books of the New Testament, memorized all of the assigned verses, and was pleased that, by the time he finished at McCallie, he was scoring 100% on Bible examinations. He attended Sunday school and church weekly, as required. Sometimes he noted that the pastor had a good speech or that he was funny. But he usually sat in the back and, at times, just read *Time* magazine. Sunday evening included vespers services in the school auditorium, which featured music, singing, and talks. One evening he was asked to pray publicly. Suddenly, he recorded, *"I became very nervous."* He was not for or against Christianity — he went to church because he was expected to and studied the Bible as part of his academic requirements. It was nothing personal.

The school was well regimented. The students wore military uniforms and underwent daily inspections of their dress and their rooms. They marched with and without rifles. They had regulations on conduct and behavior. There was a quiet hour after dinner. And the rooms were checked nightly to be sure that all of the cadets were in bed on time. As a military academy, there were talks on war, service to the country, honor, and valor. The implications of America going to war became evident to the cadets on October 16, 1940, as Jack explained, *"Today, all men between the ages of 21 and 35 register in the nation-wide conscription."* The cadets exercised daily, and each week they were weighed. On December 8, 1940, Jack weighed 169 pounds.

During the school year, Jack became more involved in the school activities and developed a circle of friends. He practiced badminton with a couple of the boys and entered the intramural tournament. He played chess and battleship and showed the other boys that he could lift weights (*"I did well."*). His increasing strength was demonstrated when *"I held out our 17 lbs. bar for 1 min 45 sec, which, in our dormitory, is a record so far."* He also attended a couple of home football games.

The academics were tough compared to Columbus High School in Georgia. Trigonometry was especially hard for him. On October 29, he had a test and failed. On October 30, he had a quiz and failed. His diary recorded hours spent day and night studying trigonometry to master this discipline. On November 14, he noted, *"I went to Trig and got a 95 on my days' work."* By the end of the six-week term, he pulled his grades up to an A. Unbeknownst to Jack, in exactly four years he would be in Germany and Belgium doing trigonometry to save his life and those of his comrades as he used his math skills to direct the fire of 105 mm howitzers against Nazi Panzer and Tiger tanks.

During breaks, Jack would visit his parents in Fort Benning via the railroad, connecting through Atlanta, Georgia. When he arrived on December 20, 1940, he met his cousin Sally and her personal nurse, Mattie. For Christmas, he got a portable Zenith radio, a pair of socks, a necktie, a bathrobe, some hair tonic and shaving cream, gloves, golf balls, and a stocking full of odds and ends. He immediately reconnected with Alfred, Joe, and other friends. He also returned during spring break and between academic school years. The time off was largely spent reading, playing golf, and going to double features with his pals.

The spring semester of Jack's junior year at McCallie was a breakout. He joined the soccer team and made the Varsity team as a fullback. He joined the Student Council. He also joined the golf team. Furthermore, his study methods became habits, and he continued to excel in the classroom. However, he did not like to attend non-essential events, choosing to go to the library or to his room to read, study, or listen to his radio. He still loved *Gang Busters*, but he also liked Red Skelton, Glenn Miller, speeches by President Roosevelt, and following the news of the growing worldwide conflict that was World War II.

The other cadets recognized the personal qualities of Jack Whitcomb, as highlighted in a letter sent from the school to Whit.

January 30, 1941

Dear Colonel and Mrs. Whitcomb:

The boys in South Hall elected Jack to represent them on the Student Council for the second semester. This is a splendid tribute to the way in which Jack has conducted himself here. This means that the boys see in Jack the finest sort of character — honesty, integrity, fair-play — and I know that you will be happy to learn of this honor that has come to him.

Sincerely,
*Neill M Watson*
Director of Admissions
The McCallie School
Chattanooga, Tennessee

*Summer Vacation, 1941*

Jack returned to Fort Benning, Georgia, between his junior and senior year of high school. He took a job at the Infantry School Book Shop, but there was plenty of time for golf. His availability to complete a foursome provided opportunities to rub shoulders with some of the top military brass in the U.S. Army. One avid golfer was General Omar Bradley. Jack played 18 holes with him on June 18, 1941, and seven holes on June 24 before it started to rain. Later, General Bradley would command all of the U.S. ground forces from the invasion of Normandy to the defeat of Germany, commanding 43 divisions and 1.3 million men. This was the largest number of American soldiers ever to serve under a U.S. field commander.

*Senior Year at McCallie School*

Jack's senior year at McCallie Military Academy was even stronger than his junior year. Upon his return, he was given one of the top honors of a military academy, representing the entire regimen. The recommendation was as follows:

# A Good and Faithful Servant

Lieutenant Clyde Goforth,
The McCallie School Commandant
Chattanooga, Tennessee,

Dear Clyde;

In regard to the existing vacancy of a Color Sergeant in The McCallie Battalion, I recommend that Corporal Jack Whitcomb be given this promotion.

Cadet Whitcomb is a member of the Senior Class and is a very fine boy of excellent character. He is of an Army family and is familiar with the principles of military courtesy and discipline. His military record last year was excellent, and I feel confident that he will make a good cadet for this position and well deserves the promotion.

With Kindest regards, I am
Sincerely yours,
*H. P Dunlap,*
Captain, Infantry, Actg. Asst. Adj General.

Jack received the promotion and led the cadets in all formal marches, parades, and public appearances.

Jack developed a love for publishing as an extracurricular activity. He worked as a reporter and photographer for the school newspaper, *The Tornado*. He volunteered as a worker for the school yearbook, the *Pennant*, and he joined the Monogram Club. Learning the principles of organizing, planning, and completing major publishing projects proved invaluable for future efforts, including the published history of Jack's unit in WWII and the first yearbook for Grace Theological Seminary.

Jack also excelled in athletics. He returned to the athletic fields to play Varsity soccer and golf — lettering in both sports. After working hard athletically, he would go to *The Junction* for a special treat, Coca-Cola®, chocolate milk, or his favorite treat of all, ice cream.[5]

In school, his grades began to reach the top third of his class. In formal intelligence diagnostic testing, he ranked third in his class of 110

---

5. Jack loved vanilla and strawberry ice cream, but his favorite flavor was lemon custard.

cadets. The school sent this report to his parents, noting that he rose from 44th in his class in his junior year. He was also noted to take more difficult classes and a strenuous workload, and "he has worked much harder than the average senior at McCallie and is to be congratulated."[6]

Jack's classmates and teachers appreciated his personal character and effort. For example, his English class acted out Shakespeare's play *Othello*, and he was chosen to play Othello.

Maps and geography remained a passion throughout high school. *"I studied the map of Africa because I am trying to learn the capitals of every country in the world,"* and *"I made a list of all the Chinese provinces and their capitals from my Asia map, checking them in the dictionary and typing out the list."* He continued his practice of carefully drawing maps of different countries of the world and drawing pictures of world leaders (see examples in Photo Group 1).

December 17, 1941, was a good day.

> *In American History I got 98 on a matching test. In Spanish I got 100 on a vocabulary test. I went to Patten Field (soccer). We practiced kicking and then played some scrimmage. I got off a lot of good kicks and played well. I got a letter from National Geographic Society acknowledging my finding of a mistake on a map.*

This type of interest and attention to detail would be a critical characteristic for the type of work for which God was uniquely preparing him.

To Whit's dismay, Jack's eyesight precluded him from applying to West Point for college. Jack was interested in the Foreign Services programs at Georgetown University, and he formally requested that Dr. McCallie write a strong recommendation for him. The letter was sent from the school to Georgetown.

School of Foreign Service
Georgetown University
Washington, D. C.

---

6. Letter to Jack's parents from William L. Pressley, head of the Department of English, McCallie School, Chattanooga, Tennessee, November 15, 1941.

## A Good and Faithful Servant

Gentlemen:

Jack Whitcomb (John Clement Whitcomb, Jr.), son of Colonel J.C. Whitcomb, 505 Baltzell Ave, Fort Benning, Georgia, is a Senior at The McCallie School this year. During his period of residence here, Jack made exceptionally good grades. We expect him to graduate in June of this year with honors. He will have 17 credits, which is more than is necessary. His grades are now averaging about 92. His deportment is perfect, his attendance record is perfect. He is one of the superior boys in this school and I recommend him without qualifications.

His grades in languages are excellent and he is a boy of unusually high character. I believe he will make a splendid record in the School of Foreign Service.

Sincerely yours.
*J.P. McCallie*
Headmaster

However, his father believed that Princeton would be a better school for Jack, with broader opportunities. Whit took charge of his son's college application process.

## Darkening Clouds of WWII

After the attack of Japan on Pearl Harbor, Hawaii, on December 7, 1941, the United States' role in WWII rapidly grew, as did the realization that the battles would be fought in two major theaters throughout the world. The news of the growing world war was ominous for Jack and his classmates throughout his years at McCallie, but it was especially so his senior year. Jack recorded the major military events and political speeches as they came across his radio.

October 31, 1941: *"An American Destroyer was sunk by a German Submarine near Iceland."*[7]

December 7, 1941: *"At 2:30 p.m. a boy told us that Japanese bombers had bombed Pearl Harbor in Hawaii and that*

---

7. The USS *Reuben James* was the first U.S. Navy ship sunk by hostile action in the European theater of World War II.

*the Philippines were attacked. We went to supper, and then to vesper service where we prayed for America."*

December 8, 1941: *"At 11:30, we all went to assembly and heard President Roosevelt ask a joint session of Congress for war against Japan."*

December 11, 1941: *"Italy declared war on the USA, and Hitler did the same. Roosevelt sent a message to congress asking for an immediate declaration of war on both Nazi Germany and Italy."*

December 13, 1941: *"Midway and Wake Island are still holding out. Received a telegram that **Dad was made a Full Colonel last night**. Hungary and Bulgaria declared war on America."*

Christmas of 1941 brought Jack back to friends and family at Fort Benning. His Christmas gifts included a pair of wool socks, a necktie, two pairs of white wool golf socks, a golf-score watch, a non-losable golf tee, shaving lotion, and a beautiful new portable Royal Typewriter, which he used daily for years. Then his mother informed him that he was to go to a dance with Pauline Vida, so *"I called her, but she said she couldn't come."* Instead, he picked up Joe and Helen Warren and Alfred and went to a movie.

*The movie was a good mystery,* The Maltese Falcon.

On February 23, 1942, Jack received a call from his dad *"to tell me to fill out my application to Princeton for the three-year accelerated course beginning in June 29."* Jack, obeying his father, went to Prof. McCallie the next day to talk to him about going to Princeton. *"He said he would write a good letter for me."* That was key, since McCallie Military Academy had a history of sending great students to Princeton. The following day a package arrived — special delivery from Colonel Whitcomb — an application to Princeton. Most of that week was spent filling out the application and getting some help from his professors on writing a personal statement on why he wanted to go to that university. He also requested an exemption to taking the science part of the entrance exam, since he would apply to the humanities. On March 2, 1942, he sent a card of commitment. A week later, Jack celebrated, *"Princeton has exempted me from the science test on the Entrance Exam."* The exam was taken on April 11, 1942, and Jack was told that he did well. On May 8, 1942, he received the good news — he was accepted to Princeton University.

> I went to history. We had an easy test on the last two chapters. I got a letter from PRINCETON, WHICH SAID THAT I HAD PASSED THE COLLEGE ENTRANCE EXAMS, AND WAS ACCEPTED IN PRINCETON! I listened to the news of a gigantic Allied-Japanese naval battle off of the Coral Sea. I typed a letter

At high school, the excellence of Jack Whitcomb as a student continued to emerge. In English, his final rank was second. In history, he ranked first. And amazingly, he also ranked first in *Bible*!

The spring of 1942 was a perilous time for the United States military. Jack continued to log the radio reports of the war:

> March 4, 1942: *"MacArthur's tiny air force sank two Jap ships."*

> April 9, 1942: *"We had a moment of silence for the fall of the Bataan Peninsula."*

One of the assignments in English was to write a poem. Jack's poem captured the moment, in 1942, as WWII was exploding, and his generation — especially those boys from a military academy — would be called upon by their country to fight a war that they neither started nor wanted. The poem hit home to the cadets in such a powerful way that they chose Jack as "The Class Poet," adopting the poem as the official *poem of the year*, and asked Jack to read it aloud to the cadets, parents, and dignitaries at the graduation ceremony. The poem was as follows:

# McCallie

## A Challenge

A doubtful nation taught in peace has met a war of hate
America has met a fellow whose strength may prove her fate
The lessons learned are costly ones for the first may be the last,
And few can say what lies in store beneath these clouds so vast.

Not long ago a rising storm lay waste our years of peace
In foreign lands it crushed all hope with worldly sin unleashed.
But heedless of its growing threat we slept in peace content
And cast aside all fear of war and what it really meant.

As long as men would fight for us on a distant unknown shore,
Our lofty creeds and high ideals would be safe for evermore.
So with these thoughts we soon climbed high into our safe retreat
And there we slept behind our walls in security complete.

But while we slept the blow was struck by arms across the sea;
our dreams were gone, And there we stood to face reality.
A bitter price we'll have to pay to see this light of day!
And whether it will come again is up to us to say.

> Jack Whitcomb
> McCallie School
> June 1942

## Graduation

In May 1942, Jack completed his education at McCallie Military Academy. He sat on the stage during the honors program and graduation, hoisting the colors of the military academy. He received special recognition of his hard work, winning some of the top academic awards, including the First-Place Faculty Medal for Overall Excellence and official Class Poet. When the time came, he stood, representing both his class and his generation, and read "A Challenge" to the crowd.

*Summer 1942*

The brief summer vacation between McCallie and Princeton was spent in Fort Benning, Georgia — reading, relaxing, and playing golf. Whit was busy with the logistics of bringing military leaders and dignitaries through Fort Benning, and Jack met many of them. These events were also recorded in Jack's diary.

## Summary

The time in spent Fort Benning, Georgia, and Chattanooga, Tennessee, stood in stark contrast to Seattle, Washington. As a nation, the United States plunged into WWII — with Whit, as a career military leader, fully engaged in the excitement and effort. As Jack became a young man, his interactions with his father strengthened as Whit took a more active and determined role in Jack's development. Jack also met and became personally acquainted with many of the top leaders of the nation. While many folks viewed them as elite demigods, Jack got to know them as regular people. He clearly appreciated their achievements but never focused on or envied social status.

A personal and life-changing transformation occurred with John Whitcomb at McCallie Military Academy. At home, he appeared to be passive and detached, as he was relegated to his room during his parents' parties and social events and cared for by servants and hired help. At McCallie he learned to take care of himself, as no servants were provided and as he observed the ways of other cadets. He learned outstanding study habits and the rewards of hard work and self-discipline. He took his "book" skills out of his room to learn writing and publishing with the school newspaper and yearbook. He found two sports that matched his interest and skill — soccer and golf — and lettered in both. He rose to the top of his class and was selected by his peers to represent his entire class on graduation day.

My father often told me how McCallie changed his life and gave him the skills and discipline needed for his future career. He also deeply appreciated the godly example of J.P. McCallie, who showed genuine interested in Jack's future — and his soul.

The impact of Professor Whitcomb as an alumnus of McCallie School is still remembered. In September 2002, the McCallie class of 1942 celebrated its 60th reunion. The class voted on whom to honor with the first and only Alumni Achievement Award. They chose "Jack" Whitcomb.

*Diary Notes*

June 7, 1942

left, Dad & I worked on my Princeton medical sheet. He went down to the airport to meet MAJOR GENERAL CLARKE, who just arrived from London with LORD LOUIS MOUNTBATTEN, SIR JOHN DILL, & General MARSHALL. General Clark came to the House with Dad, & he is to sleep here tonight. He left with Dad for a dinner, & I played 6 holes of golf at 8:00 P.M. Came home

June 21, 1942

and went downstairs to meet COL. FRANK MURPHY, who came with Dad later on. He is a JUSTICE OF THE SUPREME COURT, A FORMER GOVENOR OF MICHIGAN, ATTORNEY-GENERAL, AND GOVENOR-GENERAL OF THE PHILIPPINES. He (REF. SUPP Y)

LAST DAY OF MY SEVENTEENTH YEAR. REFER TO BOOK IV FOR MON, JUNE 22, 1942

# The Whitcombs' Military Legacy

**2.1** (Left) Dr. Whitcomb's grandfather, Col. Clement Colfax Whitcomb, MD, U.S. Military Corps, 1909 portrait. (Right) Receiving the medal of the French Legion of Honor, Tours, France, April 9, 1919.

**2.2** (Left) Dr. Whitcomb's father, Col. John C. Whitcomb Sr., U.S. Army, 1943 portrait. (Right) Col. Whitcomb in France in 1944 during WWII where he was awarded the Legion of Merit and other medals for his service.

Sun, 1941 - I got up around 7:40. It was cold outside, and the radiator was off.

At 2:30 P.M. A BOY TOLD US THAT JAPANESE BOMBERS HAD BOMBED PEARL HARBOR IN HAWAII, AND THAT THE PHILIPPINES WERE ATTACKED. WE LISTENED ATTENTIVELY TO THE RADIO, AND REPORTS CAME IN THAT THE BATTLESHIP OKLAHOMA WAS SET AFIRE, AND THE WEST VIRGINIA SUNK. THE JAPANESE DECLARED WAR ON THE U.S., THE DUTCH EAST INDIES, CANADA, COSTA RICA, AND NICARAGUA DECLARED WAR ON JAPAN. THE MALAY STATES, AND THAILAND WERE ATTACKED BY JAPAN. We went to supper, and then to vesper service, where we prayed for America.

**2.3** Copy of John Whitcomb's diary entry on December 7, 1941.

**2.4.** John Whitcomb was inducted into the Army in April 1943.

**2.5** Front view of 240 mm howitzer, the gun that Jack Whitcomb was trained on in the 5th regiment, 15th battalion, Fort Bragg, NC, April–August, 1943 (photo is from the signal corps, public domain).

## Engineer Training at Virginia Polytechnical Institute

**2.5** (Left) John Whitcomb at Virginia Polytechnical Institute, 1943–44. (Center and right) Roommates Warren Severin and B.J. Cohn.

**2.6** This was one of my dad's favorite pictures of himself. He was training for the field artillery as an engineering student at VPI, February 19, 1944.

**2.7** My dad was assigned to the 84th infantry division that was being made combat-ready in Camp Claiborne, LA, spring, 1944.

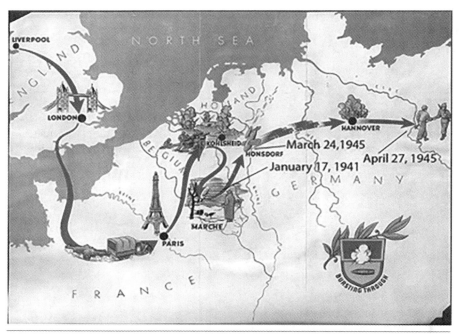

**2.8** Map developed by John Whitcomb after the war to highlight the action of the 909 Field Artillery Unit. Dates added to correspond with text.

**2.9** October 15–Nov 3, 1944. My dad joined the Red Ball Express in France. The Red Ball Express was a shipping route through France to supply the fast-moving front line. My dad worked as an interpreter commanding German POWs on loading the trucks.

**2.10** Greeting card from Jack's 84th Infantry Division, printed before the Battle of the Bulge in Belgium. The Germans called the soldiers "hatchet men" of the "Terror Division."

**2.11** Field artillery loading a 105 mm howitzer. The firing was timed by the fire command center so that all the projectiles would hit the target simultaneously (stock U.S. Army photo).

**2.12** "Finest soldier . . ." A cartoon drawing of my dad in action as the "Computer," receiving calls from the forward observers and directing the artillery units on where to aim and the type of shells and the amount of charge needed to stop the enemy. 909 Field Artillery Battalion, February 11, 1945.

145

**2.13** Jack Whitcomb and his VPI roommate B.J. Cohn meeting at Amonines, Belgium, January 17, 1945, during the Battle of the Bulge.

**2.14** Unidentified town after shelling by the field artillery (stock U.S. Army photo).

**2.15** German prisoners of war (stock U.S. Army photo). My dad often served as a German interpreter as POWs flooded in.

**2.16** Jack Whitcomb at Rheiuhausen, Germany, near Duisburg (just north of Düsseldorf and Cologne) where the 909 crossed the Rhine River into the heart of Germany, March 21, 1945.

**2.17** Symbol of the 909th Field Artillery Battalion. It also served as a cover for the History of the 909th, which my dad helped write.

## When it starts

Are you still alive? You struggle with inadequate weapons, with inadequate equipment, shaking of half-trained units. But you live. Thousand of your comrades, many of your own friends have fallen. It was bad, but you have escaped. You live. Your officers reject your thoughts that this is just a fight break. There is hope, because — you live.

Tomorrow we can start, as it all started at the Atlantic Wall, at Avranches and St. Lo. Morning: Sudden, non-stop drumfire of all calibers, rolling use of Jabos; Thousands of Flying Fortresses; Carpet bombing; Tanks, armor-piercing missile weapons and the new flamethrower. Everything that you have seen so far has been a child's game in the mountains.

Tomorrow: Hell.

The day after tomorrow it will be over, and you are either dead, a cripple or a prisoner of war. The decision may be up to you. Therefore, now consider what you will do if you are still alive, when the material battle rolls over you. Then maybe you have the opportunity to save your life. Many will have to surrender. But many will have to die because he made the choice too late.

WHICH CHOICE DO YOU MAKE?

**2.18** (Above) A psychological warfare pamphlet shot over the German lines in artillery shells and dropped from airplanes. (Right) English translation. From my dad's war souvenirs.

HEUTE LEBST DU NOCH. Du kämpfst mit unzureichenden Waffen, mit mangelhafter Ausrüstung, von halbgeschulten Einheiten umgeben. Aber — Du lebst. Tausende Deiner Kameraden, viele Deiner eigenen Freunde sind gefallen. Es war schlimm, aber Du bist noch entkommen. Du lebst. Deine Offiziere verwerfen Deine Gedanken, dass das nur eine Kampfpause ist. Es besteht Hoffnung, denn — Du lebst.

MORGEN KANN ES LOSGEHEN, wie es auf einmal losging am Atlantikwall, bei Avranches und St. Lo. Morgen: Plötzliches, pausenloses Trommelfeuer aller Kaliber, rollender Einsatz von Jabos; tausende von Fliegenden Festungen; Bombenteppiche; Panzer, panzerbrechende Raketenwaffen und die neuen Flammenwerfer. Alles, was Du bisher gesehen hast, war im Vergleich damit ein Kinderspiel. Morgen: die Hölle.

ÜBERMORGEN WIRD ES AUS SEIN, und Du bist entweder tot, ein Krüppel oder Kriegsgefangener. Die Entscheidung darüber liegt vielleicht an Dir selbst. Deshalb bedenke jetzt, was Du machen wirst, wenn Du noch am Leben bist, wenn die Materialschlacht über Dich hinwegrollt. Dann ist vielleicht für Dich Gelegenheit, Dein Leben zu retten. Viele werden sich ergeben müssen. So mancher wird aber sterben müssen, weil er die Wahl zu spät getroffen hat.

**WELCHE WAHL TRIFFST DU?**

ZG 82

**2.19** Mission accomplished! Jack Whitcomb at the banks of the Elbe River, marking the final goal of the Railsplitter's advance in WWII, April 27, 1945.

**2.20** (Left) House occupied by my dad in Sinsheim, Germany, 20 miles south of Heidelberg, Germany, from June 1946 to January 1946. (Right) The house was owned by former German soldier Rainer Ehmann and parents. My dad and Rainer became lifelong friends.

**2.21** My dad in London with Stewart Anderson. They were supporting the "Christ is the Victory" program, September 1945.

**2.22** The Statue of Liberty. This was one of my dad's favorite photos — a sight that was cherished by every American G.I. as they chugged into New York Harbor after winning WWII in Europe.

**2.23** Day of Army discharge, January 27, 1946, Ft. Meade, MD.

# Section 3

# College and Military Service

# Chapter 7

# Princeton

"I definitely accepted Christ"
June 1942 to March 1943

## The USA at War

Horrific injuries and death destroyed the lives of thousands and thousands of young American men from Jack's generation as they marched over foreign lands, crisscrossing the seven seas and soaring in the black and blue skies. By June 1942, just six months after Pearl Harbor, things appeared bleak for the Allies as casualties mounted and victories remained elusive.

Plunging deeper and deeper into the Second World War, the U.S. Military desperately needed additional young men to replace the tens of thousands of casualties in Africa, Italy, and the Pacific Ocean. In addition, the military anticipated that many more men would be needed for the invasion of Italy, France, Germany, and other European countries to destroy the Nazis. Many more men would be needed in the Asian war against the Empire of the Sun — including an invasion of Japan itself. Every young man knew that, in some way, he would serve his country in this time of all-out war.

On June 22, 1942, John "Jack" Whitcomb turned 18 years of age, officially becoming an adult and eligible to fight. Jack's father, Whit, spent the evening with Jack on his birthday discussing college life in Princeton, including the importance of good study habits, writing letters to his family, and tips on social life. The next day, Jack packed his belongings in Fort Benning, Georgia, traveled by car to Columbus, Georgia, and then boarded a series of northbound trains with his mother headed toward Trenton, New Jersey, the last stop on the journey to Princeton University.

In 1942, the Whitcombs' house in Fort Benning resembled a beehive of officers, dignitaries, and military friends of Colonel Whitcomb as the Infantry School hummed in high gear. The week before Jack and Salome departed for Trenton, for example, the Whitcombs hosted an evening dinner with their friend, Colonel Norman Schwarzkopf.[1] Col. Schwarzkopf was famous as the lead investigator in the Lindbergh kidnapping and for being the narrator on *Gang Busters* — Jack's favorite radio show as a child. He spoke at length of his impending assignment to Iran with his family. That evening, they also confirmed that his wife, Ruth, would meet Jack and Salome in Trenton, New Jersey, where the Schwarzkopfs had their home, and that she would chauffeur them over the final 18 miles to Princeton, New Jersey.

On the train ride north, Jack read *War and Peace* for entertainment. A consecutive series of trains lumbered through Georgia; the Carolinas; Virginia; and Washington, D.C., toward the final destination of Trenton, New Jersey. Ruth Schwarzkopf met Jack and his mother at the train station and took them to her house for a few hours. Ruth had a 7-year-old boy, Norman Schwarzkopf Jr., who would later plan and lead *Operation Desert Storm* to destroy the Iraqi Army and liberate Kuwait.[2] Ruth finally completed the short trip to the Princeton University campus where Jack would enter college the next morning as a freshman. His mother would continue north to visit her family near New York City. Jack was finally at Princeton.

## A History of Princeton as Defender of Truth

Princeton, like most of the great private universities in the United States, was established as a seminary. Founded in 1746 by the New Light Presbyterians as the College of New Jersey, it was one of the original Ivy League schools. It was founded during the Great Awakening

---

1. John Whitcomb diary entry, June 14, 1942. Among other notable guests to the Whitcomb home was Col. Frank Murphy, Justice of the Supreme Court, formerly Governor of Michigan, Attorney General and Governor General of the Philippines (recorded on June 21, 1942).
2. Norman Schwarzkopf Jr., https://en.wikipedia.org/wiki/Norman_Schwarzkopf,_Jr.

and, after a shaky start, flourished in the late 1700s under the Reverend John Witherspoon, signer of the Declaration of Independence and the Articles of Confederation. The foundational paradigm was the philosophy of Scottish realism — there is no conflict between reason and faith.

Following Witherspoon, a number of problems developed with both students and faculty. The Presbyterians, who wanted to maintain a stronger focus on training ministers, encouraged the founding of Princeton Theological Seminary in 1812. Unlike its Ivy League peers, Princeton and its seminary supported strong, conservative biblical scholarship until the 20th century. Notable theologians included Charles Hodge in the 1860s–1870s, whose *Systematic Theology* remains a Christian classic; his son Archibald Alexander (A.A.) Hodge, who clarified the doctrine of atonement; B.B. Warfield; John Gresham Machen; and others. Warfield was instrumental in articulating the orthodox position of the process where divine inspiration involved the human author's intellect as they expressed themselves linguistically, while at the same time being supervised by the Holy Spirit to ensure its perfection. J. Gresham Machen clarified the issues surrounding the virgin birth of Christ. B.B. Warfield remained at Princeton from 1887 until his death in 1921, while Machen remained at Princeton until 1929.

During the first 150 years of Princeton's life, the drive for the supremacy of Scripture as God's Word, and of evangelicalism of the unbeliever, emanated from faculty leaders and the administration. Consider the statement of Charles Hodge in 1868 during the inauguration of the school's new president, James McCosh, who led Princeton from 1868 to 1888. In articulating the purpose and goal for Princeton University, Hodge stated,

> We would, in a single word, state what it is that we desire. It is that true religion here may be dominant, that a pure Gospel may be preached and taught and lived, and that students may be made to feel that the eternal is infinitely more important than the earthly.[3]

---

3. Charles Hodge, D.D., L.L.D, Address of Welcome on behalf of the Board of Trustees, October 27, 1868 (New York, NY: Robert Carter and Brothers). Reproduced at https://static1.squarespace.com/static/590be125ff7c502a07752a5b/t/5f628e72747b-0077f8b00dd3/1600294515438/Hodge%2C+Charles%2C+Address+of+Welcome+on+Behalf+of+the+Board+of+Trustees.pdf, accessed August 24, 2021.

Princeton President James McCosh was a strong believer but not a theologian. Under his leadership, the University experienced remarkable growth in the physical facilities, the size of the faculty and student body, and in their reputation as an Ivy League school. But this emphasis resulted in a shift in focus from Scripture to academics. Functionally, the new aim became a race to remain in the upper echelons of academic study, along with Harvard and Yale. The changing focus on academic excellence resulted in a downgrade in the previous priorities to provide the church with orthodox and competent clergy and to provide the state with orthodox and competent layman. The respect for the Scriptures initially diminished in the college, driven by the science departments and the cosmology[4] of Darwinism.

Francis Landey Patton, who followed McCosh and served as president of Princeton from 1888–1902, was an ordained minister and strong advocate of inerrancy of Scripture and opponent of the philosophy and intentions behind "higher criticism." Although he was very popular with most of the students and the Presbyterian faithful, he was criticized as being a poor administrator by his detractors. Patton was replaced by Woodrow Wilson, who later served as the 28th president of the United States. The replacement of Patton by Wilson marked a precipitous downturn in godly leadership within the institution. But God's purposes at Princeton would not falter.

## Deterioration of Christian Institutions Outside of the Local Church

It is a fact of history that Christian organizations that become institutionalized, that attain significant financial resources and/or notoriety, and/or that are governed with a polity that deviates from the checks and balances of the local church, fail from the inside out. Princeton University suffered this fate during the late 19th and early 20th centuries. By the time John Whitcomb entered the freshman class in 1942, the last of the great Christian leaders on the school's faculty had passed away or abandoned the Seminary in protest.[5] But God did not abandon

---

4. Cosmology is the science of the origin and development of the universe. The big bang theory was created to explain the creation of the universe without a Creator.

5. J. Gresham Machen left Princeton in 1929 over the growth of liberalism, to form Westminster Seminary in Philadelphia, Pennsylvania. He was joined by Cornelius Van Til (who would plan a major role in forming John Whitcomb's approach to apologetics), Robert Dick Wilson (whose son, Christy Wilson, would play a role in John Whitcomb's

# Princeton

Princeton — He shifted the initiative to make and teach disciples from the administration and faculty to the students and alumni.

The catalyst for the secularization at Princeton University was the continued and rigorous argument between the seminary and the secular college over the issue of the accuracy and authority of Scripture in the area of science and natural revelation. The internal debate captured international attention as Charles Hodge, president of the seminary, grappled with James McCosh, president of the college, over Darwin's theory of evolution.[6] The debate continued through the time of B.B. Warfield, an evidentialist who unwittingly argued that *justification for a belief required extra-biblical evidences*. The problem with this approach is that it puts natural revelation on equal par with divine revelation. However, in apologetics, one cannot serve two masters, and the Princeton theologians subtly but increasingly rejected clear statements of the Scriptures in areas of science in favor of "natural revelation" as defined and enforced by the scientific theories of the day. Thus, the "7 days" of creation morphed into seven eons of unclear length and character by well-meaning theologians in order to harmonize the Bible with secular concepts of science — rather than *vice versa*.

The correct approach, in retrospect, would have been to harmonize measurable, physical observations with the framework and history revealed in the Bible. In the end, the faculty of the theology department found themselves trapped in a hopeless position, finding it impossible to harmonize the biblical record within the framework of the "scientific" arguments of the evolutionists in the college. As a result, by the 1930s, the voices of the divinity school in support of the authority and accuracy of Scriptures in areas of origins and natural history drowned. The legacy of great Princeton theologians ended.

When Jack Whitcomb entered Princeton in 1942 as an undergraduate, the effects of liberal and naturalistic theology had destroyed Princeton Seminary as a Defender of the Faith. Everyone at Princeton University accepted Darwin's theory of evolution, including the seminary faculty. This concession to secular scientific theory, and doubtless other areas of Christian faith and practice, resulted in the theological and spiritual

connection with the Princeton Evangelical Fellowship), and Oswald T. Allis. They were followed by others.

6. See, for example, a History of Princeton University, http://en.wikipedia.org/wiki/History_of_Princeton_University.

destruction of this once-great institution. Clear, accurate interpretation of Scripture and theologically sound answers to the secular scientific critics awaited the voices of godly men from elsewhere. By the 1930s, an atheistic-naturalistic epistemology and secular humanistic philosophy dominated the classrooms.

## Jack Whitcomb Enters Princeton

Jack was enthusiastic about entering Princeton. He was assigned room #492 in Pyne Hall, which he shared with three roommates. In addition to freshman classes, he signed up for intramural soccer, social clubs, and other activities. He wrote to his parents about his living conditions and plans.[7]

> I think that I want to be in the R.O.C.T. here and get a commission as a lieutenant in the artillery as I had planned.
>
> I signed up for swimming as my major summer sport.
>
> Last night was the first meal we had served on the campus, and up till then I had my meals in the restaurants across the street. The dining halls in which we eat are beautiful, large, Gothic structures, with many portraits and paintings hanging around the walls. The food is just perfect, and I look forward to the meals.
>
> I am finding myself slowly running out of money with all the expenses of my first few days here. We have to pay $1.00 for this and $5.00 for that so much that it is a wonder that I have any money at all left." . . . [list of expenses] . . . "I also bought a freshman cap, which all freshmen are required to wear to show that they are in the same class. We also wear black ties. This is a custom of the school and will last through until next Christmas.

On June 28, 1942, Jack wrote a separate letter to his dad. A few highlights include: "For athletics, I have signed up for swimming as the main sport," adding some more details for his dad. "In the swimming we will have practice in life-saving, and other valuable skills in case you find yourself in the middle of the ocean beside a torpedoed ship."

He also discussed his plans to obtain the prerequisites for specialized course of studies.

---

7. Letter from John Whitcomb to his mother, June 15, 1942.

What I will be taking is a definite course called the S.P.I.A. (School of Public and International Affairs). There are many boys I know of that are planning to take this course here, but only fifty of us will be admitted [to the program] at the end of our sophomore years. I am sure that if I study hard, I will be one of them.

Jack entered these classrooms with an open mind, full of anticipation but uncertainty about the future — and concern about the growing involvement of the USA in WWII. As one might expect, he was exposed to the leading minds of evolution and secular thinking. However, he gained confidence in his abilities and work ethic, as his test scores rose to the top of his class, reminiscent of his trajectory at McCallie Military Academy.[8] Furthermore, some of the McCallie alumni contacted him,

I have already seen three of the McCallie boys who have come up to Princeton during the past three years. One of them is Lester Brooks, who is the captain of the golf, and Bob Caldwell, who was the major of the battalion. David McCallie, who is the son of Professor McCallie has also come by to visit me, and he is my councilor or advisor, luckily.[9]

Shortly thereafter he also met John Parks, another McCallie alumni who was a student at Princeton. Together, the early connection of these guys with Jack in his college career would have long-term ramifications.

## Jack Chooses a Course in Geology

Most of the courses that Jack took were designed to prepare him for S.P.I.A., including languages such as German and Spanish. Jack also loved geography and maps, so he signed up for geology. As Jack got into his coursework, he wrote an update to his mother dated July 1, 1942.

My geology teacher, Prof. Mcclintock.[10] Geology is going to be a very interesting course for me, because it will have

8. Letter to Jack from J.P. McCallie, October 1942.
9. Letter from John Whitcomb to his mother, July 1, 1942.
10. Paul MacClintock, Ph.D., represented a generation of geologists that brought distinction to the department from the 1930s to the 1950s. From http://etcweb.princeton.edu/CampusWWW/Companion/geological_geophysical_sciences_department.html, accessed June 26, 2019.

a great deal to do with map work, for topographical references, etc. . . . Each week, I have three lectures in geology to
attend, and two laboratory periods. During the lectures the
professor either shows moving pictures and slide pictures, or
else just talks to us about the material covered in our textbook assignments in order to make it more clear to us. We
have many new terms to learn such as barchans, igneous,
butte, mesa, delta, tarn, esker, kame, silt, and other geological
things which refer to sand formations, wind erosion forms,
or soil compositions.[11]

To Jack's surprise, he both enjoyed geology and did very well in the
class. So, for the fall semester, he continued in geology, now under
Professor Richard M. Field.[12] As usual, Jack sent updates to his parents
on his course work.

Letter from Jack to his parents on October 10, 1942:

In geology we are spending the first six weeks of the
semester in detailed study of paleontology, which consists
of the study of ancient fossils, clams, and other things that
crawled around the bottom of the ocean millions of years
ago, and which are now extinct.

Letter from Jack to his parents on November 19, 1942:

I have a short report to make in Geology about the development of the early cave man, which must be in sometime
before Christmas. In that course, we are now studying the
prehistoric ages and eras, such as Cambrian, Paleozoic, Mes-
ozoic, and Cenozoic, during which the dinosaurs roamed the
earth and continents changed greatly in form. We have to

11. On July 16, he describes his lectures on glaciers and mountain carving by glaciers. He
also studied mechanisms of erosion, rivers, wind work, subsurface water, etc. In his
laboratory session they study topographical maps, how river erosion has carved regions
like Yellowstone Park, etc. On August 15, he wrote to his parents that "I got a 93 on my
final rock test, which was one of the highest grades."

12. Dr. Field was a famous geologist and paleontologist. He authored the textbook that Jack
used, entitled *An Outline of the Principles of Geology*, College Outline Series, 3rd edition
(New York: Barnes & Noble, 1938), 211 pages; *Geology: A Survey-outline of the Principles
of Physical and Historical Geology*, College Outline Series, Barnes and Noble, New York,
198 pages.; and *The Principles of Historical Geology from the Regional Point of View*, Princeton, N.J.: Princeton University Press; London: Oxford University Press, 1933, 283 pages.

make use of the museum there, by studying the various dinosaur skeletons, and other fossil bones.

At the end of the second semester, Jack was delighted to have among the top scores in German and Spanish, etc. But, he noted to his parents, "The best new of all was my getting a 1+ in Geology for the term."[13]

## Freshman College Life

The freshman year in college remains one of the most dangerous times of life. Here, for the first time, many young men and women become "liberated" from their parent's control and often plunge into risky and wicked behavior that leads to spiritual, emotional, and/or physical disasters with life-long regrets. In contrast, there are other young adults who demonstrate self-discipline, self-control, and long-term vision that avoid the minefields of unfettered rebellion, abandonment of principles, or mistakes conducted under coercion of peers. These individuals often succeed where others fail. Although John Whitcomb was not a believer, he displayed high moral and ethical behavior, respect for authority, dignity, and honor. He also acquired a deep respect for Christianity from the examples of godly leadership by the faculty at McCallie Military Academy. As a new freshman, he religiously attended the Episcopalian services at the University Chapel each Sunday, taking Holy Communion with a small group of other students from traditional American backgrounds.

Jack Whitcomb's diary documented extraordinary discipline and energy. The majority of his week included attending class and studying, day and night, six to seven days a week. His circle of friends hovered around room #492 Pyne Hall, representing his dorm mates. Although he spent countless hours reading and studying, his door remained open, and the neighboring freshmen often came to him for long discussions on a variety of topics. He occasionally attended campus events, including football games, but primarily spent his free time reading magazines, listening to the news of the war, and drawing maps of all of the countries of the world.

Although Jack made social events on campus a low priority, this does not imply that he was a wallflower. He kept himself in physical shape with regular exercise, including swimming, running, and playing

---

13. Letter from John Whitcomb to his parents on January 24, 1943.

soccer and football. He also got into wrestling matches with other students from time to time — just to keep them in line.

## Reserve Officers' Training Corps

American colleges and universities offered a temporary refuge for the best and brightest young men. The Reserve Officer's Training Corps (ROTC), for example, became a major program on campuses, including Ivy League schools such as Princeton.[14] Jack signed up for the Army ROTC in the field artillery and participated in classroom teaching, training exercises, and drills. However, because of poor eyesight, he was disqualified from the ROTC. Instead, he was assigned to the Army Enlisted Reserve Corps.[15] In response to this news, Jack's dad, Col. Whitcomb, sent a letter to the school. In response, Jack was given another eye exam, and he barely passed, allowing him to apply for the ROTC. However, this was very competitive, and the delay may have cost the loss of open slots. Nevertheless, Jack signed up for the Military Science course at Princeton, which is the same course that the ROTC students took. Jack was specifically interested in Army artillery and was allowed to start training with the cannoneers.

Jack was fascinated with the cannons and training. On November 6, 1942, for example, he records, *"I put on my ROTC uniform. Then in lab we had drilling and went out for gun practice with the 75's. I was No. 2 gunner."*[16]

However, the ROTC program was doomed. In fact, there were about 100,000 men who already graduated from ROTC and received commissions. The Military Brass decided that the ROTC would be suspended because the soldiers were needed *on the front lines* — not officers in reserve. Clearly, all able-bodied young men would eventually be drafted, trained, and sent east or west across great oceans to fight the Axis powers. So, the future of young men in Jack's situation became tenuous.[17]

---

14. See blog of Princeton ROTC during WWII, including training videos, https://blogs. princeton.edu/reelmudd/2010/09/soldiers-on-campus-circa-1943/.

15. Letter from John Whitcomb to his mother on July 28, 1942. The program did not result in a commission upon graduation but was helpful in getting into officer candidate school.

16. A letter from John Whitcomb to his mother describes his training on the small artillery in detail. The Princeton ROTC would later be given the new 105 mm howitzers, which was the mainstay of field artillery units in WWII.

17. In January 1945, Jack noted that all of the students who signed up for the air corps were already gone.

# Princeton

## Off-campus Activities

<u>Cane Night</u>. As a child, I remember dad making a vague reference to Cane Night. Cane Night is a Princeton college tradition dating back to the 1870s when a group of sophomores stole the fancy walking canes of the arrogant incoming freshman who failed to show the proper humility to the upper classmen. Freshmen strutting around campus with fancy clothes and expensive canes would not be tolerated. The situation led to a famous melee between the freshman and sophomores.

The historical battle became immortalized as an annual event featuring the freshman and sophomore classes and centered on wrestling for walking canes. Psychological class dominance and pride followed either the freshman or sophomores, depending on the outcome of battle. The school administration finally attempted to corral the dangerous tradition and transform it into a sporting event. Since this action undermined the spirit of undergraduate class clashes, the students would bypass all attempts of the administration to manage the traditions by secretly meeting on the football field to fight like "men."

As a freshman, Dad noted, his classmates met the sophomores on the football field at midnight on a predetermined date in October. "In the morning," he quipped, "badly beaten sophomores could be seen crawling off the field of battle." We did not know if this comment referred to a historical event, a rumor, or something that he read in the college newspaper. However, his October 22, 1942, diary entry recorded the consequences of participating in the battle specifically, noting that he had his clothes badly ripped on "Cane Night." Although Professor Whitcomb's children generally viewed their dad as a bookworm, they now believe that he was not an innocent bystander. Whether or not he administered any of the beatings (before becoming a Christian, of course) will never be known.

## Dating

Princeton, like McCallie Military Academy, was an all-male school until 1969. This did not mean that women were not allowed on campus, and many of the guys found gals to date from the community or other nearby schools. Regardless, a number of ladies "mysteriously" appeared in strategic locations and events.

There is no record of Jack dating as a freshman student at Princeton University. On Saturday, July 10, 1942, for example, he reported, *"At 6:00 we went up to supper. There were many girls here visiting for the weekend. After supper I went to my room and read some more from my Geology book. Miller went to the dance over in Palmer Square. I read several chapters from 'War and Peace' – to bed at 10:45."* What *was* recorded was a failed attempt of his mother to spawn a relation between her son and a young lady during Christmas break, 1942.

## Mom, the Matchmaker

Colonel John "Whit" Whitcomb was transferred from Fort Benning, Georgia, to Camp Butler, North Carolina, in July 1942. Camp Butler, located just northeast of Durham, North Carolina, became a major U.S. Army training and staging area for 35,000 troops at a time. Jack's parents bought a house in Durham, where his mother stayed throughout the war.

Jack spent Christmas of 1942 in Durham. The first clue that something suspicious was happening was the long telephone conversations that Jack's mother was having with a Mrs. Brimmer on the day he arrived at his new home. Mrs. Brimmer's husband, Colonel Brimmer, like Whit, was transferred to Camp Butler, North Carolina — accompanied by his wife and daughter Jacyline.

The next day, December 21, Jack returned from the A&P store where he was sent for some English muffins, and he found that Mrs. Brimmer was at his house with her daughter Jacyline. So, he sat by the fireplace with Jacyline, watching the flames and eating nuts. Jack also showed her his German album and Princeton textbooks. The Brimmers left just before supper.

The following day Jack relaxed, reading *War and Peace*, until evening, when the Brimmers came over. Jack and Jacyline started a fire, and the family enjoyed a spaghetti dinner. After dinner, Jack set up a movie projector, and they all watched movie clips and laughed. Then they listened to records and talked in the living room until the Brimmers finally left at midnight.

Jack spent December 24 at Camp Butler with his dad, watching the soldiers put Jeeps on top of the buildings with cardboard Santa Claus figures serving as drivers. That evening, Jacyline Brimmer came to their house to deliver a small gift, and they exchanged it for a gift for Mrs. Brimmer.

Christmas Day was again spent at Camp Butler, but on the way home, the Whitcombs' car happened to drive by the Brimmers' house, and it stopped to allow the Whitcombs to see the Col. and Mrs. Brimmer to wish them a Merry Christmas. Jacyline came in a little later. They finally finished their visit and went home.

On December 26, 1942, the Whitcombs had surprise visitors while Jack was doing a crossword puzzle — it was the Brimmers. Jack showed Jacyline the Christmas presents he received, and they talked in the living room while the mothers talked in the kitchen. Then they left.

On December 28, 1942, a Mrs. Morehead called to invite Jack to a dance at the Country Club. Salome returned the call and accepted the invitation for Jack, then asked him to call up a Miss Sug Nicholson, who lived across the street, and to invite her to go with him to the dance. Sug said she was going somewhere else, so Jack decided to go "stag." But his mother decided that Jack should take Jacyline Brimmer to the dance. He called, and she accepted.

Salome bought a corsage for Jack to give to Jacyline on the day of the dance. Jacyline arrived, dressed in a nice evening dress, and he presented the flowers to her. They drove to the country club in pouring rain, arriving a little early. There was a live orchestra, but *"it sounded bad."* Numerous small children, mostly girls, appeared, dancing with each other and making noise. The room was also hot, so they went downstairs to the grill to get a Coca-Cola®. But the pouring rain caused the grill area to flood.

The evening went from bad to worse. Jack recorded the events in his diary:

> *It was such a bad dance, that Jacyline and I decided to leave early. It was still raining, and we drove downtown to get something to eat. Since the Washington Duke was closed (11:40 p.m.), we ended up in a small place called "White Palace" and I had a hamburger. Then I drove her back home to the University Apartments, leaving the key in the car while I took her up to their apartment. Mrs. Brimmer had just come back from the Hone's where she and Mother had spent the evening. I said goodnight, and hurried back to the car, AND FOUND THAT IT*

# A Good and Faithful Servant

*HAD BEEN STOLEN! I rushed around in the rain to look for it, and then came home to tell Mother. She tried to call Dad, but couldn't reach him, and then phoned the police to tell them the license number and type. Mother was very nervous, & we went to bed. Then around 3:00 AM the police called again and said that they had found our car before the University Apartments and that we could come for it at the police station in the morning.*

The next morning Jack retrieved the car from the police station. The thieves trashed the car with cigarette ashes and pop bottles. They had taken the mirror and torn off the A&C ration slips. So, Jack cleaned the car and took the bottles to Piggly Wiggly to exchange them for the deposit money. When he returned home, he found his mother and Mrs. Brimmer already organizing a golf outing for the afternoon — a foursome of the two mothers, Jacyline, and Jack.

They drove to the Hope Valley Country Club, finding the grounds soaking wet with large puddles everywhere. Jacyline quit after nine holes, being bothered by a sore wisdom tooth.

On January 31, 1942, Jacyline had her wisdom tooth pulled, while Jack went to Camp Butler with his father. On New Year's Day, Jack's mother insisted that they walk over to visit Jacyline, who remained in pain after her tooth extraction and could not talk. So Jack sat at her bedside, reading magazines and doing crossword puzzles until his mother was ready to go home.

For the next three days, Salome and Mrs. Brimmer took Jack golfing, with Jacyline walking with them but not playing. But by January 4, 1943, Jacyline revealed that she was not interested in golf and recognized that Jack had no real interest in her — so Jack golfed with his mother and Mrs. Brimmer then packed his things for the trip back to Princeton the next day.

Jack recorded nothing on what Jacyline looked like; whether she was in school; if she had a job; or his personal opinion of her intellect, charm, or beauty. On the one hand, it appeared that he initially enjoyed talking to her, but he soon became bored. The situation also appears awkward, with encounters orchestrated by the two mothers. Furthermore, Jack lived in New Jersey, and he also expected a call from the Army at any time. So, while the situation may have been awkward, Jack seemed to take it in stride.

## Spiritual Life at Princeton — The Princeton Evangelical Fellowship

The decline in Christian leadership at Princeton University and growing secularization was countered by the emergence of strong student-led organizations. The first example was the Princeton Foreign Mission Society that was founded in 1883 by Robert Wilder, whose father served as a missionary to India. The goals of the Society were, first, to encourage other students to be missionaries, and second, to evangelize the Princeton student body. The Society attracted national attention, sparking a student volunteer movement across the country with the motto, "The evangelization of the world in this generation."

The most effective ministry was Princeton Evangelical Fellowship (PEF). The PEF, founded in 1931 as the League of Evangelical Students by an alumni missionary, Donald B. Fullerton, focused on weekly Bible studies for students, with Mr. Fullerton providing additional disciple-ship to interested students. However, the dedicated work of a number of Christian students at Princeton was critical to the early success. Key student members of PEF included some former McCallie students — Bob Caldwell, John Parks, and David McCallie — and other Christian students at Princeton, including David Marshall, Christy Wilson, and Bob Marshburn.

### The McCallie Military Academy Connection at Princeton

On June 29, Col. Schwarzkopf brought a truck full of furniture to Jack since their family was leaving the country for Iran. Jack carried two chairs, two lamps, and a mirror up to his room. Waiting for him was Bob Caldwell, a sophomore at Princeton, who was an alumnus of McCallie Military Academy.[18] Bob invited Jack to supper, and

---

18. Robert (Bob) H. Caldwell Jr. was a member of a prominent family in East Tennessee. After Princeton he returned to Chattanooga, Tennessee. According to his obituary, he worked as an investment advisor. He loved the outdoors and served as a prominent local figure in philanthropic and civil activities, including serving on the Board of McCallie School. He died suddenly of a heart attack at age 61 years, only a few years after finally reuniting with and marrying his Princeton sweetheart, Gina Rulon-Miller. He was remembered in the community as a devout Christian with great compassion for his fellow man. http://www.chattanoogan.com/2010/12/26/191159/Caldwell-Robert-H.-Bobby-Jr..aspx.

off they went. During supper, Bob told Jack about the PEF Bible Studies and invited him to attend. When Jack returned, he found that the bed lamp and bulb, which he left on the front lawn, had been stolen.

The following Sunday, July 5, 1942, Jack recorded, *"At 2:30 I put on my coat and went to Murray-Dodge Hall for a meeting of the Evangelical Fellowship with Jack Parks, a '39 McCallie boy in charge. Bob Caldwell, and Christie Mattheson and another boy were there."* Afterwards, Jack Parks invited him to his dormitory room in 4A Holder, and Jack took up the offer the following Wednesday to talk.

On Sunday afternoon, July 12, Jack Whitcomb recorded the follow-up, *"Jack Parks came by for me and we went up to Murray Dodge Hall where I was introduced to several boys and the teacher, Mr. Marshall.[19] We prayed and had a lesson. I said goodbye to them and returned to my room about 4:15."*

Jack Parks and a friend visited Jack Whitcomb at his room again on July 17, 1942. It was a brief visit, but apparently a positive follow-up.

On Sunday, July 19, Jack *"went over to the University Chapel and attended HOLY communion in the Episcopal Service. At 2:30 I went up to Murray-Dodge Hall and met Jack Parks and another boy there. The guest teacher arrived with some women and we had the lesson. It was pretty good."*

On July 23, 1942, Jack accepted the invitation to go to 4A Holder and join Jack Park's prayer meeting. This was the first of many prayer meetings that Jack would attend.

## Other Key Princeton Students in the PEF

On Sunday, August 16, Jack met another dedicated Christian student, Christy Wilson. Jack wrote,[20]

> *At 2:30 I put on my suit and went up to Murray-Dodge Hall for the Bible class. This was the last one for the summer. Christy Wilson invited me over to his home for tea, and I went with him. . . . I met Mrs. Wilson and his brother Stephen.*

---

19. David Marshall was a student who attended Princeton from 1941–1945. Marshall noted during the Princeton Evangelical Fellowship 50th Anniversary Diner, June 6, 1981, that Jack thought he was Donald Fullerton's physical child since he kept referring to him as "my son."

20. John Whitcomb diary entry, August 16, 1942.

## Princeton

Christy Wilson was an undergraduate student at Princeton who went on to Princeton Theological Seminary where he eventually received his Doctor of Theology degree. He was remembered as very mild, an outstanding scholar, a good but not great Bible teacher, and a very nice person.[21] He had a strong Christian upbringing, as his father, Robert Dick Wilson Ph.D., D.D., LL.D., was a brilliant conservative scholar[22] who taught at Princeton Theological Seminary before joining J. Gresham Machen in the founding of Westminster Seminary in the 1920s. Christy Wilson continued to teach Bible classes and meet with PEF students, even though his decision to go to Princeton Seminary instead of a more doctrinally conservative seminary seemed to cause some concern and tension among others in the PEF leadership.

David Marshall was a natural student leader of PEF (even though Jack Parks was President of PEF that year). He had a brilliant mind, a great sense of humor, natural leadership abilities, and he loved the Lord. In many ways, he helped establish PEF as a strong campus organization rather than a Bible study and continued to support PEF long after his graduation.

Robert (Bob) Marshburn was another strong Christian student at Princeton who took special interest in Jack. He was from a fine Christian family near Philadelphia, and he would invite Jack to his home and their home church (see below). Originally from Miami, Florida, he was accepted to Princeton University as an undergraduate and completed his degree in 1943, graduating *magna cum laude*. He continued on at Princeton Seminary, earning a Bachelor of Divinity in 1945.[23] During the summers between seminary semesters, he took courses at Moody Bible Institute. After seminary, he was ordained as an evangelist of the Presbyterian Church in Florida and then served as a missionary in Lima, Peru, then as a pastor in Georgia and Florida.[24]

---

21. Letter form Paul Pressler to the author on August 19, 2016.
22. See Brian Nicks, "Life and Work of Robert Dick Wilson," TMSJ 19/1 (Spring 2008) 91–106, available online at https://www.tms.edu/m/tmsj19e.pdf, accessed July 4, 2019.
23. Robert Marshburn, *Princeton Alumni Weekly*, Volume 46, November 2, 1945: "the first member of our class to be ordained into the ministry. . . . graduated from Princeton Seminary . . . leaving for South America as a missionary."
24. *Statesville Record & Landmark* (newspaper), May 26, 1964, page 3, http://www.newspapers.com/newspage/3114960/.

For the rest of the summer, and into the fall, Jack continued to attend the Sunday afternoon Bible studies and Thursday night prayer meetings. In the autumn of 1942, Jack also learned that the primary teacher for the PEF on Sundays was not David Marshall, but Donald B. Fullerton — the man who would become Jack's spiritual father.

## Donald B. Fullerton

Donald Fullerton, the founder and long-time leader of the Princeton Evangelical Fellowship, took a circuitous route to Princeton via Wall Street, the U.S. Military, missionary work in India, Pakistan, and Afghanistan, and a U.S. Military chaplain position. He remained a lifelong bachelor with a heart and passion for serving the Lord by teaching and discipling others.

Fullerton was born in Whitestone, Long Island, New York, on July 6, 1892. As a child, he enjoyed the luxuries of a wealthy New York City family. His father traded stocks on Wall Street, and Donald received an outstanding private education while being groomed to walk in his father's footsteps. He also enjoyed the benefits of being raised by a godly mother in a Christian home.

His educational pathway took him to Princeton University where he attended from 1910–1913, graduating in three years with a Litt.B. degree. He immediately obtained a position as a reporter for the *Wall Street Journal*, giving him access to the inner workings of financial leaders of the time. As a man of integrity who was committed to honesty and truthfulness, the financial circles became less appealing and more appalling.

With growing American involvement in World War I, Fullerton decided to serve his country as an officer in the U.S. Army. While details of his experiences are scarce, the training resulted in an officer's posture, dignity, and organizational experience. He also developed a heart for souls of young men who needed salvation, direction, and training for a life of service to God and country.

Following the Great War, Donald Fullerton decided to leave the business world and serve his Lord as a missionary to unreached people in northern India, Pakistan, and Afghanistan. Although Fullerton never spoke much about his experiences as a missionary, he did provide a succinct account of the events at the request of Dr. John C. Whitcomb Jr. in May 1954:

About nine months was spent along the Afghan Frontier and in Kashmir, including one month in Afghanistan, a land still closed to the Gospel. God taught many lessons of His faithfulness, provision and power to keep as well as to save. An enduring impression was received of how the Holy Lord is robbed of His glory through the unspeakable, degraded, idolatrous, conditions of millions living in heathen darkness. Secondly, there came a realization of the desperate needs of the mass of humanity without hope and without God. Thirdly, there was a sense of the need of our Savior for those willing to obey His command to go and make disciples regardless of the cost. Fourthly, the task is one for men. Many brave women were met standing in places of danger where men should have been. God needs MEN, UTTERLY DEVOTED TO HIM.

An independent observer and colleague of Donald Fullerton was Jock Purves, who recorded the details of Fullerton's character, bravery, and endurance.[25] Jock was sent to the city of Kohat, a British military outpost, about 100 miles west of Islamabad, the capital of Pakistan. Accompanying him were three independent Plymouth Brethren workers, Miss Flora Davidson, Miss Maria Rasmussen, and Mr. Donald Fullerton. Jock Purves wrote, "No words of mine can express [Fullerton's] worth. Together we read the Holy Scriptures and prayed, tended each other and evangelized."[26]

Kohat was a wild and dangerous city. Recognizing the strong Muslim influence, the missionaries asked the Scottish superintendent of police upon arrival about housing and their personal safety. "Well," he remarked about the residents of the city, "they may not cut off your heads the first night, but I would not be sure about the second." He offered no help or assistance, believing that missions work in this part of the world was a bad idea. But Fullerton had his eyes set on Afghanistan.

Afghanistan banned Christian missionaries, British citizens, and other undesirable people from entering the country. However, Donald

---

25. Jock Purves, *The Unlisted Legion: Part of its witness in the Karakoram and the Khyber* (Edinburgh, Carlisle, PA: The Banner of Truth Trust, 1977), DBF, 110, 113, 117–122, 173.

26. Ibid., 117.

Fullerton was American, and Maria Rasmussen was Danish, and they obtained visitor visas for one month. Immediate plans included a journey through the Khyber Pass into Afghanistan on the old Silk Road[27] and then on to the capital city of Kabul. The team took Fullerton's bedding blanket and rolled it, stuffed with portions of Scripture and copies of the New Testament translated into Arabic, Pashto, Persian, Urdu, and English. The "sleeping bag" became so heavy that the men could barely lift it. Intense prayer for the journey followed as the two "tourists" headed west toward the Afghan border, intent on smuggling the hidden treasures of God's Word to people in desperate need of the gospel.

Shortly after going through the Khyber Pass, the car they hired began sputtering, stalling, and finally died. Providentially, a native Afghan in a horse-drawn cart stopped by and agreed to transport the stranded American and Dane to Kabul, for a price. The circuitous route over mountain trails designed for the horse-drawn carts bypassed the guard-post and customs inspectors. All the Scripture arrived safely, and the team distributed God's Word to the souls whom He had chosen.

Shortly after distributing the Scriptures, a revolution broke out. Afghan leaders were assassinated, the borders were closed, and the country spiraled into war and chaos. Foreigners faced clear and imminent danger of abuse and murder. Fullerton and Rasmussen tried to flee over a mountain pass to Quetta, Pakistan. They were shot at by both government and rebel forces and were nearly killed by nomads after crashing into the lead camel of a caravan. But by God's grace, they escaped all harm. The experience clearly left deep and lasting impressions on Fullerton. Notably he admired the bravery of God-fearing women who moved forward and stood fearless in the face of danger, in part because of the *absence of brave Godly men.*

Fullerton was then assigned to teach the Bible in northwestern India. But he developed severe, persistent abdominal pain and a mysterious illness that forced his return to the United States. After convalescence, he attempted to return to India, Pakistan, and Afghanistan, but the condition flared again. He was forced to retire from foreign missions.

---

27. Map of the Silk Road, http://www.silkroadencyclopedia.com/Images2/MapSilkRoad-RoutesTurkeyChina.JPG.

# Princeton

Fullerton decided to refocus his career on the evangelism and training of qualified young men to meet the need of world evangelism and discipleship. He took advantage of the two institutions from his past where young men were being trained: the U.S. Army and Princeton University. Although Fullerton benefited from the family fortune and did not need to work, he took a position as an Army chaplain at Fort Dix, New Jersey,[28] located about 25 miles south of Princeton, to gain unrestricted access to young men in the military. He also took advantage of his status as a Princeton alumnus to gain access to young men at the university. Fullerton started weekly Bible classes at Princeton University in October 1931 and invited students to his house in Plainfield, New Jersey, from time to time for a meal, a lesson, and/or discussion. The program grew into the Princeton Evangelical Fellowship. He maintained these connections for the rest of his life.

## Personal Observations on Donald Fullerton

I met Dr. Fullerton on several occasions. Compared to my father, he appeared rather short and reserved. He impressed me with his graciousness and kind words. My father appeared extraordinarily excited in his presence and was proud to line up his children for inspection. "How could such a man be effective when he appeared so timid and quiet?" I thought. "In private," my father explained, "he could be quite direct and forceful." In retrospect, Fullerton's intellect, commitment, passion, personality, and determination were perfect for mentoring young men. Rather than being a pioneer missionary in Afghanistan, Fullerton proved to be a pioneer in forming an effective campus ministry. The PEF became the model for all major campus ministries to follow.

## Jack Attends PEF during the Autumn of 1942

Jack left a number of positive notes about PEF and the outreach in his diaries. For example, on Sunday, October 11, Jack wrote, *"At 2:30 I went up to Murray-Dodge Hall and Mr. Uncan gave us our lesson for today*

---

28. Fort Dix served as a reception and training center for men inducted under the draft. At the end of the war, the center became the separation center, returning more than 1.2 million soldiers to civilian life. On July 15, 1947, Fort Dix became a basic training center and the home of the 9th Infantry Division. From http://www.dix.army.mil/history/history.html.

*from Genesis 3. We discussed it thoroughly. . . . At 5:45 I put on my coat and went up to Jack Park's Room. Bob Caldwell came, and two other boys and I went up to Mr. Uncan's apartment across the street. His wife had prepared a nice dinner for us, buffet. . . ."* The following day he sent a letter to his mother about how impressed he was with these new friends.

> Every afternoon I have been going to a Bible class, conducted by Mr. Fullerton, who is a Chaplain at Camp Dix near here. The class was started by John Parks, who is a junior now, and who went to McCallie also. They are very interesting classes, and often are quite a few boys that attend them.

The continuous, coordinated, persistent, and genuine outreach of the McCallie boys and PEF students was having a great impact in the mind and heart of Jack Whitcomb. And Mr. Fullerton, a gentle and knowledgeable teacher who knew the Word and loved people, was presenting solid Bible teaching within the context of terrific Christian students that Jack could identify with and to learn from their examples.

## From Christmas to Christ

After returning to Princeton University from Christmas break in Durham, North Carolina, Jack became increasingly disillusioned with the direction of his secular classmates and attracted to believers. The contrasting nature of various events in January 1943 highlight the work of God in Jack's heart.

Jack returned to Princeton late on the evening of January 5, 1943. Two days later, he visited the room of Jack Parks for prayer meeting. But on Sunday, he stayed in his room and read the newspaper.

He returned to the University Chapel the following Sunday, January 17, to hear a visiting preacher from Illinois. This was a big disappointment, especially because *"he didn't follow his subject in the sermon."*

On Monday, January 18, Jack learned that being drafted into the Army was eminent. *"I will be liable for call any time after Feb 6, but in case of a delay, I can study a whole terms work in one subject in 3 weeks."*

The intensity of the interactions in Pyne Hall began growing, as Jack's friends and dorm mates (Figure below) gravitated toward drinking and partying. On Monday night, Jack noted that *"the others were playing cards in Marine's room, and I then had a great fight with Brawner."*

The following morning, Jack and Ted Fehrenbach *"cleaned up the mess when Marine vomited in the bathroom at 1:00 a.m."*

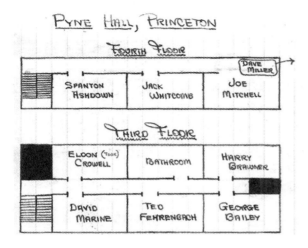

A floor plan of Pyne Hall designating the rooms of the students on the fourth and third floor. Most of the people mentioned in the diaries outside of PEF are these dorm mates.

That Saturday, Jack joined the dorm group for supper. Then Jack went to see *Yankee Doodle Dandy* at the Garden theater with James Cagney playing the part of George M. Cohan and returned to Pyne Hall where he ate *"Marine's cake, popcorn and had ham and cheese sandwiches"* with his friends. But these activities were meaningless.

On Sunday afternoon, January 23, 1943, Jack decided to attend the PEF meeting. He noted, *"Mr. Fullerton spoke to us, and I thought it was a very interesting and effective discussion."*

The following weekend illustrates the growing division in Jack's mind between the direction of his dorm mates and the students of the PEF. *"Harry and Ted discussed their little vodka party last night,"* Jack noted, *"at which Harry passed out and all of them including Ted, George and Dave and SM Keeney were drunk."*

On Sunday, Jack retuned to PEF and specifically noted:

> *Went to Murray-Dodge Hall. John Parks, who is leaving us to go into the ministry, gave a short talk. Then Mr. Fullerton spoke to us. Had some officer elections, and Dave Marshall was elected president. He nominated me for Sec-Tres, but since I am going into the Army, I declined. I intended to go to the show with Harry. Came back to the room, and as I was studying,*

*Mr. Fullerton came in to talk with me. When Harry came up, I told him to go to the show alone. After looking at maps, we discussed the truth of the Bible and the evil teachings of the University Chapel and the World. Then we discussed the value of the Schofield Reference Bible,[29] and I determined to buy one tomorrow. He left and I went to bed around 10:30.*

The next day, Monday, February 1, 1943, Jack kept his promise to Mr. Fullerton, *"I purchased a large size Schofield Reference Bible for $7.65 & took it to my room. I read the introduction to my new Bible and then we all went up for a good supper."* However, the printing was faulty, so he returned it and awaited a replacement.

Jack wrote home to his mother on February 5 with more details on his discussion with Mr. Fullerton:

> [He] asked me about when I expected to enter the army. He is a chaplain at Fort Dix, so knows a lot about camps around here. Just like Dr. McCallie, he believes that the best possible thing is to continue in a study of the Bible after I enter the army and he recommended that I get a reference Bible for my own use, with notes, explanations, and chain references for more convenient study. So I am going to get a very nice one here, at the University story for use later on (it is called the Schofield Reference Bible, and is the same kind as I used at McCallie, the best one there is).

The following diary entry from Sunday, February 7 was also telling:

> *[I] went to breakfast with Harry Brawner. Harry wasn't feeling so well because he had been drunk last night. . . . . Put on a tie and coat and went up to Murray-Dodge Hall for the Bible Class. Bob Caldwell was there and Mr. Fullerton talked to us as usual about the Bible. After the class I was to have a talk with him, so I waited. Olin Ellis asked him some questions about "whether to listen to anti-Bible sermons." Then Mr. Fullerton, Davie Marshall and I went over to 4A Holder, where he*

---

29. The diary entries refer to the *Scofield Reference Bible*. This study Bible was edited and annotated by Cyrus I. Scofield, which popularized dispensationalism at the beginning of the 20th century. https://en.wikipedia.org/wiki/Scofield_Reference_Bible.

*gave me a book to read this week, "Can A Young Man Trust."* **We discussed the qualities of a true believer, and then Mr. Fullerton told me about some of the great truths & prophecies of the Bible.** *I took a few notes. It was 6:25 so I went over to supper. Then I returned to my room and I spent a few hours reading "Can A Young Man Trust." I compared the many Bible verifications with Scripture. The book showed how the Scriptures and science coincide.*

By Monday, February 8, 1943, the evidence of Donald Fullerton's continual teaching and discussions with Jack about Christ and the Bible became even more evident.

*I went over to the University Store. Bought a lampshade and asked whether my Schofield Bible had come yet. . . . Returned to my room and spent some time reading the book of the Word given to me by Mr. Fullerton, called **"Can A Young Man Trust"**. . . . Then I ate lunch. . . . I went to the University Store to ask for my Bible. There was a long line waiting. Got a picture of a tiger and returned to my room to read "Can a young Man Trust." [went to class] I returned to my room & read some more from my book about the Word of the Lord. . . . After supper I went over to the Prayer meeting in Holder, & then returned to my room again to read the book & think about the Truth of the Bible.* **I went to bed around 10:30 & prayed awhile.**

On Tuesday, February 9, 1943, Jack summarized key events in his diary:

*At 3:30 I went back to my room again to read "Can A Young Man Trust," looking up Bible references. [went to supper] I read my N.T. Bible in the reading room before going to 4A Holder for Bible study & prayer. Returned to my room around 8:00 PM and read my book." . . . I went to prayer before going to sleep.*

Wednesday, February 10, 1943:

[Went to class] *and then finished the book on trusting in Christ, called "Can A Young Man Trust" by Arthur Gook. . . .*

*I read a few Psalms from the Bible. . . . Went up to supper & waited around until 7:20 when the prayer meeting was to start. Dick Beltram & David Marshall were there. After that I came back to my room to read "The New Boy" a pamphlet telling about a New Life in Christ. To bed early.*

Thursday, February 11, 1943:

*Studied my N.T. Bible, reading the first part of John. After supper I went to Bible Class. Bob Marshburn & I had a long talk about the Bible & the Word of God. He invited me to come to his farm home next weekend.*

Friday, February 12, 1943:

*I argued with Spanton Ashdown[30] about the Bible, but he wouldn't believe in it. After supper I went to Dave Marshall's room for Bible Class. I gave the lesson on 1 Timothy 4 and got some small pocket testaments. I studied the Bible that evening.*

Saturday, February 13, 1943:

*I went by the University Store to see if my Bible had come yet. I wrote notes into & underlined many of the passages in my New Testament. . . . I typed letters to Nana and mother.[31]* [went to supper] ***I went to my room & studied the Bible until Mr. Fullerton came. I definitely accepted Christ & decided to write home about it next week.*** *Bed at 11:30.*

This moment marked a turning point in the life of John C. Whitcomb Jr. And he never looked back. The decision to accept Christ was not a sudden, emotional response. It was based on a growing understanding of Christ, the Bible, truth, and the testimony of the lives of both Mr. Fullerton and young men his age whose lives had eternal meaning — in contrast to the ways of the world.

---

30. Spanton Ashdown was a freshman rooming on the fourth floor of Pyne Hall immediately next to John Whitcomb.

31. The letter of February 13, 1944, from Jack to his mother included this paragraph, "I have been attending Bible class every week, and in the evening, some of the boys hold a prayer meeting in one of the dormitories. I have been thinking about something that I am going to do after the war, which I will be able to tell you about later."

## Changing Life Goals and Early Discipleship

The change in Jack's life was immediately evident — with a love for God's Word, a desire to fellowship with God's people, and a mission to tell others. The first day as a Christian, a Sunday, was recorded in Jack's diary,

> *I did not go to the chapel, but stayed in my room reading the Bible. Ashdown & later Bailey[32] came in, & I talked with them about the Bible, & loaned him my pamphlet. We discussed the Bible on the way to lunch. At 2:30 I went up to Murray Dodge Hall & attended Bible Class. Mr. Fullerton made a wonderful talk to us. Returned to my room & started to do the Schofield Bible lessons he gave me. After supper* **I started to write the letter home telling about my change of plans.**

This letter was drafted and rewritten several times over the next few days, and finally sent home. The opening paragraph states:

Dearest Mother and Dad,                    February 16, 1943

I have finally and definitely decided what I would like to be and do after the war! You may be at first surprised when I say this, but I am sure so sure of it that everything else I have done before is blackened out in comparison. I want to study the Bible, until I know it well, and then either be a teacher of the Bible in the United States or be a missionary abroad. I have waited a week to think it over before writing to you about it, because I know how much of a change it is. And the more I have thought about it the more convinced I am that this is exactly the thing I want to do, and the thing I will be happiest in doing.

God's call of Jack Whitcomb to evangelism and world missions was crystal clear. His spiritual father, Donald Fullerton, set the example through a heart and passion of a missionary, and the experiences of serving in Pakistan until his health forced relocation to Fort Dix, New Jersey. Bob Marshburn, who recently graduated from Princeton

---

32. George Bailey was a freshman rooming in Pyne Hall on the third floor below John Whitcomb.

University with top honors before he enrolled in Princeton Seminary, and others had spent countless hours with Jack, discussing the Bible, leading Bible studies and prayer meetings, and encouraging him to accept Christ as his personal Savior. Like Mr. Fullerton, Bob's heart was foreign missions, and he would later serve as a missionary in Lima, Peru.

Jack Whitcomb, who loved to learn of continents and countries, languages and cultures, and politics and international affairs, immediately embraced world missions. His mind and heart said "China," sparked perhaps by the love and affection given to him by Pung, his Chinese amah who poured several years of her life into him when he was a child. Having grown up in Tientsin, China, and learning Chinese as his first language, he believed that a dormant Mandarin dialect, buried somewhere deep in his brain, would be rekindled, allowing him to clearly communicate Christ to the Chinese people. The question of career was settled in his mind and heart. He would, God willing, become a missionary to China.

*Spiritual Boot Camp*

Jack's focus and priorities immediately changed, as reflected in his daily diary entries. He now spent hours reading and studying the Bible and attending every possible Bible class and prayer meeting offered on campus. He also began reading a variety of Christian books that were recommended by Donald Fullerton and others to provide clarity and perspective on critical issues — including the creation of man by God.[33]

Bob Marshburn intensified the discipleship of Jack and introduced him to elders in the faith. On February 20, 1943, at the spiritual age of one week, Bob took Jack to Philadelphia, Pennsylvania, to spend the weekend with Donald Barnhouse. Dr. Barnhouse, pastor of the 10th Presbyterian Church in Philadelphia, was one of the most respected pastors, authors, and teachers of that generation.[34] Dr. Barnhouse

---

33. For example, on February 15, 1943, he began reading *Modern Science and the Genesis Record* by Harry Rimmer, (Eerdmans, 1937). See later chapters.

34. Donald G. Barnhouse, Th.D., was one of the leading pastors in the Presbyterian circles and evangelicals in general during the mid-20th century. He published a number of books and *Revelation*, a magazine that published his sermons, expositions, and religious interpretations of current events. Jack would subscribe to this and it became one of his favorite periodicals early in his Christian life. Jack would correspond with Dr. Barnhouse from time to time.

graciously welcomed Jack to his family and home and initiated a lasting friendship with this freshman college student. Jack attended the 10th Presbyterian Church that Sunday and heard a message on John 18:12 before he returned to Princeton.

Bob's intense effort was intentional. The winter classes were coming to an end, and Jack was a newborn Christian, with an uncertain future. How much grounding in the Word could a young man receive in two weeks?[35]

## Uncle Sam Calls Jack's Number

Two days after returning from a weekend with the Barnhouse and Marshburn families, Jack found a note in his room to immediately report to a Mr. Kelley's office at Princeton. With the dearth of healthy young men still in the workplace, the military draft began extending to college students, and Jack anticipated Uncle Sam calling his number at any time. To his relief, Jack learned that he, along with 25 other top students, would participate in a program in foreign languages so that they could serve with the occupational forces *after* the war.

This new program was designed to replace this pipeline of educated combatants provided by the ROTC and would be called the Army Specialized Training Program (ASTP). In contrast to the ROTC's purpose of developing military officers, the ASTP developed high-grade technicians and specialists, such as engineers, doctors, and linguists — Jack's forte. A series of tests and examinations would determine the aptitudes and ability of the students, with the highest scores resulting in special training. Low scores resulted in a fast track to the area of greatest need — fresh troops to replace dead and missing soldiers from the front lines in the worst locations and suffering the heaviest casualties.

Jack's freshman year at Princeton University was almost over. He finished his assignments and packed his belongings. On Sunday, February 28, 1943, he put on his coat, walked to Murray-Dodge Hall, and attended his final PEF meeting for three years. Mr. Fullerton taught on 1 John 4:11–21. "By this we know that we abide in Him and He in us, because He has given us of His Spirit." He said goodbye to Mr. Fullerton and left for war.

---

35. Bob Marshburn would continue to correspond with Jack during his Army years and beyond and proved to be a great help.

# Chapter 8

# Uncle Sam

"Engineering is against my will"
March 1943 to August 1944

Jack got up at 7:00 a.m. on Monday, March 1, 1943, in his Princeton dorm room, took a shower, packed his bags, and sent his books to his mother in Durham, North Carolina. After saying goodbye to "the boys," he boarded the 9:08 southbound train with his typewriter, suitcase, and laundry bag in his hands and left Princeton behind.

As a new and enthusiastic Christian, he immediately began reading the Bible once settled into his train car. He finished Romans, 1 Corinthians, and part of Acts on the series of railroad trains heading to Raleigh, North Carolina, where his parents met him. They loaded a truck, circled north of Raleigh to drop off Col. Whitcomb at Camp Butler, then turned southwest to their new home at 619 Morehead Ave., Durham, North Carolina.

The next morning, Jack walked to downtown Durham to find a Scofield Bible at the Thomas Books store. Though his shopping trip was unsuccessful, he had old Scofield lessons among his belongings and spent time the next day sharing a Bible lesson with his mother that was designed to prove that Jesus is the Son of God.

The fact that Col. Whitcomb was less than a 30-minute drive from Durham allowed him to visit often and for Jack to have short visits in Camp Butler. While Jack focused on developing a series of one-hour Bible studies on the Gospels for his mother, he also tried to have discussions with his father about the Bible. However, these conversations usually ended in arguments and were thereby markedly curtailed — for the time being.

Eventually, Jack found and purchased a new Scofield Bible. He used his break from schoolwork and military service to read random books from the Bible, to work on maps of the world, to organize picture albums of his family, and to read some books such as *The Robe* and *Modern Student's Life of Christ*. Family times included seeing some movies in Durham with his mother and playing golf with his father at the Hope Valley Country Club. He also decided to begin reading the Bible from the beginning, starting with Genesis chapter 1. But he never attended a church or met with any other Christians during the weeks at his new home. As a Christian, he was alone.

Jack waited in Durham for his military orders. On March 15, 1943, he was officially inducted into the army. On March 20, 1943, he received his orders to report to Fort Bragg, North Carolina, on March 31, one month after leaving Princeton.

Jack accepted his responsibility to join the military at the request of "Uncle Sam." He specifically chose the Army, honoring his father and his forefathers who served their country with distinction, often as high-ranking officers like his father. It was now Jack's turn to be tested in battle.

## The Whitcomb Military Legacy

Jack Whitcomb is a descendent of one of the earliest families in America.[1] The history of the Whitcombs is one of men with unusual physical strength and longevity, distinction of service in business and government, and leadership in combat as military men or citizen-soldiers. The first American Whitcomb (spelled John or Jon, Whitcomb, Whitcombe, Whettcomb, and/or Whetcomb) was a middle-class Puritan who came from Southern England to the Plymouth Colony in Massachusetts circa 1629 on a ship named the *Hopewell*.[2] The English

---

1. From *The Whitcomb Family in America: A Biographical Genealogy* by Charlotte Whitcomb (Minneapolis, MD, 1904), which includes Jack's grandfather, Clement Colfax Whitcomb, p. 338, https://archive.org/details/whitcombfamilyin00whit. Jack's lineage is from John Whitcomb the English immigrant (1629 and/or 1635, depending on source) to Jonathan, Jonathan, Jonathan, Abner, Abner, John, John, Clement Colfax (C.C.), and John C. (father), making him an 11ᵗʰ-generation American.

2. *Hopewell* log, http://www.geni.com/projects/Great-Migration-Passengers-of-the-Hopewell-1635/1995. Note that Jon Whitcomb was added to the log of passengers later. The *Hopewell* appears to have made several trips, and it is unclear which trip Jon was on, or if he made the journey twice.

surname "Whitcomb" originated in a small town in southern England near Dorchester named "Whitcombe." Following the Norman invasion of Southern England by William the Conqueror in A.D. 1020, all of the inhabitants of the town were given the surname "Whitcombe" for taxation purposes. The names of inhabitants of Whitcombe and their assets remain enshrined in the notorious Domesday Book.[3]

Descendants of the first American Whitcomb migrated from Plymouth to Boston and surrounding areas in Massachusetts. They fought in the French and Indian War and led the Patriots during the Revolutionary War.

A descendent named John Whitcomb became the first general of the Massachusetts Colony during the Revolutionary War.

Benjamin Whitcomb, a woodsman and citizen-soldier from Vermont, became a legend as the captain of Whitcomb's Rangers — one of four original U.S. Army Ranger units organized during the American Revolution. The Rangers fought as commandos throughout Vermont, New Hampshire, New York, and into Quebec, Canada. Dressed as Native Americans, Whitcomb's Rangers attacked the enemy with hit-and-run tactics, wreaking havoc on British forces descending from Montreal, Canada, as the Red Coats sought to divide the United States from North to South.[4] Benjamin Whitcomb's escapades became legendary after he ambushed and killed the commander of the British First Brigade, Brigadier General Patrick Gordon, on July 24, 1776 (under the general orders of George Washington in retaliation for the British hiring Indians to massacre American settlers). A reward of more than a year's pay was offered by the British for his capture — dead or

---

3. The Domesday Book is a record of the assets owned by Englishmen at the time of William the Conqueror. It was called the Domesday Book because it was given indisputable authority — just as the "books" in heaven at the last judgment (cf. Revelation 20:12) are indisputable, http://en.wikipedia.org/wiki/Domesday_Book. The assessment of the townspeople of Whitcombe — where the Whitcomb surname was established — was also recorded, http://www.domesdaymap.co.uk/place/SY7188/whitcombe/ .

4. The British describe him as "near 6 feet High, rather thin than otherwise, Light Brown Hair tied behind, rough faced, not sure whether owing to the smallpox or not. He wears a kind of under Jacket, without Sleeves, slash Pockets, leather Breeches, grey woolen or yarn Stockings, and shews, Hat flopped, with a Gold Cord round it. He had a firelock, Blanket, Pouch, and Powder Horn" (Chapter 5, page 2, https://www.yumpu.com/en/document/view/4582435/ranger-manual-benjamin-whitcombs-independant-corp-of-rangers). See also a review from Vermont, http://www.rutlandhistory.com/documents/Quarterlies/RHSQ-Vol8-4-Fall1978.pdf.

alive. Although this was the highest bounty placed by the British on any American citizen during the entire Revolutionary War, Benjamin Whitcomb was never captured.

Abner Whitcomb, a blacksmith by trade and six generations before Jack, was one of the "minutemen" who answered the Lexington call and fought the British Army on the day the shot was fired that was "heard around the world."

Abner's great grandson, John Whitcomb, fought in the Civil War.[5] He was severely wounded by a cannon ball that blew off his leg during the Battle of Seven Pines near Richmond, Virginia. Undaunted, he returned to Portland, Maine, to raise his family as a one-legged Yankee farmer.

John had one son, Clement Colfax (C.C.) Whitcomb. After graduation from the Medical School of Maine at Bowdoin College in 1891, C.C. joined the Army Medical Corps. After 19 years of service, he then returned to school to complete his surgical training at Harvard University. He served his country in the Spanish-American War in the Philippines and Cuba, and in France during World War I. Family history is that as an army surgeon, he noted that soldiers with relatively minor wounds were arriving at the army hospitals after a long trip through the trenches, dead. He developed some type of emergency surgical kit and taught the stretcher bearers how to dress wounds at the front line *before* transport. He also arranged to have huge numbers of these emergency packs constructed and distributed to all the allies. This action may have saved many thousands of lives. We are not sure about the exact details, but he DID win the Medal of the French Legion of Honor and the Medal of Honor of Poland for his extraordinary contributions as a surgeon. Clement Whitcomb, M.D., completed his service as a colonel in the U.S. Army. He is buried in Arlington National Cemetery as an American hero.

C.C. had one son, whom he named John Clement Whitcomb (Whit). Whit was trained at West Point (where he later taught and is now buried) and, like his father, became a colonel in the U.S. Army. He was deeply involved in the 1930 development of new "army doctrines," which were rapidly updated after the world saw the devastation of the *blitzkrieg* on the Polish cavalry in September 1939. Family

---

5. http://mazhude.tripod.com/Civil-War/11th-ME-Roster-M-Z.html.

history is that he recognized that General George Patton, whom he knew well, could advance his tanks 20–30 miles per day into enemy territory, but they needed bullets, bandages, gasoline for the tanks, and food for the men, and that the logistics of support was based on WWI trench warfare. So, he developed a highly flexible and dynamic supply system to support tank breakouts. When Patton's Third Army was formed in Normandy, Whit was hand-picked by Patton to be Chief of Staff of the 90th Infantry to support the tanks' breakthrough with soldiers and supplies. Whit's organizational plan and support system was a key to one of America's great battle victories of WWII (the Battle of the Falaise Pocket). We are not sure of the exact details, but he was awarded the Legion of Merit Medal for his efforts (see below). He also had one son, whom he named John Clement Whitcomb Jr. (Jack).

## Jack Whitcomb and His Approach to War

Unlike many of his forefathers, Jack was not a pugilist. Although he was passionate and competitive in areas of wit and wisdom, he intentionally avoided personal conflict — unless it was unavoidable because of personality characteristics or overriding principles. Indeed, he would rather suffer loss than argue or fight over non-essential issues.

So how did a sensitive young man with a heart for missions become a combat soldier within months after becoming a born-again Christian? And how did he grow as a Christian while away from his mentors and support groups as a soldier in the U.S. Army?

## The Impact of War on Young Men

War is a terrible — although sometimes unavoidable — thing. The minds of those who survive active combat are no longer naïve to the evil and destructive nature of man. And the effects of war on young people can last a lifetime.

The reality of the deep psychological scars of veterans became vivid to me between 1985 and 1991 as I interviewed countless WWII vets while finishing my medical training at Duke University and rotating through the Durham Veterans Administration Medical Center. It was common for WWII veterans, 40 or more years after the war, to reveal to their doctors their continual psychological and emotional suffering from what they saw, what they did, and what they endured. This generation seldom discussed what happened in WWII, as they were instructed not to talk about their experiences in consideration of their comrades in arms who may have suffered greatly. Unlike soldiers of other countries and other times, they did not flaunt their medals and commendations, but rather tucked them away — feeling that they were only doing their duty and that the real heroes gave their lives. They struggled with recurrent nightmares, anger, fear, depression, alcoholism, drugs, and loneliness — since few people without their experiences could understand their haunting memories and their inner pain. I could not help thinking about my father, and how his experiences may have affected his life.

The time between Jack's salvation and an early exit from Princeton was short — only two weeks.

I asked my dad whether he had many Christian friends in the Army. "There were very few," he said sadly as he looked down, shaking his head from side to side. "There was only one that I can remember."

"What was it like as a new Christian at war?" I asked. "Tough!" he answered. "Very tough."

Jack would be on his own — except for his Bible, the Holy Spirit, and occasional Christian friends. But he survived, grew, and emerged with maturity and determination that would never have developed without a baptism of fire.

## *Military Boot Camp — Fort Bragg, North Carolina*

Military training at Fort Bragg commenced on April 1, 1943. All newly enlisted men reported to the Reception Center. The inductees were examined physically, emotionally, and intellectually and were issued uniforms, fatigues, and basic equipment. And thus, they began basic training. The daily routine was boring, with a few drills, exercise, and special assignments such as "kitchen patrol" (KP).[6] Jack did not know anyone, and since groups of men were continually coming and going, making new friends was pointless. The evening activities included showing the same two movies from 7:30 to 9:00 p.m. The first one was a poor quality "cops and robbers" flick, and the second one a documentary on "British war maneuvers." So, Jack decided to focus on his Bible.

---

6. On May 6, for example, Jack noted in his diary that he got in late because he had to peel 90 gallons of potatoes!

It was impossible to read in the barracks, so Jack went to the recreation hall on the first evening and began to read *Visions of Heaven and Hell* by John Bunyan.

April 4, 1943, was a Sunday, and Jack reported for chapel. To his surprise, the chaplain, Capt. Milner, gave an excellent message, and about 20 men accepted Christ. Jack befriended him and also got permission to come to the chapel in the evenings to read his Bible and some Christian literature such as *Moody Monthly*.

On April 7, Jack was summoned for an interview, which lasted an hour. He was questioned about his past history, schooling, hobbies, occupations, foreign languages, and subjects taken at Princeton. At the interview, Jack learned he did very well on his intelligence examinations with an IQ estimated at 146 (placing him in the top 0.1% of the population[7]), mechanical aptitude score of 122 (well above average), and Signal Core test score of 132 (outstanding). Based on his exam scores and interview, the officer told him that he had an excellent chance of getting into an O.C. school[8] or be assigned to an F.A. (field artillery) battalion if he wanted.

Fort Bragg was a revolving door for thousands of American boys — new recruits in, new soldiers out. Jack noted that many of these guys were from places like Princeton, Yale, Duke, and other top schools that were being "cleaned out." On April 9, just over a week after Jack arrived, a group of ROTC boys came in from Davidson College — including Bob Worth, a fellow cadet from McCallie Military Academy. Bob graduated *magna cum laude* and was just ahead of Jack in class ranking. Bob was a Christian, and now Jack and his old classmate became reacquainted as brothers in Christ. Of course, as graduates of a military academy, they immediately noted that most of the other boys did not know how to march! Their reunion, however, only lasted for three days, as Jack's name was called for shipping out with 100 other guys to the Field Artillery Replacement Center.

---

7. There are multiple intelligence tests and classification systems. The Terman's Stanford-Binet original (1916) classification rates scores of 140 or over as "genius," but after 1937, the term "genius" was dropped because it was recognized that a single score was not sufficient to determine intelligence and giftedness. It also matters what the person does with their talents.

8. The initials O.C. were not spelled out in the Whitcomb diaries or letters. It may have indicated an Occupation Unit where qualified individuals with language and cultural training would work in the transition of military government to civil government.

# Uncle Sam

## *The Black Dragon*

Basic training began with a focus on becoming a cannoneer, as Jack waited for the promised Army Specialized Training Program (ASTP, initiated while he was at Princeton to replace the R.O.T.C) position with further training in linguistics and occupying a foreign country conquered by others.

Jack was quite excited about his new assignment. He wrote to his mother, "I think I am extremely fortunate to be in the outfit they have put me in, because it is the best one in the whole Army. I am in a battery of 240 mm. howitzers, which are the largest guns in the whole army, and they are really huge!" (April 16, 1943). The 240 mm M1 howitzer was nicknamed the "Black Dragon."

Jack went on to explain:

> These guns come in four parts, each of which must be pulled about by a large tractor. Each [of the four] guns costs $250,000. . . . Our battery (A) has about 250 officers and men, and we are divided into two parts — the tractor drivers and the truck drivers. I signed up for tractors, so I will be driving a huge caterpillar with a 240 mm howitzer dragging behind before many weeks are past! These guns weigh about 52,000 lbs. apiece, and they shoot a 360 lb. projectile for 10 miles. These projectiles must be lifted into the gun cranes, and it takes 4 men to carry one.

Jack also found out that it was not just his brains that got him assigned to this unit — it was his brawn. The massive size and weight of the pieces of the 240 mm howitzers required big strong men — none shorter than 5 feet, 10 inches, and many from Midwestern and Southern farms.

The primary training of the F.A. unit centered on the care of the Black Dragon. Jack drew six diagrams showing the process of setting up this gun in a letter to his mother on April 22, 1943. The process included digging a 3.5-foot-deep pit, erecting a frame, using a tractor to pull a platform over the pit, positioning the top carriage over the platform, adding the gun cradle, and then attaching the "tube" (gun barrel). The gun was then "hidden" with camouflage netting. This takes about two hours of "hard and intricate work." The team spent weeks dragging these monsters all over the training area, breaking them down in the evening, moving them at night (in pouring rain or by moonlight), and having them ready to go the next morning. They also learned vehicle maintenance for the tractors and trucks.

*Basic Military Training*

In addition to training the men to set up, tear down, and transport the 240 mm howitzers, the army had all men go through basic training as foot soldiers. Basic training was rigorous, with parade marching, long hikes with full packs, and physical conditioning. There were classes on military courtesy, battlefield hygiene, and the identification of friendly and foreign planes and vehicles. There were practical tests to learn the sounds of different guns shooting, the smell of nerve gases, and proper use of gas masks. They learned techniques of map reading, scouting and patrolling, and capturing and interviewing enemy prisoners. They trained for combat using carbine rifles (including extensive target practice, gun and ammunition handling, and gun cleaning) and arming and throwing hand grenades.

My dad was also trained (although I cannot envision it) in knife fighting!

They trained on various obstacle courses including the "commando course" (made of bombs, mud, and sand) and the "infiltration course" (in which they crawled under machine-gun fire and barbed wire and into a movement of trenches. They also learned about anti-tank defenses and how to manage land mines. Finally, they were taught first aid and how to fight forest fires.

The experience in the Field Artillery Replacement Center was not all bad. While Jack was often exhausted from long marches and complained of sore feet, he noted that the food was excellent and that his bed was very comfortable. He also was able to get passes on most of the weekends to go to Durham by reciting the "14 General Guard Orders" from memory. While his unit was blessed by having a bunch of farm boys who were strong and able to handle tractors (especially in mud), they appeared to be unable to memorize the 14 orders or march in step — so they were stuck in camp over the weekends while Jack went home.

# Uncle Sam

## *God's Boot Camp*

Jack was 18 years old when he entered the army and began intense training for a military career that would only last a few years. The training was intense and covered everything that he might face in war. Whit, who would have much greater responsibility for about the same amount of time in the same war, trained his whole life to be ready to fight military battles on earth.

Jack had a "change of plans" on February 13, 1943, when he accepted Christ as his Savior and began focusing on intense training for missionary service in China. Yet, two weeks after being saved, he was separated from his Christian friends and mentors. How did he find his way?

Although Jack was a new Christian, he already had a "running start" in the knowledge of the Bible and basic principles of Bible study. This began at McCallie Military Academy, where he excelled in memorizing aspects of the Bible and ranked number one among the cadets in his Bible classes — even though he was not a believer. His exposure to the Bible continued at Princeton with the outreach of former McCallie students who were true Christians and the work of Donald Fullerton and others associated with the Princeton Evangelical Fellowship during his freshman year. So even as a new Christian, Jack could spot a good "fundamental" and poor "liberal" Bible teacher. However, no one can thrive as a Christian alone, including Jack.

At first, it appeared that Jack would be completely alone and would need to find his own way. His long-term goals were clear, and he did the best he could to avoid the pitfalls of army life and focus on more important things. But our spiritual enemy is crafty, and there are many pitfalls to trap well-intentioned Christians.

Jack's diary recorded his journey. On Sunday, April 18, he went to church, but the chaplain's talk *"was not too good."* Later in the afternoon, *"Some of the boys went up to play basketball, & I finished reading the book of Acts in the Bible."* He spent most of his free time in the chapel or somewhere quietly reading his Scofield Bible and other Christian books, *Moody Monthly*, and as usual, *Time* and *Life* magazines. He began memorizing chapters from the Bible beginning with Romans 8. Then he developed a systematic program to memorize other chapters of Scripture. In anticipation of both the ASTP and future mission opportunities, he also began reading the New Testament in both German and Spanish.

## Being Different

Most of the boys that were drafted into the army and received basic training at Fort Bragg had a lot in common, whether in personality, interests, or backgrounds — but Jack was different. On the one hand, he could be classified as a "military brat." These are kids that grew up in a military home where the family frequently moved from place to place throughout the United States and the world. This type of background resulted in children who had an expanded worldview and a unique trait of adaptability. It may also have been known that Jack's father was a high-ranking military officer and a West Point man; therefore, low-ranking officers that mishandled Jack's situation might suffer significant consequences. Furthermore, Jack had previous military training as a cadet in McCallie Military Academy, so to some extent, he was already well trained. Then there was his brain — a brilliant student from Princeton who knew more about most things than most of the trainers. Although Jack was physically tall and strong, he suffered from allergies and poor eyesight. Poor eyesight was of minor concern to the Army — unless one was applying to West Point! But the enigma to the trainers at Fort Bragg who were expecting a warrior must have been how Jack's faith could have affected his personality and career goals such that he wanted to become a Christian missionary.

Jack did not fraternize with most of the men, whose typical goals included getting drunk and chasing skirts. Rather, he frequented the chapel, read the Bible, and witnessed to his brothers in arms. When he did get a pass, he refused to go crazy with the other privates, and instead went home to see his mother. So, as the officers organized the enlisted men into fighting units, Jack kept coming up as a "supernumeral,"[9] a polite term for a person who was not picked for the team. He would be reassigned to the next unit and move on.

The other consequence of being a bit of a loner was the antagonistic response of some of the trainers typified by a Lieutenant Stevenson. He continually harassed Jack with extraordinary amounts of kitchen

---

9. Supernumeral describes a person or object "exceeding the usual number." Based on diary entries of May 22, 1943; Sept 5, 1944.

patrol (KP) and random, distasteful tasks around the training center. Jack just did the work without complaint.

## Christian Friends

Providentially, Jack met several Christians at Fort Bragg, but their paths usually overlapped for only a short, but valuable time.

In April, he briefly ran into Bob Worth from McCallie Military Academy.

In May, he learned of a Christian in another unit named Charles L. Moon, another ASTP candidate whom Jack heard about because he was passing out tracts and witnessing to many of the soldiers. They became friends — until transfer orders sent Moon to the University of Oklahoma for technical training.

In July, he met Samuel H. Price Jr. Sam was a solid Christian who became a close friend. He was assigned a job similar to Jack's in the 309th Field Artillery unit.

When Jack had the opportunity, he witnessed to unbelieving soldiers about Christ. On July 5, for example, he *"talked to Anderson about Christ on my tractor* [used to pull the 240 mm howitzer]. *It was pouring rain."*

In August, he met Vernon P. Patterson (Pat), who was also a committed Christian. Pat often met with Jack on base and would accompany him to the chapel to discuss things of the Lord. Pat was a true student of the Word, reading his Bible as well as deep, high-quality Christian books in his free time. Jack embraced the example set by Pat and rose to contribute as much as he could to the conversations. On August 18, for example, Jack met Pat in the library *"where I showed him many of the amazing truths explained in the Scofield Bible."* This was the type of fellowship, encouragement, and support that God provided for Jack during his personal spiritual discipleship that lasted throughout basic training and onto the battlefield.[10]

---

10. Jack noted a series of Christian friends in his diary and letters. Vernon W. Patterson accompanied Jack to The Citadel. He was assigned to the 100th Division, and Com G, the 397 Infantry. Other Christians that Jack would meet included Whitney Macomber (August 25, 1943), Chester Cieplechowicz (sent to Battery A, 754 FA Bn), and Nobel Seaborn (FARTC). Alfred E.E McKenney was another Christian friend who would be assigned to the United States Coast Guard Academy, New London, Connecticut. Paul L. Fowler was a friend assigned to the Cannon Co. 272 infantry, where he was

# A Good and Faithful Servant

## The ASTP Program

Since the trip to Mr. Kelley's office in Princeton, Jack continually anticipated an assignment to the ASTP. Shortly after arriving at Fort Bragg,
Jack received word via Princeton that the ASTP program was on hold.
However, in June, word came that the experimental program was coming back on track. On June 5, Jack learned he needed to reapply for the
program. He was re-examined, and six days later he *finally* received
notification that he had been accepted. But this news did not stop basic
training — the grueling process continued for nearly three months as
he became an expert in field artillery.

Being located only 70 miles from his parents' home in Durham,
North Carolina, it allowed Jack to travel home whenever he could get
a pass. Beginning with his first pass on May 8, after one month of continuous training, he utilized this option at every opportunity through
August 1943, when he was finally transferred to his ASTP assignment.
The short respites into his home environment allowed quiet time for
reading, organizing his things, and enjoying some golf. More importantly, he redeemed the time with long discussions with his father
when their paths crossed, and especially with his mother, on the Bible
and what it meant to know Christ personally. Sunday mornings now
included occasionally attending church as a family, for the first time
since he was a boy in Seattle.

The demands of war broke up the family nest even before Jack left
Fort Bragg. On July 18, 1943, Whit was transferred to Nashville, Tennessee. Whit, now attached to the Second Army, was assigned to headquarters where he took over as a Director of the Tennessee Maneuvers.[11] The Tennessee Maneuvers Area differed from the Louisiana

---

later killed in action somewhere in France. Sam H. Price Jr. (HQ Btry. 309th F.A.)
was another friend. Two friends and roommates who were more nominal Christians
include Warren Severin (assigned to Company B of the 309 Medical Battalion [PFC] in
the 84th Infantry and would serve as a stretcher bearer and messenger) and B.J. Cohn
(who would be assigned to a mortar platoon in the 335th Division of the 84th Infantry), who would parallel Whitcomb's training and deployment in the 909 F.A. of the
84th Infantry.

11. In 1941, Whit co-authored the *Infantry Mobilization Program* by which all U.S. Infantry
units were trained in WWII. Between 1941 and 1944, the massive shift from peace to
all-out war resulted in a continuing shift in assignments and locations for military men
and their leaders. From 1941–1942, the Louisiana Maneuvers included a series of "war
games" where opposing armies put the new ideas and combat doctrines to the test. The

Maneuvers Area in terms of the terrain. The hills and mountains provided challenges and obstacles that better represented the topography of the German Fatherland. Whit's job included sending five or six divisions of infantry through a ten-week series of military "test problems" to determine fitness for combat. Salome, the trailing spouse, remained in Durham for the summer and then moved to Nashville, Tennessee, until Whit left for Europe.

## The Citadel

On August 23, 1943, Jack finally received the long-anticipated telegram informing him that he would start his ASTP training at The Citadel near Charleston, South Carolina. This was a great opportunity, as The Citadel was the "West Point of the South." President and Commander, General Charles Pelot Summerall, was a personal friend of Whit and a dedicated Christian. General Summerall was considered one of America's great generals based on his leadership in the Boxer Rebellion in China and during World War I. He also served as Chief of Staff of the United States Army from 1926 to 1930. He then became the 10th president of The Citadel, providing it with immense national prestige.[12]

Upon hearing the news that Jack was going to The Citadel, Whit wrote a personal letter to the General.

> Dear General Summerall:
>
> My son John C. Whitcomb Jr. has recently completed his basic training in Field Artillery at Fort Bragg and yesterday received orders assigning him to the A.S.T.P at The Citadel.
>
> I am very happy indeed that he has been assigned to your outstanding school and am very anxious to have him meet you personally. The last time you saw him was at Governors Island in 1927, when he was three years old. It is doubtful if either of you will remember it.
>
> I am asking him to call on you, and it is in the hope that you may be able to see him for just a few moments that I am writing this.

---

big winner was George Patton, whose revolutionary approach to tank warfare catapulted him into military leadership and international fame. In the autumn of 1942, the War Department decided to resume field maneuvers in middle Tennessee.

12. From the Citadel websites: http://www.citadel.edu/root/brief-history and http://www.my.citadel.edu/root/brief-history#summerall.

With most sincere personal regards, I am
Very truly,
J. C. WHITCOMB
Colonel, Infantry.

Three days later, the official orders arrived, commanding Jack and three other soldiers to report to duty at The Citadel immediately. The next day at 8:00 a.m., they turned in their sheets and blankets and reported for duty — but not before Lt. Stevenson pulled Jack aside and forced him to sweep the entire floor of the barracks one more time.

The Citadel was a military university. But the volume of men coming to Charlestown and the ASTP program was huge, and The Citadel became more of a triage center than a training center for the majority of the boys who were destined to become engineers. Groups of college students who passed the ASTP entrance exam were evaluated and sent on to major colleges and universities throughout the United States that were qualified to teach the specially designed curriculum anticipated to meet the future needs of the Army. The contribution of the engineers to the success of the U.S. Military in WWII cannot be overstated, in terms of logistics, construction, equipment repairs, the detection and disarming of mines, and the demolition of things that the enemy wanted.

Whit sent Jack a letter just before leaving Fort Bragg on how to introduce himself to General Summerall, a "Four Star." Upon arrival at The Citadel on August 28, 1943, Jack sent a message to the Commander informing him of his arrival. The next day, Sunday, August 29, 1943, Jack was invited to the general's home, and the two met for over an hour. Jack described him to his mother in a postcard as "a very nice old gentleman." The meeting was also "very nice," ending with a request from Summerall for Jack's mother's address and an invitation for Jack to join him and his wife the following Sunday for dinner.

Salome Whitcomb received a two-page, handwritten letter from General Summerall dated August 31, 1943. He noted, "I was delighted to see John when he called last Sunday. I never saw a more attractive young man. His courtesy, poise and intelligence could not be finer." He also promised to write strong letters of recommendation for the "O.C.S." and further training at The Citadel, if asked.

# Uncle Sam

The day after meeting General Summerall, Jack learned that he was not qualified for the linguistics program of the ASTP because he lacked three college courses: political sciences, European history, and geography (even though he was a self-taught expert in geography!). However, he was accepted as an ASTP engineer. Apparently, the rules for the ASTP had changed, and Jack's choices were limited to engineering, medicine, or advanced languages (Jack's first choice). However, the entry classes for linguistics were all closed, and only about 10% of the ASTP boys were being chosen for the languages option. Almost all had graduated from universities, had advanced degrees, and had significant government or administrative experience. However, since Jack's IQ was over 130, he was told that the decision was made that "I could do well in BASIC ENGINEERING, no matter what mathematical or scientific background I had."[13] He also noted, "That's my only choice. I am not the only boy with no background or interest for engineering who is forced to accept it."

True to his word, General Summerall invited Jack to Sunday dinner with him and his wife. Jack noted in his diary, *"Cleaned up and dressed and went over to have dinner with Gen. & Mrs. Summerall. I left at 3:20 and came back to read* God is my Copilot.*"*

Jack began attending classes on September 6, 1943, which included physics, mathematics, chemistry, and military correspondence. In the afternoon, he had exercises and marching, but also studied, played softball, and tried swimming — but the pool was cold and had too much chlorine.

Jack now had Christian friends that accompanied him from Fort Bragg. This band of brothers studied their Bibles daily and had long discussions on diverse topics such as Jesus' brothers, the nature of the Church, errors in the Christian calendar, etc. And on September 2, they spent the evening discussing evolution. Jack also began reading *Miracles of Our Lord, The Life and Epistles of St Paul, God and the Cosmos, God's Revelations of Himself to Man,* and *Preaching Without Notes,* as well as recording daily Bible study in his diary and getting passes on Sunday to attend church. This was clearly a highlight for him of his time at The Citadel.

The low point came on September 16. After supper there was a call-out of the 75 boys that would be attached to The Citadel for good.

---

13. Letter from John Whitcomb to Col. Whitcomb, August 30, 1943, from The Citadel.

Jack's name was not called, nor were most of his friends. Jack noted that, "We made such a noise about it that the Major made us go on a short road march."

Upon hearing the news, Whit provided some fatherly wisdom to his son. "But regardless of your personal feelings, the Powers-that-Be in their strange ways have decided that you can help by studying Basic Engineering, so that is that and like a good soldier it is up to you to do your best."

Unbeknownst to Jack or Whit, the Highest Power, in His wisdom, directed Jack to develop intimate knowledgeable in this area of science since it would be critical to understanding and co-authoring *The Genesis Flood* with a Christian *engineer* — Dr. Henry Morris.

## Virginia Polytechnic Institution

On October 1, 1943, Jack was transferred by train from The Citadel to Virginia Polytechnic Institute[14] in Blacksburg, Virginia, to continue his training program in engineering. His friend Warren Severin was transferred with him. They were assigned as roommates.

The first thing Jack did was to go to the library to look over some of the Christian books on the shelves. He began by reading *Holy Living and Holy Dying, Yale Lectures on Preaching*, and the Old Testament books of Judges and Exodus from his Bible. He also continued his detailed diary, tracking every announcement about the progress of the U.S. Military in WWII, his courses, his free time, his daily Bible readings, and the books he was studying.

On Friday, October 8, Jack and Severin marched over to the engineering building to register at VPI. They were assigned to math, physics, chemistry, English, history, geography, military, and physical education. The training would be intense, with classes Monday through Saturday, including Thanksgiving — with only Christmas day as a respite.

The next day, Severin and Jack meandered over to the library where Jack spent several hours reading *More Twice Born Men*. After supper there was a dance, but Severin and Jack returned to the library and studied until it closed.

The Blacksburg area had a number of good churches. On Sunday, Jack would go to the Presbyterian church, the Blacksburg Baptist Church, or both. He also faithfully attended Wednesday night services.

14. Now known as Virginia Polytechnic Institute and State University, or "Virginia Tech."

He continued a systematic study of the Scripture, beginning with copying the entire books of Daniel, Romans, John, etc. (including the study notes), by pen or typewriter. He also read more Christian books such as *Knowing the Scriptures, The Life and Epistles of St. Paul, The Number of Man,* and *Pilgrim's Progress.*

Midway through the semester, on October 29, 1943, Jack and Severin got a new roommate — B.J. Cohn. He was married and had a baby, but he was now in the Army with the rest of the boys.

C.C. Whitcomb, Jack's "Grampy," was now 75 years old and suffering from liver failure. On November 15, Jack received word that C.C. died and would be buried in Arlington National Cemetery. Whit and Salome stopped in Blacksburg on the way to Arlington to pick up Jack, but the military commander at VPI, Col. Wilson, only gave Jack a 1-day furlough — allowing Jack to visit his parents but forcing him to miss the funeral and family gathering.

On December 14, Jack found out that the ASTP students would get a one-week furlough beginning on the 1st of January 1944. However, Severin received a copy of the *Chicago Tribune* where he saw an article stating that the ASTP program might be liquidated. They continued with classes and standardized Army tests in all of the core courses. Jack received a "B" in mathematics, physics, and chemistry, with a "C" in physical education. This was not bad for a student with minimal prior background in the sciences competing with college students who had a passion for science and engineering and *chose* this path for a career.

Christmas day had no classes, so Jack went to the railway station and confirmed train tickets to Nashville, Tennessee, to see his parents during his furlough. He received some clothing from his relatives for Christmas and a silver "Parker 51" pen from mother and dad. He also enjoyed a "Huge Christmas Dinner" with many civilians and heard that Eisenhower was chosen to lead the invasion army next spring.

## Nashville, Tennessee

Jack began the year of 1944 on a series of trains rumbling from Blacksburg Virginia, to Nashville, Tennessee. He met his parents at the train station and proceeded to the Hazelwood Inn where they stayed until they could rent a house. Jack was exhausted from the previous semester and the train ride, and finally got a chance to sleep.

# A Good and Faithful Servant

The first thing that he discovered upon awaking at 9:00 a.m. on January 3 was that he had *"a big lump on the right side of my neck."* Whit sent a staff car to bring Jack to Headquarters where he met a general and a few colonels before being taken to the surgeon's office. Diagnosis: mumps. Prescription: strict bed rest and isolation for 10 days. So, Jack went back to the hotel and to bed with a copy of *The Brothers Karamazov* by Fyodor Dostoyevsky. The doctors also sent a letter to VPI that his furlough needed to be extended.

During the duration of his sickness, Jack was allowed a few visitors. His dad came the next day from the maneuvers, noting that the New River crossing test was quite muddy and discouraging for the soldiers. Whit understood the complexity of river crossings quite well, including the planning and dangers, as well as the strategic requirements. Rivers would serve as a major line of defense for the Nazis in Europe, and he demanded readiness.

The Hazelwood Hotel housed a number of military men working on the Tennessee Maneuvers. Learning of Jack's condition, General Burress (2 star), who commanded the 100th Division, and Generals Melline and Murphy, his executive and artillery officers, came to talk to Jack.

Most of the time, Jack would lie in bed and read *The Brothers Karamazov.* On Sunday, January 9, he read *"a few verses from the Bible."* In the evening, the doctor came by and gave him permission to *"sit up."*

On January 11, 1944, President Roosevelt's address to Congress asked for a National Service Act to draft all men 18–65 and women 18–50 for industry. Clearly, the Army was running out of men and would need any young man still in the States who was alive and able to be prepared for combat ASAP.

The following evening, Jack was visited by a Mrs. Fly. She was a godly woman who appeared to be of great encouragement to Jack. She brought her Schofield Reference Bible to the bedside and shared the "system Bible Study" method and some examples for Jack. He also met some other fine Christian ladies, including Mrs. Bacon, who talked to him about the Bible and fundamentalism.

After ten days of strict bedrest, Dr. Maj. Little made a house call to look at Jack's throat. It was better. The Whitcomb family had also secured a house about 10 miles from Nashville, so they began packing up their belongings for the move. On January 17, Whit and Salome took their son to a fine Chinese restaurant for his favorite food, then took him to the train station where they put their son in a Pullman car and sent him back to VPI.

## Finishing at VPI

Upon returning to VPI, Jack signed up for II History, Analytical Geometry, Principles of Speech, Physics, Military Class, and Chemistry Lab. He quickly recognized that he was far behind in all classes, especially analytical geometry.

On Wednesday, January 26, Jack and his classmates *"formed at the mess hall and marched to the T&A for a private conference (without officers) with the inspecting colonel of the Service Command."* There were many *"gripes and complaints about library privileges, medical care, shoe tickets, entertainment, etc."* The focus was Col. Wilson, who had refused a pass for Jack to go to his grandfather's funeral the previous fall. On Friday, January 28, Col. Wilson addressed the ASTP students and complained their action had a bad effect on his career. Nobody seemed to care, including Jack after Col. Wilson had denied his request to go to his grandfather's funeral.

In early 1944, the draft board recognized that it was 200,000 men short of goal of 7,700,000 men in uniform. The decision was made to eliminate the entire ASTP, with the exception of a few in medical and dental school and some specialized engineers. One hundred ten thousand students were reassigned to combat service.

On February 21, 1944, each ASTP Trainee at VPI received an official memorandum. The key sentences read,

> BECAUSE OF THIS IMPERATIVE MILITARY NECESSITY MOST OF YOU WILL SOON BE ORDERED TO FIELD SERVICES BEFORE THE COMPLETION OF YOUR NORMAL COURSE...MOST OF YOU RELEASED FROM THE ASTP WILL BE ASSIGNED TO THE ARMY GROUND FORCES FOR DUTY WITH DIVISIONS AND OTHER UNITS.

On March 25, 1944, Jack received orders to report to Camp Claiborne, Louisiana, along with 700 basic engineering students. The next day he received a certificate that said he had satisfactorily completed the course of study in General Basic Engineering at Virginia Polytechnic Institute. He would be joining the 84th Infantry Division — the "Railsplitters."

## Whit Goes to War

Jack's father preceded him on the European battlefield by seven months. In March 1944, Whit left Nashville and was assigned to Head-quarters of the Fourth Army, as "G-2" (chief intelligence officer) in San Antonio, Texas. But as D-day approached, Whit was transferred to the 83rd Infantry Division's staff as a "Reserve Colonel" just before shipping out to England on May 22, 1944. A few short weeks after shipping out, Whit and the 83rd were invading France through the beaches of Normandy.

### Camp Claiborne

Jack, Severin, and B.J. Cohn left VPI and headed to rural Louisiana. In April 1944, the 84th ID inducted Jack, Severin, B.J., and an additional 2,800 former ASTP men into the division.[15] These college-trained men were divided among three infantry regiments and were given five weeks of special training. Jack, already trained in field artillery, was assigned to the 327th F.A. unit. The training was now focused on developing fighting group organization, command structure, combat teams, and coordination.

Jack reported the situation in a letter to his father on April 3, 1943:

> They say we are going to have a hard schedule to follow, and I hope it conditions us. Many of the soldiers here say that the 84th Division is an "old man's outfit" and that 4-F men (unfit for service) are sent here from other divisions. The average age of the soldiers here is 31, and they have been training a long time. This is all rumor, but I hope the ASTP men will be able to help the division some.

Three weeks later he wrote to his mother: "Sometime next week we will take the 25-mile hike with full equipment, and that will be the big push. . . . Already they have taken out so many officers that the division can hardly operate, even with the help of acting officers."

15. Theodore Draper and Walter Chapman, *The 84th Infantry Division in the Battle of Germany: November 1944–May 1945* (New York: Viking Press, 1946), 3.

On May 5, he wrote to his mother, "I have been assigned as a fire direction man because of all of my math." His friend Warren Severin would be sent to the 333rd Infantry Division.

## A Furlough from Camp Claiborne

After about two months of training, Jack received a 15-day furlough spanning June 1 to June 15. He chose to go to Durham, North Carolina, to be with his mother — a trip that took two days by train each way. At home, he rested, unpacked the boxes sent from VPI, and talked to his mother about Severin and B.J. Cohn. On Sunday, he put on a clean uniform, drove downtown to the First Presbyterian Church and heard a *"fine sermon"* on the Trinity.

**June 6, 1944.** Jack recorded the events of D-day in his diary:

> *After breakfast I went to the front room and got the morning paper. The headlines said, "INVADE FRANCE." I rushed to the kitchen and told Mother that the Invasion of Europe had begun. We heard the radio broadcast of the invasion between Cherbourg and Le Havre. We drove out to Duke University Chapel and said a prayer for the INVASION FORCES. Came home and listened to the latest bulletins. Mother and I heard the King of England speak to the Empire. We listened to a prayer by President Roosevelt.*

## Whit Lands in Normandy

On June 17, 1944, Whit and the 83rd division landed on Omaha Beach under the fire of German artillery and strafing by Luftwaffe fighter planes.[16] Dead bodies from earlier days floated in the water, and twisted wreckage remained scattered on the beach and sea where men and machines met their fate.

The infantry was immediately deployed to an area west of Cretan, France, to relieve the 101st Airborne Division and begin the fight across France toward Germany. The fighting raged from hedgerow to hedgerow against heavily entrenched German defenses, resulting in numerous casualties with every yard of progress.

---

16. Harry C. Gravelyn, *World War II: My Experiences as Captain of Company D, 331st Infantry, 83rd Infantry Division* (Travelyn Publishing, 2016), NOOK Book.

The new U.S. Army combat doctrine placed commanders near the front line to better assess the ebb and flow of battle. This plan was highly effective in battle compared to the doctrines of the *Wehrmacht* (German army) that required all decisions to go up the chain of command, be analyzed by generals who knew little of the battlefield details, and then go back down the chain of command to the troops, often a day or two later. On the other hand, the new American doctrine resulted in great advantages on the battlefield and a rapid succession of promotions and reassignments as numerous "vacancies" were created by bullets.

On July 4, 1944, the Regimental Commander of the 83rd ID, 331st Infantry, Col. Martin Barndollar, advanced to the observation post near the front line because many of the units were being mauled by the Germans. In the moment the colonel exposed himself for a look, he was shot through the heart by a German sniper.

Gen. Robert C. Macon, the Division Commander, replaced the dead Col. Barndollar with Col. John C. Whitcomb Sr.[17] Whitcomb quickly and successfully stabilized the situation and engineered some new, effective, strategic advances. He remained with the 83rd Infantry Division for three weeks before being assigned to Chief of Staff for the 90th Infantry Division in Patton's 3rd Army. Whit's replacement in the 83rd Infantry, Colonel Ericson, was killed within days, as he was shot through the stomach by a rifle grenade. Whit would remain with the 90th Infantry Division for the duration of the war.

## Jack Completes His Military Training in the USA

On June 15th, 1944, one week before his 20th birthday, Jack arrived back at Camp Claiborne.

Upon returning to his position in the F.A., Jack was questioned by Lt. Wade, who appeared doubtful about classifying Jack as a computer for the F.A. but approved him anyway. Jack also had his share of KP — which was fine because, after cleaning pots and pans and peeling potatoes in the kitchen, he had access to their ice cream!

On June 22, Jack's 20th birthday, the men were taken to the lake. It was essential that the soldiers knew how to swim — a skill that Jack had already mastered. However, they had to swim with their fatigues

---

17. See order of battle, https://history.army.mil/documents/ETO-OB/83ID-ETO.htm, accessed June 8, 2019.

and shoes on. Jack's group started by swimming freestyle 200 yards out into the lake. They then swam another 100 yards freestyle, followed by a 50-yard swim without using their arms. The workout ended with flip turns, 20-yard chest carries, a 15-yard underwater swim, and ten minutes of treading water with their fatigue shirts inflated. The last task of the day was for the men to practice disrobing in water.

In August, the entire division was given three days of air transport operation training, which included principles of parachuting. During this time, the command of the 84th ID was transferred to Maj. Gen. Alexander R. Bolling, who would guide the Division throughout the war.

On August 15, 1945, Jack received a letter from his father in the 90th Infantry somewhere on the front lines in France:

> I hope this reaches you before you leave Claiborne, but I do hope you get over here before it is over. It is a great experience — the greatest of its kind there is, and I don't want you to miss it.
>
> This outfit has had a wild week running around the Boshe[18] Army. We have had all the top-flight news correspondents with us, but they can't mention our outfit by name. I assure you we have made some big headlines.
>
> It is a tremendous emotional thrill to be among the first into a liberated city, especially when we get in so fast the Boshe haven't time to destroy it. True, they always take time to smash and loot, even on the run, but that is nothing compared to systematic [illegible].

Col. Whitcomb was referring to a decisive battle resulting in the breakout of American forces trapped in the hedgerows on the coast of Normandy onto the planes of France.

The battle plan was named Operation Cobra. It began around July 22, 1944, with the British and Canadian armies launching a major attack against the German defenses on the north side of the Normandy beachhead. This drew German reinforcements away from the

---

18. The word *Boshe* or *Boche* was a derisive term used by the French in WWI in reference to soldiers of the German Army. It means someone with a big thick head — like a cabbage (cabbage head) — or hard head — like a nail head — and implied someone who was mentally slow, obstinate, etc.

American position to the south, just inland of the Omaha and Utah beaches.

On July 25, nearly 1,500 B-17's and B-24's dropped more than 3,000 tons of bombs along the German defenses within an area less than 5 miles wide. Another 1,000 tons of bombs and napalm were dropped by medium bombers. Immediately, the U.S. Army began pouring through the hole in the defensive line. The U.S. 90th Infantry Division turned west to attack the Germans, sealing off the Cherbourg Peninsula.

After intense attacks by the Americans, the commander of the German 2nd SS-Panzer Division realized that his units had been surrounded again by Americans and faced the threat of being completely encircled and destroyed. He sent a message about the specific and general situation up the chain of command, ending with, "I am an old tank man. This breakthrough is decisive; the war in France is lost."[19]

At noon on August 1, 1944, the U.S. Third Army was activated under the command of Lieutenant General George S. Patton. He had 25 infantry divisions, 13 armored divisions, 2 airborne divisions, and 6 supporting corps under his command. He immediately ordered the 90th ID to turn south and attack a town 88 kilometers away, secure the area around the key port area of Avranches, and prepare to move EAST, NORTHEAST, or NORTH! Under Patton, the 90th and other ID swept through Western France, captured Le Mans, then turned north to Chambois and closed the door of the Falaise Pocket.[20] The action resulted in the Germans losing entire armies and led to the liberation of France. It was a tactical and logistical success from which the German Army never recovered.

This was the battle for which Col. John Whitcomb trained for his entire career. His contribution to the war resulted in the Bronze Star with Oak Leaf Cluster, the Croix de Guerre with Palm, the Legion of

19. From "The Lions of Carentan Part III: Operation Cobra," https://warfarehistorynetwork.com/daily/wwii/the-lions-of-carentan-part-iii-operation-cobra/, accessed on June 8, 2019.
20. Details of the 90th Infantry are available at "90th (US) Infantry Division: After Action Reports — Battle of Normandy August 1944," https://www.dday-overlord.com/en/battle-of-normandy/after-action-reports/90th-infantry/august-1944, accessed June 9, 2019.

Merit,[21] and other medals. The citation for his actions leading to the Legion of Merit is as follows:[22]

> The President of the United States of America, authorized by Act of Congress, 20 July 1942, takes pleasure in presenting the Legion of Merit to Colonel (Infantry) John Clement Whitcomb, United States Army, for exceptionally meritorious conduct in the performance of outstanding services to the Government of the United States as Chief of Staff of the 90th Infantry Division from 15 July 1944 to 16 October 1945.
>
> Colonel Whitcomb through his exceptional organizational ability, tireless energy, resourcefulness and marked devotion to duty was responsible for initiating a program of reorganization in the operation procedures of the General and Special Staff Sections and redistributed and fixed the responsibilities of individual for details of administration and supply. As a result, all problems of staff reorganizations, reassignment and movement were solved without confusion.
>
> His service was invaluable.
>
> Upon the assignment of a new commander to the division, he attributed the ease with which reorganization command echelons were affected to the smooth and efficient staffs he found already functioning as a result of Colonel Whitcomb's program. At the very outset of the Division's "Breakthrough" from Normandy, Colonel Whitcomb

---

21. The Legion of Merit is awarded to those in key positions of responsibility and power, for their service and achievements. It is also the first U.S. medal to be awarded to citizens of other nations for their outstanding service, fidelity, and loyalty in combat or non-combat positions. It is awarded in four degrees to distinguish the person it is awarded to, including Chief Commander (a head of state or government), Commander (equivalent to a U.S. military chief of staff or higher), Officer (rank of colonel [army and air force] or captain [navy or coast guard]), and Legionnaire (any recipient that does not meet the requirements above). Except for the Medal of Honor, the Legion of Merit is the only United States military medal that is worn around the neck. From https://www.medalsofamerica.com/blog/legion-of-merit-details-and-eligibility/, accessed December 29, 2021.
22. Citation is available at https://valor.militarytimes.com/hero/95211, accessed December 29, 2021.

rendered invaluable service as counselor and advisor on policy and morale.

During a campaign, characterized by rapid advances and intense fighting, he constantly, with effortless ease, directed and supervised the operation and security of the widely separated echelons of the division and subordinated staffs, thus relieving the Division Commander of much distracting concern.

By his thorough understanding of staff problems and their solution, his enthusiasm and tact, and his devoted loyalty to his Commander, Colonel Whitcomb has contributed in a large measure to the success of the Division.

Jack Whitcomb was proud of his father. But though Jack too trained and fought in this world conflict, he was still planning to take a different career pathway that would result in a different type of battle — a battle for *truth*.

# Chapter 9

# The 909

"We have been very busy"
August 1944 to May 1945

It struck me as odd, while growing up, that my father always wore a hat with the first autumn chill outside our northern Indiana home. As the temperature dropped with approaching winter, he would wrap his face with a scarf and hold his gloved hand over his forehead as he ventured out into the cold to start the car or dash from the car into a seminary building. He said this hypersensitivity came during the horrible winter of 1944, in the Battle of the Bulge, when his face was frozen.

## America's "Greatest Generation"

There is nearly universal consensus that the generation of American men who were willing to sacrifice everything for God and country, who fought the forces of evil on a massive two-front war, who saved the world, and who made America a superpower was the greatest generation that this nation has ever seen. I agree. My father was among this generation.

### Jack Goes to War

In August 1944, Whit was in the midst of battle in France as Chief of Staff of the 90th Infantry Division within Patton's Third Army. Jack was still in basic training down in Camp Claiborne, Louisiana. It was clear that something dramatic was happening in Europe because Jack began to see groups of German POWs being detained in the middle of the USA!

During the last week of August 1944, the 84th Infantry Division packed all of the equipment used in training into boxes labeled "TAT" (to accompany troops). With the major equipment in boxes, the troops cleaned up the camp and cleared out the barracks in preparation for a month-long journey to the European Theater.

On September 5, 1944, three days before infantry division boarded the troop trains at Camp Claiborne to move east, Jack received an unexpected order. Again, he was designated as a "supernumeral" — this time in the 327th F.A. unit. He was transferred to the 909th Field Artillery Battalion to fill a missing piece in that unit. Jack had to adapt to an unfamiliar team at the last moment, just before deployment to fight the Nazis. The good news was that the 909th was one of the best field artillery units in the 84th Infantry and would later be recognized as one of the best in the U.S. Army.

The troop trains were filled with men and materials and lumbered out of Camp Claiborne on September 8, 1944. On that day, Jack began keeping track in a tiny 2 x 3.75-inch leatherbound pocket booklet of every place he visited. The route was circuitous, taking three days to reach Camp Kilmer, New Jersey, which was the final staging grounds and a port of departure for Europe.

Jack's mother, Salome, moved from Nashville, Tennessee, to Highland Park, New Jersey, to be near her family as both of the men in her life departed for war. Jack, for a brief time, was now 30 minutes south of her at Camp Kilmer. Receiving a 24-hour pass allowed mother and son to meet each other in New York City — revisiting favorite sights, sounds, smells, and tastes from their grand time together five years prior.

On September 20, 1944, Jack's unit reported to Pier 54 in New York Harbor. They boarded the *Sterling Castle*, a troop transport ship, headed for England. Jack unpacked his duffle bag on the top deck near a window with a view. The longshoremen completed their tasks, the ship was untethered, and they headed out to sea on a foggy afternoon. Navigation and communication methods lacked today's sophistication, and the *Sterling Castle* crashed into a barge somewhere on the way to the deep blue sea. The troop ship suffered some damage but was able to return to NYC.

Upon arriving back in NYC, Jack received another 24-hour pass — and shocked his mother by showing up at the front door of the

Highland Park house without warning. Though she was happy to see her son, she feared that Jack was AWOL!

In their time together, Salome told Jack of Whit's selection for Patton's Third Army in the 90th Infantry Division. Jack informed his mother that his own role in battle would be in the headquarters, armed with maps, slide rules, compasses, and a headset as a fire-direction computer for the 909 Field Artillery unit — and NOT on the front line in a rifle company. Salome breathed a sigh of relief with the knowledge that her son would not be shot at — directly.

The *Sterling Castle* was repaired by September 29. Jack returned to the same cabin and settled in for the 10-day excursion across the pond. On the first day at sea, Jack ran into B.J. Cohn, his second roommate from Virginia Polytechnic Institute.

Fortunately, the transatlantic crossing occurred with good weather and without attack by Nazi submarines. The ship schedule remained tightly organized. All soldiers were expected to rise at 1:30 a.m. (which is ~7:30 a.m. England time). Breakfast was at 2:00 a.m. (~8:00 a.m. England time) in a huge dining hall. The GIs were fed two meals a day, but according to Jack, "the English food was starchy and unattractive." Everyone had jobs — Jack carried sacks of coal on his back from the hull to the D deck kitchen. In his free time, he was able to talk to B.J. Cohn and enjoyed some friendly fellowship. He also noted talking to a German Jew who had escaped Germany and was now returning to kill Nazis. Apparently, it was the young Henry Kissinger[1] who was on the same boat! Jack was also fascinated by a teacher who knew a lot about European history and culture, likely Theodore Draper,[2] who would be chosen as the "historian" for the 84th ID.

Like many of the American GIs, Jack entered England through the port at Liverpool. The TAT boxes were unloaded from the ship and loaded onto trains. The Americans were transported across England, bypassing bomb-damaged London (although Jack could see search-light beams in the sky and hear the air raid sirens). They finally arrived

---

1. Henry Kissinger was a Jewish soldier who went on to become a famous American diplomat and political scientist. He served as National Security Advisor and Secretary of State in the administrations of Presidents Richard Nixon and Gerald Ford.
2. Theodore Draper was author of *The 84th Infantry Division in the Battle of Germany: November 1944–May 1945* (Nashville, TN: The Battery Press, 1946), 260 pages and a 140-page Roster of Officers and Enlisted Men.

at the Lopscombe military facility "somewhere between London and the English Channel" at 2 a.m. on October 11, 1944.

Shortly after arriving, Jack discovered that he, along with 8 officers and 192 other enlisted men, would be sent to France immediately. The task was to support the Red Ball Express — the convoy of trucks, cars, tanks, troop transporters, and anything else on wheels that must be transported from the landing site at Omaha Beach to the front line. He wrote to his mother on October 29 to explain, "Our job has been to haul supplies in France [Cherbourg to Paris and up to the front lines]. I was not a truck driver, but I went along as a basic." Jack was chosen for this mission because the majority of men loading and unloading the trucks were German prisoners of war, and Jack's language skills were needed to provide instructions and orders in German. So, on October 15, even before he received key equipment (such as a sleeping bag), he boarded a transport ship in England and crossed into France to become part of the Red Ball Express.

The remainder of the 84th Infantry Division, including the 909th F.A., crossed the English Channel to Omaha Beach on Thursday, November 2, 1944, on a ship called the *Leopoldville*. A few days after the 84th ID disembarked, the *Leopoldville* circled back to England and returned with another load of troops. This time on its way back, a Nazi submarine attacked it with torpedoes. Although the ship did not sink for several hours, the Congolese, Belgian, and British crew abandoned the ship, allowing it to slowly drift out to sea as the hull filled with water. For hours, the Americans on board tried desperately to contact any and all Allies for help — but no one answered. The *Leopoldville* finally capsized and sank. Over 800 American GIs died in the freezing waters that day — the greatest loss of American soldiers' lives while crossing from the USA to Europe of the entire war. The despicable action of the Belgian and British crew resulted in a massive disaster and an international scandal.

*Campaign #1 — The Siegfried Line*

Jack was reunited with the 909th F.A. in France on November 5, 1944. The next day, the entire 84th Infantry Division was rushed north by truck to Wijlre, Holland, by truck, regrouped, and then east to the region of Aachen, Germany, just after it fell to the American Army. Jack recorded in his little book, *"Rhineland, Germany; \*COMBAT\*; Kohlscheid. Arrived at 1ˢᵗ position, 10:00 AM, Friday, November 10."* His battalion would move through 50 different positions by the end of the war.

The soldiers with the highest likelihood of being killed are those entering battle for the first time. Almost none of the soldiers of the 84th Infantry Division had any combat experience whatsoever, so there was concern as to how they would fare against the seasoned German Wehrmacht. History proved that they were not only capable; they were outstanding. As Major General Alexander R. Bolling noted in his official review after the war, "The Railsplitters could accomplish anything!"

One of the key features of the 84th ID that led to this distinction was the 2,800 former ASTP students who were smarter, more disciplined, more mature, and more creative than the average GI Joe. Indeed, the Railsplitters distinguished themselves in three different types of warfare — breaking the Siegfried line, holding an emergency, makeshift defensive line at Marché in the Battle of the Bulge, and a history-making breakthrough across the Roer River with sweeping advances across the heart of the German Fatherland to meet the Russians at the Elbe River.

By November 1944, the Allies finished pushing the Nazis out of France and Belgium and into Germany. Following WWI, the Germans constructed a massive defensive fortification from the Northwest tip of Germany to the Black Forest and Switzerland. This defensive line was called the Western Wall by the Germans and the "Siegfried line" by the Americans. The fortification included reinforced concrete pillboxes, anti-tank traps, land minds, barbed wire, and powerful artillery guns. Fighting along these lines was intense, and advances were measured in meters rather than miles.

The 84th Infantry's first assignment focused on breaking through the Siegfried line at Geilenkirchen, just North of Aachen, Germany — a major city that fell to the Allies 10 days earlier after fierce fighting. The 84th would replace exhausted, bloodied, and victorious American soldiers.

By mid-December, the 84th ID conquered the fiercely defended Frelenberg–Grundschule sector by pounding through the Siegfried line, and poured into the Fatherland. Their success earned promises of desperately needed rest. But rumors of a massive German offensive just to their south, and a possible breakthrough of the American lines in the forested hills of the Ardennes region of Belgium, began spreading like wildfire among the troops. On December 21, 1944, orders came for the men of the 84th ID to grab their gear packed with two days of K rations and a canteen of water and to pile into transportation trucks for immediate departure. Secret destination: Marché, Belgium. Mission: plug a massive hole in the American lines caused by the German offensive.

*Campaign #2 — The Battle of the Bulge*

Hitler recognized that Germany could no longer fight a two-front war. Therefore, he concocted a plan for multiple Panzer armies and support troops to attack the Western Front through the weakly defended Ardennes Forest of Belgium. The primary objective focused on capturing the port of Antwerp, Belgium, a major port city, to become the primary entry point of Allied men and supplies following its reopening for the Allies in November 1944. Hitler believed that achieving this objective would cause the Allied alliance to crumble, allowing him to negotiate a peace treaty so that he could transfer all his remaining resources to the Eastern Front and destroy the Russians.

*Surprise, Surprise*

Early on the morning of December 16, 1944, Hitler launched a surprise attack with a quarter of a million men led by three Panzer armies. Hitler predicted that the Allies would need a few days to organize a response. Furthermore, he assumed attacking at the junction of American and British lines would result in further delays, as the nations would thus negotiate who was to respond, when, and how. He surmised these negotiations would paralyze his victims until his objectives were met.

The initial attack included 2,300 tanks blasting through the American 106th Infantry Division, which killed over 400 soldiers, wounded 1,250, and left 7,000 missing in action. More than 7,500 Americans surrendered at one time. That was one of the largest surrender of troops of the war. Day one was a massive success for the Germans. But sustained success of the German salient would be denied by the rapid, tenacious, and innovative American response. Hitler and his top Nazi generals never anticipated the flexibility, creativity, and resolve of America's greatest generation.

To the surprise of the German High Command, the American GIs responded rapidly and in unexpected ways. The Germans failed to recognize the degree of initiative and training that was given to corps and company commanders on the front line (i.e., the new American war doctrine), allowing for immediate and decisive responses during the ebb and flow of battle. They underestimated the *unwritten* American doctrine that major army groups, with no pre-battle relationships, could unite on the battlefield and fight as one. They underestimated the tenacity of the American defenders at key defense sites that cost the Germans both time and resources. These courageous defensive stands stalled and weakened the attacking German armies, so no full breakthrough was ever achieved. Hitler miscalculated the time lag between the initiation of the attack and the tactical reaction of the American forces. All these things led to an *American* victory.

## Massacre at Malmedy

On December 17, 1944, an event occurred that brought anger and a terrible resolve among the Americans soldiers. The Germans overran the 285th F.A. battalion near Malmedy, Belgium, and they surrendered. The American soldiers were then herded together and executed. Eighty-six American men were murdered by Nazi SS troops on that day, in a frozen field, in cold blood.

Knowledge of the massacre rifled through Allied troops, resulting in rage, a resolve for revenge, and refusal to surrender. It would be a fight to the death.

## Surrounded at Bastogne

Bastogne, Belgium, is one of many small towns where the Americans fought courageously against all odds. The story became the posterchild of the Battle of the Bulge because the famous 101st Airborne Division (the Screaming Eagles) and other units were completely surrounded by the Germans in an apparently hopeless situation but refused to surrender. The German Commander, boasting that the American situation was hopeless, gave the American commander two hours to surrender

— or be annihilated. General McAuliffe, the American commander in Bastogne, responded with one word, "Nuts!" Instead, the Americans fought desperately while, in a seemingly impossible tank maneuver by America's most audacious general — George S. Patton — the airborne unit was rescued.

*Final Defensive Line at Marché, Belgium*

On December 20, 1944, two days before the "Nuts" reply at Bastogne, Jack and the 84th Infantry Division made a secret emergency dash from their battle lines near Aachen, Germany, to Marché-en-Famenne (Marché), Belgium, via a 14-hour, 75-mile drive overnight! Although Marché was only a small market town, it was of major strategic importance because it was the intersection of multiple key roads and was located at the geological divide between the forest and the plains. The plains were the optimal terrain of the German Tiger tanks; forested hills were their worst nightmare.

The race to Marché was won by the 84th by a mere four hours. This was due in part to the demolition engineers of the highly decorated 51st Engineering C Battalion. Almost single-handedly, they blew up every bridge and barricaded every road as fast as they could during their retreat from the German advance. These actions significantly delayed the German advance to Marché, causing the Germans to arrive behind schedule. Furthermore, the Germans were exhausted and decided to rest for a few hours before parading into the undefended town of Marché.

The urgent repositioning of the 84th Infantry Division from Aachen to Marché filled a huge gap in the American defenses on the southern flank. The rapid deployment of all available forces formed a new defensive line across Belgium, from north to south, right along the divide between the Ardennes Forest and the central Belgian plateau. The American plan, but not the British plan, was to prevent the German tanks from entering the central plateau and slicing Belgium in half on their way to the port city of Antwerp.

Upon arriving at Marché late in the evening of December 20, the 84th Infantry Division commanders learned that the town was to come under attack at any moment. Indeed, German tanks were at the outskirts of town, planning to shell it during the night and stroll into town the next morning. The American defense was stretched desperately thin — one soldier every 150 yards across the front line. The 84th Infantry's Commander Collins radioed his superior, General Bolling, to ask if they should pull back or hold. The order came to "hold." Shortly thereafter, the order was updated: *"Hold at all costs!"* No retreat, and certainly *no surrender.*

When the Germans awoke on the morning of December 21, they discovered that the "undefended" town was occupied by the Americans! The 84th Infantry Division and the 909 F.A. now had four German Panzer divisions in the cross hairs of their guns. The Germans had no idea as to the size or strength of their new opponents, and the commanders of the 84th used the deception of widely spread soldiers to fool the Germans as to the strength of their defense.

Lieutenant Robert Fowler Jr.[3] was a forward observer for the 909th F.A. in front of Marché. He was among the men who spotted the enemy and called back to Jack Whitcomb at central command with details of the enemy's location, movement, strength, and progress. My father considered the forward observers as the bravest of men (Chapter 17).

Robert Fowler Jr. recalls what he saw:

> I was the forward observer from the 909th Field Artillery, 84th Division, assigned to the 335th Infantry to shoot artillery for them and also direct fire from other artillery units in the division's artillery if needed. We dug in and waited for the Tiger tanks to come at us. In a few hours they came. A line of tanks a mile long with some infantry with them. They were trying to get through the pass into Marche. I started shooting artillery, 105 mm and 155 mm shells, at the first tanks along with another forward observer on the opposite side of the pass. We did get them stopped in the pass. Some tanks were on fire, others were disabled enough to block the pass. There the Tiger tanks fanned out over the floor of the valley in front of us and started shooting at us. During the first 24 hours, the 909th Field Artillery fired over 400 rounds of ammunition at the tanks and held them out of town. We

---

3. Robert Fowler Jr. was contacted by the author in spring 2014. He lived in Clearwater, Texas, and had vivid memories of the events, at age 94. He died on October 12, 2015, at age 95.

continued to fire at the tanks in the valley, day and night. . . .
The Panzer units were stopped with artillery fire and some
very brave soldiers in the 335th Infantry, 84th Division.[4]

Over the next few days, the 84th Infantry Division fought off multiple
attacks by various *kampfgruppen*[5] of the German Wehrmacht.

One of the most effective strategies of the artillery battalions was to
coordinate the fire of all the guns at once. During a 30-minute artillery
barrage, for example, the most effective projectiles to kill enemy soldiers were the first ones to hit since the soldiers had not yet scrambled
for cover. The American artillery computers (e.g., Jack Whitcomb)
learned to organize all of the howitzers by altitude and distance from
the target, then have them fire their guns in rapid sequence at a determined trajectory so that all of the projectiles from all of the guns hit
the target at the same moment. Furthermore, they had a new invention called the *proximity fuse* that caused detonation of the shell at a
predetermined distance from the target — making it many times more
lethal to enemy troops. The coordination of the howitzers and use of
the new shells could spell annihilation of entire panzer divisions at the
hands of the 84th infantry field artillery.

The U.S. Army forbid the soldiers from keeping diaries in case
of capture or death with potential military secrets falling into enemy
hands. The pages of Jack's diary remained blank. Military censors literally cut sentences out of letters or destroyed them. Jack, completing a shift in the map room, penned a letter to his mother that got
through the censor's scissors. It began, "From somewhere in Belgium,"
and then summarized the desperate battle with these words: **"We have
been very busy."**

*Americans Under British Command*

To the dismay of the Americans, on December 20, 1944, General
Eisenhower transferred command of Hodges' U.S. First Army and
Simpson's U.S. Ninth Army to the command of British Field Marshal

---

4. Description sent by Robert Fowler, http://www.veteransofthebattleofthebulge.org/
   vbob/wp-content/uploads/2011/03/2001-Aug.pdf.
5. A *kampfgruppe* — an ad hoc task force or combat group with combined arms formation usually containing tanks, infantry, artillery, and other elements as needed for a
   specific objective.

Bernard Montgomery to coordinate the American and British defense against the surging German salient. The Americans were already engaged in a rapid defensive counterattack and were ready to throw their reserves into the fray. Montgomery was more cautious and wanted to wait and plan a more organized response from farther to the west rather than sustain a series of isolated actions.[6]

The 84th was putting up a historic fight against the Germans far to the east of where Montgomery was planning his defensive line. Reinforcements were urgently needed to fill in the gaps in the wavering American defensive line and to cover the flanks of the 84th ID to prevent them from being surrounded, as the 2nd Panzer Division discovered that there was no defense south of Marché and began outflanking the 84th ID. However, Montgomery was determined to fall back, an action that would have resulted in Marché being surrounded and becoming another Bastogne — or worse yet, Malmedy.

Help for the 84th ID came in a creative way — without directly disobeying the orders of Montgomery. The American generals generally opposed Montgomery's caution and perceived miscalculations. They planned to deploy their reserves to counterattack the German bulge to the south and west of Marché, but Montgomery said no.

The message with Montgomery's orders was relayed to the 2nd Armored Division by the American commander under Montgomery. The coded message was sent with intentionally ambiguous terms: position yourself between town A and B and only attack if attacked. The 2nd Armored Division, located in central Belgium well behind the 84th Infantry at Marché, was under the command of "Lightning Joe" Collins. Collins now commanded Patton's old "Hell on Wheels" tank division that Jack remembered from Fort Benning, Georgia. The aggressive commander of the 2nd Armored Division looked on the map and saw *two* towns that could be "A" and *two* towns that could be "B." One A-B combination meant "fall back"; the other meant "move forward," thus giving the 2nd Armored an opportunity to "misinterpret" the command. A "correct" interpretation of the message was "fall back." Needless to say, the Americans moved forward and attacked!

---

6. Hitler was counting on the slow and cautious approach of Montgomery. In addition to underestimating the American soldier, he failed to anticipate Eisenhower's transfer of command of American armies to the British to have a unified attack.

On December 23, the skies cleared, and the American and British air forces joined the melee with ferocious attacks. Many Nazi tanks and supply vehicles were destroyed as the soldiers ran for cover.

Unaware of the high-level politics, the 84th ID fought bravely and successfully. The 116th Panzer Division suffered near total annihilation on the outskirts of Marché by relentless artillery and the rifle companies. The 2nd Panzer Division finally determined that Marché was too heavily defended and bypassed Marché to the south, only to have their supply lines shredded, in part by the accurate long-range fire of the 909 and other F.A. batteries. The 9th Panzer Division and Panzer Lehr of the 5th Panzer Army also failed in their attacks on Marché and withdrew to Bastogne.

Between December 26 and 30, the American 2nd Armored Division pounded the German 2nd Panzer and 9th Panzer Divisions south and west of Marché, while the 909 Field Artillery and 84th Infantry blocked reinforcements and prevented retreat with continuous artillery fire. Without supplies of fuel and ammunition, the Germans were sitting ducks. By December 27, the 2nd Panzer Division suffered near complete annihilation, losing 100 of their 120 tanks and most of their half-tracks and trucks. They ceased to exist as a fighting unit. Hundreds of soldiers were killed, nearly 500 were taken prisoner, and only a remnant of badly beaten German soldiers escaped the onslaught by dashing through the woods back to the land from whence they came. The commander of the German forces, General Manteuffel, now realized that any further attempts to reach the Belgian River Meuse, the first major objective on the way to Brussels and Antwerp, would be futile. His two best Panzer divisions were too weak for further offensive operations.

The Railsplitters had stopped cold the German advance at Marché. This marked the end of the German offensive. On New Year's Eve, December 31, 1944, the 909 fired a midnight volley of high explosives into the ice-cold night air to welcome in 1945. The next morning, the Railsplitters turned over their stronghold to the British 53rd Infantry Division and withdrew for a brief rest. It would not be long before they returned to the field of battle to eliminate the remnant of the Nazi bulge into Belgium and to begin their own offensive into the heart of Germany.

*The Shrinking Bulge*

The routine for men of the 84th Infantry Division was to fight on the front line for days to weeks at a time, and then be given a vacation. After the battle at Marché, the 84th was sent for some rest and relaxation at the beautiful European resort town of Comblain-la-Tour, Belgium. This was a time to shower, shave, wash clothes, write letters, and relax. Jack spent his time alone, reading and writing letters to family and friends. These respites were short lived, however.

The Railsplitters, now linked to the 4th Cavalry Group and 2nd Armored Division, led the counteroffensive against the German salient, capturing La Roche and Amonines, Belgium. Finally, on January 16, 1945, private Rodney Himes from the 334th Infantry of the 84th Division noted an American soldier walking outside of the house they were hiding in near Houffalize, Belgium. Himes ordered the soldier to identify himself. The soldier came from the 11th Armored Division of Patton's Third Army. The southern part of the bulge was closed and only mop-up operations were needed to finalize the victory.

On Tuesday, January 30, 1945, as the bulge was being cleaned by the armed forces, Jack was ordered to headquarters and the office of General Bolling. Perhaps they had found his sleeping bag! To his surprise, he met his father, Whit, who entered the battle from the south as part of Patton's Third Army. They were able to spend a splendid afternoon together. Whit noted in a follow-up letter to Jack, "I would have loved to see your mother singing and dancing when she heard that we were able to meet in Belgium."

Jack described the reunion in a personal letter,

> Mother Dearest,
>
> The great day finally arrived! I saw Dad yesterday! It was around 10:30 in the morning that a telephone call came to our C.P. ordering me to report immediately to the Chief of Staff of the 84th Div. I was taken over there in a jeep and went into the division headquarters. There was Dad with our commanding general, and the Chief of Staff! I was sorry to hear that he could stay with me for only an hour or so, and then had to return to the 90th. The general sent us over to his private dining room, where we had a swell chicken dinner.

In just an hour's time we had so much to talk about that it was hard to think of the most important things. We spent about 30 minutes in the General's war room where all the big campaign maps are on display, and it was really interesting. If Dad could have spent a couple of days with me, we could have gone to Brussels that afternoon, but as it was, things were quite rushed. After about an hour at the division hq. we rode in Dad's jeep back to the town where our battalion is located. We had a nice *cool* ride through snow blanketed country and finally reached the place. Unfortunately, our colonel was not there, and the CP was busy with a conference, so Dad left to get an early start back to his division. He left me a box full of candy, toilet articles, sweaters, sox, and gloves, which ought to keep me going for a long time!

*Campaign #3 – The Roer River Breakthrough*

After the Allies pushed the Germans back to the battle lines that were established before the Battle of the Bulge, the Railsplitters found themselves in approximately the same spot that they had initially been assigned, just north of Aachen, Germany, in view of the Roer River. With experience and success in Belgium, the confident Railsplitters were ready to advance quickly. However, in a desperate attempt to slow the invasion of the Fatherland, Hitler commanded the opening of the gates of the dams controlling water levels on the Roer River Dam, flooding the lowlands between Holland and Germany. It would be nearly impossible to advance through the mud and flood plains, thus delaying the advance of the American, British, and Canadian armies.

The 84th ID was stuck in a small town just north of Honsdorf, near Linnich, Germany, and less than 25 miles north of Aachen and 40 miles west of the Rhine River. Jack experienced several notable events that he was finally able to relate to his mother in a letter, dated March 16, 1945. The details of danger appear to be minimized in the letters to his mother, especially linked to the death of men in his unit. A notable story was Jack's description of seeing the first version of Hitler's *Vergeltungswaffen* (vengeance weapon), or V-1 rocket (the "buzzbomb").

## "Robot Bombs"

Jack first heard a V-1 rocket during the Battle of the Bulge in Marché, Belgium, but began seeing them while camped in Honsdorf. He noted the "loud rumbles as they pass overhead is frightening indeed." He goes on to describe his experiences in Honsdorf:

> This was my first real view of one. They look like a small airplane with square wings, and out of the back end comes flashes of light at rapid, regular intervals, this makes their straight courses visible at night. They don't go very fast, only about 300–400 miles per hour, but they make plenty of racket, like a wagon on a cobblestone street. Our town must have been right on their line of travel because they all went over our heads, in the direction of NW.
>
> Well, one night our experience with buzz bombs came to the final climax. One landed in our battery area. We had all heard the familiar rumble in the distance, and the approach, but this time it just got louder and louder until it seemed as though it would enter our room. The crash that followed sent us staggering to the cellar, but falling plaster was the only result, and we knew that there would be no more explosions. The robot bomb had landed 300 yards from our house, making a crater 30 feet across and 12 feet deep. I don't know yet what made it fall so suddenly without its motor stopping.
>
> Another week went by with nothing but mines and Robot bombs to worry us (because from then on, we ducked when we heard them going overhead!). The one night we visited the cellar again when German heavy artillery opened up on us. More than a hundred shells came whistling down on our area, but none of them hit anything. Our next incident was a bomb dropping into our area by one of our own planes.[7]

## Roer River Crossing and Breakthrough

The Roer River is much smaller than the Rhine, but it still offered a major obstacle because of the flooding and the organized German

---

7. The incident of friendly fire was when a 500-pound bomb prematurely fell off of an Allied airplane and destroyed the mess hall, killing the cooks and servers. It was a "sad day" for the unit.

defense. The crossing of the Roer River by the 84th Infantry Division was a masterpiece of American strategies designed by Brigadier General[8] John H. Church, Assistant Division Commander. Indeed, it continues to be studied at American war colleges.[9] The strategy was to put the forward observers inside of the tanks of the 2nd Armored Divisions and put the tank field observers back at the fire direction headquarters. This markedly improved the coordination between the fast-moving Sherman tanks and the highly accurate and deadly howitzers.[10]

The Railsplitters snuck up to a narrow part of the Roer River just east of Honsdorf. They spent two consecutive nights with artillery barrages and smoke screens along the river, far from the actually crossing site. The Germans rushed to the areas of bombardment, anticipating a crossing, which never materialized. On the third night, the defending Germans were more complacent in their response to the artillery shelling and the smoke screens shielded the view of advancing infantry.

The artillery laid down a massive barrage, only yards away from the front-line soldiers. When the bombardment stopped, the soldiers jumped into rubber boats and paddled across the river under machine gun fire. Pulling ropes and wires behind the boats, they spanned the river, constructed floating bridges, and began streaming tanks and infantry across the Roer. The soldiers' greatest fear was landmines on the enemy's shoreline, but the wires and mines were cut and disabled by the artillery barrage. The German commanders, alerted of the crossing, expected the insurgents to press directly east toward Berlin. Information went up the chain of command to the generals, and a defensive move was ordered to concentrate their defense to the east of the crossing.

*The Breakthrough*

Instead of charging forward from the landing site, the infantry turned left, traveling north. The German defenders in the adjacent sectors

---

8. A *brigadier general* has one star and is ranked immediately above a colonel and below a major general.

9. *CSI Battlebook 19-B: Roer River Crossing* (Fort Leavenworth, KS: Combat Studies Institute, 1986).

10. The 105 mm M2A1 (M101A1) howitzer was the standard light field artillery with a range of 7 miles (11,270 meters). The propelling charge consisted of a base charge and six increments, forming seven charges from 1 (the smallest) to 7 (the largest). It gained a reputation for its accuracy and powerful punch.

assumed that they were out of danger since no directives from high command trickled down to them.

Charging perpendicular to and well behind the defensive lines, the Railsplitters suddenly entered and immediately captured entire towns filled with unsuspecting and defenseless German soldiers within minutes rather than days. Stories ran rampant of GIs over-running unsuspecting German military stations in the early morning, collecting all of the guns, and forcing the enemy soldiers to surrender without a shot. After the surrender, the GIs sat down in the town's banquet hall and ate the Germans' breakfast!

An eyewitness account of the breakthrough was written on March 9, 1945, in a letter from Jack Whitcomb to his mother.

> In my other letter I was telling you about our stay and the small town of Honsdorf, on the west side of the Roer River. It was three weeks ago today that we started the big push, and I have been on the Rhine for a week and a half already. Before we even made the river crossing, we were told to expect a breakthrough, and to leave our duffel bags behind us to make room for extra gasoline and rations.
>
> It took our infantry and engineers only a few hours to get across the Roer in rubber boats and start working on the bridge. In the meanwhile, our guns were firing constantly to give them support, and I was computing down in the fire direction center when we gave the first command to fire the preparation for attack early that morning of the 23rd. After firing across the river for several hours, we hear the report that our infantry had taken the small towns of Rürch, and Korrenzig, thus securing our bridgehead. Two days later the bridgehead had expanded enough for our field artillery battalion to move over the river on the pontoon bridge to give the troops closer support in their drive due north. As we crossed over the pontoon bridge, I noticed that the river was quite small, but it had been our barrier for months. Across the river from Linnich, we passed through Korrenzig on our way northward. There were guns and trucks everywhere off the road and on it. Engineers were still repairing bridges and filling in craters near the road. There was little

thought of camouflage or concealment, because speed was the motive, and no time was wasted. That night we set up our CP in the cellar of a house in Doreren. We had to bail it out to use the basement (the Roer must have partially flooded over this town, or else there had been plenty of rain like back on Honsdorf). By the next day our infantry had achieved a breakthrough to the north, and our tank columns had spear-headed 10 miles north, bypassing the city of Erkelenz and taking Wegberg.

So we packed up and took off after them. By the night we were in Wegberg, having gone through Houverath, Golkrath, Hoven and Schwanenberg on the way. I had ridden in the back of our "weasel," a small boat-shaped vehicle with tracks, capable of moving on the land or water; so in this manner I could have a fine view of the countryside. During the ride I could see small fires on either side in the distance and the distant boom of artillery. The civilians in these towns had just awakened to the fact that they were behind our lines a few hours after our tanks had rushed through. That night in Wegberg our battalion and attached AA units captured a dozen German soldiers in the town, because the infantry had passed through in too great a hurry to clean them out. The MP's had formed a temporary PW cage in the town with about 140 prisoners in it. They were all jammed into 2 trucks and taken down the road to other PW cages. (In the follow-ing days we didn't even bother to take them back with guards — just let them walk to our rear lines alone!) That night, the only thing the Germans could do was to bother the town with mortar shells and a few 88 mm's. You see, our division was actually forming a spearhead into enemy territory, only about 3 miles wide, with Germans on either side of the path we were making. We were sacrificing security for speed in this situation, because the Germans were disorganized and too dazed to accomplish anything. So the tanks plunged on ahead, with infantry following in trucks, then the artillery, and leaving the German soldiers for the rear echelons to take care of!

With the Roer River breakthrough, the Americans were behind the Germans' major defensive line, and progress toward Berlin was as fast as the Autobahn. The major problem was no longer German combatants — although the remnants of the German army fought on — it was the German prisoners, who surrendered to the Americans by the hundreds of thousands.

*Speaking German — Instructions and Surrender*

The artillery did more than fire high explosives and armor piercing shells at the Germans. They also fired messages to the German solders encouraging immediate surrender. My father kept one of the messages, written in German, as a war souvenir. A translation of *"Wenn Es Losgeht"* reads:

**When it starts**

Are you still alive? You struggle with inadequate weapons, with inadequate equipment, shaking of half-trained units. But you live. Thousands of your comrades, many of your own friends have fallen. It was bad, but you have escaped. You live. Your officers reject your thoughts that this is just a fight break. There is hope, because — you live.

Tomorrow we can start, as it all started at the Atlantic Wall, at Avranches and St. Lo. Morning, Sudden, non-stop drumfire of all calibers, rolling use of jabos; thousands of Flying Fortresses; carpet bombing; Tanks, armor-piercing missile weapons and the new flamethrower. Everything that you have seen so far has been a child's game in the mountains. Tomorrow: hell.

**The day after tomorrow it will be over** and you are either dead, a cripple, or a prisoner of war. The decision may be up to you. Therefore, now consider what you'll do if you're still alive, when the material battle rolls over you. Then maybe you have the opportunity to save your life. Many will have to surrender. But many will have to die because he made the choice too late.

**Which choice do you make?**

Jack preferred a more direct, personal, and positive dialogue with the Germans in their own language. Jack initially used his German with soldiers helping with the Red Ball Express. He explained to his mother in a carefully crafted letter (since all letters were reviewed and censored):

> It was interesting to have an opportunity to talk to German prisoners who were working for us at our camp. We are not allowed to speak with them except to give orders, and explain the work to be done, but I had good practice doing that for three days. The army is highly discouraging speaking with the German civilians, so I hope to learn my German by reading the signs on the roads & newspapers.

Jack continued to be called upon to use his language skills in Germany. During the battles, Jack rotated with other technicians of the 909th F.A. unit in 6-hour shifts. His favorite job was as a G-2 Intelligence officer where he would compare aerial photographs with detailed maps in headquarters to discern the location and activities of the enemy. The rest of the time he was assigned to proceed with the advanced units into newly captured towns to tell the German peasants and citizens that they were now under American jurisdiction, and the following rules applied: *"Die amerikanische Armee werde dich nicht töten. Die Soldaten werden in Ihrem Haus bleiben. Sie können Ihre Küche im Laufe des Tages zu verwenden."*[11] In addition, Jack, along with a few other German-speaking members of the Railsplitters, such as Henry Kissinger, spent hours interrogating and directing German prisoners of war — a significant endeavor since 1.5 million German soldiers surrendered to the Allies on the Western Front. This was where Jack spent most of his time, working to improve his German language skills, helping Germans with their English, and telling them about the Lord.

Jack Whitcomb related another incident in a letter to his mother that happened after the Roar River breakthrough sometime between February 28 and March 3:

> I was chosen to go along on the forwarding party, because I could get along with German fairly well. A forwarding party

---

11. Translation: "The American army will not kill you. The soldiers will stay in your house. You may use your kitchen during the day." They would need to get out of the house at night, staying with other families because the Americans needed their house to rest.

is a small group that went ahead of the main body with the purpose of finding a place to stay, possible gun positions, and routes. We started out with the general plan of looking for positions on the other side of St. Tönis, the next large town ahead. We ended up riding into Krefeld itself amid the on-looking German population which didn't know quite what to do at their first sight of American soldiers! Some cheered, and others put their hands over their heads. White flags hung from doors and windows. **We later discovered that we had gone right into the part of Krefeld that had not yet been taken because our infantry had bypassed it, swinging to the north again.** The people seemed to be happy to see their war experience ended so suddenly, and we had no trouble at all. We stopped on the street to look for a nice CP. Many homes were still intact and occupied by German families despite the general destruction and ruin of their town, caused by previous bombings. I guess they had no place else to go to with all of Germany in a similar plight. In looking around the area we saw a large castle like building with thousands of civilians grouped around it. This was a large air raid shelter or "bunke" where they lived for security. St. Brooks, my chief of section and I walked beyond it, looking for our CP. **As we approached a large schoolhouse, six German soldiers rushed out with hands up.** They were in green uniforms and had packs on. We brought them back to where the trucks were, and after searching for weapons, sent them along back on the road to St Tönis where the MP's would either pick them up or send them further back. By this time we had found a nice place for the whole battery of stay. It was in the cellar under a bombed out hospital. Electric lights, running water, plenty of cots were among its attractions.[12]

Most of the Germans that Jack encountered in France and later in Germany were not hardened Nazis; they were German boys that had been conscripted into the army. They were deeply depressed and tired of fighting. Their country was in shambles. Their friends and many family members were dead or missing. And now they anticipated

---

12. Letter from Jack Whitcomb to his "Dearest Mother," dated March 16, 1945, 9th Army, Germany.

execution by the Americans — another lie of their propaganda ministers. Thus, Jack had a message of hope for many Germans, telling them of God's grace and mercy. He did not see the German POW as enemies, but as people who needed Christ. And he did witness to them — but carefully, privately, and without the appearance of "fraternizing with the enemy"!

*Between the Rhine and the Elbe Rivers*

The 84th ID advanced to the Rhine River near Homberg, about 45 miles away, in only 10 days. They stopped on the west side of the Rhine for a rest and then crossed the Rhine at Wesel on March 24, 1945, following, and then joining, the 5th Armored Division. Once across the Rhine, it was almost a wide-open race across the final 250 miles to the Elbe River, just west of Berlin.

The next major objective was Hanover. The city suffered an enormous pounding by the Allied air raids and artillery — with the city falling into the hands of the 84th Infantry on April 10, 1945. The shock came to the soldiers with the liberation of a Jewish concentration camp on the Northwestern outskirts of Hannover in the town of Ahlem.[13] The survivors appeared as "living skeletons," affirming the rumors of Nazi atrocities among the American soldiers that "none of it has been exaggerated."[14] Four days later, the town of Salzwedel, Germany, fell to the Americans, who found the streets of the city filled with feeble women, just freed from another concentration camp, dressed in rags, rummaging through the city in search of scraps of food or pieces of clothing.

Jack's eyewitness account of the concentration work camp in the town of Salzwedel was conveyed in yet another letter to his mother:

> The 4th of April was the day we advanced 60 miles from Münster to the Weser River south of Minden. Then after we crossed the Weser, we took Hannover in 4 days, and continued eastward. At the city of Salzwedel we liberated many thousands of Jews, Poles, Russians, Hungarians, Italians, and

13. Photodocumentry by one of the U.S. soldiers from the 84th ID: http://www.jou.ufl.edu/documentary/angelofahlem/angelofahlem.html.
14. Captain William J. Kilcoyne, *History of the 909th Field Artillery Battalion in World War II* (Heidelberg, Germany, 1945) 31 (arrangement and layout by Tech 4 John Whitcomb, Cpl. Hartley Harrison, and Cpl. William Wakeland).

French men. The city was mad with joy. The first tank had entered at noon, and we went through at 3:00 P.M.

## The Final Days of WWII

By April 16, 1945, the Railsplitters reached the Elbe River at Seehausen Germany, less than 50 miles from Berlin. But orders came to stop the advance. This was as far as they were to go — for political reasons. The artillery continued to fire shells across the river to harass the withering German army.

At 3:30 p.m., April 30, 1945, Hitler had committed suicide deep in his bunker below the Nazi Chancellery building in Berlin. The final days of conflict witnessed large numbers of Germans desperate to surrender to the Americans. "It was a strange sight to see hundreds and thousands of them crossing the river in small boats, swimming, floating on rafts or anything that would support them, as they sought to get to our side before they were overtaken."[15] On May 2, nearly 16,000 Germans successfully crossed the swift river, while those who perished remained unnumbered. Later that day, the Americans and Russians met on the East bank of the Elbe. The fighting, for the 84th Infantry and 909th F.A. was over.

Finally, on May 9, 1945, Germany unconditionally surrendered to the Allied armies, and the European part of World War II was over.

*Wrapping Up*

Both Jack and his father survived the war. Colonel John Clement Whitcomb Sr. was exhausted, being driven day and night by Patton, and required several months of rest to recuperate. Fighting with the 90th Infantry, Colonel Whitcomb's soldiers discovered Nazi gold at Merkel,[16] and his efforts to secure the site were documented.[17] He was

---

15. Ibid., 34.
16. Made famous by *The Monuments Men: Allied Heroes, Nazi Thieves, and the Greatest Treasure Hunt in History* by Robert Edsel with Bret Witter (New York, NY: Center Street Hachette Book Group, 2010) and by the movie *The Monuments Men*, co-produced by Columbia Pictures (in association with 20th Century Fox) 2014.
17. Bernstein's April 18, 1945, memo, "Report of developments ill removal of treasures from Kaiseroda mine at Merkers, Germany" (page 66). From the Clinton Presidential Library/Clinton Digital Library, https://clinton.presidentiallibraries.us/files/original/e9f43ddbc252798c59c537cb509c5f78.pdf, accessed February 1, 2014, and January 3, 2020.

awarded the Legion of Merit for exceptionally meritorious conduct in the performance of outstanding services to the Government of the United States as Chief of Staff of the 90th Infantry Division from 1944 to 1945. Despite multiple recommendations for promotion from colonel to general, by Patton and others, this lifelong ambition was never achieved. General Marshall made sure of it (Chapter 5).

## Memories of the War

The American men and women who sacrificed everything to win WWII are called the "Greatest Generation." However, they are also called the "Silent Generation," as they seldom spoke of what they saw and heard.

Seventy years after the Battle of the Bulge, I asked my father about his memories of the fight. As a soldier, he told me, little was known about the details of the battle. He was now fascinated to return to Belgium and to the German salient from a *historical* perspective. At the time of the battle, German spies dressed as American GIs could be anywhere, and thousands of Allied soldiers would be put in eminent danger if key pieces of information fell into the wrong hands. The less the battling GIs knew, the less they could tell the enemy if they were captured or deceived by an imposter. My dad heard almost nothing of the details of the battles — except "we won!"

I asked him how he felt that he had performed under pressure. He just nodded, noting that he did his job to the best of his ability — but it was his colleagues on the front lines that deserved the credit. However, Sergeant Joe Mitchell, who worked with Jack throughout the war, saw things differently. He later drew a cartoon of Jack at the Fire Direction Center with the caption "Computer," adding, "J. Whitcomb. One of the finest soldiers I've ever seen."

My father's perspective from ground zero includes the freezing cold, missing a sleeping bag, and the sense of desperation during the first days of the battle. His job as a fire direction computer placed him in the basement of a convent near Marché, continually marking the targets as seen by the forward observers. He remembers the grateful nuns bringing him hot soup.[18]

---

18. The 909 Battalion CP was located in the basement of a convent. In recording the history of the 909 (page 20), the authors (including John Whitcomb) noted that the cold guards were often warmed by a bowl of hot soup from the nuns who made every effort

Some specific events also remain crystal clear. He remembers a howitzer battalion radio operator yelling into his headset, "No need to call in coordinates! We can see them coming! The German tanks are directly in front of us!"

Another night, just after being replaced from guard duty, a mortar round hit the spot where he had been standing — instantly killing the GI who replaced him. "At that point in time," he recalls, "I knew that God had other plans for me."

He remembers trudging to an old barn in search of a place to escape the bitter cold and get some sleep — since his sleeping bag *still* had not arrived — only to find the barn stacked like cordwood from floor to ceiling with American soldiers killed in battle and frozen solid in the agonizing contours of death. This was an unimaginably sad moment epitomizing the haunting finality of every human life, some much younger than others.

### What Makes a Fine Soldier?

Napoleon noted, "The first quality of a soldier is constancy in enduring fatigue and hardship. Courage is only second." I doubt that these were the qualities that distinguished Jack from his comrades in arms.

The perception of many who have never served in the military and who form their views of battle conditions from history books, movies, and video games is that a fine soldier is a brash, cigar-smoking, machine-gun toting, heartless brawler with a foul mouth and dirty face. It seems paradoxical that, from the perspective of a true battle-hardened sergeant of the 84th Infantry Division near the end of World War II, the "finest soldier" he "had ever seen" was a mild-mannered, academic, supernumerary with bad eyesight who wanted to be a missionary to China.

I asked my father years later, "What do you recognize as the characteristics of a fine soldier?" He answered, "Complete commitment to the cause. Immediate obedience to the wishes of the commanding officers." And then he paraphrased 2 Timothy 2:3–4, which says, "Suffer hardship with me as a good soldier of Jesus Christ. No soldier in active services entangles himself in the affairs of everyday life, so that he may please the one who enlisted him as a soldier."

---

to make them comfortable with what conveniences they had available. The first death of a member of the 909 was Lt. Eugene Green on December 26, 1944.

# A Good and Faithful Servant

Jack never complained about hardships — a characteristic displayed as early as July 1937 when he broke his arm on Mount Olympus. Second, he had great respect for people in positions of leadership and strived to please them with discipline and meritorious achievements. Third, he was smart, had great attention to detail, and was dedicated to performing a technically demanding job with perfection. Fourth, he was a man of compassion, who cared for the well-being of others — a rare quality in the middle of a massive war. Finally, he completed his service to Uncle Sam and marched forward in a new direction, following the example of the Apostle Paul, "forgetting what lies behind and reaching forward to what lies ahead, I press on toward the goal for the prize of the upward call of God in Christ Jesus" (Philippians 3:14).

But in many ways, the war clearly changed Jack. His cousin Sally noted that he was much more sober-minded and focused on religion after the war — a change that may have actually begun on February 13, 1943, in his dorm room in Princeton. Dad remembers that he and other veterans returning to Princeton after the war often remarked, "We matured ten years for every year of war."

# Chapter 10

# Bill

"God has revealed to me once again that He wants me to serve Him."
May 1945 to January 1946

The war in Europe ended on May 8, 1945, with Jack standing at attention at the Guard of the American Flag in front of the Command Post in the tiny municipality of Wallstawe, Germany, 30 miles west of the Elbe River, Position #50.[1]

The dash from the Rhine River to the Elbe River across the heart of Germany was completed at record pace with heavy use of the Autobahn. Large areas of the country were bypassed, and groups of German raiders and elements of various army groups continued to fight and harass the Americans. Jack sat on the bank of the Elbe River for only a short time after arriving at the destination earlier in April. Groups of soldiers from his unit were immediately dispatched for a variety of tasks that are important for an occupying force in hostile territory.

Jack's first task was to help in the "mopping up" operations in the vicinity north of Seehausen along the Elbe River. Much of this was clearing wooded areas of the few remaining German fighting units that would harass the troops with small arms fire and mortars. But for the most part, the country was wrecked, and the people defeated.

The battalion was then transformed from a fighting unit into special task force with jobs of taking care of prison camps, helping displaced persons, and picking up guns, ammunition, and war junk.

---

1. Most of this history comes from letters sent from John Whitcomb to his mother. He only made a few brief entries in his diary during 1945–1946, usually noting the time they left one position and arrived at the next. Most pages are blank.

237

For many of these tasks, Jack was well prepared, now fairly fluent in German, well organized, and resourceful. He was transformed from a soldier to a military police (MP), an interpreter, a map reader, and often served within forwarding parties to enter captured cities, set up a military government, or establish garrisons. He was still hoping that he would be able to join the Army of Occupation in Germany, rather than be shipped to the C.B.I.[2] with the other men in the 84th who had less combat time than seasoned soldiers such as those of the 90th ID who fought from Normandy through France and Germany with Jack's dad.[3]

## The Russians

On April 27, 1944, a detachment of 14 soldiers, including Jack, was sent to Berkau, Germany — a few miles from Bismark — to complete the liberation of a Prisoner of War camp filled with Russian soldiers. Jack was expecting to see hundreds of starving, sick soldiers begging for food. Instead, they found a well-organized camp with Russian officers and doctors in charge. There were about 350 soldiers, but at the time they had nowhere to go since the Russians and Americans had just made contact with each other along the Elbe River near Torgau, about 125 miles south of Seehausen. Jack was sent from Berkau to Bismark to tell the local *bürgermeister* (mayor) that the town was to provide supplies for the Russian prisoners. The support from the local Germans was unexpectedly good! Jack noted in a letter,

> We are the only Americans in the vicinity, including Bismark, for 15 miles around and everyone comes here with their problems and troubles. We have the town carpenters building things for the camp and four young Hitler youths helping us in our work. They are hanging around us constantly, asking about America and about our army. They are all around 16, 17, 18 and want to come back to America with us. They work hard all day, and come back the next day for

---

2. C.B.I. was the China-Burma-India Theater where army planners were going to send the 84th Infantry Division, unless V-J Day (Victory over Japan) came quickly!

3. The U.S. Army developed a point system, based on time in the army and time in battle. It took 85 points to get out of the Army — and Jack only had 37. Only one person in their battalion of over 500 men had 85 points, so everyone was expecting to be fighting the Japanese soon.

more, just to be with us. I cannot understand these people, because they try to do anything for us.[4]

On April 30, 1945, Hitler committed suicide in his bunker in Berlin.

May 1 was "May Day," a special holiday for the Russians. Jack helped organize a special event for them by bringing in food and cloth under the supervision of Captain Webb, the commanding American officer. Some local women made a large Russian flag and an American flag out of scraps of cloth. The celebration started with all 350 Russian soldiers marching in formation in front of the flagpoles on the parade grounds, wearing their various uniforms. The flags were then raised together as the soldiers gave "three cheers"! The Russian commander made a speech (in Russian) and then the flags were brought to half-mast in honor of President Roosevelt. This was followed by a series of speeches to Russian soldiers who did not speak Russian (e.g., those from the Ukraine, Mongolia, Turkestan, Siberia, etc.).

Following the speeches, the Russian soldiers marched back into camp where three long tables had been erected and set with white tablecloths, plates, and utensils for all 350 prisoners. The Germans from the town served a banquet of potato and sauerkraut soup followed by sauerkraut, potatoes, and black bread. The Russians ate everything.

After dinner, the Russians moved to a field where they met 24 prisoners from a Yugoslavian concentration camp near the same town. The purpose was a soccer game. The Russians won the game.

Jack wanted to stay in Berkau for many weeks, especially since he was staying in a well-built and modern German house, and because all of the cooking, KP, and laundry was now done by the efficient German and Polish women! However, after one week, on May 4, he was ordered to go to Schnega, located 40 miles northwest of Berkau and between Uelzen and Salzwedel where, less than three weeks earlier, Jack's division had liberated many thousands of Jewish women and other prisoners. Their job was to search for more concentration camps in the 30-mile section between the two towns.

On May 8, 1944, Jack was in the small municipality of Wallstawe, Germany, just 15 miles southeast of Berkau. There he learned that the war had officially ended. That day Jack took off his steel helmet forever!

---

4. Letter from John Whitcomb to his mother, May 1, 1945, 9th Army, Germany.

From then on, the soldiers sported polished shoes and pressed uniforms — primarily to impress the German civilians (in Jack's opinion).

On May 11, 1945, Jack was promoted to the rank of Technician fifth grade (T/5). This rank was given to technicians with specialized skills. They were addressed as "corporal." Jack's final rank as an enlisted soldier was T/4 —addressed as "sergeant."

## New Perspectives on Germany

In contrast to western Germany, which was almost completely destroyed by aerial bombardment and artillery, central Germany was largely untouched by the war, except for key industrial sites and the center of some major cities. The smaller cities were largely bypassed during the dash to the Elbe River.

As an occupying force, the Americans usually worked through the *bürgermeister* of each town. Jack was struck by the efficiency and organization of everything, including each home. However, they were not "beautiful homes" like in England. Furthermore, the people appeared harsh in appearance and conversation. Jack noted:

> Even the women have harsh nasal voices and seem to be yelling at you all the time when they converse. When we have to move into a German house and the occupants must move in on neighbors, it is just like a madhouse with everyone screaming at once. The lady of the house demands to know why we didn't take Frau Schmidt's house instead & the aunts and uncles dash around grabbing mattresses and pillows to take with them. Children ask for chewing gum and chocolate.[5]

Jack's unit began hopping from town to town back toward the French Port where American troop ships were slowly transferring soldiers to the United States. With the war in Germany over, the army censors also stopped slicing up letters. On May 19, 1945, Jack wrote this to his mother about their next move, 150 miles southwest of Salzwedel to Alfeld, Germany:

> I am taking the advantage of my first opportunity to write an uncensored letter! So from now on I can tell you

---

5. From a letter from John Whitcomb to his mother on May 15, 1945.

where I am and where I have been. . . . At present I am in the picturesque little town of Alfeld on the Leine, about 30 miles south of Hannover. We are in in the mountains here, but it is really pretty scenery around here. We are about 1 mile east of the Weser River. ... We are staying in a large mansion owned by some people who make their living by going to Africa & India to get animals for the big Hannover Zoo. Right across the street is their menagerie where most of the animals are kept. I have visited it several times looking at the elephants, giraffes, zebras, lions, tigers, leopards, pumas, baboons, monkeys, alligators, parrots, flamingoes, hippos, camels, ostriches, llamas, buffalos, gnus, and many varieties of deer, goats, sheep & birds. . . .

As always — great attention to detail!

The next stop took Jack southwest to Reinerbeck, Germany, for a week then south to Leutershausen, Germany, a quaint town of ~2,400 people located 100 miles east of Heidelberg, Germany. He stayed in the mansion of a count (age 14), whose father had died two years earlier. The countess (mom, Gräffin von Wiser), the young count (son), and two daughters now worked in the fields to survive. The house was run down, but its previous grandeur and nobility could be seen with beautiful portraits, paintings, gilded furniture, great libraries, manuscripts, suits of armor, statues, and pictures of the family in their nobility.[6] This stop lasted 11 days, and the time was spent taking some day trips and looking around the area.

## Sinsheim, Germany — Position #54

On June 11, Jack Whitcomb arrived in Sinsheim, Germany, just 20 miles south of Heidelberg, Germany. The 909th F.A. Battalion was assigned to the Seventh Army, now the third army in which Jack's unit served. He was assigned to live in the same fine house as their colonel but had to sleep in a room in the attic. He expected to be there about two months before orders came regarding the C.B.I. campaign — hopefully including a short stop in the USA on the way to the Far East. In the meantime, he learned that the U.S. Army was organizing and sponsoring a variety of activities to keep the inactive soldiers busy,

---

6. From a letter from John Whitcomb to his mother on June 7, 1945.

such as sightseeing tours, task-oriented trips, building projects, and college courses.

## A Nice Vacation

Finally, on June 20, Jack was given a furlough — one year after his last furlough from Camp Claiborne, Louisiana, to Durham, North Carolina. By accident, he learned about a trip for members of the 909th F.A. leaving from Heidelberg and that there were two open slots. The trip was to Nice, in Southern France on the famous French Riviera. He jumped on the opportunity, got urgent furlough papers from his commander, scrambled into a mail truck heading to Heidelberg, and caught the others who were boarding transport trucks to head south. He documented every city, changes in mode of transportation (to a train), and recorded the things he saw out the window along the long journey. He arrived in Nice just in time to celebrate his 21st birthday. The entire city, including all the hotels, were given over to American GIs, with a cost of $2.00 per day. Best of all, the Red Cross offered free Coke and ice cream! Jack took every tour, side trip, and boat trip available, seeing many of the places that his mother had visited just before the war.

The trip back was eventful. The train stopped in Nancy, France, at midnight, and the group went to a hotel called the *Cité Universitarie*. Jack had a hot shower and a good night's sleep, but the next morning, July 1, there was no sign that the group was leaving (Jack thought there was a truck shortage), so he went to church. He then went to the Red Cross club to write some letters and eat doughnuts, but when he returned to the hotel, everyone had left!

He found out that there was transportation back to his station the next day, so he made his own day pass and spent the day seeing the city. He found some infantrymen from the 84th, so he went to their camp in the Corps Rest Area. He was given a bed, blankets, and a "real" pass to town. He drew his PX ration of candy, soup and fruit juice, and ate ice cream. Then he rented a bike and toured the city. The next morning, he had a great breakfast and caught a truck to Mannheim, just west of Heidelberg, Germany. He arrived just after his unit, whose truck broke down, and they spent a miserable time getting back to Mannheim. So it worked out perfectly!

Upon returning to Sinsheim he spent most of his time answering the phone and helping develop a weekly newspaper for the 909th F.A. called the *Cannoneer's Post*. He helped with writing articles, setting type, and editing the newspaper, with 1,000 copies printed in Heidelberg and distributed to the battalion. He also read some books (e.g., *David Copperfield* and *Quo Vadis*), studied geography, and played chess.

Sadly, Jack entered Europe without his *Scofield Reference Bible*, had no access to good Christian books, had no solid Christian friends, and he seldom spoke to others about Christ. There was also no record in his diaries or letters that he attended church or chapel, except for the first Sunday in France. When it came to discipleship and spiritual growth, he could not go it alone. Jack had fallen away from Christ and Christianity. And despite the interesting things around him, he was unhappy.

The 909th, successfully achieving all goals in Germany, and began training for battle in the Pacific. Formal training focused on radio use, mechanics, agriculture, languages, and literacy. On July 10, Jack learned that the 909 would remain in Germany until about January 1946. This meant that he could take some advanced college courses and do some more sightseeing.

## Higher Education

When Jack learned of an opportunity to study at a major university, he immediately filled out an application to go to Sorbonne University in Paris for courses in French language and civilization. He thought he was an excellent candidate. But to his surprise, dismay, and disappointment, his application was rejected. Unbeknownst to him, this was Divine intervention.

On July 18, 1945, Jack wrote to his parents about a different opportunity:

> I have been chosen as one of the men in the Division to attend school in England under the Army Education Program. It will be an eight-week course at the Army University Center No. 1, Shrivenham Barracks, England.[7] I am leaving tomorrow, July 19 so that I can be in England on the 25th."

---

7. Also known as Shrivenham University, http://www.iwm.org.uk/collections/item/object/205202248. Shrivenham is also the site of the Defense Academy of the United Kingdom.

# A Good and Faithful Servant

The toughest part of the war for Jack was isolation from Christian fellowship and the lifestyle examples of godly men such as Donald Fullerton. Basic training was tough, but a believer here, a believer there — ones who shared a love of the Savior and a dedication to His service — continually encouraged him. Europe was different. Europe was a spiritual desert engulfed by the atrocities of wicked men. The battles were intense — with horrific destruction and suffering.

It was during this hiatus between combat and college that God, in His providence, brought Jack into contact with an old acquaintance. These two men, now seasoned veterans, independently and seemingly randomly stumbled through the rubble of post-war Europe until a providential meeting.

## Bill

Jack packed his bags and headed out of Sinsheim by truck and train on his way to the English Channel, and on to the Shrivenham, England, 80 miles west of London.

Jack stepped out of his train car at a train station along the way to stretch his legs. Suddenly, he heard an unexpected voice crying, "Hey, Jack Whitcomb!" Jack was shocked to see Bill Eerdmans, a former classmate at McCallie Military Academy.[8] Jack knew Bill as a "bad boy," rightfully expelled from the school just a week before graduation for his disobedient antics. In contrast, Bill remembered Jack as "witty, bright and personable" and that "he always spoke with at least six reasons why, always numbering them off his fingers."[9]

The son of the famous founder and president of William B. Eerdmans Publishing Company of Grand Rapids, Michigan, Bill displayed both brilliance and boredom, leading to continual mischief. Bill, a Yankee, never felt at home with the culture of the Deep South in Chattanooga, Tennessee and remained the odd man out as he pushed the limits of the school's tolerance of behavior. Finally, a week before graduation, Bill was caught drinking beer, which was not allowed. The consequence of this, and numerous other infractions of the code of conduct, resulted in his dismissal with a few other

---

8. Larry Harmsel with Reinder Van Til, *An Eerdmans Century: 1911–2011* (Grand Rapids, MI and Cambridge, UK: Wm. B. Eerdmans Publishing Company, 2011).
9. Email from William Eerdmans to the author on January 16, 2015.

boys. The incident loomed large in Bill's personal and family history, as the author of the Eerdmans' 100-year journey records: "It was a hard blow for Bill, and perhaps harder for his father, who drove the long road back to Michigan in stony silence, now and then staring balefully at his abashed son."[10]

William Eerdmans Jr. decided to join the army. Assigned to the 36th Infantry Division, his army group remained engaged in intense combat for more than 400 days, scrapping and grinding from Casablanca in the Northwest African country of Morocco to Italy, France, and Germany. Casualties exceeded 3,600 killed in action and 13,000 wounded, including Bill. In February 1944, during the prolonged battle at Monte Cassino, Italy, an exploding shell peppered Bill with shrapnel from head to hip. Severely wounded, Bill struggled through multiple surgeries and rehabilitation in a military hospital near Naples, Italy. During these days, Bill read *A Leatherneck Looks at Life* by Cornelius Vanderbreggen, a Dutch American second lieutenant in the Marine Corps who made the case for following Christ. The book made a huge impact on Bill, as did other events of the war. When his condition improved, the Army returned him to his combat unit, still at Monte Cassino, and he continued to fight.

On April 29, 1945, deep in the heart of Germany, Bill's unit overran two Nazi concentration camps linked to Dachau. Hundreds of dead Jews formed piles of bodies organized into rows. The bodies, naked or thinly clad in striped pajamas, showed "no sign of blood, strangling, bullet holes, or the like . . . bones covered merely by a layer of skin — sunken eyes, chests, drawn-in stomachs that went back to the spine."[11] Bill noted in a letter to his family that deeper into the camp they found "another pile of Jews — these were headless, armless, legless — cut in half — beaten to pulps — probably those of the Jews who offered some resistance or who cried out for mercy — these Jews, these victims of these heartless Godless German vermin!!" ... "It seems that all around me I see nothing but death, torture, cruelty, & people in love with Hell." Nine days after Bill witnessed the atrocities at the Nazi death camps, the war with Germany finally came to an end.

---

10. Larry Harmsel with Reinder Van Til, *An Eerdmans Century: 1911–2011* (Grand Rapids, MI and Cambridge, UK: Wm. B. Eerdmans Publishing Company, 2011), 53, 55.
11. Ibid., 63.

Bill was a changed man. As soon as the war was over, Bill Eerdmans began tirelessly traveling throughout Europe with an evangelistic message and evangelist's passion.[12]

Jack, who became a Christian the year after graduating from McCallie Military Academy, and who had become discouraged and depressed with the lack of Christian friends and fellowship, could not believe what he saw and heard. Jack described the events in a letter to his mother on July 26, 1945:

> A very wonderful thing has happened to me on this trip to England! God has revealed to me once again that He wants me to serve Him. I was riding on the train just after we left Frankfort, Germany, and we were preparing for a two- or three-day train ride across France. At one station the train stopped & I walked out on the platform to look around, when I heard someone call my name. I looked up, and there was a boy leaning out of the window in the next car, whom I didn't recognize at first. When I got closer, I remembered him as being Bill Eerdmans, a boy that lived in East Hall at McCallie School for a whole year with me. I never had associated with him very much while at McCallie because he had a low character and spent all his time with the worst men in McCallie. Finally, two weeks before graduation, he was expelled from McCallie along with three or four others, & I never saw him again. He joined the Army, & fought in Italy, France, & Germany. In Italy he was wounded & had been saved. He accepted Jesus Christ as his Savior, and God gave him a new life right there. Remember the words that Jesus spoke in John 5:24 – "Verily, verily, I say unto you, He that heareth my word and believeth on him that sent me, hath everlasting life, and shall not come into condemnation; but is passed from death into life."

---

12. Bill Eerdmans seldom communicated with family or friends during the early part of WWII, and he was thought to be dead by the staff at McCallie Military Academy who sent two letters of condolence to his parents in Michigan. Later, as a changed man, he reestablished his contacts. His letters to the faculty at McCallie were so profound that they rescinded his dismissal and gave him his high school diploma as part of the class of 1942.

So Bill Eerdmans believed on Jesus Christ, & he was saved, and born again. Ever since that time he has been a real Christian & has dedicated his life to serving Christ.[13] So among all those thousands of people, from all over Europe, we were brought together by God, & what joy it was to hear that he too had been saved by the Lord! When we had been at McCallie, neither of us cared for the Gospel of Jesus Christ & neither of us believed that Jesus, the Son of God, had died for our sins.

Jack and Bill traveled together on the train, in the staging area in Le Havre, France, crossing the English Channel on a ship, and on to Shrivenham, England. They were assigned to the same dorm and took ancient history and speech classes together. Together they started a Christian fellowship group to study the Bible, encourage other Christians, and witness to others, following the pattern that Jack experienced with the Princeton Evangelical Fellowship three years earlier. On August 3, Jack wrote his mother, "I have been studying the Bible with Bill quite a lot lately, & we are having a wonderful time studying & having prayer together."

This time with Bill Eerdmans, and reflection on God's providence, represented a major step forward in Jack's thinking and life commitment. He explained to his mother:

> *I have never been so happy as now, because God has told me that I am chosen to serve him.* So what else could I do but follow? God and Christ are real, and the Bible is true! I have done none of this myself, and none of it is conclusions from my own thinking. The truth is, I have failed to follow the light that has been before me all this time, & for that reason I have fallen away from Christ, especially after we reached Europe. And I never could understand why I was unhappy in this condition. But now God has opened my eyes again![14]

---

13. Bill returned to Grand Rapids, Michigan, to work with his father in the Christian book publishing industry. He eventually succeeded his father as president in 1963 and ran the company until age 90, when he stepped down in 2013.

14. Personal letter from John Whitcomb to his mother on July 26, 1945, from Shrivenham, England.

# A Good and Faithful Servant

On August 6, 1945, an American airplane released the first tactical atomic bomb on the city of Hiroshima, Japan. Two days later, the Soviets unleashed a vicious attack on Japanese-occupied areas in China, including Manchuria, Inner Mongolia, and northern Korea. The next day, another atomic bomb fell from an American airplane onto the city of Nagasaki, Japan, instantly evaporating 50,000 citizens. The emperor of Japan realized that his empire faced annihilation, and he suddenly sought peace. These shocking news headlines forecast a rapid end to war for the exhausted Allied armies in Europe. Jack immediately recognized the plummeting likelihood of being transferred to the China-Burma-India Theater. Transformation from U.S. Military service fighting the Axis powers to full-time Christian service fighting an invisible enemy would commence immediately.

On August 9, 1945, Bill gave a 10-minute talk on the wonderful work that the men could and *should* do for the Lord — in partial recognition of the free gift of salvation that He gave to each of us. Then, from 9:00–10:00 p.m., the men met in a dorm room for a prayer meeting and Bible discussion. The group included about 20 men and continued to flourish throughout the summer until Bill, and others, began receiving the long-anticipated order to return to the United States.

During the summer of 1945, Jack and Bill made numerous trips to London, about a two-hour train ride due east of Shrivenham. Shortly after reaching England, they made a trip to the capital city to attend church at the Metropolitan Tabernacle at Elephant and Castle. The large Independent Reformed Baptist church thrived under the preaching of Charles Haddon Spurgeon. But the famous building suffered almost complete destruction from Nazi fire-bombs on May 10, 1941, during the Battle of Britain. Only the facade, built using classic Greek architecture in honor of the Greek language used by God to communicate the New Testament to man, survived. Loss of the building did not destroy the congregation, as believers continued to worship in the basement. The building was eventually rebuilt and continues to thrive. Forty years in the future, Professor John Whitcomb would begin returning to the site of the Tabernacle many times again to support an ally in the faith, the Reverend Peter Masters.

Jack completed 80 hours of advanced language training at Shrivenham American University, with consistent grades of "Excellent." He was then selected to attend the Army University Center in England for an additional eight weeks of study.

Despite the destruction, Jack was amazed at the post-war gospel revival sweeping the city. This resulted in many return trips to London. An evangelical campaign called "This is the Victory" drew thousands of people to hear the gospel each night. Evangelist Tom Rees, for example, preached at Martin Lloyd-Jones' Westminster Central Hall with over 4,000 attending. Floods of people formed long lines in hopes of getting into the buildings for one of multiple meetings through the weekends. Bill and Jack participated in services through the "United Nations Gospel Team" and gave their testimonies. Bill recalled, "I stammered a bit while Jack, with his seven points and more, didn't."[15] Jack and Bill participated in a number of other additional gospel meetings throughout eastern and southern London. It was a fantastic experience.

It struck Jack that the "This is Victory" campaign originated and grew through the efforts of a U.S. Army sergeant and other U.S. servicemen. The movement stood in stark contrast to the liturgical formality of the clergy that Jack witnessed in the Anglican Church with his parents as a child. He explained to his parents that the revival featured "preachers who were not ministers, but have civil services jobs, are teachers, publishers, businessmen, servicemen, etc. None of us seem to go for the black robes and gowns very much!"[16] Many of these lay preachers may have come from the patterns established by Spurgeon, who stressed the study of Scripture by the common man, or the strong Plymouth Brethren influences in England, as illustrated in America by Donald Fullerton, founder of the Princeton Evangelical Fellowship who led Jack to the Lord.

Jack not only observed these meetings but also became an enthusiastic participant. On Sunday, September 2, 1945, for example, Jack met another American soldier at service in London who provided him with German gospel tracts. Jack learned that a group planned to help in an evening service in Bromley South on the southeastern side of greater London. "Twenty of us made up the group, including Canadians, Americans (soldiers, sailors, & officers), Australians,

---

15. Email from William Eerdmans to the author, January 16, 2015.
16. Personal letter from John Whitcomb to his mother and father, September 4, 1945.

Scotchmen, a Dutch sailor, British service women. We had a wonderful program. There were five boys in the congregation that were converted that night."[17]

On September 25, 1945, Jack packed his belongings and left Shrivenham, England, for Sinsheim, Germany, and the 909th Field Artillery Battalion. As planned, he obtained 40 hours of college credit and visited many historic sites in England.[18] But of greater significance was God's confirmation of Jack's calling to serve Him, with the "random" meeting of Bill Eerdmans, the encouragement of the strong preaching of Christian laymen in London, and the rallies of Allied soldiers serving in God's army through the United Nations Forces Witness Team. Jack's life purpose, direction, and mission became crystal clear and laser focused.

Years later, Jack and Bill would meet again and many times after that. This time it would be in Winona Lake, Indiana.

## Back to Germany and Position #54

The sudden end of WWII in August 1945 changed the direction from one of retooling to rapid demobilization. By October, the men were leaving at a rapid rate, resulting in continued reorganization and promotions to fill the vacancies.

In addition to his daily work at the phones in Sinsheim, Jack worked with Captain William Kilcoyne, Corporal Hartley Harrison, and Corporal William Wakeland to write a short book, *History of the 909th Field Artillery Battalion in World War II*.[19] He also worked on the battalion newspaper, the *Cannoneer's Post*, published weekly from July to November 1945. The battalion helped open a swimming pool and movie theater as some members of the unit systematically departed for home, based on the point system.

But Jack's heart was now different, with a renewed missionary spirit. He began in the house in which he was staying. The owners of the house had a son, Rainer Ehmann, who fought with the German Army, was captured, and held in a POW camp. He was released and traveled

---

17. Ibid.
18. On Labor Day, Jack visited Canterbury.
19. Captain William J. Kilcoyne, *History of the 909th Field Artillery Battalion in World War II* (Heidelberg, Germany: Dr. Johannes Horning, 1945), 59 pages (arrangement and layout by Tech 4 John Whitcomb, Cpl. Hartley Harrison, and Cpl. William Wakeland).

70 miles to his home by foot, only to find an American soldier living in his house. However, Jack and Rainer became friends, although no record of their friendship exists since Jack feared being fined, or worse, found "fraternizing with the enemy." Rainer was a broken man, exhausted and disillusioned, being lied to by the Nazis and witnessing the destruction of his country, the loss of his friends, and learning of the atrocities of his leaders. Jack worked with Rainer to improve his German and continuously witnessed to him.

For years, Jack kept in touch with Rainer, initially by sending food and other essentials, then with Christmas cards and occasional letters. In 1970, Jack returned to Germany and found a "Rainer Ehmann" in the Sinsheim phone book. He called the number and asked if Rainer Ehmann lived there. The answering party paused, then exclaimed "Johan!" Professor Whitcomb changed his itinerary to return to Sinsheim to see his old friend again. Rainer welcomed him to his home for a fine dinner and introduced him to his believing wife and three children. Professor Whitcomb provided some words of encouragement, some Christian literature, and bid farewell. One week later, Rainer dropped dead of a heart attack. Only God knows if they will meet again in heaven.

*Three-day Pass to the Bavarian Alps*

In mid-October, Jack learned of a trip to the Bavarian Alps at the Austrian-German border. On October 27, 1945, he and 40 other men from the Division jumped into 2 ½-ton army trucks and headed to a resort hotel in Oberjoch, the highest ski resort in Germany. Jack noted, *"We were assigned beds in a hotel, and had supper after washing up. The luxurious accommodations was [sic] really a surprise, after 20 months of crude conditions."* Previously the hotel was occupied by the 55th Fighter Group, who named the Haus Ingeburg Hotel the "Mustang Manor III" after their P51 Mustang fighters.

The following day was spent hiking and taking the cable-car two miles up the slopes. During the silent lift, they saw a wild fox resting near a tree, a deer, and finally mountain goats in the snow below them. Jack went on about his trip in a detailed letter typed to his parents on November 1, including visits to the Neuschwanstein Castle near Füssen, Germany (which served as the model for the Sleeping Beauty

Castle at Disneyland, Anaheim, California), and other sites. His description of post-war Bavaria was particularly interesting.

> In driving through this section of Germany, there are several features I noticed that set it apart from the rest of Germany. One of these is that there is no cultivation of the land down there. All the land is just grass, meadows, and rolling hills, with thousands of dairy cattle grazing. When we drove through the small villages in the evening we would have to drive very slowly to avoid bumping into the cows that fill the roads. You can hear the cowbells for miles, when they start their evening journey homeward. Also, the farmhouses are quite distinctive, looking just like the pictures of typical Alpine houses with murals painted on the outside walls, brown woodwork, balconies, overhanging roofs, and pots of red flowers in the windows. Also, the green shutters against the brown background is quite distinctive. The men wear green pants, jackets, and hats with feathers in them, while the children are dressed in leather shorts with little crossed suspenders on. Their dialect seems to be different from the Heidelberg area, and they tend to roll their R's like the Spanish.

Upon returning to Position #54, Jack completed his work on the Battalion history. Printing of 1,200 copies of the book was paid for with Battalion funds. In addition, he completed a "five color" map of the journey of the 909th Infantry Division from Liverpool, England, to the Elbe River.

On the home front, he learned that his parents decided to purchase a home in Washington, D.C. But the date of Jack's potential departure from Europe kept changing, so the date of the reunion after nearly two years (when Jack suffered from the mumps) remained a mystery.

*Trip to Poland*

In November 1945, Jack was selected as a translator to escort 250 displaced Poles from Mosbach, Germany, to Dziedzice, Poland (50 miles west of Cracow), on a train.[20] On November 16, Jack told his parents:

---

20. The details of the trip, including sightseeing in Prague on the way home, were published in *The Railsplitter* newspaper on December 9, 1945, by T/4 John Whitcomb, "30 Redlegs Escort Poles Home on Train — Enjoy Mixing Business, Pleasure."

In order to impress the Russian soldiers in this area we travel through (only a few Americans have gone this far East), we will wear dozens of metals, badges, insignia, emblems, patches, stripes and decorations, even though we have not earned them! Captain Fralish will be train commander, and he too will wear many medals, by order of General Bolling!

Letter of November 20, 1945:

I am sitting in a box-car at the Nürnberg station, and it is 1:30 AM. But so far it is the most comfortable trip I have made in Europe. There are only 3 of us in this new, clean box car, & we have two nice stoves set up. Also we each have cots, & places to hang clothes, etc. The other two persons in the car are Capt. Fralish, the train commander, and a sergeant, who is the Polish-Russian interpreter. I am supposed to be the German Interpreter.[21]

There were over 200 Polish people in the other 15 cars, brass bands and all! It took us until 4:00 PM to get loaded and arranged, putting telephone lines between the cars. Finally, after a few more Polish band selections, & cheers from the crowd, we left Mosbach.

Letter of November 21, 1945:

We have stopped here in Prague for a couple of hours, and another freight train full of Poles has just pulled up beside us. They left Stuttgart also on Monday evening, and are heading for the same place we are. They seem to be really getting the Poles out of Germany in a hurry. All of these box cars full of Poles are decorated with flags, pine branches and their Polish home town chalked on the sides.

Letter of November 23, 1945:

We arrived here in Poland early this morning, around 12:15 AM. It is now 4:00 AM and we are still sitting here in the railroad yard waiting for morning. . . .

---

21. Most of the Poles could speak German, so translation between English and German was useful and important.

# A Good and Faithful Servant

> Since I wrote to you from Prague day before yesterday, we have gone through Kolin, Pardubitz, Böhmisch, Trübau in Bohemia, Hohenstadt in the Sutedenland; Olomovc, Weisskirchen, and Mähr Ostrau in Moravia, and arrived here in Dziedzice in Poland this morning.

Letter of November 24, 1945:

> The situation in Poland is pretty bad. What the Germans left behind in the way of rolling stock,[22] cattle and goods of any kind, the Russians are now taking away. The result is that Poland is worse off than any other country in Europe. It was a strange situation to see trainloads of Poles coming back from Germany in a very happy, flag waving mood, while dozens of people who had seen the country begging us to let them ride with us to Czechoslovakia. We saw long lines of Polish repatriates standing before the main office building in Dziedzice, waiting to get their papers, etc. And mingling in every crowd were always the menacing looking Russian soldiers with their sub-machineguns slung over their shoulders, and wearing long overcoats, boots, and fur caps with the red star in the middle. . . .
>
> After everyone was unloaded, we said goodbye to the Polish train commander and our two Russian escorts. Then the train was then sidetracked, and each box car was cleaned out. In the meantime, many people came up to our car begging us for a ride across the border. A French couple, a Czech woman, a German PW, three Polish men and a British Soldier came by at different times to show us their papers and ask for a ride. But the Russians and Czechs have strict orders against anyone leaving Russian territory, so we could do nothing.

On the way back, there were many halts and train inspections in the Polish and Moravian areas until they got back to Prague. The train stopped for three days in Pilsen, Czechoslovakia, so the three Americans were able to get a passenger train back to Prague, Czechoslovakia, for a brief visit, even though it was in the Russian zone.

The world was changing.

---

22. Vehicles that can be used on a railroad track.

Bill

## Returned to the USA — Mission Complete

On January 11, 1946, Jack sat in the driver's seat of a parked truck in the port city of La Havre, France, immediately north of the Normandy beaches where thousands of service men died and where he entered the war 15 months earlier. He ate donuts while watching the German POWs, returning from detention centers in the United States, vacate the SS *Waterbury Victory* to make room for him and his brothers in arms. These German prisoners, following final processing, received freedom to return home to the rubble of the crushed Third Reich, just days before Jack himself would arrive to his new home at 612 North Abingdon St, Arlington, Virginia.

The soldiers, carrying their belongings in duffel bags, loaded the SS *Waterbury Victory* in short order, and by 16:00, the ship set sail and entered the English Channel. The ship was no luxury liner, and Jack was soon seasick. The SS *Waterbury Victory* was number 842 of 890 planned "Victory ships," the mass-produced cargo carriers that could be built in about a month.[23] The ships were small, about 450 feet long and 110 feet wide. With the abrupt end of the war, their utility ended, and most of them were mothballed. The SS *Waterbury Victory* only served the Navy for 83 days, was sold to a private company in 1947, and eventually scrapped.[24] For Jack, crossing the North Atlantic on choppy seas in January proved to be cold and miserable. Finally, on January 22, 1946, the Statue of Liberty passed by the vessel on the port side, indicating that American soil would soon be under foot.

Discharge from the U.S. Army followed standard protocol. The returning troops were transferred by ferry from the New York Harbor to Hoboken, New Jersey, then by train to Camp Kilmer, where Jack and 2.5 million other soldiers were processed. After two days, he was transferred to Fort Meade, Maryland. Finally, on Saturday, January 27, 1946, Jack received his mustering out pay of $1,000, a new uniform, ribbons, and signed discharge papers. He proceeded to the chapel to be officially discharged, while his parents watched from the balcony. After a happy reunion, the Whitcomb family drove to their new home.

---

23. See https://en.wikipedia.org/wiki/List_of_Victory_ships and ship photo https://ww2db.com/image.php?image_id=6993, accessed August 25, 2021.

24. See https://www.joc.com/maritime-news/ss-waterbury-victorys-war-service-commemorated_19950830.html and http://shipbuildinghistory.com/merchantships/2victory-ships.htm, accessed August 25, 2021.

# Chapter 11

# Mr. F.

"Therefore Stand!"
January 1946 to June 1948

## Return from War

Saturday, January 27, 1946, marked the end of Jack Whitcomb's service to Uncle Sam and a return to civilian life. But going to battle and returning as a veteran of a foreign war is different than going to summer camp. The camper is typically no different than when he left — except for a suntan, new temporary friends, some scrapes and burses, and perhaps a broken arm! In contrast, an individual returning from war often becomes a different person, having personally seen and experienced death and destruction of enemies and friends.

A P-47 Thunderbolt fighter pilot, interviewed for a documentary taped ~50 years after WWII, recalled the fighting experience with passion, emotion, and energy, and in incredible detail that was seared into his long-term memory. "After the war," he continued, "the rest of life seemed trivial and insignificant. I got married and sold life insurance." Another soldier from the 84th Infantry commented that, after fighting the Nazis, "the rest of my life was a footnote."

This was not the case with Jack. The amazing coincidence of meeting the converted and evangelistic Bill Eerdmans immediately after the fighting ended, his witnessing powerful revival services in London, and his recognition that God saved him *personally* for His service provided Jack with a purpose and direction that made *WWII* seem relatively insignificant! God taught him some unforgettable lessons of His divine providence and protection. For Jack, life's purpose extended far beyond fighting the Nazis — it would be fighting the invisible god of the Nazis and other, more sinister forms of evil on a *spiritual* battlefield. Indeed, "we wrestle not against flesh and blood, but against principalities, against powers, against the rulers of the darkness of this world, against spiritual wickedness in high places. Wherefore take unto you the whole armor of God, that ye may be able to withstand in the evil day, and having done all, to **stand**" (Ephesians 6:12–13; emphasis added).

The relationship between Jack Whitcomb and his family changed. No longer was he a quiet, observant boy, managed by servants and relegated to his room during house parties with Army brass. Jack became his own man, and he was on a mission that his parents could not understand or appreciate. His immediate plans included leading his parents and relatives to faith in Jesus Christ. His family, however, remained resistant to the gospel for many years, and only God knows which ones believed. Jack continued his witness to each of them as he contemplated the next step of his life's mission.

A Princeton University education lost its appeal during the three years Jack spent serving his country. Should he return to school or not? What was the value of a secular education to a missionary? These were the questions that Jack wrestled with in the winter and early spring of 1946.

## Advice of Donald B. Fullerton — Mr. F.

Jack sought out his old mentor and spiritual father, Donald Fullerton, to receive some wise, godly counsel. Mr. Fullerton recommended that he return to Princeton and complete his secular education and then consider seminary. Fullerton noted that God uses different people in His plan in different ways.[1] And although there are not many "wise according to the flesh" (1 Corinthians 1:26), there are *some*. God gives gifts to men, including gifting some as teachers "to equip the saints for works of service to the building up of the body of Christ" (Ephesians 4:8–12). The proper use of God's gifts requires training and hard work. For Jack, his intellectual gifts were obvious, and for Jack's specific future, Mr. Fullerton believed that he needed the best formal undergraduate

---

1. The Church, the body of Christ, has many members with different functions as summarized in Romans 12:4–8 and 1 Corinthians 12:4–31.

education, followed by the best possible seminary training. So, Jack Whitcomb returned to Princeton.

On March 1, 1946, Jack Whitcomb packed his belongings in his room at his parents' new home in Arlington, Virginia, and then boarded the train from Washington, D.C., to return him to Princeton, New Jersey. He checked in to school and carried his belongings to a new dorm room at 111 Joline Hall. George Shirk met him, a scholar from Irvington-on-Hudson near New York City, who became his new roommate. Jack found an old friend and classmate, Harry Brawner.[2] After a compelling invitation, Harry joined Jack for church on March 3, 1946 — the day before classes began. The hiatus in his formal educational process officially ended. Classes began, as did his participation in the Princeton Evangelical Fellowship (PEF).

The transition to student life during this period of time remains obscure, as the diary entries are sparse, and my dad's specific memories have faded. However, we know that the term continued until mid-June. On Sunday, March 31, 1946, Jack noted in his diary that he attended the University Chapel in the morning to hear Dean Wicks and then he went on to the PEF meeting at 3:00 p.m. In addition to old PEF friends, Jack made new friends though PEF, including John Rea, "a tall, blond haired, blue eyed young man that could have been Jack's twin."[3] On June 20, 1946, he returned to his family's new home in Arlington, Virginia.

## Summer of 1946

On Saturday, June 22, 1956, Jack Whitcomb celebrated his 22nd birthday with his parents. As a present, they took him on a short road trip to the University of Virginia at Charlottesville and the home of Thomas Jefferson at Monticello. The next day, Jack took his mother to the Metropolitan Baptist Church in Washington, D.C., to hear Dr. K. Owen White speak on Hebrews 11. His father found other things to do.

As new homeowners, remodeling and updating the house and yard became the focus of the Whitcomb family for the summer. The small house in Arlington, Virginia, underwent a thorough cleaning in

---

2. Alexander Harrison Brawner Jr., known as Harry, https://library.princeton.edu/mudd-dbs/memorials?qname=PAW&SUBJECT=Brawner&CLASS_YEAR=1945&CLASS_GRADE=, http://www.thomasleejones.com/memories-of-mother-and-other-things/.
3. Viewpoint of Sally Salvador, John Whitcomb's cousin, spring 2014.

anticipation of the arrival of "Nana," Jack's recently widowed paternal grandmother, who was coming to Washington, D.C., by train from St. Petersburg, Florida.

Nana arrived safely. She loved the Whitcombs' little house and took Jack's room during the stay — leaving him to sleep on the living room floor. The backyard arbor required an update. Colonel John C. Whitcomb Sr., as Chief of Staff of the 90th Infantry Division of Patton's Third Army during the liberation of France and Germany, embraced this new challenge in the USA with Jack as the infantry. The new task force successfully located and purchased green and white garden chairs and some porch furniture from Hecht's and Sears department stores.

Nana, who was Whit's mother, viewed religion with contempt. Jack recommended going to the Clarendon Baptist Church to hear the Rev. Frank L. Snyder preach on salvation — but in the end, he attended alone. On July 4, Nana celebrated her 77th birthday in the arbor. For the next few days, Jack tried, in vain, to witness to Nana. Nana finally left the house to stay with General and Mrs. Ireland in downtown Washington, D.C. To Jack's knowledge, she never came to know the Lord.

Jack began a full-fledged effort to serve the Lord in the nation's capital. Clarendon Baptist Church held evangelistic tent meetings from July 7 to 13, and Jack attended every service. On Tuesday evening, he convinced his father and mother to attend a meeting, but otherwise they refused, and he attended alone. At the end of the week, Nana completed her visit and boarded the train back to St. Petersburg. Not much progress was made in evangelism, and the Washington, D.C., area in July sweltered in heat and humidity. Jack and his mother decided to pack their things and return to Limekiln Lake, New York — exchanging the hot and humid atmosphere for a cool and relaxing environment. Whit remained in Arlington, Virginia, working in Georgetown, Maryland, and at the Pentagon.

### Limekiln Lake — 1946

Limekiln Lake remained a peaceful and quiet refuge from much of the world, but their old campsite suffered decay after years of neglect while the country — including Whit and Jack — focused on the destruction of Nazi Germany. The remainder of the summer included rebuilding the boat dock, fixing the porch screen and awning, and cleaning the campsite.

Jack's diary reflected the days of summer — a bad sunburn; a few odd jobs such as chopping wood for people; and helping at Kalil's Grocery;[4] with produce runs to the city to get milk, meat, and drinks — no comparison to the Red Ball Express.[5]

The family cottage, located across the lake from the store, required multiple trips by rowboat for various necessities, including newspapers, and additional trips for fun. Aunt Juliette, cousin Sally, and some friends from the New York City area came to visit from time to time. Jack entertained 9-year-old Sally by blowing bubbles, playing board games, and painting "Sunset Point" on a big rock near their cabin. Jack also enjoyed swimming across the Limekiln Lake. But in spite of surviving WWII, his mother insisted on accompanying Jack during his long-distance swims by rowing a boat alongside him. However, after several weeks, the rugged life and inconvenience of the remote vacation cottage lost their charm, and the family relocated to the Porcupine Lodge.

*Genealogical Chart of the Hebrew Kings*

The days at the lake also provided time for discussion with family and friends on various topics, and time to read. Jack caught up on his reading of world events, the history of Europe, French history, and the biblical books of 1 and 2 Samuel, 1 and 2 Kings, Isaiah, and John. On August 13, 1946, after studying 1 and 2 Kings, Jack began outlining a genealogical chart of the kings of Israel and Judah. This would be the first step in the development and publishing of his Bible Charts, which, with important revisions and new insights from the work of Dr. Edward Thiele[6] and others, became the standard tool for Old Testament

---

4. The diary entry of July 24, 1946, included the processes of selling butter at 90 cents per pound, steak at 85 cents per pound, frankfurters at 55 cents per pound, peaches at 25 cents, cheese at $1.00, eggs at 69 cents per dozen, milk at 20 cents a quart, bread at 15 cents a loaf, canned shrimp at $1.10 per can, and tomatoes at 35 cents a pound.
5. The Red Ball Express was a truck convoy system during WWII that supplied Allied forces moving quickly through Europe after breaking out from the D-Day beaches in Normandy in 1944. In order to expedite cargo to the front, trucks emblazoned with red balls followed a route similarly marked with a red ball. The Express operated 5,958 vehicles and carried about 12,500 tons of supplies a day. See Chapter 9.
6. Edward R. Thiele, Ph.D., was a missionary and scholar who published his doctoral thesis at the University of Chicago in biblical archaeology in 1943 and published his thesis in 1951 titled, "Mysterious Numbers of the Hebrew Kings." This solved the apparent discrepancy in the royal genealogies of Judah and Israel during the time of the divided kingdom by proving that the two nations used different methods of recording the king's year of accession to the throne.

Bible scholars. Over 1,000,000 copies were eventually printed as stand-alone charts or included in various study Bibles.

*Return to Washington, D.C. — Late Summer of 1946*

Jack and his mother left Limekiln Lake on August 15 and returned to Arlington via Harrington Park, New Jersey, arriving in the capital late on August 16. Jack attended a Youth for Christ rally the next day, featuring Clifford Lewis of Nashville, Tennessee. The next day, Sunday, Jack visited the Wallace Memorial United Presbyterian Church to hear C.E. Hawthorn while his mother tended to the house and his father worked in the yard.

Jack spent the next two days helping his father build a back porch and retaining wall. Initially, he hauled rocks from the creek bed to the back porch, but he sprained his right foot on the front steps and couldn't walk. He resigned himself to mixing cement while hopping on one leg. He decided that construction was *not* his thing and that he would seek opportunities to serve the Lord in ways that were more reminiscent of the gospel teams that he so enjoyed while he was in England the previous summer.

Although he loved his dad, Jack believed that his time was better spent serving the Lord directly rather than undertaking home construction projects — which was neither his gift nor his interest. He therefore visited the Service Men's Victory Center in Washington, D.C., to find out about opportunities for Christian service in the area. They recommended *construction work* at the new Washington Bible Institute. *"So,"* he wrote, *"I went over and told them I would work for a month without pay."*

## Washington Bible Institute

The Washington Bible Institute (WBI) was a fledgling organization that was formed between 1938 and 1940 with the merger of three Washington area Bible schools: Washington Bible College, The American Home Bible Institute, and The Washington School of the Bible.[7] The founding president resigned in 1944 to work with servicemen returning from

---

7. History of Washington Bible Institute: https://www.lbc.edu/dc/history/. Washington Bible College and Capital Bible Seminary ceased operations in January 2013, and their academic program was acquired by Lancaster Bible College, which continues to provide college and seminary education.

war, and George A. Miles became president. The new school faced many challenges, but they did own some facilities on the northeastern side of Washington, D.C. The facilities required major renovation. Jack joined the cause — demolishing old walls and building new rooms to become useful classrooms. Although he disliked construction, this appeared to be where God wanted him for now. He then changed his attitude about this non-scholarly manual labor and decided to contribute his efforts to this project to the best of his abilities.

While the details of Jack's efforts are not important, the time that Jack spent with George Miles and other Christian workers proved invaluable. Indeed, Jack benefited from daily personal time with Mr. Miles, as he would swing by Jack's house in Arlington, Virginia, each morning to drive him to WBI and drive him home each night. In addition, Mr. Miles involved Jack, and the other young workers, in various Christian activities such as Youth for Christ rallies, witnessing to men on chain gangs, and encouraging young believers in their faith. Specifically, Jack learned of the importance of structured, systematic Christian education as he, Mr. Miles, and others prepared the new facilities. By mid-September, the renovations were sufficient to move desks and chairs into a classroom so that the fall semester in Washington, D.C., could begin.

The work of Jack Whitcomb in the summer of 1946 at WBI contributed in a small but important way to a great work of God. Under the leadership of Mr. Miles, the Washington Bible Institute flourished. In 1956, the name was changed to Washington Bible College, and it received accreditation as a school of higher education. In 1958, Capital Bible Seminary was founded as an extension of the college. Years later, Professor Whitcomb would return to Washington, D.C. on many occasions — not to wield a hammer, but the Sword of the Lord — teaching seminary students from the Word of God. In 1992, the WBI legacy became even more precious, as one of Professor Whitcomb's close friends and colleagues from Grace Seminary, Dr. John Sproule, became the fourth president of Capital Bible Seminary.

## "Therefore Stand"

During the evenings of August and September 1946, after a day of construction work at WBI, Jack studied his Bible and read various

Christian books. On August 28, he began reading a book by Wilbur Smith,[8] *Therefore Stand.* The book, considered the greatest work of Wilbur Smith and one of the great Christian books of the 20th century, focused on Christian apologetics in an age of liberalism[9] and higher criticism[10] that appeared to be unanswered by Bible-believing Christians. The book is credited as helping to spark an international revival of evangelical scholarship. This 522-page masterpiece greatly impacted the young Jack Whitcomb.

The premise of the book was that conservative Christians abandoned their duty to biblical scholarship and defending the faith, resulting in the destruction of the faith by liberal theologians. On September 4, for example, Jack studied Smith's treatment of the account of Paul's addressing the secular scholars on Mars Hill (Acts 17:16–33). Interpretation of this passage formed the premise of Smith's argument for approaching unbelievers with thoughtful and unanswerable arguments related to God, beginning with areas of common ground shared

8. Wilbur Smith taught at the Moody Institute from 1938–1947. He resigned from Moody to join Charles Fuller and Harold Ockenga in founding Fuller Theological Seminary and subsequently taught there from 1947–1963. He later left Fuller in protest to the erosion of their stand on biblical inerrancy. He concluded his 33-year collegiate teaching career at Trinity Evangelical Divinity School from 1963–1971.

9. The term "liberalism" is used here in terms of biblical interpretation and theological discipline, rather than in a political sense. Liberalism in theology allows everyone to interpret the Bible as they wish, without criticism or opposition. In contrast, "conservative" theology insists on Divine inspiration and inerrancy of the Scriptures (in the original), and on careful study of the historical, grammatical, and contextual elements to correctly understand the Word of God, with the intention of obeying it (Acts 17:11). The natural consequence of liberal thinking is that there is no such thing as "heresy" and that everyone should "do what is right in their own eyes" (cf. Judges 17:6, 21:25). The challenge with the conservative position is in determining where the line is drawn between truth and error, what denotes heresy, and where the authority lies for theological discipline. Liberal politics, in contrast, believes that people are inherently good and focuses on freedom from any restrictions imposed by authority on one's way of life or behavior and believes in the role of the government in ameliorating social or economic inequities. Conservative politics recognizes that humans are flawed and that immorality and laziness lead to destruction. They focus on encouraging personal responsibility in moral, ethical, and social settings, with the role of government limited to providing national defense, supporting an effective infrastructure for community services, and enforcing just laws by punishing evil-doers. Theological and political views of "liberal" and "conservative" tend to overlap in the thinking and practice of many people, but they are not the same.

10. "Higher criticism" of the Bible focuses on searching for evidence that the Scriptures are not true. "Lower criticism" of the Bible focuses on comparison of various copies of the Bible to help determine words of the original text.

with the unbeliever. Smith argues that conservative Christians abandoned their duty to scholarship, and therefore, true Christianity continued losing the battle of ideas and thought to intellectual theological liberals.

*Therefore Stand* focused on three areas of crisis among Bible-believing Christians: the Resurrection of Jesus Christ, the creation of the universe, and the final judgment. Smith sought to provide as much information as possible to his readers with extensive quotations from leading scholars, since many of the potential readers lacked access to scholarly libraries.

While the entire book contains valuable material, the chapter on the "Creation of the Universe" deserves special attention. The chapter contains two sections. The first section provided strong arguments for the greatness, the omnipotence, and the omniscience of the Most High God. The second section wrestled skillfully, but inadequately, with the problem of the fossil dinosaurs and (unquestioned) scientific evidence of an earth thought to exist for billions of years. Smith argued for the "gap theory" to explain these observations and theories.

The book concluded with a call to action — and Jack responded. His diaries document a transformation from a more casual observer and general supporter to a motivated man of action. September 1946 marks the beginning of intense, passionate, unrelenting, and tireless dedication to scholarship and to reaching others for Christ, even above and beyond the efforts of Donald Fullerton. Smith fired the starting gun, and Jack leaped out of the starting blocks, like a rocket fired from a cannon, into the race. And he never stopped.

*Therefore Stand* provided some strong and inspiring perspectives, but years later, Jack became uncertain about the validity of some of the arguments. With time, experience, and consideration of an alternative view of biblical apologetics (Chapter 17), Professor Whitcomb recognized that pure intellectual arguments were ineffective in bringing unbelievers to Christ. It was not that they were spiritually ignorant or misguided — they were enemies of God and spiritually dead! The most effective answers to unbelievers came through faithfully preaching the gospel and trusting the Holy Spirit to bring conviction and salvation — and *then* the arguments of apologetics could work effectively in their new mind, being alive in a new relationship with God, and with a new ability to understand the Scriptures with the Holy Spirit as their guide and helper. Skillful and accurate biblical arguments played an important role in different ways for believers than convincing the unbeliever — it exposed the error of false teaching and strengthened the faith of true believers. Thus, while the issue of using intelligent arguments as the basis of evangelism proves inadequate, it remains central in the area of apologetics — to be able to give an answer, defense, argument, or explanation (Greek, *apologia*) for the hope that is in you (1 Peter 3:15). Jack helped prove this point with the writing of *The Genesis Flood*. But the value and use of these approaches rest in believers, not unbelievers.

Jack now understood why he was at Princeton — he had a rare opportunity to master humanistic arguments as a target for destruction by correct biblical arguments (2 Corinthians 10:2–5). Furthermore, he needed to act, using his opportunities on the Princeton campus with students and alumni to bring others to a better understanding of Christ and His Great Commission.

Jack Whitcomb returned to Princeton for the fall 1946 semester with a new perspective and urgency to reach others on campus for Christ and to begin the life-long discipleship process. Rather than only being a participant in the PEF meetings, Jack now stepped into action, actively and tirelessly promoting the spiritual programs and emerging as a leader by example. He joined forces with John (Johnnie) Rea, his close friend and classmate with a similar passion and dedication to the work of the Lord.

## Mr. F.

Jack desperately needed the advice, guidance, and mentorship of Donald Fullerton (see short biography in Chapter 7). Fullerton, (referred to as Mr. F. in Dr. Whitcomb's diary) took on an intensifying role as Jack's spiritual father — much as Paul served as Timothy's spiritual father (2 Timothy 1:2). Mr. Fullerton not only provided teaching and advice, but he taught by example. Jack would continue to work closely with Mr. Fullerton until his death on April 9, 1985. The humble teaching and commitment to students at Princeton by Mr. F. made such a profound and lasting impact on Jack and other students who went into full-time ministry that Professor Whitcomb succeeded in securing an honorary Doctor of Divinity degree for Donald Fullerton at Grace

Seminary. Professor Whitcomb also personally honored Dr. Fullerton by naming his second son Donald.

**Jack and Johnnie Energize the PEF**

In the fall of 1946, Jack Whitcomb became proactive in PEF and became a catalyst for new growth and effectiveness on the campus of Princeton University. In addition to regular college classes, he documented in his diary his own personal Bible study and memorization, reading essential Christian literature, visiting friends and other students on campus, and involvement in multiple works of service on a daily basis.

Jack and his colleagues began by formalizing a schedule for the year, including prayer meetings on Wednesday and Bible classes on Thursday led by Jack and other students in the dorm, and the regular PEF Bible class on Sunday afternoons taught by Donald Fullerton. Jack, Johnnie Rea, and other students also volunteered to distribute invitations for students to join PEF and set up the room for the weekly Bible study.

Jack's diary entries from late September and October 1946 illustrate the renewed zeal, attention to personal growth, and outreach, in addition to his heavy academic work as a Princeton University student.

*Diary entries during the first six weeks of class at Princeton — Fall 1946*

Bolded names are people that Jack met or reached out to.
- September 26, 1946 (Thursday) – *"After History 311 precept . . . I spoke to **Prof. Mommsen** about the historical certainty of the Resurrection, & he promised to read part of 'Therefore Stand' which I borrowed from Art." At our 7:30 weekly Bible Class, Johnnie taught from I Peter 1. Then 4 of us distributed PEF cards in half of the dorms."*
- September 27, 1946 (Friday) – *"In the afternoon I gave out more invitation cards. To Patton, 'O1. & Laughlin Halls."*
- September 28, 1946 (Saturday) – *"Studied Leviticus after supper. **David Miller** came by for a couple of hours in the evening."*
- September 29, 1946 (Sunday) – *"**Johnnie Rea, David Hostetler**, and I went to the Second Presby Church to hear Dr. Charles*

*Wilson preach on the Restoration Fund. I called on **George Shirk** after lunch, but he wasn't in. At 2:00 we went up to arrange the room and Murray Dodge for our meeting. Mr. Fullerton spoke on John 5:30-47 after we sang hymns at the piano. **Bob Dickerson, Herb Schwartz, Garry Glover, Bud Gammon** and **Bob Dunn** were there. At 7:30 Mr. Fullerton took Dave and me to New Brunswick to the Bible Church and spoke to Rev. Malmberg about teaching a class."*

- September 30, 1946 (Monday) – *"History 311 lecture Prof. Mommsen gave 'Therefore Stand' as one of the outside reading options on the Resurrection. Our prayer meeting[11] was at 7:30."*
- October 1, 1946 (Tuesday) – *"Prof. Mommsen lectured on the beginnings of the Church."*
- October 2, 1946 (Wednesday) – [only notes on schoolwork – e.g., History 313].
- October 3, 1946 (Thursday) – *"In the evening we had our first student Bible class at Murray Dodge. **White, Fan Syclen** and **Mr. Jolleff** came. We discussed 1 Tim 1."*
- October 4, 1946 (Friday) – *"We had our prayer meeting at 7:30."*
- October 5, 1946 (Saturday) – *"Did some Bible study & memory work with Johnnie in the evening. **George Slunk** called and stayed till midnight."*
- October 6, 1946 (Sunday) – *"I went to Trenton at 9:03 with **Art Schuler & Olin**. We attended a 'rally' service at the Church of the Open Bible. Came back at 1:00, having had lunch there. I called on **George Slunk**, & invited him to Bible Class. Mr. Fullerton spoke on Leviticus types of Christ because of the Jewish New Year was recently celebrated. Two new fellows came, one being **Lenox Palin**,[12] & the **other** one still in the Army. We*

11. Prayer meeting is abbreviated as "pm" or "p.m." throughout.
12. Lenox G. Palin was a Princeton football star who went on to the ministry, attending Fullerton Seminary. He pastored congregations in New Jersey; two in southern California; and the Calvary Bible Church in Neenah, Wisconsin, near Lake Winnebago and Oshkosh from 1986–2000 (https://cbcneenah.org/), and he finally retired in southern California where he could be close to family and serve as a part-time pastor to senior citizens. During his tenure in Wisconsin, the church grew significantly, resulting in the decision to purchase property and build a new church. In addition to leading the building program, he had a heart for missions, resulting in increased commitment to missions. He died on May 17, 2018, https://paw.princeton.edu/memorial/lenox-g-pal-in-50, accessed on August 26, 2021.

*talked awhile at our room & studied all evening."*

- October 7, 1946 (Monday) – *"I called on **Harold Davenport** at the Seminary and he gave me some pamphlets."*
- October 8, 1946 (Tuesday) – *"We had our prayer meeting at 7:30 & seven attended. I studied 1 Tim. 2 & Numbers at the library."*
- October 9, 1946 (Wednesday) – *"Van Dusen of Union [Seminary][13] spoke on the ecumenical movement. I went with **Konrad Mueller.**"*
- October 10, 1946 (Thursday) – *"Mr. Harbison lectured on Divine Right & Sovereignty. . . . During the afternoon I read a few chapters on 'The balance of Tomorrow' by Strausz-Hupe & prepared my paper on 1 Timothy 2. We had our Bible Class in Rev. McClain's office, & 8 attended."*
- October 11, 1946 (Friday) – *"For History 313, I read a very interesting essay by Thomas Aquinas on the relation of faith to reason. . . . We had an evening p.m. and I studied 1 Peter."*
- October 12, 1946 (Saturday) – *"**Olin, Johnnie** and I bicycled over to the Penns Neck to see if the Baptist Church there needed any help in SS."*
- October 13, 1946 (Sunday) – *"Johnnie and I took the train to P.J. and walked back to Penns Neck to attend the Princeton Baptist Church. Rev Chew was a very modernistic minister.[14] Got a ride back. I called on **Fred Beebe** in 12 M. Dod Hall. At the 2:30 meeting our regular group + **Lennox Palin** came. After supper I cycled over to Plainsboro to attend the Young People's Meeting at 7:30. Rev McClure was an excellent fundamental minister. I determined to go there on Sundays and help out with classes."*
- October 14, 1946 (Monday) – *"During Mr. Estey's History 313 precept we discussed the weakening of the Church during the*

---

13. Henry Pitney Van Dusen, Ph.D., was a theologically liberal theologian who was the new president of Union Theological Seminary and a leader in the ecumenical movement. He played a prominent part in the founding of the World Council of Churches. See https://www.bu.edu/missiology/missionary-biography/t-u-v/van-dusen-henry-pitney-1897-1975/, accessed August 26, 2021.

14. Even as a young Christian, John Whitcomb had conviction and discernment; he immediately terminated his involvement with this church and moved on to another one that was committed to accurately teaching and following the Word of God.

*14th & 15th centuries. Mr. Mommsen gave a lecture on Augustine & his theology.. . . . I stamped 'Bible Class' on some John's Gospels for library distribution."*

- October 15, 1946 (Tuesday) – *"I got a nice letter from Dannie James & Stewart Anderson, who were London Gospel team friends.. . . . After prayer meeting I studied Augustine's Confessions at the Library.* **Thompson** *asked me questions concerning his conception of good & evil."*
- October 16, 1946 (Wednesday) – *"Mr. Harbison gave a lecture on Church history during the 14th & 15th centuries. . . .* **Ken Duprey** *came by in the evening during our prayer meeting and argued against Christianity."*
- October 17, 1946 (Thursday) – *"Spent some time preparing my I Timothy 3 lesson for tonight. . . . At the Bible class.* **Wallace Ham** *came."*
- October 18, 1946 (Friday) – *"Johnnie Rea and I cycled over to Rocky Hill (4 mi.) and called on Mrs. Gooselink, the Dutch Reformed Minister's wife.* **Herb Schwartz** *came over for PM and spent the evening talking to me."*
- October 19, 1946 (Saturday) – *"Johnnie and I discussed geography, and after supper, church history. The* **YOKANA brothers** *called on me."*
- October 20, 1946 (Sunday) – *"Johnnie and I cycled over to Plainsboro, and Johnnie led a girl's SS Class. I called on* **B. Caldwell,** *but not in, also* **John Witherspoon.** *At the PEF meeting Mr. Fullerton spoke on Isaiah 53 fulfilled in the N.T.* **Wallace Ham & Walli VanSiclen** *were there. After supper I borrowed Johnnie's bike and went to the Young People's meeting at Plainsboro. Returned early and typed letters to missionary societies. . . . We looked over the PEF files."*
- October 21, 1946 (Monday) – *"Had orange juice at Balt with* **Dave Baird** *& went to History 313 precept. Discussed medieval outlook on life."*
- October 22, 1946 (Tuesday) – *"I went out for football, & we won by default."*
- October 23, 1946 (Wednesday) – *"Spent the evening bickering for Court Club."*

- <u>October 24, 1946</u> (Thursday)– *"During History 311 we had an interesting discussion of Church authority & a Catholic was there. . . . I spoke with* **Harry Brawner** *about Christianity at the Club. . . . Prepared I Tim 4, & played football for Court. At the 7:30 meeting no new men came."*
- <u>October 25, 1946</u> (Friday) – *"At Zavelle's bookstore I looked over their second-hand Christian books in the basement. Bought Ploetz' 'Epitome of Universal History'. . . . Had a p.m."*
- <u>October 26, 1946</u> (Saturday) – *"***Jonnie Rea** *& I went up to Za-velle's to make a list of the good Christian books."*
- <u>October 27, 1946</u> (Sunday) – *"I had breakfast at Charter with Johnnie & we cycled over to Plainsboro for SS & Church. After lunch I called on* **Fred Beebe** *and* **John Witherspoon**. *At the meeting 20 people came – 3 seminary students, Olin's parents,* **Dwight Livingston**, *three girls, Rev. McCloy,* **Walli VanSiclen** *& our group.* **Mr. Fullerton had a talk with Fuller about the Seminary,**[15] *and came to our room. I cycled over to Plainsboro and attended the C.E. Class on a discussion of John 5."*
- <u>October 28, 1946</u> (Monday) – *"At Zavelle's I bought 4 Christian books. . . . At p.m.* **Ken Duprey** *came around & stayed all evening reading up on apologetics & criticizing it."*
- <u>October 29, 1946</u> (Tuesday) – *"After p.m.* **Paul** *and I walked over to the Grad. School to visit his brother, but he wasn't there."*
- <u>October 30, 1946</u> (Wednesday) – *"In the evening I ran down to Wash. Rd. & back with* **Dave** *[Hostetler] &* **Johnnie** *[Rea] after p.m."*
- <u>October 31, 1946</u> (Thursday) – *"Spoke to Dean Brown about taking Greek in the Seminary. Went over & called on Dean Roberts. Prepared I Tim. 5 for tonight. At the meeting* **Ernie Wright** *stayed. Afterwards the 4 of us had a long talk about prayer and fellowship in the PEF."*

---

15. This was a critical meeting. Mr. Fullerton had major concerns about Princeton Seminary and was searching for an alternative. Fuller Seminary was starting, and Wilbur Smith, author of *Therefore Stand*, was leaving Moody Bible Institute to join the seminary. Jack was very interested in going to Fuller to study under Smith, but after the meeting between Fullerton and Fuller, Fullerton sensed some major problems and steered students from then on to Grace Theological Seminary to be trained by Alva J. McClain and company. Professor Whitcomb later used the case of Fuller Seminary as an illustration of the dangers of evangelicalism and a compromise on the authority of Scripture.

## Lifelong Habits

Maxwell Maltz, M.D., a plastic surgeon in the mid-20th century, is credited for popularizing the self-help idea that "it takes 21 days to form a new habit."[16] Whether or not this statement is true, or applies in all situations, is debatable. What is not debated is that the new patterns established by John C. Whitcomb Jr. during the fall of 1946 continued for the rest of his life.

Two complementary personal attributes of Professor Whitcomb came together at this time. First, Whitcomb already displayed incredible stamina — he could work tirelessly, 18 hours per day, 7 days a week. Second, his intelligence, focus, and attention to detail allowed complex areas of knowledge to be mastered. Wilbur Smith's book *Therefore Stand* both clarified and focused Professor Whitcomb in developing and using his gifts, abilities, and divine calling. The guidance and encouragement of Mr. F., combined with Jack's conviction of a personal call to action from the Lord, resulted in an amazing, 75+-year marathon of service.

Professor Whitcomb was once asked about how he maintained the frenetic pace of his daily life in service to the Lord. He answered,

> It was like I hit the road running from the time I was born. Endless moving. I almost get nervous when I am not moving somewhere. I start packing when I am unpacking or else I feel like I am out of the will of God.[17]

The key was not just movement but moving forward with a Divine purpose and enablement. It was discerning areas of need within Christianity, determining if this was an area where he was gifted, and giving 100% effort to meet the need.

*Jack Helps Revolutionize the Princeton Evangelical Fellowship*

After establishing a pattern of weekly prayer meetings and Bible studies, Jack, Johnny Rea, Olin Ellis, and a few Christian friends began thinking more broadly and strategically about the needs and opportunities to evangelize and disciple students at Princeton. They planned

---

16. From James Clear, "How Long Does it Actually Take to Form a New Habit? (Backed by Science)," http://jamesclear.com/new-habit, accessed February 6, 2016.

17. Interview of John Whitcomb by Paul Scharf, May 2003.

series of initiatives to expand the influence of the PEF throughout the campus and direct more students to personal faith in Christ, centered on the solid Bible teaching of Donald Fullerton. As the fall semester progressed, Jack's strategic plans were initiated.

First, PEF needed resources to support new initiatives. For financial and prayer support of PEF, Jack decided to reach out to former students touched by Mr. F. *"At Nassau Hall,"* he wrote in his diary, *"I got the addresses of 50 Alumni interested in the PEF."* Each would be sent a letter, approved by Donald Fullerton. This effort proved to be invaluable for the success of future programs through both prayer and monetary support.

Second, Jack's own experience of conversion as a college freshman highlighted the need to focus evangelistic efforts on new students. He developed a form letter to be signed by himself and other upper classmen to be sent to each student as they entered Princeton — just as Bob Caldwell, John Parks, David McCallie, David Marshall, Christy Wilson, and Bob Marshburn had reached out to him. *"At the First National Bank,"* Jack noted in his diary, *"I ordered 800 copies of our form letter to be mimeographed. I bought paper and envelopes at Zavelles."* The next day, he began stamping Gospel of John booklets and stuffing them into envelopes. He then went to the registrar's office and *"found that there were 611 members of the Class of 1950."* Since multiple copies of the Gospel were left over, he went to the library and passed them out to other classmates.

Third, Jack, Johnny, and other members of PEF continued to invite and encourage other Princeton students to attend Mr. Fullerton's Sunday afternoon Bible studies, to participate in prayer meetings in the dorm, and to make personal visits to students. Of note, throughout Jack's diary are comments about all the people that he went to call on, all that came to him, and the fact that they often spent several hours in deep discussions about the Bible and related topics.

By the end of the fall semester, there was a palpable change in the visibility and effectiveness of the PEF.

When Jack returned to Princeton from Christmas vacation on January 5, 1947, he was met by Mr. Fullerton. Fullerton wanted to discuss PEF meetings that were planned for the next month and to think more broadly and strategically about the future as Jack had suggested in the fall. Fullerton, following up and endorsing Jack's plans, also provided a more extensive list of names of potential PEF supporters. Jack would obtain their addresses from the alumni office.

The next day, Jack obtained the addresses of *"friends of PEF."* He also picked up the 800 mimeographed letters directed to the Class of 1950 and 300 invitation cards. Working with Olin Ellis, they personally signed the letters to the freshmen and sent them out.

## The God of Creation

Jack was also considering ways to attract and engage the broader Princeton community. He learned of a film that was produced by Moody Bible Institute (specifically, the Moody Institute of Science) called *The God of Creation*.[18] On January 24, 1947, he wrote to Moody to get information on renting the film. The response from Moody was positive, and on Monday, February 24, Jack presented his idea to the group, and they discussed having an evening showing of the film on campus.

The film, *God of Creation*, was the first of a series of 39 educational films, produced by a Moody Bible Institute graduate and former pastor, Irwin A. Moon.[19] While most fundamentalists were convinced that the study of science leads directly to atheism, Moon believed the opposite to be true and founded the Moody Institute of Science, a division of Moody Bible Institute. The revolutionary approach of film series directed by Moon was rapidly embraced by Christian believers worldwide. Between 1947 and 1948, for example, the film was shown 9,000 times in churches and schools to over 1.4 million people.[20]

Jack Whitcomb's plan was approved, and the date of Tuesday, April 29, 1947, was set for the showing. Over 200 came, and attendees took 70 Gospels of John. At the prayer meeting the following Wednesday, they decided to show the film again on May 19, and Jack sent Moody Bible Institute an additional $10 as a rental fee.

Monday, May 19, 1949, was set for the second showing. Jack ordered 25 new placards to advertise the film. They got approval to show

18. The film can be viewed on YouTube, https://www.youtube.com/watch?v=Om8w8f3aBnA.
19. Irwin Moon obituary, http://articles.chicagotribune.com/1986-05-24/news/8602070324_1_rev-moon-educational-films-moody-bible-institute.
20. James Gilbert, *Redeeming Culture: American Religion in an Age of Science* (Chicago, IL: The University of Chicago Press, 1997), 135, accessed January 2016.

the film in the Frick Chemistry building auditorium again. The group sent out invitations and, one week before the showing, posted placards for the film throughout the campus.

The event became a highlight of PEF history. Jack Whitcomb noted in his diary that evening, *"At 7:30 we showed 'The God of Creation' at Frick. Over two hundred came, including Albert Einstein."* Seeing Einstein leaving the building after the showing, Jack walked up to him, gave him a Gospel of John, and thanked him for coming. Einstein thanked Jack for the offer and took the Gospel of John.

The report of the PEF to the Moody Institute of Science about the showing also documents this event. "Among those who came was Albert Einstein, and the audience, which saw him come in was greatly impressed by the reference to him that was made in the film. Afterwards over seventy Gospels of John were distributed."[21]

While the showing of *The God of Creation* remained a highlight of the spring semester, Jack's diary records the continuous seven-day-a-week pattern of systematically studying for school, mastering the Scriptures by focusing on one book at a time, and continually reaching out in evangelism to students and encouragement of friends.

The transformation of Jack over the 24 months from summer 1945 to spring 1947 were remarkable, changing from a discouraged young Christian to a sterling example of a student, who was 100% committed to Christianity, the Bible, and Christ. Even Bob Caldwell, the McCallie Military Academy graduate who, as a sophomore, met Jack Whitcomb as a freshman and invited him to Donald Fullerton's Bible studies, now sought out his younger friend for advice. Bob believed that he was a born-again Christian but, after seeing the transformation in John Whitcomb's life, felt that he had no power in his own Christian life. Jack spoke to him, encouraging him and urging him to join his colleagues in Christian service through participating in the PEF.

Donald Fullerton was a gifted Bible teacher, but he also developed very strong personal father-son relationships with a few of the students based on their mutual love of Christ and His Word. This was the case before WWII with Dave Marshall, whom Jack thought was Mr. F.'s child, as he kept referring to him as "my

---

21. Ibid.

son." Mr. Fullerton poured his life into Dave, and it was mutually beneficial.[22] During the spring of 1947, Donald Fullerton began pouring his life and energy into Jack Whitcomb and Johnny Rea. Johnny Rea and Jack began joining Mr. Fullerton regularly for Sunday evening dinner following the PEF meetings. The evening would continue either by taking Mr. Fullerton to the room of a classmate for a special visit or to spend hours talking about things related to Christ, the Christian life, or the future.

The transformation of the PEF from a Sunday afternoon Bible study to a major Christian campus ministry through the efforts of Jack and others also inspired Mr. Fullerton. Fullerton began spending much more time at Princeton, especially with Jack. He began visiting for entire weekends rather than a few hours on Sunday afternoon, and began inviting Jack to his home in Plainfield, New Jersey, or to accompany him for special events in the area.

## Jack Whitcomb Becomes the Leader of PEF

In May 1947, the PEF had an election of officers for the new academic year. Jack records the outcome,[23] *"Paul Kent is secretary, Ernie Wright the Treasurer, and I am pres."*

As the official PEF president, Jack began reviewing and sorting books and files which were largely disorganized. Among other things, Jack found a copy of the PEF Constitution.[24] Jack decided to institute a series of additional upgrades and changes to PEF.

- The Constitution was copied and distributed to the leaders as a foundation for their program.
- A library was needed to provide access of important Christian books to PEF members. Jack asked Donald Fullerton to help by contributing some key evangelical books to the library. All of the books in the PEF library would be stamped with Fullerton's name.[25]
- An official letter of invitation to PEF would be delivered to all freshman each year.

---

22. Letter to the author from Judge Paul Pressler, August 19, 2016.
23. John Whitcomb diary entry, May 20, 1947.
24. John Whitcomb diary entry, May 29, 1947.
25. John Whitcomb diary entries, May 29, 1947, and September 2, 1947.

- Specific follow-up plans would be in place for all students who responded to the letters and other invitations.
- A series of Christian leaders would be invited to speak on campus.
- The film series would be continued.
- The PEF office would obtain a telephone.
- An alumni-student banquet would be established.

In addition, Jack encouraged his colleagues to officially join the PEF. As the spring semester ended, Jack took pictures of the PEF students and made copies for everyone. He then wrote to each of them individually, enclosing copies of the photographs.

*PEF – Fall Semester, 1947*

Jack returned to Princeton during the summer in order to graduate in June 1948. He used the time to prepare for the academic year and the incoming freshman students. Jack asked Mr. Fullerton to draft an alumni letter to be mimeographed, signed, and mailed. On August 21, 1947, Jack found that it would only cost $13.50 to have 900 freshmen letters printed, and the presses rolled.

When the students arrived, Jack led the effort to visit all of the dorms to pass out letters of invitation and to meet the new students. At their regular Thursday evening dormitory Bible study, seven freshmen came and *"seemed interested."* On Sunday, five new students came to hear Mr. Fullerton speak. The organization and planning were paying off.

*PEF Film – God of the Atom*

After the success of the *God of Creation* film in the spring, the PEF decided to order another film from the Moody Institute of Science called *God of the Atom.* Jack again printed placards and distributed them around campus. The film was shown on October 16, 1947. Jack noted, *"About 300 came for the 1ˢᵗ showing, and 180 for the second. I made a short speech about the PEF before each. 110 booklets were taken."*

**Opposition to PEF**

*Faculty evolutionist.* The PEF had become highly visible on campus! But, the day after showing *The God of the Atom*, as Jack removed the placards from the graduate school and college, *"a professor accosted me at the station about our movie.*" Then, on October 23, Jack noted in his diary, *"Got a letter from Prof. Field of the geology department,*[26] *who complained about our movie, God of the Atom. I called him up.*" On November 19, 1947, after meeting with Professor Field, Jack sent him a letter. No resolution was noted.

*Gospel Bombs.* The growing notoriety and effectiveness of PEF on campus also raised opposition from the Dean and the President of Princeton Seminary. Some of the PEF students created the "Gospel Bomb," a tract, invitation card, and gospel that were wrapped in red cellophane and distributed on campus. About 120 students responded to the "bomb." But Jack also noted that *"Glenn Peters and Marvin Jacobs came over to tell us how Dr. John A. Mackay [President of Princeton Theological Seminary] reacted against the gospel Bombs, and how Dr. Christy Wilson had defended them before a special meeting.*"[27] Later, Jack *"was told by Johnny and Herb Schwartz that Dean Aldrich had made some derogatory remarks about P.E.F. in Chapel.*"[28] In addition, various people began attending the PEF Bible studies to hear what was happening firsthand. For example, Jack noted that *"Rev. MacLean came to hear a talk on the second coming of Christ and was very overwrought about our literalism.*"[29] Later, Jack met with Marvin Jacobs to hear about some Gospel Bomb contacts he had visited. But, he noted, *"Dr. Mackay disliked tracts"* and that they didn't want to offend him again.

*Atheist meeting.* On May 17, 1947, Jack was surprised to find that there was an unexpected meeting following their Bible class. *"There was an atheist meeting, with about 75 attending. I stayed to listen in, and it was quite foolish. The man who spoke was from the American Association for the Advancement of Atheism.*"

*Competing organizations.* The PEF was not the only Christian organization on campus. However, as the broadening visibility and success of the programs increased, and as more and more students became involved, it began attracting attention from "competing" groups. One of them was the Student Christian Association (SCA).[30]

---

26. Whitcomb had taken Professor Field's geology class in the fall of 1943. See Chapter 7.
27. John Whitcomb diary, May 14, 1948.
28. John Whitcomb diary, May 23, 1948.
29. John Whitcomb diary, June 3, 1948.
30. According to a Princeton University website, "The Student Christian Association and its predecessors were the dominant religious organizations at Princeton University for

Jack was asked to meet the director of SCA to discuss campus ministry organization and cooperation. At 4:00 p.m. on October 10, 1947, Jack and Johnny *"went up to Murray-Dodge to have a conference with Rev. Burton MacLean. He put great pressure on us to join the SCA. We discussed it at the d.p.m [prayer meeting] and all agreed not to join."* Later, pressure for the PEF to join Intervarsity Fellowship and a Baptist campus ministry would be considered and rejected, preserving the unique goals and purpose of PEF (Chapter 14).

*Challenges in religion and philosophy courses.* Jack also faced opposition in class. In his Religion 204 class, Professor Thomas made it clear that he did not believe in a literal interpretation of the Old Testament.[31] He did, however, believe in Providence and God working through evolution.[32] Jack decided to write his term paper on "Signs of the Times and Biblical Prophecy." Jack noted that Dr. Thomas *"returned the term papers and he refused to give me a grade because it was too Biblical."*[33]

The situation was more challenging in his philosophy class. Jack decided to write his term paper on the weakness of Nietzsche's attack on Christianity when he did not consider Christ's Deity.[34] On August 14, Jack *"Had a heated discussion with Prof. Kaufmann on my philosophy paper on Nietzsche."* In response, he took extensive notes on Nietzsche's *Twilight of the Idols* in order to write another paper on his theory of morals. He finally wrote his paper, "Criticism of Nietzsche's Ethics," and turned it in. Jack's opinion of many of the philosophers was captured on August 22: *"Phil. Discussion on religious views of ten philosophers (they should have remained agnostics)."*

## History

John Whitcomb's major at Princeton was in Ancient and European History, where he graduated with honors.

---

almost a hundred and fifty years. The Philadelphian Society, founded by a small group of students in 1825, was the quasi-official campus religious agency by the beginning of the twentieth century. In 1930 the Student-Faculty Association (SFA), organized by the Dean of the Chapel, took over the Society's programs, focusing on community service. In 1946 the Student Christian Association (SCA) replaced both the Society and the SFA, coordinating both religious and community service activities in campus. The Student Volunteers Council succeeded the SCA in 1967." (Quoted from http://findingaids.princeton.edu/collections/AC135, accessed June 18, 2016).

31. John Whitcomb diary, March 25, 1947.
32. John Whitcomb diary, March 28, 1947.
33. John Whitcomb diary, May 29, 1947.
34. John Whitcomb diary, August 12, 1947.

In contrast to religion and philosophy, Jack's history professors were interested in his views and supportive of his independent studies. As noted above, on September 26, 1946, Jack spoke to Professor Mommsen about the historical certainty of the Resurrection, and he promised to read part of *Therefore Stand*. In response, on September 30, 1946, Professor Mommsen gave *Therefore Stand* as one of the outside reading options on the Resurrection for History 311.

During the introduction to History 312 on February 17, 1947, Professor Mommsen sat next to Jack, and they talked. Later, Professor Mommsen asked Jack to look over *Christianity and Classical Thought* by Cochran, as he planned to use it for his course the following fall.[35] On April 14, Jack responded by recommending some Christian histories to Professor Mommsen.

For History 312, Jack met with his advisor, Dr. Palmer, and decided on the topic of "18th Century England and John Wesley" for his 8,000-word junior independent paper.[36] On Monday, June 2, 1947, Jack noted, *"I got my junior independent work on Wesley back. Prof. Palmer said it was good."*

During the summer semester, Jack wrote another paper for history, this time on John Knox.

The senior thesis represented the culmination of the education process in the History Department at Princeton. On September 30 at 7:30 a.m., Jack attended a senior meeting where they were instructed about writing their senior thesis. Jack noted, *"I spoke to Prof. Harbison about mine (perhaps on D. L. Moody)."*

Jack determined to do an outstanding job. Not only was the thesis carefully documented with numerous references, including Mrs. George W. Loos, grandniece of Dwight L. Moody, and David Packard, grandson of Dwight L. Moody, but he also corresponded with Mrs. W.R. Moody, daughter-in-law of D.L. Moody.

The thesis was submitted on April 15, 1948, to the Department of History, Princeton University. The thesis is 92 pages in length with 15 primary references and 16 secondary sources. One of the references was by Dr. Charles R. Erdman[37] of Princeton Seminary, to be

---

35. John Whitcomb diary, March 28, 1947.
36. John Whitcomb diary, March 4, 1947.
37. Charles R. Erdman, *D. L. Moody: His Message for Today* (New York, NY: Revell, 1928), 154 pages.

interviewed on December 4, 1947. Another reference was by Wilbur Smith,[38] who had captivated Jack with his book, *Therefore Stand*. Jack contacted Smith and, on December 1, 1947, *"received a lengthy and helpful letter from Dr. Wilbur M. Smith on my Moody thesis."*

The thesis' title was "Dwight Lyman Moody: The Apostle of the Nineteenth Century." It was divided into four chapters: I. The Young Zealot, II. The Mighty Apostle, III. Moody the Educator, and IV. The Abiding Influences. Jack concluded that "from 1870 to 1900 the Church launched the greatest missionary enterprise in its history and won more converts than in any earlier period of like duration." During his life in the 19th century, Moody preached to an estimated 100,000,000 people. And despite the fact that there were many famous preachers and teachers in England and America, "no Christian leader in that aggressive age can compare with Moody."

The faculty in the history department was duly impressed with the quality of research and writing of the thesis. This thesis secured Jack's recognition as a top scholar and his graduation with honors.

But one of the interesting side notes was Jack's interview with David Packard, a Princeton student. Jack was concerned that Moody's grandson was not a believer. He invited David to the Sunday Bible class to hear Mr. F. Jack wrote in his diary on Sunday, November 23, 1947, *"Mr. F spoke afterwards with Dave Packard (D.L. Moody's great grandson). Dave accepted Christ."*

*PEF Special Events*

As described in Jack's presidential plan, the PEF began inviting special speakers to visit and lecture to the students. This included W.A. Dean, who spoke on "The Foundation of Christianity," and Dr. Vansteenberghe of the Belgian Gospel Mission, who spoke on "Christ the Mediator." In addition, Emil Pearson came to speak on "Light in the Dark Continent," Frank J. Newberg spoke on "The Birthday of the King" just before Christmas, and Rowan Pearce spoke on "The Preeminence of Christ." This program began attracting many of the top Christian leaders and proved to be an invaluable complement to the faithful teaching of Donald Fullerton.

---

38. Wilbur M. Smith, *Dwight Lyman Moody: An Annotated Bibliography* (Chicago, IL: Moody Press, 1948), 221 pages.

## *PEF Alumni-Undergraduate Banquet*

To better connect with former PEF members, Jack planned the first alumni-undergraduate banquet. The event was held on December 12, 1947, at the Princeton Inn. The event was so successful that it became an annual event.

## *PEF Newsletter*

Jack also initiated the PEF Newsletter. On Sunday evening, December 14, after the Bible study, Mr. F. spent the evening talking about PEF and a possible newsletter, the PEF News. This was sent out in December 1947. The newsletter focused on the events of the PEF, the need for deeper spiritual commitment, and a commitment to prayer. It also highlighted excerpts from missionary testimonials delivered at the banquet and from letters of encouragement sent from former PEF students who were serving the Lord around the world but who could not attend the banquet.

## *Radio Ministry*

On November 19, 1947, Jack had the opportunity to talk to Ted Gartrell about giving Bible lessons on the Princeton radio station, WPRU. PEF was given a time slot from 12:05 to 12:10 a.m. weekly, and the program began on December 9. Jack spoke on the program on multiple occasions, including January 6, 1948, when Jack spoke on passages from Isaiah 53 and John 3, 12, and 14.

## Outside of Princeton

Donald Fullerton believed that Jack needed to expand his perspective and experience beyond the ivory towers and begin organized ministries in the neighboring communities. He invited Jack, Johnnie Rea, and others to events and meetings off campus but also encouraged two specific outreach opportunities for Jack.

## *Teaching Sunday School*

On Sunday, September 7, 1947, Jack began teaching Sunday school to boys at the Christ Presbyterian Church. Three boys attended the first week, but with time, the Sunday school class grew to about 8 to

10 regulars. In addition to teaching, he emphasized the importance of memorizing Scripture and would check them on reciting memory verses. Jack continued teaching through the end of his senior year.

*Street Meetings in Town*

In April 1947, Jack learned that some evangelical Princeton Seminary students were planning to hold evangelistic street meetings in town. Jack began supporting the effort and tried to encourage more involvement from PEF and other seminary students. The meetings would be held on Wednesday and Saturday evenings.

On Saturday May 10, for example, Jack noted in his diary, *"In the evening I went to Witherspoon St and made a short talk in a street meeting put on by Mr. Smith and some seminary students. My bicycle was stolen."* Undaunted, he went again on Saturday, May 17 with *"Johnny, Mr. Smith, Lenox to give talks and testimonies."*

The street meetings became more effective when, on July 16, Jack noted, *"We had loudspeakers which were very helpful. Gave out many tracts."* But on July 23, he noted, *"At 6:15 I went over for street meeting and took a picture. Ten Univ. Men came by. . . . The police forbade our use of loudspeakers."* Nevertheless, Jack continued to support this ministry through the summer.

## Choosing a Seminary

Jack was convinced by George Miles and Donald Fullerton that to be an effective Christian leader, he would need seminary training. The ultimate goal was the mission field, and the specific target was China. Although Jack forgot the Mandarin dialect he learned as his first language, his early affection for a Chinese "amah" and the warming familiarity of Chinese foods and smells and people served as persistent reminders of this mass of humanity. And the need in China was great. Jack focused on the China Inland Mission, started by Hudson Taylor in 1865, a visionary and passionate man who championed the cause for Christ in China.

Jack had already memorized the names of all of the provinces and their capitals and posted a map of the East, with pins marking each of the China Inland Mission stations.[39] But he also had some concerns.

---

39. John Whitcomb diary, August 1, 1947.

He attended a special service to hear the Reverend Ralph Toliver, a missionary from the China Inland Mission who was in the United States on sabbatical.[40] The message was less inspiring than he was expecting, noting only that the speaker *"wore a gown."* Jack's vision of his work in China remained vague, although he anticipated that communication with the Chinese would be a strong asset, as the forgotten Mandarin vocabulary, embedded somewhere deep in his brain, would be easily resurrected.

With the urging of Donald Fullerton toward seminary and missions, the core PEF group actively discussed and investigated a number of religious graduate schools. Jack recorded debates on specific seminaries under consideration on a frequent basis. First, it was clear that Donald Fullerton had grave concerns about Princeton Seminary and recommended that students consider going elsewhere. However, some of the men supporting PEF were Princeton Seminary students, and some of the undergraduates still aspired to attend Princeton Seminary. The school still had a great library, interesting speakers such as Jack Wyrtzen (founder of Word of Life),[41] and some godly faculty — remnants of a better time. Jack and Johnny had taken Greek at the seminary in spring 1947, and they had an inside track to admission. But they also knew the leadership and direction of the school, especially with regard to the inspiration, clarity, and authority of the Scriptures in all areas of life.

On May 31, 1947, Jack and Arsen Gulian discussed Westminster Seminary, a school started by former Princeton Seminary faculty, but Jack decided against it. On June 19, 1947, during summer break in Washington, D.C., Jack met a Mr. Bishop from Grace Theological seminary while Jack was helping George Miles at the Washington Bible

---

40. John Whitcomb diary, December 15, 1946.
41. One of the key contacts made through Princeton Seminary was Jack Wyrtzen, who was there for a visit. Professor Whitcomb would remain in contact with him, and the Word of Life Bible Institute, for life. John Whitcomb noted in his diary on April 15, 1947, *"I went to the seminary and met Jack Wyrtzen, director of the Word of Life Hour. – Eight PEF men were there."* In the *"evening heard Jack give an excellent talk. He wants three of us to give testimonies in New York."* Whitcomb then wrote out a "one minute" testimony. On Saturday, April 26, 1947, John Whitcomb and John Rea took the 4:11 p.m. train to New York City. They met Jack Wyrtzen and his friends and had a prayer meeting. Then they *"went on the Air at 8:00 pm and Johnny and I gave one minute testimonies."* They took the 10:05 p.m. train back to Princeton.

Institute. David Marshall, who helped mentor Jack as a freshman, previously attended Grace for a summer and offered glowing praise. A month later, Johnny Rea and Jack received Grace Seminary catalogues in the mail. On July 27, Jack discussed Fuller Seminary with Donald Fullerton. This was Jack's first choice, in part because Wilbur Smith, author of *Therefore Stand*, was joining their faculty. However, Fullerton had growing concerns about the school's foundation and direction after his meeting with Fuller the previous fall, and he dissuaded Jack from enrolling in that school.

## Graduation

June 15, 1948, marked graduation day. As Jack and his parents traveled from Washington, D.C., to the Princeton campus for this great event, Jack suddenly realized that he had forgotten to order his cap and gown! However, one of each was secured. Jack noted, *"so we feared the worst, but everything went well."*

## Reflection of Mr. F.

On February 6, 1950, Donald B. Fullerton sent a letter to John Whitcomb, now at Grace Theological Seminary. "My heart is filled with praise for the way He caused you to grow spiritually in those days, preserving you and preparing you for His service and for your labors unto Him in the PEF subsequently. Your diligence in the spiritual leadership, as well as in the executive and paper works meant a great deal in forwarding the effectiveness of the witness on the campus."

Judge Paul Pressler entered Princeton in the fall of 1948. He immediately gravitated to Donald Fullerton and his deep Bible teaching. Pressler added, "Mr. Fullerton admired [John Whitcomb] as he admired few people. He never had anything but good things to say about [him] and he is one of only a few people like that. All of the attendees at the PEF considered [John Whitcomb] a tremendous leader and we were in awe when his name was spoken. I always felt that he was both quiet and outgoing. He was a leader."[42]

---

42. Letter from Paul Pressler to the author, August 19, 2016.

# Princeton, Pre WWII

**3.1** Jack Whitcomb entering Princeton, age 18.

**3.2** Donald Fullerton (left) and David Marshall (right) were key leaders of the Princeton Evangelical Fellowship (PEF) both before and after WWII.

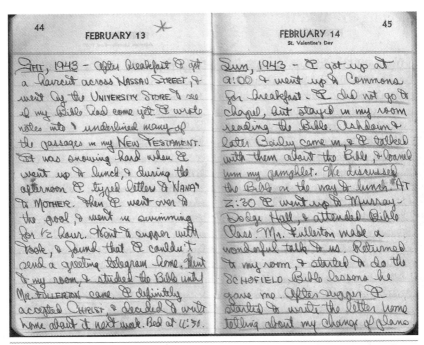

**3.3.** Diary entry affirming a decision to accept Christ (February 13) and start in a new career direction as a missionary (February 14). Shortly after this decision to follow Christ was made, young Jack Whitcomb was drafted into the U.S. Army.

## Post-WWII / Princeton

**3.4** Post-WWII picture of Jack with his paternal grandmother, "Nana," under the grape arbor at their home in Arlington, VA, July 6, 1946. She cared nothing of Christ or the Bible. Jack was conflicted as to his future plans.

**3.5** George Mills, president of Washington Bible Institute, mentored Jack during the summer of 1947. In addition to refurbishing a building to make new classrooms, Mr. Mills transported Jack back and forth from his parents' home in Arlington, VA, to the campus on the east side of Washington, D.C. This provided time for many discussions on the importance of a Christian education and planning for a life of service to the Lord.

**3.6** Jack Whitcomb portrait 1946, before returning to Princeton.

**3.7** Middle Dod Hall on the campus of Princeton University. Jack lived there from September 1946 to June 1948.

**3.8** The PEF headquarters was at Middle Dod Hall also, including the PEF library, one of Jack's initiatives in 1946.

**3.9** Donald Fullerton talking to Ray Lozier, spring 1947.

**3.10** Christy Wilson was an undergraduate PEF student at Princeton University who stayed engaged with PEF as a Princeton Seminary graduate student. He did much of the teaching and provided continuity at key times throughout the 1940s.

**3.11** Princeton Evangelical Fellowship students, May 27, 1947. Back row: John Rea, Lenox Palin, Dick Sharrett, Bob Deming, Dave Hostetter. Front row: Ernie Wright, Ed Gammon, Olin Ellis, Jack Whitcomb, Paul Kent.

**3.12** WWII father and son veterans in Florida at the home of Jack's grandmother, 1946.

**3.13** The Whitcomb family at Thanksgiving dinner on November 28, 1946, Harrington, NJ. Left to right, Jack, John Sr. (Whit), Sally, Adele (Auntie), Salome (Jack's mother), and Juliette.

**3.14** Gospel street meeting in the town of Princeton, July 30, 1947.

**3.15** Jack's boys Sunday school class at the Christ Presbyterian Church, Trenton, NJ.

**3.16** Jack's mother, Auntie, and cousin Sally dressed up in their finest for the graduation. Sally remembers the whole family going down to Princeton: "They were so proud of him."

**3.17** Jack Whitcomb enters the world of educated people —
with honors! Another job well done.

**3.18** Jack Whitcomb and Johnny Rea both graduate from Princeton University with honors, June 15, 1948. They continued to be classmates three months later at Grace Theological Seminary.

**3.19** A woman at Hephzibah Heights believed to be Ruth Paxson, a former missionary to China who had a great impact on John Whitcomb between college and seminary (summer 1948). Summer Bible conference retreats were popular in the past and highly recommended to PEF students by Donald Fullerton.

**3.20** Group picture of the key workers and teachers of Hephzibah Heights in the summer of 1948 near the chapel. The man in the center is Eddie Samson. Ruth Paxson may be to Rev. Samson's right. Jack attended at the urging of Donald Fullerton, who believed that these summer retreats were critical for spiritual refreshment.

**3.21** Jack Whitcomb earned his keep at the summer conference center working on the grounds and helping with maintenance. His home was this little hut that he called the "Prophet's Chambers." By the end of the summer, he was ready for Grace Seminary.

**3.22** It was an honor for me (left) to finally meet Dr. Fullerton during his visit to Grace Theological Seminary in 1976. I was amused as well since my father referred to him as "a giant," while he appeared to me to be of rather slight stature!

**3.23** Dr. Fullerton was very proud of his PEF disciples and the impact that they were making in the Lord's work, as reflected in this photograph taken by Dr. John Whitcomb during his visit.

# Section 4

# Seminary & Christian Service

# Chapter 12

# Grace

"Dr. Alva J. McClain: my theological father"
June 1948 to 1950s

Professor John C. Whitcomb Jr. spent the majority of his professional career teaching at Grace Theological Seminary (Grace) in Winona Lake, Indiana. Although Grace was relatively new when Jack Whitcomb was a Princeton University student (it was meeting in rented space), Donald Fullerton began directing his Princeton Evangelical Fellowship (PEF) disciples to Grace in the late 1940s and continued this trend for decades. PEF students remember Fullerton's rendition of 1 Corinthians 13:13 as applied to seminaries: "And now abideth Faith, Dallas and Grace, these three; but the greatest of these is Grace."[1]

In the fall of 1948, three Princeton University graduates enrolled in Grace Theological Seminary: Olan Ellis, John (Johnny) Rea, and John (Jack) Whitcomb. Several major events that occurred over the next few years transformed Jack Whitcomb into Professor Whitcomb. Among the most important was coming under the mentorship of his "theological father," Alva J. McClain, at Grace.

## Spiritual Retreat

Donald Fullerton believed in the value of escaping the daily routine in the secular world by going to a secluded location for a time of spiritual revival with dedicated rest, reflection, fellowship, and

---

1. The King James Version of the Bible reads "And now abideth faith, hope, charity, these three; but the greatest of these is charity." Modern versions translate "charity" as "love." Besides Grace, the recommended seminaries were Faith Theological Seminary, now in Baltimore, Maryland, and Dallas Theological Seminary in Dallas, Texas.

spiritual encouragement. Fullerton recognized Jack Whitcomb's passion, commitment, disciplined study habits, and organizational skills, but he also recognized that he missed the spiritual nurturing and maturing that naturally occurs in a true Christian home. Fullerton believed that Jack would benefit from a full summer in a spiritually nurturing environment before entering the scholastic environment of a seminary. Thus, Jack Whitcomb, after graduation from Princeton, followed Mr. Fullerton's recommendations and headed north from Princeton, New Jersey, to Monterey, Massachusetts, for a summer at Hephzibah Heights.

## A Godly Old Lady

Hephzibah Heights[2] was a summer retreat for the Hephzibah Ministries, headquartered at Hephzibah House, a brownstone residence at 51 W. 75th Street in New York City. Hephzibah House was an outgrowth of the Young Ladies Christian League, which had been established for the purpose of promoting the spiritual welfare of young women all over the world. Although the Young Ladies Christian League folded in 1917, the godly spirit and dedication to prayer and foreign missions continued through Hephzibah Ministry.

Donald Fullerton, a New York City native with many personal connections around town, developed a close working relationship with the ministry at Hephzibah House, including taking PEF students there during the summer for evangelistic work. As David Marshall (Princeton, 1941–1945) remembers, "Mr. Fullerton would have me go out to the street corner five days a week to draw a crowd, then he would come down and preach to them."[3]

In 1928, Hephzibah Ministries purchased 200 acres of land near Monterey, Massachusetts, in the southwest corner of the state. The ministry built a summer conference center on top of Chestnut Hill, with residential buildings, dining rooms, and a chapel, and named it "Hephzibah Heights." The program included a series of special speakers who would minister to the attendees for one week at a time during the summer.

---

2. A detailed history of Hephzibah Heights and Hephzibah House are available online at https://hhouse.org/our-history/, accessed August 26, 2021.
3. David Marshall, 50th anniversary of the PEF dinner, June 6, 1981.

# Grace

Jack arrived at Hephzibah Heights on June 16, 1948, following the recommendations of Mr. Fullerton. He served as a summer staff member, with the primary task of groundskeeping. He also attended the Bible teaching and preaching sessions and enjoyed opportunities to meet and interact with some great Bible teachers. Among the prominent speakers that summer were Clarence Jones (HCJB radio station, Quito, Ecuador), Kenneth Masteller, and Alfred Kunz. After being at camp for nearly a month, the camp directors asked Jack to preach. This occurred on July 11, 1948, nearly three years after his first opportunity to speak in London, England, after WWII. Fullerton made several visits to Hephzibah Heights during the summer to encourage, mentor, and challenge Jack. But the key person was an older woman named Miss Ruth Paxson, a missionary to China who was forced to retire due to poor health but who continued to serve the Lord as a popular author and speaker in the United States.[4]

Jack kept a diary of the daily events in his life from age 11 years onward. But for his spiritual development, he was advised to also kept a record of weekly events under three categories: Prayer Request, Answered Request, and Special Blessings. These entries documented the spiritual transformation that occurred under the lessons taught by Miss Paxson.

On a personal note, I never remember hearing my father mention Hephzibah Heights in my life, until I specifically asked him in 2015 about the transition from Princeton to Grace. Upon reflection, he became excited about his wonderful memories of that summer, emphasizing on multiple occasions the importance of this time in the development of his spiritual life. He added, almost embarrassed to say, "A lady there taught me about the Holy Spirit and living the Christian life. And she taught me how to pray."

The Special Blessings notes included entries from Jack highlighting the impact of Miss Paxson's lessons on his mind and heart.[5]

---

4. Ruth Paxson wrote multiple books, and some are still in print. These include *The Wealth, Walk and Warfare of the Christian* on the Book of Ephesians (Fleming H. Revell Co., 1939), 222 pages, *Caleb the Overcomer* (Faithful Life Publishers, 2003), *Rivers of Living Water* (Moody Publishing, 1978), *Life on the Highest Plane: God's Plan for Spiritual Maturity* (Kregel Classics, 1996), and others.
5. The sentences, capitalizations, "*," and abbreviations are directly from John Whitcomb's notes in 1948.

- *Fourth week in July*. "Evening talks at Keswick[6] by Miss Ruth Paxson on Life of Christ. Deeper Sense of Christ's indwelling presence." "Talks by Miss Paxson at Hephzibah Chapel on Christ, our Pattern and Provision for Victory." "Great Blessing from Miss Paxton's Wed. morn. Talk on our Identification with Christ in His death & resurrection & ascension by faith in God's statements in Rom. 6." "Bondslaves of Christ. My first true realization of this fact."
- *Fifth week in July*. "Great blessing and conviction following Miss Paxson's talk on the capital 'I' of self as opposed to 'I in you' of Christ." Special blessing - "Her Thursday eve. talk on European crisis – need for Bible classes." "Friday morning on warfare of Christian against Satan in the power of Christ's finished work." "Fri. evening's talk on Victory over our circumstances and environment. Sins of complaining." "*Sat. morn talk on the Holy Spirit. First came to a clear understanding of the baptism and infilling of the Holy Spirit."
- *First week in August*. "Miss Paxson's Sunday morning talk on grieving the Holy Spirit." "Very stirring morning communion service, conducted by Mr. F and Mr. Woodbury." "Miss Paxson's afternoon talk on Manifestation of the Infilling of the Holy Spirit."
- *First week in September*. "Telling Ernie [Wright] of Miss Paxson's talks & prayer with me on the PEF."

The summer of 1948 proved to be the perfect preparation for seminary. Miss Ruth Paxson, in the pattern of Priscilla[7] in Acts 18, demonstrated the powerful influence of a godly woman who knew God's Word and His ways. Her impact on the spiritual life of John Whitcomb continued for the rest of his life. She died the following year at 60 years of age.

## Transition to Indiana

On Monday, September 6, 1948, Jack left Hephzibah Heights by car to NYC, where he caught a bus to Harrington Park, New Jersey. He again witnessed to each of his relatives individually and then proceeded to

---

6. *New England Keswick* is a year-round Christian retreat and conference center located in Monterey, Massachusetts, near Hephzibah Heights.
7. See Acts 18:2, 18, and 26.

Princeton to catch up with the students helping with the PEF reply cards for new students. The new PEF annual plan was already behind schedule — an ominous sign.

The next day, Jack visited the home of his friend and Princeton classmate Ernie Wright and stayed for supper. After supper, he got grilled by Ernie's father, a professor at Johns Hopkins University in Baltimore, Maryland, about why he was going to Grace Seminary and about evangelical Christianity in general. Jack noted in his diary, *"He seemed to be quite bitter against fundamentalism."* But Dr. Wright was not the only parent who showed concern and even disdain for the work of the PEF. Other parents, with great ambitions for their children's worldly success, blamed the PEF for altering the career goals they set for their children. Time after time, the Princeton boys, like Jack Whitcomb, became true Christians and changed their life goals to follow the leading of their newly found heavenly Father rather than earthly father and to study at a seminary or pursue other avenues of Christian service.

After supper at the Wrights, Jack caught the night train to Pittsburgh, arriving at 8:00 a.m. on the morning of September 8, 1948. Johnny Rea was there to meet him. Johnny had just bought a "Kaiser" car,[8] and they drove it to the Rea farm, about 50 miles from Pittsburgh, to meet the Rea family and watch Johnny say farewell.

The next morning, Jack Whitcomb and Johnny Rea drove from Johnny's parents' home to Winona Lake, Indiana, to begin seminary. Dr. Herman Hoyt, dean of the Seminary, met them and took them to the home of Mr. Downden, where they would rent second-floor rooms of an old wooden house near the school.

The next day, Jack and Johnny walked over to the Free Methodist Publishing Company building and took the stairs to the 3rd floor to register for classes in the rented space serving as the seminary. They met some of the key faculty such as Dr. McClain, president of the seminary, Dr. Homer Kent Sr., and Robert D. Culver, Th.M. They also met some students, including Jim Marshall, the older brother of David Marshall — the Princeton classmate of Jack and Johnny and former

---

8. Kaiser Motors Corporation made automobiles from 1945 to 1953 before a series of mergers, eventually becoming part of American Motor Corporation (AMC). The residual component of the company makes the U.S. Army Humvee and civilian Hummer H1.

PEF student leader. Jack was now an official student at the fledgling Grace Theological Seminary.

## A History of Grace Theological Seminary

The story of Grace, from its inception in the 1930s through the 1960s, is also largely the story of John Whitcomb's third father,[9] Alva J. Mc-Clain. The circumstances leading to the establishment of Grace is preserved in a special yearbook, published in 1951 to commemorate the opening of McClain Hall on the new Grace campus in Winona Lake, Indiana. The editor, with a deep interest in history and the actions of great leaders in times of crisis, captured the critical events that shaped the seminary through the eyes of the founders. The editor of the volume would be John C. Whitcomb.[10] The following story relies heavily on this yearbook.

### The Dunkards

Grace Theological Seminary traces its roots to the "Dunkards," a name given to the German Baptist Brethren who baptized new believers by total water immersion — similar to other Baptists, except believers were immersed three times forward. McClain provided a detailed history of the movement,[11] beginning in 1708 when Alexander Mack, "a well-educated and Bible-loving Calvinist," and his colleagues questioned whether the Reformation had fully brought the Church back to a New Testament Church model. They chose to accept only the Holy Scriptures as their infallible rule of faith and practice. Holding this fundamentalist position led to persecution by both the German Catholics and Lutherans, resulting in the emigration of the entire congregation from Germany to Germantown, Pennsylvania, a town on the northwest side of downtown Philadelphia.

---

9. See John Whitcomb's four fathers, Chapter 1.

10. *The History of Grace Theological Seminary, 1931–1951*, ed. John Whitcomb, 1951, 125 pages.

11. The origin and practices of the German Baptist Brethren differ from the Plymouth Brethren, who originated in Ireland and England in reaction to actions of the Church of England (Episcopal Church), with the first congregation forming in Plymouth, England. An early and prominent leader was John Nelson Darby, who became instrumental for articulating and popularizing dispensational eschatology with a pre-millennial, pre-tribulation rapture — which was later adopted by offshoots of the German Baptist Brethren.

History remembers the Brethren as "men of education, who had their minds trained in some of the best universities of Europe, and some of them were themselves instructors in universities. They could read the Scriptures in the original languages [Hebrew and Greek], and could give an unbiased translation of them in the language of the common people."[12] The congregation included many outstanding men, including Christopher Sower, who established a printing company and printed the famous "Sower Bible,"[13] the first German Bible printed in America.

Although the founding members of the Dunkards established an effective denomination in America, the general character of the members and the leadership changed to some degree with each subsequent generation — a phenomenon common to all human organizations. In the mid-1800s, a reactionary leadership arose, stressing conformity to traditional customs of dress, a legalistic view of salvation,[14] the authority of church conferences over local congregations, an opposition to formal education, and a rejection of foreign missionary activities. This led to a split in the denomination in 1889, with the "progressives" who opposed these tendencies becoming the "Brethren Church," while the conservative arm continued as "Church of the Brethren." The division also led to some important reforms in the thinking of the "conservatives," who reconsidered the oppressive positions of some of the older elders on education and missions.

## Ashland College

In the midst of the debate leading up to the split, a group of Brethren men in Ohio started Ashland College, which fell under the control of the progressives after the split. The college constitution, established

---

12. McClain in *The History of Grace Theological Seminary* (ibid.), quoting Edwin E. Jacobs, "A Brief history of Ashland College, page 3."
13. See https://hsp.org/blogs/question-of-the-week/christopher-sower-printed-and-published-the-first-american-edition-of-which-book.
14. The nineteenth-century Brethren appeared to be strongly influenced by Arminian views of salvation and the role of "works" in pleasing God and maintaining their eternal destiny than their predecessors, who came from a more Calvinistic perspective. The Arminian view is that salvation is accomplished through the combined efforts of God (who takes the initiative) and man (who must respond) — man's response being the determining factor. The Calvinist view is that the entire process (election, redemption, regeneration) is the work of God and is by *grace* alone. Thus, the word "Grace" in Grace Theological Seminary is a statement of the Calvinistic view.

in 1888, stated their purpose — "the training of suitable men for the ministry of the Gospel shall always be sacredly regarded as one of the main objects of this institution."[15] The school developed an undergraduate major in Bible, but there was no seminary. However, the progressive branch of the Brethren Church had two branches of its own: those who were theologically conservative but who opposed the enforcement of non-biblical traditions and polity of the Church of the Brethren, and those who were theologically liberal and opposed the authority of the Scriptures in life and practice.

The school, seeking to gain student enrollment from a broad base and to establish high academic credentials, appointed a highly regarded but theologically liberal scholar and ordained Brethren pastor, Dr. J.L. Gillin, as the school president (1907–1911). Gillian's views reflected the perspective of higher critics, recommending, for example, that the authority for Christian faith and practice for Brethren be changed from "the infallible Bible" to "religious experience." Gillin also undermined theological discipline in church membership by recommending toleration of frank heresy, such as unbiblical views of the deity of Christ. For example, Gillin wrote,[16] "A person may be a member of the Brethren Church . . . and be an Athanasian[17] on the subject of the nature of Christ, or on the other hand he may be an Arian[18] and still be

---

15. From Ashland College university's charter and constitution, quoted from https://www.ashlandsource.com/history/ashlands-dream-of-a-college-became-reality-in-1878/article_fa83f4aa-9eec-11eb-9122-4fcf9fd4233d.html, accessed December 15, 2021.

16. Quote in Alva .J. McClain, "The Background and Origin of Grace Theological Seminary," in *The History of Grace Theological Seminary, 1931-1951*, ed. John Whitcomb, 1951, p. 12.

17. The Athaniasian view of Christ, articulated in a 4th-century creed in opposition to the Arian view (footnote below), includes the statement, "We worship one God in trinity and the Trinity in unity, neither confusing the persons nor dividing the divine being. For the Father is one person, the Son is another, and the Spirit is still another. But the deity of the Father, Son, and Holy Spirit is one, equal in glory, coeternal in majesty. What the Father is, the Son is, and so is the Holy Spirit." The creed further states, "That our Lord Jesus Christ, God's Son, is both God and man. He is God, begotten before all worlds from the being of the Father, and he is man, born in the world from the being of his mother — existing fully as God, and fully as man with a rational soul and a human body; equal to the Father in divinity, subordinate to the Father in humanity. Although he is God and man, he is not divided, but is one Christ." These statements are considered consistent with biblical doctrine of the essence and personality of our Lord Jesus Christ.

18. The Arian view of Christ was that the Son of God did not always exist but was created by God the Father and was therefore subordinate to Him. Thus, he was not fully God. This view is recognized as heretical.

a good member of the Church. These things are of minor importance." The theologically liberal arm of the movement focused more on issues of social injustice than evangelism and discipleship.

The majority of the progressive churches that made up the new Brethren Church held theologically conservative views of biblical interpretation and practice. Although alarms on liberal and heretical trends at Ashland College rang through the conservative churches, no organized opposition could be mounted. Furthermore, the leadership of Ashland College and their supporters began using political and parliamentary procedures to take control of the National Conference. But in times of church crisis, God often raises up extraordinary men of faith who stand on God's truth without compromise. God's man for this crisis was Alva J. McClain.

## Alva J. McClain

Alva J. McClain was born on April 11, 1888, in Aurelia, Iowa.[19] His father, Walter Scott McClain, grew up in the rural southwestern Pennsylvania town of Masontown. Walter was of Scottish heritage, while his wife, Mary, was German and a Dunkard. They joined the local German Baptist Brethren church, where Walter later became ordained as a lay preacher. When the denomination split in 1889, they joined the progressive movement. Walter and Mary discarded their traditional Pennsylvania Dutch garb for more colorful and fashionable clothing and modern methods. Walter established the family's Christian traditions by reading the Bible each evening during dinner. Then he would go and sit by himself in his favorite chair and read the Bible and other materials until late in the night.

*Wandering Farmers*

Seeking new opportunities, the McClains moved to Iowa to become hog farmers and establish an agricultural nursery. Alva's birth gave Walter his first son among seven children. Upon receiving his son into his arms to hold for the first time, he lifted the child toward heaven and proclaimed, "Here is our preacher." However, as Alva grew up, he showed no interest in the Bible, in church, or in the Lord.

19. The primary source of the history of Alva J. McClain's childhood is from Norman B. Rohrer, *A Saint in Glory Stands: The Story of Alva J. McClain, Founder of Grace Theological Seminary* (Winona Lake, IN: BMH Books, 1986), 136 pages.

# A Good and Faithful Servant

The young McClain family left their Iowa hog farm for the Arizona Territory in 1897 to establish an agricultural farm with government-supplied irrigation near Phoenix. But the promised water for irrigation never came. They got back into their covered wagons and wandered west to Los Angeles, California, and then north to Sunnyside, Washington, in 1900 to join other members of the German Baptist Progressive Brethren who were relocating from South Dakota to establish the Christian Cooperative Colony.[20] Sunnyside, located in south central Washington State, was a tiny town of 7 families until the immigration of the "Dunkards" in 1900–1902, who bought the entire town to establish a Christian utopia. The new Brethren community became the first town in the state to adopt a self-governing plan with an elected city council with the responsibility for policy making, hiring a city manager, and overseeing the government administration offices. The city council established laws for the new town prohibiting *alcohol, dancing,* and *gambling* as a condition for the purchase of every parcel of land that was sold.

The young Alva McClain, now a teenager, was a non-conformist among the Progressives. A talented and accomplished athlete, he also gained a reputation as a prankster and troublemaker. He loved dancing, smoking, and carousing with his buddies. His intellect became obvious as he skipped through school with horrible class attendance but excellent marks. He would do so by quickly reading the assigned books and then acing the tests. He loved baseball and football, where he played quarterback. He led his high school football team to the Yakima Valley championship for three years in a row.

After graduating from high school, Alva entered the University of Washington to play college sports. He became a quarterback for the Huskies in the fall and made the baseball team in the spring. But a sports accident involving baseball cleats to his lower leg nearly killed him. The flesh and bone became seriously infected and evolved to life-threatening blood poisoning. Although he recovered, the injury ended his athletic dreams, and he returned to Sunnyside to join his father in the new business of raising pedigree fruit trees, specializing in apples.[21]

---

20. https://en.wikipedia.org/wiki/Sunnyside,_Washington.
21. The efforts of the McClains to produce high-quality saplings to plant orchards contributed significantly to the world-famous Washington State apple industry. Alva apparently contributed as well, identifying a Rome apple that was all red, rather than having a red face and green back. This was selectively bred and represents the beginning of

He also met a newcomer to town, a Miss Josephine Gingrich, who soon became his wife.

## Fulfillment of Prophecy

In August 1912, the Brethren of Sunnyside, Washington, sponsored a special speaker to come from Los Angeles, California, for a week-long conference on prophecy. Walter McClain gave his son time off from work to attend the services.

The speaker, Louis S. Bauman, served as the pastor of the First Brethren Church of Long Beach California, known to the parishioners as "Fifth and Cherry" because of its location at the intersection of these two main streets. As a pastor, conference speaker, and author, Bauman was loved and respected throughout the United States by the Brethren, and internationally known for his emphasis and service in supporting foreign missions.

A few people still remember him. Gordon Austin, a 1961 graduate of Grace Theological Seminary, attended Fifth and Cherry as a child and recalls,[22] "He preached very long sermons and a lot of his messages were on prophecy. In fact his initials (L S Bauman) stood for 'Long Sermon Bauman.' . . . Dr. Bauman loved people and would encourage them with personal notes written in beautiful handwriting. Children felt free to approach him, although he would sometimes tease them by sticking a big pin through his pants and deep into his artificial leg!"

Alva McClain decided to go and hear L.S. Bauman preach. He strutted down the main street of the town, dressed in the finest style of the day, wife on one arm and a big fat cigar in the other. They entered the church, found a pew, and Alva settled back to see if Bauman had anything to say that he had not already heard over many years of Bible teaching.

Bauman preached, as usual, on biblical prophecy. McClain became overwhelmed by the realization that God could write history ahead of time and put the events of tomorrow into a book before they occurred. At the end of the service, Alva and Jo went to the front of the church

---

the all-red Rome apples. From Norman B. Rohrer, *A Saint in Glory Stands: The Story of Alva J. McClain, Founder of Grace Theological Seminary* (Winona Lake, IN: BMH Books, 1986).

22. Gordon Austin, personal communication to the author, May 30, 2016.

and accepted Jesus Christ as their Lord and Savior. And McClain was a changed man.

## Theological Training

Following his conversion, McClain poured his mind and soul into studying the Bible and any other Christian books he could obtain. He decided to leave Sunnyside and follow Bauman to Long Beach to sit under the teaching of this man of God. Bauman urged McClain to complete his education, beginning with courses at the Bible Institute of Los Angeles (BIOLA). McClain transferred to Xenia Seminary[23] in Xenia, Ohio, where he qualified for a Th.M. but could not graduate because he never finished his bachelor's degree. During this time, he served as an itinerant youth pastor in three local Brethren churches.

At the 1917 Brethren Church National Conference in Ashland, Ohio, McClain was ordained as a minister of the Brethren Church and was elected to membership in the Foreign Mission Board. A delegate from the First Brethren Church of Philadelphia met him and asked him to come to speak on several occasions. In 1918, he became the pastor of the First Brethren Church of Philadelphia.

While in Philadelphia, McClain gained a national reputation for both his preaching and his pen. Challenged by members of his congregation on the merits of the Free Masons, he conducted a thorough investigation and then preached a sermon called "Freemasonry and Christianity."[24] The sermon was transcribed and printed, catapulting McClain into national attention as a man who was thorough and fair, but clear and uncompromising on Scripture. He also published multiple articles in the *Sunday School Times* and taught apologetics in night school at the Philadelphia School of the Bible. But one of the most

---

23. Xenia Theological Seminary was a conservative Presbyterian seminary. It began as Service Seminary (Service, Pennsylvania) in 1792 by the Associate Presbytery of Pennsylvania. Service Seminary moved several times, landing in Xenia, Ohio, where it became Xenia Theological Seminary in 1850. In 1920, Xenia Theological Seminary moved to St. Louis, Missouri. In 1930, Xenia Theological Seminary combined with the Pittsburgh Theological Seminary of the United Presbyterian Church of North America to form the Pittsburgh-Xenia Theological Seminary. Pittsburgh-Xenia Theological Seminary (1930–1959) and Western Theological Seminary (1827–1959) consolidated into one institution in 1959 to become Pittsburgh Theological Seminary.

24. The sermon underwent multiple printings. See Alva J. McClain, "Freemasonry and Christianity," (Winona Lake, IN: BMH Books, 1951, 1953), 32 pages.

impactful writings from a historic perspective was a statement written in 1921 called "The Message of the Brethren Ministry."

As noted above, the majority of churches and pastors in the new Brethren Church denomination strongly opposed the theologically liberal views that found their voice and political power at Ashland College in the early 1900s. The initial opposition was led by Dr. Louis S. Bauman,[25] who brought the issues to a head in the 1921 General Conference of the Brethren Church, forcing a vote on a statement of faith, "The Message of the Brethren Ministry," written for the conference by Alva J. McClain. The statement of faith was overwhelmingly adopted by vote of the delegates to the General Assembly. The statement became a rallying point for the poorly organized, but theologically conservative, members of the socially progressive Brethren.

"The Message of the Brethren Ministry" was considered a theological masterpiece. Following Brethren principles, it specifically presented doctrinal statements from Scripture that were tightly held by the theologically conservative members but avoided the non-Brethren policy of "church creeds." McClain did this by linking short doctrinal statements with the Scriptures from which they were derived. The only "creed" was "the whole Word of God."

The opening line of each statement is given here:

1) We believe in THE HOLY SCRIPTURES;
2) We believe in THE ONE TRIUNE GOD;
3) We believe in THE LORD JESUS CHRIST;
4) We believe in THE HOLY SPIRIT;
5) We believe in THE CREATION AND FALL OF MAN;
6) We believe in SALVATION BY GRACE THROUGH FAITH;
7) We believe in RIGHTEOUS LIVING AND GOOD WORKS;
8) We believe in THE EXISTENCE OF SATAN;

---

25. Louis S. Bauman (1875 to 1950) was the son of an itinerant Brethren minister and evangelist. Dr. Bauman served as pastor of the First Brethren Church in Philadelphia, Pennsylvania; Mexico and Rowan, Indiana; Long Beach, California; and Washington, D.C. His pastorate at Long Beach continued for 34 years (1913–1947), building a membership of over 1,900 and attendances nearing 2,500. He published over a dozen books and numerous magazine articles. His efforts also helped launch the Brethren foreign missions programs.

9)   We believe in THE SECOND COMING OF CHRIST;
10)  We believe in FUTURE LIFE, BODILY RESURRECTION,
      AND ETERNAL JUDGMENT;
11)  We believe in THE ONE TRUE CHURCH;
12)  We believe in SEPARATION FROM THE WORLD.

This statement of faith, and the "covenant of faith" that was to follow, served critical purposes of officially documented, specific biblical doctrines and principles that could be applied to define orthodox truths, and thereby also define heretical teaching, rules of membership, and principles of conduct within a legally defined organization. In this way, the "message" worked as organizational bylaws so that those who opposed the official position of the organization could be dismissed both biblically and legally. But it also served as a "living" document rather than words "written in stone" so that it could be continually modified and improved as the people gained a better understanding of Scripture.

The overwhelming vote to adopt the Message sent a clear message to the more liberal opponents. McCain recalled[26] that adoption of the statement of faith had several important results: First, it provided a rallying point for the evangelical ministers of the church. Second, a number of liberally inclined ministers left the Brethren Church and entered other denominations. Third, Dr. Gillin stopped attending the General conference, and the few remaining minsters who supported the theological "liberals" suffered a marked decline in influence. Fourth, the churches temporarily gained a larger voice in the affairs of Ashland College.

## McClain and Ashland College

McClain decided to resign from First Brethren Church of Philadelphia and returned to Long Beach, California, to complete his B.A. degree at Occidental College, where he graduated with honors. With his undergraduate degree, he qualified for and received his Th.M. from Xenia Seminary on the same day.

In 1925, the Board of Ashland College called McClain to a Bible-teaching position at the college, with the view of developing a seminary-

---

26.  Alva J. McClain, "The Background and Origin of Grace Theological Seminary," in *The History of Grace Theological Seminary, 1931–1951,* ed. John Whitcomb, 1951, p. 12.

level training program for the Brethren churches. McClain accepted the position with a vision of an effective, God-honoring seminary with high academic standards taught at the graduate level. It would be another decade before the pieces would come together.

After arriving in Ashland College, McClain began realizing the challenges in advancing his vision of a graduate-level seminary program. Despite the wishes of the board, the school administration appeared content with an undergraduate Bible program. Many of the faculty and students retained theologically liberal views of the Scriptures, leading to a double standard of practice and behavior on and off campus. Both subtle and overt opposition to biblical standards emerged, and many of the undergraduate students who were dedicated to full-time Christian ministries were leaving for other institutions. After two years, McClain, disillusioned at the prospects of starting a seminary at Ashland College, resigned and moved back to Los Angeles to teach at BIOLA. He worked from 1927–1929 to develop a detailed curriculum for a new seminary in Southern California in association with Louis S. Bauman.

When McClain was appointed Minister of Education at the First Long Beach Brethren Church, the administration at Ashland College recognized that his plan to start a seminary represented a threat to their educational leadership position for the Brethren Church. They responded by offering to launch a graduate-level seminary in Ashland with McClain as associate dean, using the new curriculum outlined by McClain. By the spring of 1930, despite major reservations, Bauman, McClain, and others agreed to the plan "as an experiment." The premise for the experiment was that (a) the "more central" location of Ashland, Ohio, would better serve the majority of Brethren churches; (b) the need to strengthen the spiritual climate on the Ashland College campus; and (c) the financial benefits to the denomination offered by a combined college and seminary on the same campus.

The seminary was started in the fall of 1930 and was enthusiastically supported by the Brethren Churches. The emphasis of the school would be orthodox belief, spiritual living, thorough scholarship, and practical application. By 1932, the seminary student body rose to an enrollment of 18 students, but conflicts rapidly emerged between college and seminary.

The first area of tension was the Statement of Faith, based largely on "The Message of the Brethren Ministry," which was adopted as the biblical standard for the school's doctrine and practice by the Board of Directors for Ashland College and Seminary in 1933–1934. The statement was accepted by the seminary but largely ignored by the college. Many of the college students felt some statements (e.g., #7, Righteous living and good works; #12, Separation from the world) were too legalistic, so they opposed signing any such statement of faith and conduct. Furthermore, it was clear that the seminary was not the desire of the college but was rather forced on them by the churches.

A second issue was a rejection of school accreditation by the secular North Central Association. This was blamed, in part, on McClain and the new Bible-centered graduate program. McClain responded, "The test of an adequate theological seminary is not some standard erected by a set of men who are antagonistic to historical Christianity, but rather this — Does our Seminary adequately prepare our men for the task to which they have given their lives? Namely, for the ministry of the Gospel in the Brethren Church. For this purpose, the approval of the North Central means precisely nothing."[27]

The third divisive event occurred when the president suddenly stopped three seminary professors from teaching Bible classes in the college and ruled that no college credit would be given to college students taking Bible classes in the seminary. Finally, in June 1937, the "experiment" came to an end, with the seminary faculty resigning or being dismissed.

On June 2, 1937, Alva J. McClain, Herman Hoyt, Louis S. Bauman, and others met in a private home for prayer. Suddenly, Bauman rose, took out his pen and checkbook, wrote something, and stated, "I want to give the first gift to the new school."

A new board and organizational officers were assembled for the new seminary. They traveled to Philadelphia to make the school official and agreed to name the new school "Grace Theological Seminary." The school began immediately in the Ellet Church of Akron, Ohio, with a student body of 39, including all but two of the students previously in the Ashland Seminary.

---

27. Quote from http://www.higherpraise.com/preachers/mcclain.htm.

Grace

The Brethren churches found themselves in a dilemma — whether to support the Ashland group or side with the Grace group. In the end, about half of the churches split from the Brethren Church, named themselves the National Fellowship of Grace Brethren Churches, and moved their seminary and national headquarters to Winona Lake, Indiana.

*Growth of Grace Theological Seminary*

Dr. Herman A. Hoyt, a top student at Ashland College and Ashland Seminary who eventually joined the faculty and became dean of Grace Theological Seminary, recalled the early days of the school.[28] He noted that of the 20 students at Ashland Seminary in 1937, 18 withdrew with the intention of joining the new Grace Theological Seminary. To the amazement of everyone, 21 additional students joined the seminary, for a total enrollment of 39 students. The reputation of the faculty and the standards at Grace spread rapidly, resulting in an explosion of growth. The uncompromising dedication to both the mastery of theology and the personal application of the Scriptures to life that McClain demanded for a school of theology resonated with God's people and made a permanent impact on the history of the Church.

Grace Theological Seminary, relocating to Winona Lake, Indiana, continued in the fall of 1939 with 28 students. The numbers grew each year from 28 to 37, 38, 54, 69, 73, 78, 79, 85, 99, and 144 by 1949. The seminary would continue to grow to over 400 students by the 1970s. A college division was added in 1948 to help prepare academically unqualified students for graduate-level seminary, with the number of college students growing from 32 to 45 and 50 in the first three years. This was the beginning of Grace College.

**The Impact of McClain on Whitcomb**

The appearance of three Princeton graduates at Grace Theological Seminary for graduate-level training made a strong, unspoken statement about the quality of the new school. And the three students, including Jack Whitcomb, distinguished themselves both academically and spiritually — thanks to the personal mentoring and teaching of Donald Fullerton. The details of John Whitcomb's ministries are summarized in later chapters.

28. Herman A. Hoyt, "An Academic History of Grace Theological Seminary," in *The History of Grace Theological Seminary, 1931–1951*, ed. John Whitcomb, 1951, p. 40–47.

There were many outstanding teachers at Grace, but none were equal to Dr. McClain. Dr. McClain soon provided a new example for Jack who would be complementary to his spiritual father, Donald Fullerton. McClain represented a godly man with profound theological insights, firm conviction of the authority and practicality of God's Word, great teaching, and leadership in battles for the truth. While Fullerton was a great Bible teacher and mentor, McClain was a true theologian — an academic skill that addresses the technical issues of doctrine using tools of language, history, logic, etc., to address the being, attributes, and works of God, and the interpretation and use of the Scriptures. McClain's personal interest in mentoring and guiding John Whitcomb proved invaluable during his early years of teaching and guiding the generations of men to follow.

John Whitcomb quickly distinguished himself as one of the top students in Dr. McClain's classes. As the responsibilities of a rapidly growing seminary, the building of a new campus, and ever-expanding class size grew, Dr. McClain began asking young John Whitcomb to help grade term papers and assignments in theology and other classes for a small hourly wage. Dr. and Mrs. McClain would often invite the young bachelor Whitcomb over to their house to review and grade papers and then to join the McClains for supper, discuss theology, the seminary, and other topics.

Professor Whitcomb remembers his mentor with fondness.[29] "Dr. McClain seemed to me to be a reserved person, quiet, with long-term goals. As I graded papers for him, we developed a warm friendship, as may be seen in letters he wrote to me."

*Theological Humility*

Like the Apostle Paul, McClain became spiritually strong in the context of physical weakness.[30] Although McClain excelled as an athlete

---

29. Personal interview by the author with John Whitcomb on June 2, 2016.
30. Dr. McClain in his later life could echo the testimony of Paul in 2 Corinthians 12:7b–10: "There was given to me a thorn in the flesh, a messenger of Satan to torment me — to keep me from exalting myself! Concerning this I implored the Lord three times that it might leave me. And He has said to me, 'My grace is sufficient for you, for power is perfected in weakness.' Most gladly, therefore, I will rather boast about my weaknesses, so that the power of Christ may dwell in me. Therefore I am well content with weaknesses, with insults, with distresses, with persecutions, with difficulties, for Christ's sake; for when I am weak, then I am strong" (NASB 1995).

in high school, his college injury and the development of an abdominal disorder plagued him for much of his life, leading to half a dozen operations and long periods of convalescence. The doctors of the day also followed the standard practice of prescribing months of "rest" to allow a "tincture of time" to bring healing. It appears that the combination of experience as a pastor and frequent ailments tempered and molded his personality. In his dealings with the weak and suffering, he provided compassion and encouragement. But in spite of his physical limitations, he rigorously embraced the clear teachings of God's Word and remained uncompromising on doctrine, principles, and practice.

On several occasions, McClain was ordered by his medical doctors to rest and seek medical help at some expert centers. Since he was unable to rest in Winona Lake with all of the seminary activities and visitors, and since the small town lacked medical specialists, he would go to McAllen, Texas, with his wife, where they had access to great doctors and were able to regain their strength in a small trailer towed behind their car. From there, he would write his books and send letters to John Whitcomb and others. The letters to John Whitcomb were typically of a technical nature, with teaching and guidance flowing between the lines.

One example is a letter dated February 19, 1952. By this time, John Whitcomb was helping with both grading papers and teaching. The issue was that many of the students were academically average men whose desire was to become a competent pastor and care for God's people. They had neither the ability nor calling to be the technical apologists that Wilber Smith described in *Therefore Stand*. Apologetics was John Whitcomb's calling, and his academic standards reflected this lofty goal.

Whitcomb may have wanted to fail a number of students and dismiss them from graduate school, but he first wanted to know how McClain would handle students who fell behind. They discussed one student in particular, including McClain's response in the February 1952 letter. McClain suggested, "If [the student's] mark is not too low, I would like to do what we can for him. Perhaps assigning him some extra work in Theology so as to get him through with a D." For others with delinquent papers, McClain suggested that rather than failing them, Whitcomb should give them an incomplete and reduce their overall grade by 1% per week of delay until their assignments were complete. But, he added, "I shall trust your judgment." In this way, Mc-Clain gently provided the guidance of a godly pastor who cared about people as well as a theologian who cared about academic standards. These men were not heretical in any way. Although not equipped for some tasks, they were each equipped in different ways with special gifts for God's service. A good teacher will do all they can to help struggling students without compromising the rules or standards of the school.

After McClain finished the letter, he wrote in the margin, "I trust you are enjoying the Lord's rich blessings in your teaching ministry."

The opportunity that John Whitcomb had to learn directly from Dr. McClain was unique. McClain was internationally recognized as a leading conservative theologian through the many lengthy articles and books that he published on numerous topics, including *Law and Grace; Daniel's Prophecy of the 70 Weeks; Romans: The Gospel of God's Grace; Bible Truths; The Inspiration of the Bible; Freemasonry and Christianity; Christian Theology*; and others. He was also a popular conference speaker, traveling throughout the United States for week-long Bible conferences. Furthermore, he kept busy with the details of being president of a seminary, which included administrative duties, fundraising, facilities management, etc. He was a charter member of the Evangelical Theological Society and served on the Scofield Reference Bible Revision Committee.

Two of his works were particularly enduring. The first was his curriculum with a detailed syllabus for each course. These have been adapted and utilized in seminaries and Bible schools throughout the world. In addition, he wrote *The Greatness of the Kingdom: An Inductive Study of the Kingdom of God*,[31] a masterpiece of dispensational theology.

## Reflections

On September 10, 1966, Professor Whitcomb wrote a special letter of appreciation to Dr. McClain to be included in a *Teacher Memorial Book*, prepared by students and faculty and to be presented to Dr. McClain. Whitcomb wrote,

Dear Dr. McClain:

---

31. Alva J. McClain, *The Greatness of the Kingdom: An Inductive Study of the Kingdom of God* (Winona Lake, IN: BMH Books, 1959), 556 pages.

I am confident that one of the main factors used by the Lord to lead me into the teaching ministry at Grace Seminary was your own faithful use of a very rare gift of unfolding the riches of God's Word. I can vividly remember the daily joy I experienced in your theology classes as I saw how you rejoiced in the depths of the riches we have in our Lord Jesus Christ. And now that the responsibility has fallen upon me to teach two of these courses in Christian Theology, I ask your prayers that I might reflect at least in part your skill in handling the Word of Truth and make its message clear and unforgettable to your students. I gladly acknowledge, under God, my deep debt to you in this great ministry.

John C Whitcomb Jr,
Professor of Old Testament and Director of
Postgraduate Studies.

Two years later, on November 11, 1968, Alva J. McClain died in Waterloo, Iowa, at the age of 80.

## Legacy

In the early 1970s, Professor Whitcomb began organizing his thoughts on the contributions of Alva J. McClain on Grace and in the Christian world. He noted that the McClain era was characterized by several healthy trends, namely an incorporation of the best of early 20th century fundamentalism into the pattern of teaching for which Grace Seminary became known throughout the Christian world. These patterns included:

1. Holding high the grace of God in every aspect of our salvation and a withdrawing from Arminian positions.
2. A strong commitment to the absolute inerrancy of the original text of Scripture, with the logical corollary of an emphasis on exegetical (rather than historical, philosophical, or creedal) theology.
3. A renewed focus on our Lord's Great Commission in Matthew 28, along with a definite turn away from the social gospel and from other neo-evangelical and ecumenical emphases [circa 1957].

4. A strong stand against the charismatic movement with its dangerous subjectivism, self-and-experience-centeredness, and its disastrous divisiveness.
5. A commitment to 24-hour creation days and a rejection of the theory of evolution [late 1950s].
6. An acceptance of God's covenant promises to the nation of Israel and thus a recognition of the distinctions (as well as similarities) between Israel and the Church in history and eschatology.
7. A new appreciation for the global dimensions of the Great Commission of Christ in terms of home and foreign missions.
8. Stronger emphasis on godly Christian character, personally and in the home, apart from which no theological position can be credible.
9. Even greater outreach into the church-planting and high-level indoctrination in America and overseas.
10. [Emphasis on the importance of] Christian schools.

Alva J. McClain was a truly great man that stood firmly on the Scriptures. His brilliant mind, his insights into difficult theological problems, his administrative skills, and his tremendous teaching skills changed the evangelical world forever. He was not only a great role model for John Whitcomb, but he also cared for him and nurtured him as a parent would for his own child. McClain stands alone as Whitcomb's "theological father."

Years later, Richard Grant, former editor of the Brethren Missionary Herald Publishing Company, sent a letter to Professor Whitcomb summarizing some conversations he had with Dr. McClain on the Scriptures, and specifically the gap theory.[32] In the last paragraph, he added,

> "Dr. Jack — Dr. McClain was proud of you and was most complimentary about you. Think of that!"

---

32. Letter from Richard Grant to John Whitcomb, June 11, 1992.

# Chapter 13

# Sib

"Serving El Señor"
July 1948–1961

## CHINA!

John Whitcomb's earliest and happiest childhood memories were from China. He knew of the suffering of the Chinese people economically, politically, and spiritually. He loved the Chinese people and determined to spend the remainder of his life as a missionary to China.

As John Whitcomb entered Grace Theological Seminary in September 1948, he was 100% committed to missions work in China and considered *no* alternative career pathways throughout his Master of Divinity training. He was also gifted in languages, being fluent in Spanish, capable in German and French, and learning Greek and Hebrew. Although he had completely forgotten Chinese, it had been his *first* language. He believed that the seeds of Mandarin remained buried in his brain, and perhaps God had intentionally planted the remnants of Chinese deep in his memory so that with proper nurturing, the linguistic seeds would rapidly sprout, grow, and blossom into fluent Mandarin.

But future plans of serving the Lord never negate immediate service. Paul instructed the Colossians to "Conduct yourselves with wisdom toward outsiders, making **the most of the opportunity**. Let your speech always be with grace, as though seasoned with salt, so that you will know how you should respond to each person" (Colossians 4:5–6; KJV; emphasis added). John Whitcomb and his closest friend and colleague, John Rea, took every opportunity both *inside* and *outside* the classroom to serve the Lord in every way possible in the city, county, and states that surrounded them.

John Whitcomb spent nearly all of his "free time" from graduate studies at Grace Theological Seminary in Christian activities: reading Christian books and other literature, teaching children and adults, witnessing in private and in public, and counseling or encouraging his fellow students. As in his final years at Princeton, the Whitcomb diaries testify to his incredible energy, stamina, and dedication to serving the Lord around the clock. Days were filled with seminary classes and studies, with an occasional afternoon break to play a pick-up football game with his classmates. His evenings and weekends were filled with complementary activities, including completing classroom assignments, reading Christian books, writing letters, and joining others in multiple evangelical service activities. Even Friday, Saturday, and Sunday nights focused on service to the Lord, as did academic trips and holiday vacations.

The activities that consumed his free time could be summarized in five categories: (1) Foreign missions with an initial focus on China, (2) Gospel Teams linked to Grace Theological Seminary, (3) Boys Clubs, (4) Sunday school teaching in churches, and (5) Crises management in the Princeton Evangelical Fellowship (PEF, see next chapter).

## Foreign Missions in China

From the time John Whitcomb became a Christian as a freshman at Princeton, he felt both God's calling and leading to foreign missionary service in China, and his certainty grew with time. But the book *Therefore Stand* also sparked his academic acumen and intellectual curiosity to find ways to defend the faith (Chapter 15)! He continually studied intensely and intentionally, as someone called to accurately defend the Word of Truth through use of strong literal hermeneutical principles and Scripture-based arguments. The two definite callings consisting of serving in foreign missions and concentrating in apologetics proved to be God's leading indeed! But not in the ways he expected.

Immediately before starting seminary, Donald Fullerton sent Jack Whitcomb to Hephzibah Heights for a summer of spiritual growth and exposure to missions-minded people. Providentially, he met Miss

Ruth Paxson, the retired missionary to China. By communicating personal stories, conveying desperate needs, and clarifying areas of unfinished work, she deepened the convictions in his mind and heart to service to the Lord in China. He also learned more about the China Inland Mission (CIM, founded by J. Hudson Taylor), made important contacts with missionaries, and began a "recommended reading" book list including *China's Millions*,[1] which he would begin studying in the fall of 1948.

## China Prayer Fellowship

On Saturday, September 11, 1948, just before starting classes in Winona Lake, Indiana, John Whitcomb joined Johnny Rea and Jim Stauffer[2] on a trip to Chicago, Illinois. The drive lasted three hours in each direction, providing ample time to talk before and after a visit to Moody Bible Institute — and to meet Elaine Johnson, John Rea's fiancée! During the trip, the three men discussed the many ways in which the Lord had blessed them individually and decided to form the China Prayer Fellowship at Grace. Although both Johnny Rea and Jack Whitcomb were committed to going to China as theologically sound missionaries, many red flags were already being waved.

## Evolution of Modern China

Historically, European nations dominated China through the mid-20th century. The USA was also involved, as seen by little Buster Whitcomb and his time in Tientsin, China, during the 1920s. In addition to the European and American influences in central and southern China, the Japanese Empire invaded China in the 1930s based on a desire for colonial expansion. Japan dominated the northern Chinese landscape from the late 1800s to 1945.

The Japanese invasion and domination of China in the first half of the 20th century was especially brutal on the Chinese. Japanese leaders, after a careful study of the colonial expansions of European

---

1. *China's Millions* was edited by J. Hudson Taylor and published in 1890. The book is a classic on missionary work in China and remains available online: https://archive.org/details/chinasmillions00tayl, accessed July 15, 2016.
2. Jim Staffer was a Grace Seminary student one year ahead of Jack and Johnny who was also interested in foreign missions.

nations, transformed it into an empire[3] with modernized and powerful armies, navy, and (later) an air force. The territorial expansion began with the conquest of Korea during the Sino-Japanese War of 1894–1895 with annexation of Korea in 1910. Japan proceeded into northern China (Manchuria) and defeated the Russian army in the Russo-Japanese War of 1905–1906, claiming rights over both Manchuria and Korea. The conquest continued with the invasion of the rest of China in 1937 as the Empire of the Sun swept through eastern China and as part of their plan to dominate the Eastern Hemisphere.

But WWII did not end as Japan had planned, culminating with a loss of their colonies, their air force and navy, firebombs destroying Tokyo and other major cities, atomic bombs evaporating Hiroshima and Nagasaki, and a massive invasion of the Russian Army into Northern China after the fall of Nazi Germany. The Japanese Empire collapsed. This left a political vacuum in China.

Two main factions emerged in China, leading to a civil war. Chiang Kai-shek (also known as Jiang Jieshi) led the Nationalist Chinese against Mao Zedong, who led the Communist and the Red Armies. In 1946, President Truman sent General George C. Marshall to China to mediate an end to the conflict and to form a coalition government. This mission failed, leaving the USA, a new global superpower, with a dilemma on what to do. Privately, the Americans believed that Jiang was a corrupt politician that could not be trusted, that no amount of American aid could save the Nationalist Chinese, that Mao (who helped American pilots who ditched their airplanes over China after bombing Japan in WWII) was not that bad, and that Western Europe more urgently required U.S. funding.

*The China Prayer Fellowship*

The China Prayer Fellowship began in Winona Lake, Indiana, shortly after the academic year began. On Friday, September 17, 1948, the men held their first prayer meeting on the China mission field, attended by Jim Stauffer, Jim Marshall, John Rea, and John Whitcomb in Jim

---

3. The transformation of Japan in the 1800's to a world power is known as the *Meiji Restoration.* The period began in 1868 when Emperor Meiji eliminated the last shogun and took control of the nation. The 2003 movie, *The Last Samurai,* starring Tom Cruise, is cast within this epic battle. A brief, representative history of the times is given on the following website: http://www.fsmitha.com/h3/h48japan5.htm (accessed July 16, 2016).

Stauffer's rented bedroom. The group met monthly, with focused areas of prayer, a practice that continued throughout graduate school. However, the Whitcomb diary entries revealed ominous developments. As early as Monday, November 8, 1948, he wrote, *"Attended prayer meeting for China. We considered the desperate need of China as communist armies capture MuKden."*[4]

In August 1949, the State Department released its "white paper" explaining Truman's administration's position on China and their prediction of a communist victory. The Truman Doctrine defined U.S. policy post-WWII in Asia as "non-involvement in China and Asia, with the exception of the rebuilding of Japan."[5] The Truman Doctrine had many repercussions that continue to reverberate, including the eventual invasion of South Korea by 75,000 soldiers from the North Korean People's Army under the assumption that the United States would do nothing.

Two months after the white paper, on October 1, 1949, Mao declared the founding of the People's Republic of China. The Nationalist Chinese, lacking leadership, money, and support from potential allies such as the United States, retreated to the island of Formosa (now called Taiwan). The political position of Truman toward China divided the USA, as many Americans believed that China was intentionally being lost to the Communists, in part, because of Communist infiltration of the State Department and other influential departments of the U.S. Government.

Whitcomb closely monitored the situation in China. On December 30, 1949, while spending Christmas break with Donald Fullerton, he made a special side trip to Philadelphia. He boarded the 9:30 a.m. B&O Railroad line in Trenton, New Jersey, headed for Wayne Junction, Philadelphia, arriving at 11:00 a.m. He proceeded to the China Inland Mission headquarters and talked to Mr. Griffin about the outlook for missionary candidates and the situation in China. The foreign

---

4   MuKden was a key city of northern China (Manchuria), located just west of North Korea. In 1905, it had been the site of one of the largest Asian land battles between Russia and Japan, with Japan pushing the border of Russia to the north. The city is now called Shenyang, the capital of Liaoning province of China, with a population of about 7 million people.

5.   From "Harry S. Truman: Foreign Affairs," online. See http://millercenter.org/president/biography/truman-foreign-affairs, accessed July 14, 2016.

missionary endeavors in China were in complete turmoil, and the future looked bleak.

In early 1950, the intention of the Chinese Communists became even clearer as Mao and Stalin agreed to a mutual defense treaty. This treaty signaled the unification of communist efforts and expansion, soon to threaten South Korea, Vietnam, and other countries where the Americans eventually fought, and many died. The treaty also bolstered a national alarm, fanned by Senator Joseph McCarthy, known as the Second Red Scare.[6]

Whitcomb continued to read *China's Millions*. On March 6, 1950, he received a book on Pastor Hsi[7] from the China Inland Mission. On April 22, 1950, he started reading *Hudson Taylor in Early Years*.

The interest in missions to China at Grace remained. On September 18, 1950, Dr. Arthur Taylor of the China Inland Mission was invited to come to Winona Lake and speak to the faculty and students. By this time, it was clear that the door to Mainland China for American missionaries was closed.

*Change of Plans*

By the time of Whitcomb's graduation from Grace Theological Seminary in May 1951, there were no opportunities for new missionaries in China. Instead, Drs. McClain and Hoyt offered John Whitcomb the unexpected opportunity to teach at Grace and continue his education toward a doctorate in theology. His thesis would be an exegesis of biblical evidences of "Noah's Flood."

Although Professor Whitcomb never got back to China until the 1980s, he always had China on his mind and in his heart. While growing up, I remember having canned Chinese food for dinner several times a week, such as Chun King chow mein or La Choi® chop suey — always with white rice and crispy noodles. As kids, we learned to use chopsticks — a skill used to impress our friends and colleagues for years, especially those from Asia. And for special occasions, the family would pack themselves into the Ford station wagon and drive to

---

6. The First Red Scare was the American panic in the early 20th century over widespread fear of communism spurred by the Bolshevik revolution in Russia and anarchist groups threatening worldwide domination.

7. Possibly *Pastor Hsi (of North China): One of China's Christians* by Mrs. Howard Taylor. First edition, December 1903.

a nearby town to enjoy a favorite Chinese restaurant. Even in his 90s, my father chose a good Chinese buffet to celebrate any grand occasion.

## Gospel Teams

The seminary students at Grace organized and staffed a number of outreach ministries collectively called "The Gospel Team."[8] The major activities included "Street Meetings" in Warsaw, Indiana, typically on Saturday evenings; visitation to Alfran Nursing Home on Sunday afternoons; a "Jail Team"; and similar ministries in Columbia City, Indiana, about 25 miles east of Winona Lake.[9]

*Street Meetings*

Warsaw, Indiana, is the county seat for Kosciusko County, located on the northwest side of Winona Lake, with the town of Winona Lake and Grace Theological Seminary to the east of the lake. The towns are only separated by a few miles, so few stores or shops survived in the little town of Winona Lake, except for Christian bookstores, a roller-skating rink, a diner, a post office, and a fire station/town hall. Most of the inhabitants of Winona Lake were employed or serving in some type of Christian organization or ministry or were seminary students. The "city" of Warsaw represented the closest opportunity for outreach to unbelievers.

The Gospel Team led evangelistic meetings every Saturday night, as weather permitted, on a street corner in Warsaw. John Whitcomb joined this activity on the first Saturday that was possible, September 18, 1948. At 7:15 p.m., he noted in his diary that he "and Johnny Rea drove to Warsaw to support the street meeting." During the first meeting, they gave out tracts. The following week, they returned to the street meeting and gave their testimonies, and "John talked to a young boy."

The street meetings included a primary speaker and support workers that would hand out tracts and talk to people one-on-one. They also took advantage of a local artist named Joe Dombek.

Joe would strap a large blank piece of white paper to an easel and then begin using big chunks of colored chalk with broad strokes to

---

8. From *The History of Grace Theological Seminary, 1931–1951*, ed. J.C. Whitcomb.
9. Columbia City, Indiana, is the county seat of Whitley County, immediately to the east of Kosciusko County where Grace Theological Seminary is located.

build the background for a drawing. The drawing would continue with more and more refining details until a landscape and foreground were complete. He would use white chalk to dot the sky and bright highlights on key structures to emphasize a rising or setting sun. The final strokes of the colored chalk would bring the entire effort into context. Black chalk would reveal an empty cave in a hillside, and brown chalk would outline three empty crosses on a hilltop. He would then stand back and switch on a series of lights from the top of the easel, highlighting different shades and colors to give the picture life, beginning with a black light to highlight the white "stars" in the sky, red to illustrate the early dawn, and white to slowly transition into the day.

Joe would say little to nothing — just draw and stand back. But he would open the door to a strong gospel message, focusing on the essentials of the gospel — "that Christ died for our sins according to the Scriptures, and that He was buried, and that He was raised on the third day according to the Scriptures."[10] Then the Gospel Team would step in and give the details of the message depicted on the easel and lead anyone who would come forward to meet the Lord.

As usual, the Whitcomb diaries recorded his weekly activities, including participation in the street meetings. For example,

- Saturday, October 30, 1948 — *"In the afternoon I folded tracts. Drove to Warsaw for the street meeting. There were crowds in town for the Republican convention of Governor Creighton. We had a very fine street meeting. Talked to two young boys, one being Lee Williams of Claypool, Ind."*

- Saturday, November 6, 1948 — *"I was in charge of the Street meeting and we finally got the equipment into the cars. There were few people at the meeting, but we gave out many tracts."*

- Saturday, November 13, 1948 — *"At 6:00 we met with several others at the Seminary for prayer. Johnny drove Dr. Hoyt, Jim Marshall and me out to Tippecanoe [Indiana] to Hohenstein Church. We gave testimonies, and Dr. Hoyt preached on Luke 9. Got home by 10:00 & had a pint of ice cream."*

---

10. 1 Corinthians 15:3b–4 (NASB).

- <u>Saturday, November 20, 1948</u> — *"At 7:00 PM we met at the Seminary for prayer and went downtown for the street meeting. The loudspeaker went off several times while Drury preached. At 8:00 we went to the high school to a Youth for Christ rally, where 'The Voice of the Deep' was shown."*

- <u>Saturday November 27, 1948</u> — *"Went to the street meeting. Spoke to a young boy and to a skeptical college student."*

- <u>Saturday November 12, 1949</u> — *"We went to Columbia City for a street meeting. About 25 showed up. Dombek drew and Dr. McClain gave a testimony. After 30 minutes it began to rain so we went home."*

- <u>Saturday, May 6, 1950</u> — *"Joe Dombek did a chalk picture. A good crowd gathered to watch Joe draw, so after I preached, Jack Teeter and Olin Followed. One boy from Burket, Ind. Chauncey Bennett, accepted Christ."*

In reviewing the historical documents and diary entries of my dad and trying to determine *where* the street meetings were held, I suddenly recalled a memory from early childhood when I was likely three or four years old (circa 1958). I remember sitting on a park bench in downtown Warsaw, Indiana, across the street from the Kosciusko County Courthouse on the southwest side, facing east. I remember a warm summer evening with the sun slowly setting behind us, the clear blue skies, and a few puffy clouds. I remember sitting by my mother, tying to remain on the bench and sit still. I can see my dad, standing about 8 to 10 feet in front of us, facing north, talking to a shorter man with a white collared shirt. Dad had some papers in his hand and was deeply engaged in discussion. I remember asking my mom whom he was talking to, and she said that she did not know — it was a stranger. I remember asking her several times about why he was talking to someone he didn't know and was told that he was talking to the man about the Bible. I remember being satisfied by the explanation, sitting quietly and watching my dad on a warm summer evening, in rural Indiana, serving the Lord.

*Nursing Home*

On Sunday afternoons, John Whitcomb faithfully joined the Gospel Team for outreach to the 50 residents of Alfred Nursing Home, about 5 miles east of Warsaw. The program lasted about two hours, beginning with a service held in the front hall, then an hour of visitation with the residents individually in their rooms.

The nursing home team was led by Calvin Roy and Herman Hein and included 15 other seminary students. John Whitcomb spoke during the teaching time on several occasions but participated more actively in the personal visitation and encouragement of the residents. Several elderly people received Christ as their Savior, and others, who were already Christians, were spiritually strengthened.

*Jail Team*

John Whitcomb, with pride rather than embarrassment, could truthfully say that he spent considerable time in jail! He began this ministry with the Gospel Team on October 3, 1948. His notes from that Sunday state, *"In the afternoon went to visit the jail and spoke to an Amish man. Afterwards I gave out tracts on the street and talked to three boys."*

Typical after-action reports include:

- Sunday, October 24, 1948 — *"I attended a jail service in Warsaw with Jack Zielasko* [a middler[11]] *and* [Fredric] *Fogel* [a senior]. *The two prisoners we spoke to were unreceptive."*

- Sunday, November 28, 1948 — *"Went with Jim Marshall, Fred Fogel and Jack Zielasko to jail and spoke with a rather unresponsive man from Claypool* [Indiana]."

- Sunday, February 6, 1949 — *"Jail – service – Arthur Sharp, 18 professed to accept Christ."*

- Sunday, June 12, 1949 — *"Had a brief testimony service, and I led Dorsey Wolfe to Christ. He lives 2 miles from Winona."*

---

11. A middler is a student in the second-year class of a three-year program.

- <u>Sunday, January 22, 1950</u> — *"At the jail were 12 men – 10 of them caught for stealing - from Pierceton. We spent 2 hours with them, and several made decisions."*

*Sib – Spanish World Evangelism*

To emulate foreign missions and improve his relational skills with internationals, Whitcomb specifically targeted the Mexican immigrant population who would come through the area to pick tomatoes and perform other manual agricultural tasks.

In January 1950, a student by the name of Sibley Marvin Edmiston entered Grace Theological Seminary. Sib was from the Long Beach Grace Brethren Church, a prominent church among the Fellowship of Grace Brethren Churches,[12] and a strong supporter of Grace Seminary. When their pastor, Dr. Lewis S. Bauman, heard that Sib had entered Wycliffe Summer School of Linguistics in Saskatchewan, Canada, to study Spanish, he contacted Sib and asked him to consider helping to start a missionary effort to Mexico — after additional training at Grace Theological Seminary. Sib, with his wife, Willetta, and three young children agreed to make the move to Winona Lake, Indiana.

John Whitcomb and Sib Edmiston began speaking to each other in Spanish, as both men wanted to practice and improve their Spanish for ministry purposes. They would meet at Sib's house for conversation and dinner, prepared by his wife. Willetta, also known as Willie, impressed John as an excellent cook, a devoted mother, and a fine Christian woman. Willie remembers John as always being clean cut, well dressed, and *very* well mannered.[13] John and Sib soon joined forces with another Spanish-speaking friend, Florent Toirac, and traveled to towns and farms in rural Indiana to meet with Mexican migrant farm workers and to hold evangelical meetings and Bible studies for them in Spanish.

Sib went on to become a Grace Brethren Missionary in San Ysidro, California, near Tijuana, Mexico. Florent became the founder of the

---

12. The Fellowship of Grace Brethren Churches represents a group of independent churches that share a common statement of faith and basic doctrinal positions. Unlike a typical denomination, there is no authoritative structure above the local church. The independent churches cooperate in supporting a mission board, a college and seminary, and other tasks that are beyond the capability of smaller congregations.

13. Letter to the author from Willetta Edmiston, February 2015.

Winona Lake–based radio ministry, Spanish World Gospel Mission, that broadcast gospel messages to millions of people throughout Central and Southern America for decades.[14] John Whitcomb would become Chairman of the Board for the Spanish World Gospel Mission. Throughout his career, he focused on supporting foreign missions, especially presenting *El Señor* to Spanish-speaking people in Latin America, rather than *Yesu Jidu* (耶穌 基督) to the Chinese people in Asia.[15]

## Boys Clubs

John Whitcomb had a heart for young men and believed that his many years in the Boy Scouts of America prepared him for leading Christian boys clubs.

### Presbyterian Boys Club, Part I

Prior to attending Grace Theological Seminary, John Whitcomb was a member of the Wallace Memorial United Presbyterian Church, Washington, D.C. So, he considered himself a Presbyterian.

Upon moving to Winona Lake, Indiana, John Whitcomb began looking for a good Presbyterian church to attend. On Sunday, October 10, 1948, he took the bus to Warsaw and attended the adult Sunday school class and the main worship service at the First Presbyterian Church. The sermon, he recalled, seemed a bit solemn. There were very few young people and only a scattered congregation. Afterward, he met the pastor, Dr. Goodlet Watson, who told him of some of the work there. John discussed his own background and desire to minister, and the pastor invited him to teach the adult Sunday school class.

---

14. Florent Toirac, a Cuban national, was a missionary to Cuba, Haiti, France, and Spain for 28 years, where he became aware of the difficulties of reaching the masses in remote areas. He was convinced that radio was a way to reach them and established Spanish World Gospel Mission with the radio program, *El Camino de la Vida* ("The Way of Life"). It was broadcast into Spain and Latin America. To accomplish the discipleship process, national missionaries were added to the ministry and supplied with literature, New Testaments, and Bibles to assist them in their evangelistic efforts. From http://spanishworld.org/a-brief-history-of-spanish-world-ministries/, accessed November 3, 2019.

15. John Whitcomb remained active in multiple foreign mission groups throughout his life, including the Grace Brethren and Conservative Grace Brethren with missionaries in South America, Africa, India, Europe, Japan, the Philippines, etc. — but never mainland China, although he often spoke at Chinese retreats and conferences in the USA.

# Sib

On Sunday, October 17, 1948, Whitcomb took the bus to Warsaw and taught his first adult Bible class at the church with only eight people attending. In the evening, he returned to attend a Christian education meeting at church: "It was quite dull." Dr. Watson offered him a young boys class to teach, starting the next week.

The following Sunday, Whitcomb taught his adult class and began his first Christian education class to six boys and three girls. In addition to a Bible lesson, he started them on a Scripture memorization plan developed by the Navigators.[16]

By mid-November, Whitcomb began having concerns about the church. After Rev. and Mrs. Schuey invited him to their home for Sunday dinner, it became clear that the Rev. was *not* a conservative Presbyterian, but rather favored the philosophical and biblically destructive trends of Princeton University and Seminary. In the evening, Whitcomb taught Acts 1 to three boys, but *"they were very inattentive and noisy."* That evening, he went on to attend the Baptist evening service and heard a good sermon on power over sin.

Whitcomb was given charge of the evening Christian Education class beginning Sunday, November 14, 1948. He decided to read the "Susie and Johnny" adventure series[17] to the boys to maintain their attention and to use the stories as a segue for evangelism and discipleship. He also discussed plans with the kids for starting a boys club on Sunday evenings. They seemed interested. He went home and read the section on "games" from a book, *Reaching Boys.* The following Saturday, Whitcomb hitched a ride to downtown Warsaw where he got a haircut and picked out a ball for the boys club.

The first Boys Club met in the Warsaw Presbyterian Church on Sunday, November 21. Joined by his friend Johnny Rea, they came 30 minutes early and set up the room. Ten boys came, but the adult pair struggled to maintain control. After some time, they calmed the chaos, and the two seminary students presented plans for a Christian Boys Club. They also gave out memory verses and pledge cards.

---

16. The Navigators was started in 1933 by a lumberyard worker in California who believed that memorization of Scripture was a key to a successful Christian life. The non-denominational ministry has headquarters in Colorado Springs, Colorado, with branches in over 100 countries. See https://www.navigators.org/Home.
17. The "Susie and Johnny Series" are adventure books written by J.C. Brumfield with strong Christian messages.

Over the next few months, only five boys attended regularly. By early February 1949, they decided that they needed to energize the program and challenge the boys. They decided to start a monthly contest for efforts in track-distribution, verse memorizations, and special projects.

The attendance fluctuated widely. On May 8, 1949, only one boy attended, but, Whitcomb noted, *"I had a good lesson with him."* On May 23, only one boy, named Don, came, but Whitcomb happily noted in his diary that "Jim led Don to Christ." On June 5, 1949, the Boys Club had their final meeting for the summer.

## The Chicago Boys Club

The Chicago Boys Club (now the Chicago Boys & Girls Clubs) was part of a national nonprofit Boys & Girls Clubs of America (BGCA) that runs after-school clubs centered around sports, recreational activities, and schoolwork and offers programs on character and leadership development, the arts, health, and life skills. One of the highlights of the Chicago Boys Club for underprivileged kids was to go to a summer camp at Winona Lake, Indiana.

Whitcomb decided to continue his focus on young men by volunteering to be a camp counselor. On Sunday, June 19, 1949, he visited the Chicago Boys Club directors, Rev. and Mrs. Cook. He was accepted into the program for the summer.

On Wednesday, June 29, 1949, the key staff members arrived by train from Chicago. Whitcomb was assigned as a counselor to Cabin 4 (the Wildcats). Unfortunately, Whitcomb felt that the introduction was more of "indoctrination" to the camp philosophy. Later *"We spent the evening around the camp, being devoured by mosquitoes as Thad Zubrzycki pointed out various plants and trees."*

Whitcomb met the other counselor for the Wildcats, Rich Carney, and had a talk with him on the Bible and salvation in their cabin. He continued to witness to Rich and talk to him about various topics such as the Bible, salvation, and eschatology. On July 6, he gave Rich a "Pilgrim Bible" and showed him some key verses. He talked about his own conversion experience. He invited Rich to church (the invitation was declined), but they did go to the Winona Lake Bible Conference meetings at the Tabernacle. On Sunday, July 10, Billy Graham preached.

They also had Bible studies together in the dining room, around the campfire circle, or in the dorm.

On July 7, the first group of 250 campers arrived from Chicago. Jack and Rich had nine boys that would stay through July 19 and were then replaced by the next group. However, the Whitcomb goals for the campers did not play out as planned.

On July 15, Whitcomb had a talk with Thad Zubrzycki concerning speaking to his boys on the Christian faith. *"He told me I should not confuse their minds."*

On August 4, Whitcomb was summoned to the camp headquarters, where he had a two-hour talk with Thad Zubrzycki on proselytizing campers. The next day, another leader, Bob Oliver, accosted him about witnessing to his boys. He had further talks with Thad and the others while preparing for a barbeque picnic.

On August 6, it was clear that "proselytizing campers" would not be permitted. He therefore announced his decision to leave the camp as soon as they could find a replacement. This led to another one-hour talk with Thad on proselytizing.

The next morning was Sunday, August 7. Whitcomb recounted, *"At 9:45 AM Rich and I took the 12 protestants to the open-air church. . . . I led singing and taught 6 boys John 10. Talked with John Rice on salvation, and later with him and Bob Oliver."*

The next morning, Mr. Clark told Whitcomb that another counselor had arrived and that he could leave. So, Whitcomb left the Wildcats and made arrangements to continue to meet with Rich Carney during his off time.

For the rest of August, Whitcomb faithfully rode his bicycle to the Boys Club for one-hour bible studies with Rich. They studied Old Testament men who emulated types of Christ, like Joseph, Noah, and Moses. On August 9, they studied Daniel 1 and 2. On August 11, they studied Daniel 3, 5, and 6.

On August 16, he went to the Boys Club to meet Rich but didn't see him. The next day, he had short session on Joel, and later studied Revelation 6–12 for 1.5 hours. On August 21, he received a message that Rich Carney wanted to meet in the afternoon, and they spent an hour by the stream on Revelation 13–17. On August 25, they finished the Book of Revelation.

When summer ended, Rich Carney returned to Chicago. However, John Whitcomb continued to keep in contact with him, encouraging him to consider accepting Christ as his Savior and to study the Bible, and he offered to help him sort through concerning personal and family matters.

## Presbyterian Boys Club, Part II

In the fall of 1949, John Whitcomb restarted the boys club at the Presbyterian church. As before, the attendance waxed and waned. Whitcomb decided to merge the boys and girls into one group for a Christian Education (CE) program. He continued to prepare Navigators cards for the CE. On December 11, Whitcomb noted in his diary, *"At the CE meeting, I went to the basement with the boys, & just wasted time with them."*

But the CE program was not the only problem. In early October, Dr. and Mrs. Watson were seriously injured in a car accident and were hospitalized for an extended convalescence. The following Sunday, the former pastor spoke, and Whitcomb decided not to return until Dr. Watson returned. The following Sunday, Whitcomb taught his adult Sunday school class then bicycled back to Winona Lake and the Brethren Church for Sunday worship service.

By March 1950, it was obvious that Whitcomb disappeared immediately after Sunday school, and the parishioners wanted to know where he was going. In fact, he regularly attended the Baptist church for morning worship. He announced that he would be giving up the CE meetings. By April, he was attending the Baptist church in the morning and the Brethren church in the evening, with the afternoons spent in nursing homes or in jail!

On Sunday, May 14, 1950, Dr. Watson finally returned to the pulpit. However, Whitcomb noted in his diary that *"He was not the same as he had been before the accident."* The following week, he taught his last adult Bible class at the Presbyterian church in the morning and then transitioned to Grace Brethren churches for the rest of his life.

The importance of teaching young people cannot be understated. Indeed, dedicated and skilled teachers are needed for this task. But it became clear that teaching children was not Whitcomb's primary calling. His place was with college students, graduate students, postgraduate teachers, preachers, and missionaries.

**Personal Outreach Efforts**

The energy and commitment of John Whitcomb to evangelizing and teaching went well beyond the "Gospel Team" activities. Upon relocating from Princeton, New Jersey to Winona Lake, Indiana, he took every opportunity to serve and help others in their ministries. His diaries are filled with notes on people that he encouraged or counseled, letters that he wrote to help friends and acquaintances, and volunteer work of every type. Since he was not married until 1953, he could spontaneously change plans and join in various outreaches or prolonged activities on his own schedule.[18] On Friday, September 24, 1948, for example, John Whitcomb suddenly decided to take off to Bourbon, Indiana, with Robert Nitz, a recent Grace graduate, to give out tracts and do personal work. The evening was a happy and productive one. John also noted in his diary, *"We sang hymns on the way out and back."* It was joyful service indeed.

---

18. See Paul's comments, 1 Corinthians 7:32–35.

# Chapter 14

# PEF

"If your father had not stood behind Mr. Fullerton, the PEF
would have died"
Judge Paul Pressler to the author, August 19, 2016
July 1948–June 1955

When Jack Whitcomb and Johnny Rea graduated from Princeton in
May 1948, the PEF was in excellent shape (see Chapter 11). Their
departure left a student leadership vacuum that was hard to replace, especially since their class tended to be older and battle-tested during the
years of WWII. Over the next few years, a number of events transpired
that threatened to end the PEF. Although Jack left Princeton University,
he never left the PEF, remaining engaged for decades, playing important
roles in supporting and transforming the PEF into an even more effective organization that persisted for at least the next 70 years.

Continued support for the PEF stemmed from his affection for
Donald Fullerton as his spiritual father, a deep appreciation for the
effectiveness of Fullerton's ministry, a sense that it was the PEF (more
than the university) that was Whitcomb's *alma mater*, and the value of
the PEF as a source of future students at Grace Theological Seminary.
This final theme reflected Whitcomb's happiness with the faculty and
students at Grace; the excellent theological training he was receiving;
and the personal encouragement and mentoring that could be offered
to PEF graduates by himself, Johnny Rea, Jim Marshall, and other PEF
alumni that were also at Grace.

Whitcomb's continued correspondence and engagement with
Donald Fullerton and PEF students proved to be critical to the future

of PEF, as the organization faced some challenges in student leadership, in mentoring, in organizational structure, in identity and purpose, and in relation to other ministries on campus and in the community.

Fullerton was an outstanding Bible teacher but was less comfortable with organizational and leadership roles. Fullerton served as executive secretary for PEF but surrounded himself with former PEF students, such as David Marshall, via an Advisory Council. Upon graduation from Princeton in 1948, Johnny Rae was immediately added to the council, but Whitcomb was not. However, Fullerton grew to trust Whitcomb's perspectives and advice, especially on theological matters. With seminary training, demonstrated wisdom, and continued involvement as a *de facto* counselor, John Whitcomb was not only added to Mr. Fullerton's Advisory Council, but he also became one of Mr. F.'s closest friends and confidants and was respected for his unselfish sacrifices of time and energy in support of the cause.

The key theological principle that Whitcomb advocated was uncompromising commitment to obeying the Word of God as the final authority for truth and practice. Further, he believed in the *perspicuity of Scripture*, the principle that the Bible can be understood by individual, regenerate ("born again") people through the enlightenment of the Holy Spirit and that people need to search the Scripture and judge for themselves what it means,[1] using proper hermeneutics. Finally, he also taught biblical separation, in opposition to the ecumenical movement, such that an individual and Christian organizations must be able to articulate their beliefs from the Scriptures and refuse to join with other groups who would dismiss theological and doctrinal principles in exchange for unity. It was the strong support and encouragement of Whitcomb for Fullerton, and the clarity in articulating and applying these principles, that played a great part in the ongoing success of the PEF.

---

1. Larry D. Pettegrew, TMSJ 15/2 (Fall 2004) 209-225. https://www.tms.edu/m/tmsj15i. pdf. Accessed online on December 14, 2019. The doctrine means that "Scripture is clear enough for the simplest person, deep enough for highly qualified readers, clear in its essential matters, obscure in some places to people because of their sinfulness, understandable through ordinary means, understandable by an unsaved person on an external level, understandable in its significance by a saved person through the illumination of the Holy Spirit, and available to every believer whose faith must rest on the Scriptures."

## 1948–1949 PEF President: Ernie Wright

Ernest (Ernie) B. Wright replaced Jack as the president of PEF in the spring of 1948. The new year got off to a slow start as Ernie became ill in the spring of 1948 and had to drop out of school for a significant amount of time. The new PEF student leadership continued the yearly calendar of events started by Jack Whitcomb. They chose three outside speakers to visit, including Richard Seume, Th.M., of Paterson, New Jersey, in October (a Baptist pastor and well-known conference speaker); Dr. Allan A. MacRae of Faith Theological Seminary in November; and E.A. Shank, Th.M., Director of S. African General Mission in December. They planned the Annual Reunion Banquet conference in December. They also planned another Moody Bible Institute film, "The Voice of the Deep," for October 5, 1948.

John Whitcomb returned to the Princeton campus on Monday, September 6, on his way from his relatives' home in Harrington Park, New Jersey, to Winona Lake, Indiana, to start seminary. He boarded the 9:00 p.m. train from New York City to Trenton, finding Ernie Wright sitting in the same car. They got to Princeton late that evening and spent the night in Middle Dod Hall.

The next day was spent talking and praying with Ernie and visiting several other PEF members, as well as arranging files, crafting letters, and providing advice for the coming year. That evening, Ernie invited Jack to his parents' house in Philadelphia. After supper, Ernie's dad asked questions about Grace Theological Seminary and evangelical Christianity. It became immediately clear that this man was "quite bitter against fundamentalism." Jack left the Wrights' home to catch the 11:45 p.m. train to Pittsburgh, where he would meet Johnny Rae and complete the trip to Winona Lake, Indiana, by car.

### PEF After Jack and Johnny

In early September, Ernie sent out a letter to the freshman (class of 1952) that was nearly an exact copy of the letter that Whitcomb had developed and sent the previous year. The letter included a brief welcome and introduction to the Princeton Evangelical Fellowship, noting that they meet twice each week for the purpose of studying and discussing the Bible and its applications to the individual life. The letter stated, "We believe that the knowledge of the Bible is essential for a complete education and that participation in Christian activities is a most important part of undergraduate life."

John Whitcomb continued a robust interaction with PEF, sending letters to Ernie on September 8, 10, 14; October 14, 16, 28; November 13, 23, 30; December 4, 11, 12, etc. He also maintained a close correspondence with Donald Fullerton, Stuart Hayes, Olin Ellis, Eddie Sampson, and other student members of the PEF.

On the positive side, there were some encouraging letters from Ernie, including plans to link a new believer one-on-one with a more mature believer for discipleship. On Tuesday, November 30, 1948, he said, "We received a long letter from Ernie telling of the 2 Timothy 2:2 plans — he with Bob McDougal, Olin Ellis with Dave Packard, Bob Snable, & Paul Till, Len with Bob Agee, Paul Kent with Archie, and Dick with Sam Van Culen." These revealed tangible efforts to mentor new believers.

However, some of the letters raised concerns. Whitcomb noted in his diary entry of Thursday, October 28, 1948, *"Got a long letter from Ernie, telling of PEF apostasy, Bob McDougal's conversion & Stu Hayes' growth, & coming 'Seume' meeting."* The details of the "apostasy" were not included, but a prompt reply was sent. On November 5, 1948, Whitcomb wrote a letter to Eddie Sampson, *"who has decided against Bible School in favor of 'remaining in simplicity.'"*

*Competing Interest*

Jack Whitcomb, and the PEF student leadership, had previously rejected the offer for the PEF to join the Student Christian Association in 1947 (Chapter 11). The issue centered on the authority of Scripture and obedience to biblical teachings based on clear hermeneutical exegesis and sound doctrine and respectful separation from those who reject these fundamental principles. This made PEF distinct from other student Christian organizations that seek to expand membership by accepting any so-called Christian on the premise that the Scriptures are unclear, filled with errors, unknowable (except for a few things), and that alternative interpretations to central doctrines of the faith are equally legitimate — if the person holds them sincerely. This is also the direction that Princeton Seminary had taken and why many of the faculty with a conservative view of biblical interpretation had left Princeton to start Westminster Theological Seminary near Philadelphia in 1929. Thus, the issue with other Christian organizations was not that they or their leaders had bad intentions, but rather that this was a slippery slope with no foundation for truth and no incentive to study, master, and obey the Scriptures.

In addition to the Student Christian Association, both the Intervarsity Fellowship (IVF — also known as the Intervarsity Christian Fellowship, IVCF) and a new group called the Baptist Students of Princeton began parallel programs. While these two new groups were strong evangelical organizations, the issue of insisting on biblical authority and separation from others with theologically liberal theologies was minimized for the sake of ecumenical unity. For new believers and immature Christians, this caused tremendous confusion and divisions (see below).

## Intervarsity Christian Fellowship

Back in Winona Lake, on Saturday, October 16, 1948, John Whitcomb was met by Cleo Buxton, a reginal IVF staff secretary. He met Whitcomb as a former PEF member and president and invited him to attend a state IVF conference in Indianapolis. They had a good talk, and Cleo joined Jack for lunch to continue the discussion. The issue was that the PEF was a completely independent organization committed to teaching the "Whole Counsel of God" as an inerrant and authoritative guide to salvation and a godly life. IVF was a large para-church organization and campus group that sought to be non-denominational and inclusive of all so-called Christians, despite with differing doctrinal beliefs — except for the "essentials." Therefore, PEF could not agree to "not teach" many clear Bible doctrines as a prerequisite for joining forces with IVF. Furthermore, since there was a strong, coordinated evangelical program on the Princeton University campus, there was no need for IVF to start another one. Although IVF understood and sort of agreed with this situation, Mr. Buxton would meet John Whitcomb again on the issue of IVF and PEF the following year with a new "plan," as IVF quietly continued to press forward to extend its network to Princeton.

## Christmas Break, 1948

Since John's parents were in Lima, Peru, he planned to return to Harrington Park, New Jersey, to be with his aunts and uncles — and cousin

Sally. However, he also used the trip east to visit Princeton to meet with PEF students and Donald Fullerton.

On Saturday, December 18, 1948, John boarded a train heading east to Philadelphia, Pennsylvania, to meet Ernie Wright and spend time encouraging him. They attended church together the next morning and spent the afternoon discussing PEF activities. That evening, they made the short trip from Philadelphia, Pennsylvania, to Princeton, New Jersey, to meet with Olin Ellis and other PEF members. On Monday, December 20, Jack spent the day meeting and praying with various "PEFers." The next morning, he proceeded to Plainfield, New Jersey, to the home of Mr. F.

Mr. F. and his "son" Jack Whitcomb spent the next three days together. Jack joined Mr. Fullerton in some Christmas shopping, visited various people, and dropped off Christmas presents. This afforded time for deep discussions and reflections on the past, present, and future of both PEF and Mr. F. Whitcomb urged Fullerton to come visit Grace, and since he would be in Gary, Indiana, in January, he promised he would.

On Christmas Eve, Whitcomb moved on to New York City and 51 W. 75th Street to Hephzibah House. There, he met many of the friends of Donald Fullerton and new acquaintances that Jack had made the previous summer at Hephzibah Heights (Chapter 12). After a short visit, he continued his journey to Harrington Park for Christmas with his family.

On December 27, 1948, John Whitcomb returned to Philadelphia to meet with Ernie Wright and Stuart Hayes (Stu), who would be the upcoming PEF president. They planned a retreat in a remote cabin that belonged to Stu's family to spend a couple of days together focusing on PEF and some theological issues. Tragically, Stu could not join them because his 12-year-old sister had just died. Ernie and Jack decided to go to the cabin anyway and spent important time together.

After the wilderness experience, Whitcomb returned to Harrington Park for a couple of days then headed back toward Winona Lake, Indiana, with a short stop at Princeton. He was able to meet with Olin Ellis and Lenox Palin, who agreed to come and visit Grace on January 25. After spending the night at Princeton, Whitcomb welcomed the new year of 1949 with a train ride back to Grace.

# A Good and Faithful Servant

On January 6, 1949, Mr. Fullerton and David Marshall came down from Gary, Indiana, to sit in some of Dr. Herman Hoyt's classes and then meet with Dr. Alva J. McClain. McClain, who had an upcoming conference in Lancaster, Pennsylvania, in March agreed to visit Princeton for the first time and give a talk to the PEF students.

However, Donald Fullerton was clearly discouraged about the student leadership of PEF under Ernie Wright, which was further diminished as Stu Hayes, the upcoming president of PEF, was also in the ROTC and was called to Fort Bragg, North Carolina, for special training. Olin Ellis, who had been a strong student member of PEF, was graduating and leaving for Grace Seminary. There were some promising freshmen, but they were linked with the new Baptist fellowship and would not make a firm commitment to the PEF. Fullerton began wondering if his time at Princeton should end, giving him the opportunity to return to the mission field where there were so many people who had never heard the good news of the gospel.

By the end of the 1948–1949 academic year, the PEF looked to be unraveling — as summarized by a letter from Donald Fullerton to "Dear old Jack," dated July 28, 1949:

> As to Princeton Evangelical Fellowship there is no clear leading for the future. Quite possibly our Lord may be preparing to move me to another field of labor. . . .
>
> On my part there is a desire to devote my time more fully to reaching the unreached in the regions where Christ is not known. There is no certainty whether that means going to the foreign field or helping prepare young men to go - The Lord knows the way I take and is able to direct my steps into His way. That's all I want.
>
> Dear old Stuie should return shortly from Fort Bragg N.C., and then we can talk over "things." As "presi" he faces a situation that takes much prayer and dependence on the Lord. From the human site the outlook is not bright. But in the past the P.E.F. has been at lower ebb. Always our Lord has shown Himself strong and able to do more than meet every need. Regardless of the opposition we can confidently trust His over-ruling power and wisdom. We covet your prayers for the accomplishment of His will in PEF.

## 1949–1950 PEF President: Stuart Hayes

The following academic year, Stuart Hayes replaced Ernie Wright as president of PEF. Paul Pressler, who attended Princeton from 1949 to 1953 and was the new PEF treasurer, remembers Stu as a quiet and reflective gentleman who loved the Lord and was an outstanding servant of the Lord. Pressler also noted that "In addition to being a Physics Major, Stu was in the ROTC, faced hostilities from his home, and had not been in a significant leadership position before."

Stu began his tenure as president following the organizational patterns established by Whitcomb several years before. The leadership invited only one speaker, Dr. O. Vansteenberghe of the Belgian Gospel Mission, to speak. Student participation in PEF met a new low. Few were attending the Sunday Bible studies, and only four students were meeting together, just once a week, for prayer. The Baptist Students of Princeton group was growing, and IVCF continued to make a push onto the Princeton campus even though there was an agreement to focus on other campuses where there was no evangelical student fellowship. The IVCF issue was also pressed on John Whitcomb in Winona Lake by Cleo Buxton of the North Central IVCF region, who was joined by David M. Howard of FMF.[2] But the greatest disaster was an attack by Stu's father on Donald Fullerton that caused Fullerton to resign and threatening the end of the PEF.

The details of the attack on Donald Fullerton were unknown to the former PEF students at Grace until a letter was received by Olin Ellis (to be shared with Jack and Johnny) on December 17, 1949. Fullerton recounts the events leading to his decision:

> Back in September Stu called me on the phone saying that he had to resign from the PEF in deference to his father's wishes. Then a week later he called again saying he had heard I was planning on going to Palestine. If that were so and I would not be in Princeton he could remain in PEF. The way to Palestine did not seem ripe, the estate could not be closed

---

2. Foreign Mission Fellowship was a student organization at Wheaton College in Wheaton, Illinois. David. M. Howard wrote the history of the organization (which had several name changes) in *From Wheaton to the Nations*. It is the story of cross-cultural missionary outreach from Wheaton College. Published by Wheaton College, first printing (January 1, 2001).

and I took the Sunday PEF meetings as I continued to plan on leaving Princeton and finding a successor.

Suddenly a letter came from Stu's father the last day of October. It was the nastiest I've ever seen, full of false accusations and charges against me and some against Stu. He threatened that if the assurance were not given that I would have no contact whatever with Stu he would "expose" me to the University authorities. So far as I know poor old Stu never saw the letter nor does he know of its contents. Of course, the whole thing is untrue, but you know the enemies of our Lord and His Gospel are willing to believe things against His servants. There are real problems involved to protect Stu and the PEF. Stu's father was even coming to 9 Middle Dod and talking to students. This situation was impossible for the President and Executive Secretary who could not meet and discuss the plans.

A letter was sent in reply in an attempt to clarify, assuring the man his charges were not based on fact and telling him that I would have no contact with his son simply because it was the wish of a father. But I continued to go to PEF several times though Chris [Wilson] was secured to take over the Sunday class — I have told him to feel his way carefully and if it seems possible and our Lord's way — to swing it to the I.V.C.F. eventually.

Although I met the conditions laid down by Stu's father, it was discovered he had sent a copy of his letter to me, to Dean [Francis R.B.] Godolphin. Thus the man proved his own words could not be trusted. He sent the copy the same time as the letter to me, never allowing any time for the demanded reply. Dean Godolphin has been visited. He had Mr. Beebe, Mr. MacCleann's successor[3] sitting on the interview. Mr. B is the product of Princeton Theological Seminary and Union [Seminary] of New York. A copy of my reply is being sent to Dean Godolphin, "to complete the file" as he put it.

Dr. John Glasser saw both letters, was incensed highly and has written the father and the Dean in all probability.

---

3. Burton MacLean (1946–1948) and H. Keith Beebe (1949–1954) served as Assistant Deans of the Chapel.

There has been the feeling that our Lord let this thing come because he laid it on my heart to get into other work last spring, but I was too slow in making the definite move. At any rate, when the vile communication came our Lord was asked to prepare my heart to reply in accord with His will. In the regular morning reading the passages were 1 Peter 2:19-24, Hebrews 12:1-5!! What a comfort and strength for the task.

Though no reply or retraction has come, the father was called on the phone with a request to meet with me and Chris. He flatly refused, making some very insulting remarks and finally gave himself away by expressing and reiterating his "hatred" for the fundamental position.

Now you ask of my plans — Nothing is settled. Certain things obstruct a move from this location just yet. But I'm watchfully looking to our Lord Jesus for His will.

The future of PEF is in His hands. I'm sorry I.V.C.F. is proceeding as in the past, seeing everybody, more or less, except me.

On December 14, 1949, George L. Bate, class of 1945, now teaching physics at Wheaton College, sent a letter to PEF alumni:

I am writing this letter informally in [*sic*] behalf of some alumni of the Fellowship who are giving a Christmas offering to Fr. Donald B. Fullerton, Executive Secretary of the Fellowship, who formerly taught the Bible classes at Princeton. It was originally intended, before we knew his plans of leaving Princeton, that this offering be an expression of our appreciation for his continued work at Princeton, and it is with regret that we must now regard it as a farewell token of our appreciation. . . .

As to Mr. Fullerton's plans, it must be confessed that efforts to assemble enough information to include in this letter have been largely unsuccessful today. The best that can be ascertained is that he has been looking to overseas missionary activity, possibly in Palestine. This propose gift will be for his own personal needs and other support in his undertaking, and as has been suggested, it will be accompanied with the designation: "To Mr. Fullerton as a small token of appreciation for his long and faithful work with the P.E.F., to be used for himself in pursuing the Lord's work whatever the Lord may lead."

Bate also provided some instructions on making the contribution, adding,

> Enclosed will be found informal note stationery, on which each contributor is asked to at least sign his name and in addition (preferably so) to including some personal word of greeting, appreciation, or expression of Godspeed in future work, to Mr. Fullerton, as each one feels led.

With Fullerton's resignation, Stuart Hayes believed he could continue to serve as the president of PEF, while Dr. Christy Wilson Jr., class of 1944, taught the Sunday afternoon class and Rev. J. Anthony Cunio, pastor of the church of the Open Bible in Trenton, New Jersey, would drive up to Princeton on Thursdays to conduct a Bible class. However, this arrangement could only be temporary because Dr. Wilson was planning to leave the USA the next summer as a foreign missionary, and Pastor Cunio could not lead the PEF because, according to the bylaws, the leaders must be Princeton graduates.

*Whitcomb Takes Action*

John Whitcomb immediately reached out to Donald Fullerton with plans to come and help. He soon received a letter from Fullerton stating, "Of course I wanted to see you and will be glad to have you visit me anytime convenient to you after Dec 26. Will have a bed for you, as in the past, for as long as you would like to remain. It will be great to hear all the news from Grace and points west."

Whitcomb arrived in Plainfield, New Jersey, on December 27, 1949, to meet Donald Fullerton. They initially met over dinner to discuss the letter and various missions. John himself was still planning to go to China, so they had much to discuss indeed.

The next day, Whitcomb and Fullerton were met by Christy Wilson, who arrived from New York. Jack updated everyone on Cleo

Buxton's plans about IVCF in the eastern United States. They discussed the possibility of keeping PEF separate from the seminary, even if IVF took the undergraduate leadership.

On December 29, 1949, Whitcomb was given the letters Fullerton had received from Stuart Hayes' father and also one to him by John Glasser. Fullerton went to Washington to meet with Bill Oncken, a PEF Advisory Council member and Executive Council member, concerning the upcoming PEF Executive Counsel meeting planned for January 7 in Princeton. While Fullerton was in Washington, Stu Hayes arrived, and he and John discussed the PEF and related issues at length. John noted that Stu was having problems with the prayer meetings and some intellectual difficulties.[4] They had prayer together, and he left at midnight.

On December 30, 1949, while in Philadelphia to visit the China Inland Mission and meet with his friend Ernie Wright, Whitcomb noted in his diary, *"I talked to Ernie about Grace, and he discussed deciding to go the Princeton Seminary and ideas on a 'broad' ministry like Niebuhr.[5] We discussed this for several hours and had prayer."*

Whitcomb visited some other friends then returned to Winona Lake with Olin Ellis by car on January 2, 1950. Seminary classes began, and they returned to their usual routine.

---

4. John Whitcomb diary, December 29, 1949. Of note, Stuart Hayes grew up an "Episcopalian choir boy" but became an atheist after reading some critics of Christianity. After attending some of Donald Fullerton's Bible studies, he suddenly understood justification by faith and became a Christian. However, he began struggling intellectually when Fullerton told him that "If I found one mistake in the Bible — everything will collapse." He had many genuine historical questions, but rather then approaching them as John Whitcomb did (e.g., *The Genesis Flood*), he suffered many years of doubt, afraid that everything might collapse. After Princeton, he served in the military (including a tour in Korea) then earned a Ph.D. in physics at the University of New Mexico and a B.D. and S.T.M. from Faith Theological Seminary. He had a career in teaching physics and mathematics in several universities and in a private prep school near Princeton. He finally came to terms with his doubts by a careful study of the Gospels, resulting in the book, *The Gospel of John: Does it Have Historical Validity?* (WestBow Press, January 15, 2016).

5. Reinhold Niebuhr was an influential political philosopher in the mid-20th century. He pastored a church in Detroit and became opposed to capitalism — then joined Union Theological Seminary in New York City where he taught theology, wrote books, and lectured. He opposed liberal theology but was a political socialist and became a left-wing, anti-Communist Democrat in the 1940s. His writings focused on the intersection of Christianity and politics, and justification for war and political actions. From http://www.britannica.com/biography/Reinhold-Niebuhr, accessed June 19, 2016.

# A Good and Faithful Servant

## Heartfelt Letters and Renewed Dedication

Donald Fullerton, writing as the executive secretary, sent out a letter on the same day as Stuart Hayes. Fullerton communicated that the Executive Board of the PEF met in special session on January 7, 1950, to consider a course for the immediate future. A new executive secretary was needed, but that the current volunteers of Rev. Cuneo and Christie Wilson could not fill that role. It was decided that they should seek a new executive secretary to replace Fullerton who was a Princeton graduate without outside affiliation.

In response to George Bate's December 14 letter, former PEF members and friends began pouring in incredible letters of support and appreciation to Donald B. Fullerton to the designated address. Jack, Johnny, and Olin joined the effort by telling Mr. F. directly how his personal care and dedication to them, his clear and unapologetic Bible teaching, and his example had changed their lives. More importantly for Jack, Donald Fullerton had led him to the Lord and become his own spiritual father. By the end of January, the notes to Fullerton were compiled, and in early February, they were handed to him by the PEF treasurer.

Shortly thereafter, Whitcomb received a personal letter, dated February 6, 1950, from Donald B. Fullerton to Jack.

> Your part and generous remembrance and gracious expression of appreciation of the PEF activities, touched my heart deeply. It was late when I returned from Princeton with the precious packet in my pocket. When Paul Pressler handed it to me, it seemed best to delay investigation until I was alone with our Lord. A bit weary in body, in the wee small hours, I sat up in the bed and read the notes one by one, thanking and praising our Lord Jesus for His work in each life and for the joy of our fellowship together with the Father and His beloved Son.
>
> As the times in Princeton are thought over, there are deep regrets over failures to have been used more greatly, but there are also great rejoicings of heart for those things our Lord has been accomplishing in many hearts.
>
> There is a special joy in the way he brought you and Johnnie and Olie to Himself just before your entrance into

military life. How thankful I am for you in this respect! Army life and action without the Savior is a devastating thing to spirit and soul, as well as body. My heart is filled with praise for the way He caused you to grow spiritually in those days, preserving you and preparing you for His service, and for your labor unto Him in the PEF subsequently. Your diligence in the spiritual leadership, as well as in the executive and paperwork meant a great deal in forwarding the effectiveness of the witness on the campus.

As you complete your preparation in the next sixteen months, may the blessed Holy Spirit have free reign in your heart, mind and life, that in all things Christ may have the preeminence unto the accomplishment of the will of God. . . . The Lord bless you abundantly, beloved son, until He comes again. May you ever be a fragrance of Jesus Christ.

Yours ever in His deep and joyous hands,
Donald B. Fullerton.

On February 22, 1950, two letters were sent out to the friends and members of the PEF. One letter was from the executive secretary, Donald Fullerton, and the other one from the PEF president, Stuart Hayes.

Fullerton noted that as he stepped away, Pastor J. Anthony Cunio of the Church of the Open Door in Trenton, New Jersey, would teach the Thursday evening Bible class, and Dr. J. Christy Wilson would teach Sunday afternoon — but this would be a temporary accommodation. Fullerton would *continue* as executive secretary until a replacement could be found.

Stuart Hayes' letter summarized the departure of Donald Fullerton, noted the poor attendance in the fall, etc., and ended with this comment:

I feel that all of us here in the P.E.F. need a renewal and a revival in our own hearts. We need really to live and experience the New Life which is promised to us in the Bible. We need zeal to do God's work and a courage to do His will. And we need to be united by the love with which Christ loved us that we might work and pray with one accord.

In the meantime, the Baptist Students of Princeton were also having some growing pains.[6] They noted that individual students at Princeton did not have sufficient time to follow up with interested students. They had difficulty finding good speakers, and with different speakers at each meeting, there was no effective chain of thought. They wanted a fulltime worker to come to Princeton to lead the effort and also felt that the town of Princeton needed a good Baptist church supporting the effort.

While Fullerton was central to the PEF, he was not a fulltime campus minister (as the Baptists wanted); he lived outside of the town of Princeton in Plainfield, New Jersey, and he only made trips to Princeton a couple of times a week at most. He also recognized the need for a good Bible-believing church in the town of Princeton. Indeed, he had urged David Marshall to consider coming to help start a Baptist church and serve as pastor.[7] However, Fullerton was concerned that the Baptist Students of Princeton was too ecumenical and was developing strong ties to Princeton Seminary and therefore had a dangerous future. The group was also splitting the time and effort of the students attending PEF, and new or young believers who followed the Baptists Students of Princeton would not be getting the solid, systematic Bible teaching and encouragement that PEF offered. And he was right.

*Whitcomb and Rea's Response to the Unraveling of the PEF*

The Princeton men — Whitcomb, Rea, and Ellis — were tied up with schoolwork, so they invited Mr. Fullerton to come to Winona Lake for a visit. He arrived on Sunday, March 19, 1950, which coincided with the Annual Missionary Conference at Grace, and he stayed through the morning of March 22.

The former PEF members and mentor spoke at length about Princeton and PEF. For the first time, Mr. F. seemed to be encouraged about PEF, highlighting the efforts of Paul Pressler, Waring Jones, Dick Sharrett, and Bill Whipple. He also had the privilege of leading three more students to the Lord. That evening, Fullerton gave a 20-minute

---

6. A newsletter from the Baptist Students of Princeton to "Dear Brothers in Christ," dated June 1950 from H. Paul Pressler, John S. Riser, Ted M. Martin, Grady L. Smith, George Dawkins, Dan Blalock, L. Jack Caudell, Stanley Powell, and M. Dale Larew (Executive Committee, 1950–1951).

7. Whitcomb diary, Monday, March 20, 1950.

talk on John 15 to support the Missionary Conference. Jack and Johnny began making arrangements to return to Princeton as soon as possible and help strengthen the effort.

*Jack and Johnny Return to Princeton*

After making arrangements in Winona Lake, Jack and Johnny took a train to Princeton, arriving on May 24, 1950. Whitcomb reported on this trip in a letter to the alumni and friends of the PDF, dated June 2, 1950. He stated,

> When I arrived in Princeton on the evening of May 24, I went directly to 9 Middle Dod Hall (our campus HQ since 1946), expecting to find three or four students there. But my heart was overjoyed when I discovered ten students gathered for prayer. As I was introduced to the new members, I was told that the prayer meetings are held every night now, instead of twice a week, and that much progress has been made in attendance and spiritual power in recent weeks. To me, vital and powerful prayer meetings are the key to fruitful campus evangelism; and that is why I ask each of you to join me in praising God for his continual faithfulness (II Tim. 2:13) and asking great things of Him for the coming year, to the glory of Christ our Lord.

Jack continued his letter with an update on the detailed plans for the coming fall, including plans for key student leaders (mostly sophomores and juniors) to come to campus early in preparation of meeting the new students. The PEF headquarters was to move to 33 Blair Hall, where Ted Martin, class of 1952 (the new PEF president), was rooming with Paul Pressler and Bill VanderHooven (a new believer). With regard to Mr. Fullerton, he wrote,

> Mr. Fullerton has not ceased his active interest as Executive Secretary, even while Christy Wilson has graciously taken responsibility of teaching the Sunday class this year. As Christy expects to leave the country this summer, it is quite possible that Mr. Fullerton will resume teaching Sunday class in September.

Jack concluded his letter to the alumni by urging them to show support in three ways. (1) <u>Continued intercession</u> in prayer for this vital work. (2) <u>Personal contact</u> by letter or visiting the campus to encourage students in their Christian lives and testimonies. (3) <u>Material assistance</u>, whether it be Christian literature for the PEF library or monetary contributions that the work of the Lord may be carried on efficiently to the glory of Christ in the days of increasing unbelief. Signed, "Jack Whitcomb '46."

*Summer of 1950*

During the summer of 1950, John Whitcomb traveled to Lima, Peru, to spend time with his parents. He continued an active correspondence with Donald Fullerton, who kept him abreast of the situation.

One of the letters received by John from Donald Fullerton while in Peru, dated July 30, 1950, provided some encouraging developments:

> The G.A.R. Baptist[8] are proceeding to establish a work in Princeton. We hope they will cooperate with the PEF in days to come. I met with them down in Princeton in June. Paul Taber's pastor was there, Pastor Stowell. He is much interested and seems to be an able, true and understanding servant of the Lord. This will need much prayer.

There was hope for the future.

**1950–1951** *PEF President: Ted Martin*

Ted Martin was now president of PEF. Ted was from El Dorado, Arkansas, and his father was president of the Lion Oil Company. He was the roommate of Paul Pressler, whose father was a vice president of Exxon. Judge Pressler recalls[9] that Ted's father was not a believer, while his own father had trusted the Lord in his teenage years and had not grown spiritually because of the failure of his pastor. He continued,

---

8. *Greater Association of Regular Baptist* (GARB). This is a conservative, fundamental group of independent Baptist churches. Doctrinally, they were closely aligned with the PEF and Fullerton (a Plymouth Brethren — differing only on polity such as the definition and role of elders and deacons), especially with respect to the inerrancy and authority of Scripture. This new development was in line with Fullerton's desire to see a new, independent, Bible-believing church planted in the town of Princeton, New Jersey.
9. Paul Pressler III, Letter to the author, August 19, 2016.

"It was funny when we would get together because Ted and I did not drink and had a very clear testimony for Christ. The fathers would slip away and go drink a little bit when the two families would get together. Usually it is the other way around!"

Judge Pressler remembers Ted was the most giving, caring person he had ever known. He was kind, thoughtful, and had a real compassion for leading people into a saving knowledge of Jesus Christ. Ted ultimately led all members of his family to Christ. After Ted graduated from seminary, he went on to Campus Crusades for Christ and became head of their Institute of Biblical Studies. He wrote most of the training materials for Campus Crusade and was a fabulous Bible teacher with a real compassion for lost people.

Following John Whitcomb's advice to the PEF students the previous spring, the new leadership met late in the summer and made plans for the coming year. This included inviting nationally known Bible teachers to Princeton, without any funds for travel or honorarium, and without discussing any of their plans with Donald Fullerton. However, the decisions, made in "good faith," worked out well.

On October 21, 1950, Ted Martin Jr., president of PEF, sent an update to the Friends of the PEF. He wrote, "Late last spring the Lord richly blessed the work here on campus as a number of fellows turned to the Lord for that salvation which is found in none other. We are persuaded that this blessing was a result of certain Christians praying for us. *"The effectual fervent prayer of a righteous man available much"* (James 5:16). We again find ourselves in need of prayer by strong Christians." He specifically noted the plan to have Harold John Ockenga, Ph.D., D.D., Litt.D., LL.D., come to campus for four lectures on the subject of the knowledge of God, scheduled for November 27–30, 1949.

## Ockenga Meetings

Dr. Ockenga served as pastor of the famous Park Street Church, Boston, Massachusetts. He was one of the most important pastors among evangelical Christians at that time.[10] Fullerton was quite anxious about the

---

10. Under Ockenga's leadership, the Park Street Church grew to support over 100 missionaries on foreign fields. They began broadcasting the morning and evening services throughout the eastern United States with great effect. In addition, they conducted an evening Bible school with 586 students attending in the 1950 session. Dr. Ockenga was named president of the new Fuller Theological Seminary in Pasadena, California, although he remained in Boston. He also authored eight books and lectured throughout the world.

logistics of bringing Dr. Ockenga to Princeton and worked hard behind the scenes so that the itinerary, travel arrangements, visit, and honorarium would not be an embarrassment to the PEF student leaders.

The Ockenga meeting would be the make-or-break event of the PEF that fall. Four meetings would be held on a Monday through Thursday night, November 27–30, 1950.[11] Paul Pressler, president of the Baptist Students of Princeton, threw the full support of this organization behind the PEF, assisting in advertising and supporting the event. A glossy bulletin was also developed and widely circulated.

Eight days before the lectures, a young man named Shelly Ivey came to the Sunday Bible afternoon class of Dr. Fullerton and asked to speak to him afterwards.[12] Fullerton spent the afternoon and evening with this young man, and at 10 o'clock that night, he accepted the Lord as Savior. After that evening, Shelly would remark, "It's all too wonderful!" Shelly, who knew little of the Bible, responded by inviting all his friends to the Ockenga meetings.

Dr. Ockenga's messages were "very scholarly, true to the Word, exalting Christ and clear in the salvation message."[13] About 200 people attended each night, including a few members of the faculties of the university and seminary.

Shelly Ivy also came each night, accompanied by groups of his friends. Some of them would accept Christ and then would follow up with Fullerton. The exception was on the third night, when Shelly cracked his head on the floor in a wrestling match and was confined to the infirmary. Despite the fact that he missed the meeting, he took the opportunity to witness to another sick student, who then met with Fullerton the next day.

Fullerton noted that "the series was used of God to start thinking, to stir up interest, and direct hearts to Christ."[14] He later recognized this as a major turn in PEF. Not only were the messages excellent, but the event created a sense of urgency and united the students to a common cause. But most importantly, Shelly, the little Jewish student who

---

11. The messages were: "The key to the solution of your intellectual difficulties with Christianity," "The Word of God," "The Everlasting Gospel," and "The renaissance of the Soul."
12. Letter from Mr. Fullerton describing the results of the Ockenga meetings and Princeton University, December 6, 1950.
13. Ibid.
14. Ibid.

Fullerton noted "was not impressive to look at," really challenged the other PEF members to go out and reach others for Christ.

*The PEF Reaches New Heights*

Fullerton sent a three-page, single-spaced letter to "PEFers and friends of the PEF" in March 1951. The letter included an update on a missionary trip to Mexico during January and an update on the year's activities on campus:

> Of course you want to know the news of our Lord's work on the campus. This has been a most blessed year. In the last four months about a dozen students have professed to receive Jesus Christ as Lord and Savior or have returned to a faith in Him which has been badly shaken. Most of them are going on well. The P.E.F. has as strong and vital a testimony as at any time in the past twenty years of its history. . . .
>
> On the return to the campus in February, P.E.F. was clicking well under the leadership of Ted Martin '52, Bill Whipple '53 and Sam Rochester '53. . . . The Sunday afternoon Bible classes range from 12 to 25 in attendance, with splendid interest. The daily prayer meetings have increased so that in March there is an attendance of 9 to 14 students each evening. . . the Exec. Sec'y has made many trips to "the best old place of all" on week-days to talk with students concerned about their spiritual welfare. Our Lord has enabled and blessed abundantly, in meeting their problems and needs.

Fullerton finished the letter describing the PEF missionary conference with five missionaries and Christian workers from Africa, the Philippines, and Haiti providing visions of the "privileges, responsibilities, hardships and joys of serving our Lord in this dark world, and to realize the tremendous need for men to go to those who have never yet had the opportunity of hearing the message of salvation for the first time."[15] The final page gave brief updates of former PEF students, most

---

15. A clip of the event in a newspaper reported, "The Princeton Evangelical Fellowship marked the twentieth anniversary of its activities on the Princeton campus earlier this month by holding a Missionary Conference, highlighted by the presence of five missionaries from Africa, the Philippines and Haiti and by the showing of the color

of whom were missionaries, pastors, Christian workers, or in seminary training. He finished the page noting that "I'm thankful to report that all\* the above are most happily married, busily raising lively families in addition to their other activities." The "\*" led to a footnote at the bottom of the page that read, "Except Jack, who is still an unclaimed blessing."

## 1951–1955, Confusion and Division – IVCF

The Apostle Paul wrote some interesting words about divisions among those claiming to be Christians in his first letter to the Corinthians:

> For, in the first place, when you come together as a church, I hear that divisions exist among you; and in part I believe it. For there must also be factions among you, so that those who are approved may become evident among you (1 Corinthians 11:18–19).

The issues being discussed are often technical issues of biblical interpretation and their application to practice. They are not obvious in their content or implication, as some fall under the rubric of Christian liberty and preferences, and some under the category of secret heresy.[16] Tragically, with any division, there are some that take one path, and others another — "and that makes all the difference."

The desire and intent to do something that is "good" is not enough. As the old proverb warns, "The road to Hell is paved with good intentions." Amazingly, the right answers to every question pertaining to life and godliness is in the Word of God.[17] Thus, when conflicts do arise, it is certain that there are nefarious motives on one side or both that are not often obvious and requires both the study of Scriptures for truth and searching of the soul for motive.

On the campus of Princeton University, the activities of multiple Christian groups were a source of major concern to Donald Fullerton and the PEF.

The Christian Student Association was not evangelical or Bible believing (i.e., as inerrant and infallible). They had their own problems;

---

film 'Oh for a Thousand Tongues,' presented by the Wycliffe Institute of Linguistics. The Baptist students of Princeton cooperated in the arrangement for the two-hour sessions."

16. See, for example, Acts 20:27–32; 2 Corinthians 11:13–15; 2 Peter 2:1; and others.
17. See, for example, 2 Timothy 3:16–17 (especially within the context of this chapter); 2 Peter 1:3–11, 3:14–18; etc.

Unitarians demanded membership that was opposed by the Episcopalians. The issue was settled with membership based on no doctrines, except that the individual states that they accepted "Jesus Christ as Lord and Savior." Thus, they became irrelevant as a Bible-believing organization.

The Baptist Students of Princeton had strong student leadership and was a strong supporter of PEF. Paul Pressler, as the president of the organization, was an outstanding young Christian man who vigorously supported the principles held by the PEF on the inspiration, infallibility, and authority of Scripture, etc., but also continued to support the Southern Baptist Convention. Indeed, he would lead a major effort within the Southern Baptist Convention in the 1990s on these very principles because *this* was *A Hill on Which to Die*.[18] However, student leadership continually turns over, and there were no older, experienced, and seasoned Bible teachers or pastors to provide oversight, direction, and guidance.[19] This made the organization highly susceptible to missteps or to be taken over by entities that had views on the Bible and mentoring of young men that were unacceptable to the principles of the Bible held by PEF.

Finally, the IVCF continued to push their agenda on the Princeton campus. The issue here was not a disagreement on "core doctrines" but rather the ecumenical view of IVF that rejected teaching of doctrines that were considered by the IVF to be non-essential and potentially divisive. PEF would not compromise their organization by refusing to teach some controversial portions of Scripture for the sake of unity. Thus, while there was mutual respect for the leaders and intentions of each organization for the other, they could not work together on a small campus, and the presence of both was a growing problem.

18. See Paul Pressler, *A Hill on Which to Die: One Southern Baptist's Journey* (Broadman & Holman, 1999), 362 pages, https://www.alibris.com/A-Hill-on-Which-to-Die-One-Southern-Baptists-Journey-Paul-Pressler/book/2904824. Description: "The battle for conservative control of the Southern Baptist Convention lasted for decades. It cost people their jobs, their family stability — and even their faith — as moderates and conservatives fought to dominate the nation's largest non-Catholic religious group. *A Hill on Which to Die* is the story of how conservatives brought the denomination back to the Word and will of God, in what many call the most important religious event of the 20th century."

19. The importance of elders and overseers in the Church cannot be underestimated. The qualifications are given in 1 Timothy 3:2–7, and some guidelines for elders and warnings to young men are given in 1 Peter 5:1–7.

*Decisive and Divisive Actions of PEF Related to the IVF*

The leadership of the PEF wrote a joint letter to Mr. C. Stacey Woods, General Secretary, Inter-Varsity Christian Fellowship, Chicago, Illinois, on May 8, 1951, to state their grievances with the IVCF's actions on the Princeton campus over the past year. Excerpts from the letter include:

> The Executive Committee of the Princeton Evangelical Fellowship at its annual meeting in Princeton, April 28, 1951, unanimously requested its Executive Secretary to write you concerning the activities of representatives of the Inter-Varsity Christian Fellowship on the Princeton University Campus.
>
> We want you to know that we are most thankful to God for the way He used your organization on many campuses where previously there was no sound witness for our Lord Jesus Christ. Prior to your entry into the United States, Dr. Howard Kelly of Baltimore and Mrs. R. B. Haines of Germantown assured our Executive Secretary that IVCF was coming into this country with the distinct understanding that it would not work on campuses where Evangelical work already existed. Even today several hundred colleges in the U.S.A. are said to be without a sound Christian testimony.

The letter went on to outline the work of PEF, which had predated the IVCF by over a decade, including descriptions of the high quality of the Bible teaching, weekly prayer meetings, and strong student involvement. It continued:

> IVCF activities on our campus this academic year have detracted from this established work and brought division. This — when so many college campuses are without any established sound Christian testimony.
>
> It is our belief that God directs His servants in different ways and methods, and that each must respect the labors of others, provided they are in harmony with God's Word. Because our methods do differ from yours, our Executive Secretary has declined invitations to address IVCF chapters for the past fifteen months lest any misunderstandings might arise.

# Sib

Some years ago, as General Secretary of the I.V.C.F., you gave your word to Mr. Donald Fullerton, Executive Secretary of our work for the last 20 years, that as long as he was working in the Princeton Evangelical Fellowship and that organization maintained its sound position in the things of the Lord Jesus, the I.V.C.F. would not interfere on the Princeton campus. Because of our differences this seemed important. We seek to maintain a pure witness in the power of the Holy Spirit, in obedience to God's Word, without compromise, recognizing we are in the world for Christ but not of the world. Maintaining such a position in His grace we attempt to reach as many men as possible for the Lord. Then we seek to establish them in the faith through regular, consecutive studies in God's Word conducted by mature Christians qualified to teach the Bible. Generally your practice seems to be student gatherings around the Bible without such leadership. We believe. . . .

Another difference between IVCF and us centers on God's prohibition to His children to submit themselves to unsound theological teachers, as contained in 2 Timothy 2-3. The commands to purge one's self from such as "from such turn away," call for obedience. We are in close proximity to the local seminary, which we cannot recommend to students because of its present Barthian position and ecumenical emphasis.

The letter then outlined the actions of IVCF in support and cooperation with Princeton Seminary, while refusing to support or recommend any evangelical seminaries. It highlighted numerous examples of misinformation related to PEF and other issues that had arisen. On the final page, the letter addressed the immediate problem:

IVCF activities in Princeton University have brought confusion on thought, some disintegration in our Lord's work, and perplexity, hurtness and disillusion in true Christian hearts. We do not want such division among believers to be used by the enemies of Christ and His Gospel. It is possible that not all of your staff secretaries are fully informed on conditions in Princeton University or on the way our Lord has led in establishing His work on this campus. Our Savior has stated that when His children stand uncompromisingly for Him and the Word of God there will be opposition. But it is grievous when Christians choose to misunderstand and cause difficulties in work He has established.

...this letter is written in the hope you may be willing and able to take steps which shall remedy this distressing situation.

Your brethren in His joyous service by His grace,
The Executive Committee.[20]

On May 29, Fullerton sent a brief letter to Whitcomb:

Here with a mimeograph copy of the letter sent to IVCF in protest against their activities here.

Surely God has blessed the activities of our little group in a most unusual manner this year — we are closing the season with 24 members, only 3 of whom graduated. The freshmen number 12 and they are a keen lot. They will be in need of much protecting, sustaining grace and intercession during the summer months.

A reply letter, dated June 3, 1951, came to Donald Fullerton from C. Stacey Woods.

Thank you for your letter of May 8th. Such a letter requires careful and prayerful consideration.

Will you be so kind, therefore, as to regard this note merely as an acknowledgment of receipt of your letter.

Will you please convey to the members of the Princeton Evangelical Fellowship our Christian greetings, and ask them to pray with us that all concerned may be enabled to discern the mind of the Lord, the will of the Spirit, and be granted the grace of obedience, regardless of the cost.

### 1951–1952 *PEF President: Sam Rochester*

The PEF continued to benefit from the revival of the previous year and under the leadership of strong senior students. The events were

---

20. Signed by Paul H. Taber, William Oncken Jr., David Marshal, Ted Martin Jr., Sam Rochester, Bill Whipple, John A. Flack, and Donald B. Fullerton.

well planned and well attended and highly successful. Fullerton now considered moving to Princeton to set up permanent headquarters, "staffed with a full-time worker" . . . "possibly complete with a wife." They worked on building up the library that Jack Whitcomb had started years earlier. There was little mention of IVCF, suggesting that — for the time being — PEF would be respected on the Princeton campus. But their involvement would continue.

In a letter to "Jack, beloved in the Lord," dated May 22, 1952, Fullerton updated Whitcomb on the concerning situation with the Baptist Students of Princeton:

> Ted Martin and Ramsey . . . leaving.[21] We need much prayer about the coming year. Except for Sammie Rochester there is not too much evidence of deep spiritual insights and devotion to our Lord. Then the Baptist group is strong for "South-Western." **They expect to use as chaplain, a man from South Western who will be studying in Princeton Seminary.** As their group has incorporated many of the PEF this may be confusing in doctrine as well as position. Pray that our students will be enabled by the Holy Spirit to see the need of real separation unto God from sin, the flesh, the world and religious unsoundness. I will need your prayers, Jack, there are many difficulties but our Lord Jesus is ever able to give His victories, in His strength, peace and joy. May He grant all these to you continually. The Lord bless and keep you until he comes.
>
> In his deep bond of love.
> Donald B Fullerton

## 1952–1953 *PEF President: Don Robinson*

The PEF continued to mature and grow. From an organizational standpoint, PEF updated its constitution and was incorporated under the laws of the state of New Jersey.

On campus, there continued to be strong undergraduate interest with 12 freshmen joining the group and serving. The established meetings were also successful.

---

21. Paul Pressler also graduated in May 1952 and left.

In the spring, Fullerton took them to visit Whitcomb in Winona Lake and to speak at Grace. However, the wear and tear of the battles were taking their toll. Fullerton wrote back to Whitcomb in response to a letter of thanks and appreciation, "If the students were blessed I can assure you it was all of our Savior, **for never have I felt more empty or helpless.**"

### 1953–1954 *PEF President: William M. Counts*

The PEF continued to struggle with competing groups on campus that appeared to have identical agendas to PEF but were more tolerant and accepting of various views and doctrines.

In May 1954, the Faculty and Board of Trustees of Grace Theological Seminary conferred on Donald B. Fullerton the honorary degree Doctor of Divinity. Dr. Fullerton accepted this honor in great humility. However, it was both fitting and useful in his ongoing role with students and friends on the campus of Princeton University.

### 1954–1955 *PEF President: Harry A. Hoffner Jr.*

On one hand, PEF continued to have strong student involvement and strong Bible teaching and mentoring. But growing influence of other campus ministries was taking its toll.

On December 1, 1954, Dr. Fullerton sent out a long Executive Secretary's Letter. He summarized the conditions on campus using three words: Blessing, Abundance, and Confusion. To the final point, he wrote:

> 3. CONFUSION. In the last five years five other groups have sprung up on the Campus, each considered evangelical, each more or less seeking to do the very work that P.E.F. has been doing for more than 23 years. Not one of these seems able to discern the dangers of Neo-Orthodoxy (Barthianism), of sitting under its teachers, or having pleasures in them that do. God's command to turn away from those who hold a form of godliness but deny the power thereof, (2 Tim 3:15), is treated lightly. The argument used today, "it's all a matter of interpretation," is the same that was propounded to Eve in Eden in the face of God's clear words. Last August it was enlightening to

be handed a book published in Europe, examining this theological philosophy. The European title was "Neo-Modernism." But liberals introduced it to this country as "Neo-Orthodoxy." Because of the foundational teachings of Neo-Orthodoxy, the P.E.F. holds that if it is to continue an effective work in the power of the Holy Spirit to the praise of our Lord Jesus Christ, there can be no compromise along this line.

During this term a number of members who had professed to receive Jesus Christ through P.E.F. activities, have been attracted to one or another of these groups. Of course, there is confusion, perplexity, division and undermining of a strong united testimony in the truth and love of Christ. We on the campus need to realize what it means to give Jesus Christ that supreme place in our affections which makes all other love seem like hate by comparison. We need to render Him and God's Word, unquestioning obedience, regardless of human philosophies and high-sounding arguments of men. We need to trust the work of the blessed Holy Spirit, drawing hearts to Christ, incorporating them into His body and Church. We need to learn to trust Him and not princes, with their schemes, methods, plannings and organizations. We are so prone to forget God has called us into His work to be co-laborers with Him in what He is doing. What a tremendous, high calling! In Christ He has provided every need of ours for life and godliness. (2 Peter 1:3)

WE NEED YOUR PRAYERS CONTINUALLY!!!

At the end of the letter, Fullerton added a personal note to John Whitcomb: "Could you possibly get away to bring a week-end of messages to the P.E.F?"

He agreed to come on April 29–May 1, 1955.

On December 15, 1954, Dr. Fullerton sent a follow-up letter to John Rea:

**The Situation on campus is critical.** But our Lord is able to maintain His testimony. "Donn Moomaw" football hero of the West Coast, leader in Campus Crusade, having the aura of having been in "Billy" Graham's party in England and Europe, football coach in Princeton University while attending

Princeton Seminary has caused quite the difficulty.[22] He came on our campus early last fall with four other Princeton seminarians to organize and help evangelical testimony. The Baptist group got him working with them.

Their chaplain is once more a graduate of Southwestern Baptist Seminary doing graduate work in Princeton seminary. The Baptist work on campus, by report, has a good number of Princeton Seminarians helping and attending. I cannot help but think the same breed of thinking is what turned Jack Ives so far from the faith that it deflected him from Dallas to Colgate, Rochester. The same mold of thought and influence is what unsettled Sam Rochester. (what's in a name)

Also, we have I.V.C.F., Moral Re-Armament (Buchmanism)[23] and a few Young Life fellows: none of whom will accept our position of the need of separation from false teaching.

These groups seem willing to cooperate with S.C.A.,[24] especially the Baptist. Our P.E.F. students for the main part feel the Baptists are the only place they can attend Church services. The Baptist preempt Murray–Dodge Sundays, 10:00

---

22. Donn Moomaw was one of the greatest football players of UCLA, two-time All American, and first round draft pick of the Los Angeles Rams. Following his time at Princeton Seminary, he became a Presbyterian minister, serving at the Bel Air Presbyterian Church near Los Angeles, where he became friends with Ronald Reagan, until he was forced to resign in 1993 following a sex scandal (see https://en.wikipedia.org/wiki/Donn_Moomaw).

23. Moral Re-Armament (MRA) was an international moral and spiritual movement that was developed by American minister Frank Buchman. MRA was an ecumenical network based around "Four Absolutes" (absolute honesty, absolute purity, absolute unselfishness, and absolute love). It encouraged its members to be actively involved in political and social issues. It appeared to influence the post-WWII reconciliation of France and Germany. In 2001, the MRA movement changed its name to Initiatives of Change and is based in Caux, Switzerland (see https://en.wikipedia.org/wiki/Moral_Re-Armament).

24. S.C.A. – "The Student Christian Association and its predecessors were the dominant religious organizations at Princeton University for almost a hundred and fifty years. The Philadelphian Society, founded by a small group of students in 1825, was the quasi-official campus religious agency by the beginning of the twentieth century. In 1930 the Student-Faculty Association (SFA), organized by the Dean of the Chapel, took over the Society's programs, focusing on community service. In 1946 the Student Christian Association (SCA) replaced both the Society and the SFA, coordinating both religious and community service activities in campus. The Student Volunteers Council succeeded the SCA in 1967." (Quoted from http://findingaids.princeton.edu/collections/ AC135, June 18, 2016.) This is the group that John Whitcomb, John Rea, and the PEF leaders refused to join in 1946 — see Chapter 11.

a.m.–noon; 7-9:30 p.m., for Sunday School, Church, Discussion hour, and Evening Service.

The only solution some of us can't see as a possibility, is an Independent Bible Teaching Church with a Christ-centered life and ministry. There are a number of people in the town who now have to go to Trenton or New Brunswick to attend church. Please pray about this, that our Lord's will may be done and His Name honored in Princeton. Please let Jack and Ramsey see this note.

## Progress is Made

In late February 1955, a permanent residence was secured for "the Executive Secretary" that included a room and a kitchen at 15 Edwards Place, just off campus. This allowed Dr. Fullerton to provide individualized counseling for nearly a dozen students during the week and to invite guests in for supper and Bible studies.

A new group of students was elected to office including Don Williams, treasurer; Dave Goetschius, secretary; and Kurt Finsterbusch, president. Fullerton noted that "They feel like Moses who replied to God's call to responsibilities, 'Who am I…?' "

The concern continued to be surrounding discipleship of new believers. After effective evangelism by PEF, nearly half of the students were drawn away to other organizations that did not always hold to the fundamentals of the Christian faith. Furthermore, many of the campus Christians were confused as to who was who, what the differences were, and why it mattered.

## Whitcomb Visits Princeton

John Whitcomb finally arrived at Princeton on Friday, April 29, 1955, after an overnight train ride from Indiana. He was met by Dr. Fullerton, who took him to his new apartment for a "delicious meal in the pressure cooker." The afternoon was spent talking with Lew Knight then Ron Hurd. They left to attend a PEF prayer meeting then had dinner with Bill Counts before the evening service at the Engineering Lounge. Whitcomb spoke on Colossians 3:1–3,[25] showed some color

---

25. Colossians 3:1–3, "Therefore if you have been raised up with Christ, keep seeking the things above, where Christ is, seated at the right hand of God. Set your mind on the

slides from Rome, then headed back to Fullerton's apartment for long discussions with the PEF students.

Saturday, April 30, started with a meeting with PEF Advisory Council members George Bate, Dave Marshall, and Paul Taber. This was followed by an Executive Board meeting and a Trustees meeting. He then had lunch with Harry Hoffner (immediate past president of PEF) and Ron Hurd, followed by "a couple of hours" with Kurt Finsterbusch, the PEF student president, to discuss everything from creation and evolution to PEF and seminaries. At 4:30 p.m., he spoke at a PEF meeting about Lot, followed by another prayer meeting and supper at Fullerton's apartment with Mr. F. and Harry Hoffner. At 7:30 he spoke again to PEF on 1 John 3:1–3 then talked with Mr. F., Sutherland McLean, and Lew Knight until 12:30 a.m.

On Sunday, May 1, Whitcomb joined Mr. F. and four PEFers on a trip to New Brunswick for church. After lunch, he met again with Harry Hoffner, Bill Counts, Bob Griffith, and Dave Goetschius. At 4:30 he presented slides of the Holy Land and described the life of Christ. He met Bob Smith for dinner then spoke at Clio Hall to the PEF and "a few Baptists." Mr. F. then talked with him as he headed back to Trenton to catch a train back to Indiana, catching the 12:55 a.m. to Warsaw.

*Results of the PEF Visit*

Two days after Whitcomb returned to Grace, Donald M. Williams, PEF treasurer, sent him this message,

> Many of us truly feel we must reevaluate our position about Princeton Seminary because of what you said to us Friday night at Mr. Fullerton's and we ask your prayers concerning this decision that it may be truly Biblical. We also appreciate the advice that you gave us on seminaries. Many of us will have to make this decision soon also and your words were taken to heart.

At nearly the same time, John Whitcomb was writing his reflections on the visit, which he sent to the PEF students:

---

things above, not on the things that are on earth. For you have died and your life is hidden with Christ in God" (NASB 1995).

As I think back upon my many profitable interviews with PEF members, I realize now, as never before, how utterly vital it is for me to pray that each of you might grow in grace and in the knowledge of our Lord Jesus Christ. Surrounded as you are by so many shades of "Christianity" (so-called), you, as a group, will need to draw your lines of demarcation with the same degree of sharpness as the New Testament does; learn how to love all men, especially those who are of the household of faith, and yet how to contend earnestly for <u>the faith</u> once for all delivered unto the saints, as Paul did when he contended at Antioch against Peter (Galatians 2); and learn how to put <u>all</u> of your support behind the one group on campus that is proclaiming the whole counsel of God (Acts 20:27), and thus accomplish in the long run the most for God's glory and the salvation of men. Be assured that these are the lines along which I will be praying for you.

The challenge for the students was then articulated by Kurt Finster-busch, president of PEF, in a letter to John Whitcomb in June 1955:

As far as our problem is concerned, we are still in a state of confusion. None of us think much of Princeton Seminary, but some of us do think highly about some of the fundamental Christians at the seminary. I think your remark about placing our time in the most profitable place for the Lord is really the answer. . . . but another thing that makes it difficult for us, some of the PEFers, to see and act exactly as Mr. Fullerton would have us do, is that we have some very dear friends who we would greatly offend and maybe caused to stumble if we did. However, I realize it may be like Abraham's love for his father which hindered him or like Adam's love for Eve which caused his downfall.

However, the issues now became clear. Those who committed to continuing with the leadership of the PEF based on their understanding of biblical principles strengthened the organization in amazing ways, and those who were torn by pragmatic politics fell away. The foundation of the PEF stood firm and flourished.

## Post-script

The fulltime ministry of "Mr. F.," Dr. Fullerton, on the Princeton campus, with a strong infrastructure and renewed commitment to leading young college students to Christ and then teaching them to follow him with 100% commitment and effort, impacted the world.

In 1956, more of Dr. Fullerton's prayers were answered, as an independent local Bible church was opened known as the Westerly Road Church. The church was pastored by Edward Morgan, class of 1938, "offering sound refreshing exposition of God's Word" (Executive Secretary Letter, June 1957).

Professor John Whitcomb remained engaged with Dr. Fullerton and the PEF. He returned to Princeton on March 7–9, 1958, for example, for a series of lectures. He spoke five times on Isaiah 53. But after the evening meetings, he would have informal get-togethers at Mr. Fullerton's apartment. At these, Dr. Whitcomb discussed the Christian attitude toward evolution — as he was actively involved in writing *The Genesis Flood* and was fully engaged and excited about this topic. As Michael Rusten, president of PEF that year, reported, "He showed that the Biblical account of Creation is the only explanation which does not lead to a maze of contradictions. These informal talks opened the eyes of many of us to the inconsistencies of the evolutionary hypothesis and taught us to 'turn away from the profane babblings and oppositions of the knowledge which is falsely so called' (I Tim 6:20)."[26]

The heart and soul of the PEF was Dr. Donald B. Fullerton. This was his life and his ministry. Through this little man, who was brilliant, humble, caring, and selfless; who, standing securely in the hand of the Almighty, was courageous, fearless, unshakable, and resilient; who was completely obedient to the Word of God and teaching these truths; who never married but had many mighty sons who had a rippling effect, now to the fourth generation, the world was changed.

In what way did John Whitcomb play a role in the life of PEF? Judge Paul Pressler, who was a PEF member during the late 1940s and early 1950s, reflected on the impact of Dr. Whitcomb on Donald Fullerton at these critical times and his molding of the future of the PEF. Judge Pressler, in writing to the author, noted:

---

26. PEF President's report, June 1958, by E. Michael Rusten.

**I feel that if your father had not stood behind Mr. Fullerton, the PEF would have died** and with it a great deal of useful things for Christ would not have occurred. Mr. Fullerton never married and I am sure he was quite lonely. Your father and Johnny were the ones that supported him and gave him the backing and encouragement that he needed to stay at Princeton. I think that also he might have gone to the mission field against the doctor's orders if your father and Johnny had not persuaded him of the necessity of keeping the ministry going at Princeton. So in affect [*sic*] many of Mr. Fullerton's accomplishments through the PEF can be traced to your father.[27]

---

27. Letter from Paul Pressler to the author on August 19, 2016.

# Chapter 15

# Darius

"Publish or Perish"
July 1948–1961

## Introduction

The phrase "Publish or Perish" summarizes the pressure on faculty within academic circles to immediately and continually publish academic work to retain employment and advance through academic ranks to the top, which is "Professor, with tenure." The pressure typically comes from the school's administration, as the institution's notoriety and attractiveness to high-quality students and donors relies on the reputation of the faculty. The path to recognition involves both the quality and quantity of work demonstrated by books, articles, and newsworthy communications — it is much harder to become recognized for outstanding teaching since that quality is expected in all teachers. *This chapter documents the complexity of Dr. Whitcomb's work.*

Publications are the currency of success in both humanities and the sciences. Continued grant funding requires that the faculty member's team (mostly students) completes the proposed work from start-up funds or grants, and if the results are not published, then they didn't do it! Publications are graded by both quality (the reputation of the journal or publisher) and quantity (how many books and papers are published per year). "Publish or Perish" is not a myth; it is a reality in academics.

## Seminaries

Seminaries can be a strange and variable blend of church functions and academic institutions. Jesus gave a clear commission to the 11 disciples, saying, "All authority has been given to Me in heaven and on earth. Go therefore and make disciples of all the nations, baptizing them in the name of the Father and the Son and the Holy Spirit, teaching them to observe all that I commanded you" (Matthew 28:18–20; NASB 1995). The *method* of teaching was not directly stated, although Jesus Himself spent three years setting an example of how to teach disciples.

Paul followed Jesus' example with Timothy, Titus, and others, but he also established a more formal system of teaching in Ephesus. He initially taught in a synagogue, but after three months, he was forced out. So "he withdrew from them and took away the disciples, reasoning daily in the school of Tyrannus. This took place for two years, so that all who lived in Asia heard the word of the Lord, both Jews and Greeks" (Acts 19:9b–10; NASB 1995). These events occurred in a time of transition, as the church of Ephesus was being formed for the first time. Later, as Paul wrote letters back to the church of Ephesus, he provided clear instructions on the roles of elders, pastors, and teachers for equipping the saints *within* the Church. The goal was not to train the trainees for a career, but rather for ministries to strengthen the church body.[1]

The primary challenge to the Church is not persecution, it is *false teaching*. There are many defenses against false teaching and false teachers that are given in the Scriptures, but two of them are highlighted here. The first is that the selection of elders is *not* based on their academic credentials — but rather on their *character* and ability to teach, as confirmed by the ongoing observation of the church members.[2] The second, according to Scriptures, is a continued *testing* of the words of a teacher *by the people* who must determine if the teaching is of God or of the devil.[3] If the teaching is not clearly from God, then the response is not to fight — it is to run, completely avoiding the false teacher.[4] This process requires church members to continually study the Scriptures, to test the teachers and preachers as they teach by word and deed in the community, to determine who is correctly teaching the truth, and to follow their teaching and example! The hidden element in this process

---

1. Based on Ephesians 4:11–16.
2. See 1 Timothy 3:1–7; Titus 1:5–9; 1 Peter 5:1–6; etc.
3. Examples of Bereans in Acts 17:10–12; 2 Timothy 3:14–17; the Ephesians in Revelation 3:1–3, in contrast to 2 Corinthians 11:3–4, 13–15.
4. Examples: John 10:5; 2 Timothy 2:23–26; 2 Timothy 3:5; etc.

is the work of the Holy Spirit, who leads truth-seeking believers to the truth and directs their steps in its application.[5]

## Challenges in Biblical Teaching

Formal and systematic teaching of the Scriptures is the work of the local church. However, in small congregations, there may not be enough qualified teachers to fully equip the saints and teach future teachers. In this case, multiple smaller churches often form cooperative fellowships and support a program of systematic teaching. The trap is that the local church may relinquish their responsibility of teaching the "full counsel of God." The typical member begins to believe that careful study is for the clergy, and the responsibilities for teaching and learning are delegated to others. The local church may justify this idea by sending some money to support a seminary or by sending some of their young people to attend them. But a more ominous trap exists that has derailed the effectiveness of countless thousands of young students of the Word and has destroyed entire denominations. This trap is the movement toward an independent academic model of seminaries that is separate from oversight and governance by church congregations.

## Academic Model for a Seminary

In an academic model, the teachers (faculty) are chosen on academic accomplishments and stature in the academic world. Academic leaders are those who publish. Publishing requires that some research is completed, data analyzed, and that the conclusions drawn are either more clear, novel, or provocative. In the academic model, the professors test the students; the students do not test the teacher. In the academic model, the lifestyle of the professors is not closely observed, in the way that they are in a local church, and if problems arise, the students cannot easily "flee." Removing professors who begin admixing false teaching is often challenging. When it does occur, the professor just goes to another academic institution for a new job, based on his accomplishments and fame rather than his character and ability to "rightly divide the Word of Truth" (2 Timothy 2:15). Thus, the design, organization, and administrative structure of an academic seminary (and other parachurch organizations) have inherent flaws when it comes to discerning and maintaining biblical truth. Instead, it is the

---

5. John 7:17, 16:13; Romans 8:14; 1 John 5:6; etc.

"household of God, which is the church of the living God, [that is] the pillar and support of the truth" (1 Timothy 3:15; NASB 1995).

Another problem with an academic seminary model is the character and accountability of the trainee. The students come through an application process, typically after high school or college, that demonstrates their *academic* abilities. Upon completing the academic requirements, they are now "clergy" and immediately look for a full-time job within a church. This bypasses the guidelines of 1 Peter 5:5–8 (NASB 1995): "You younger men, likewise, be subject to your elders; and all of you, clothe yourselves with humility toward one another, for God is opposed to the proud, but gives grace to the humble. Therefore humble yourselves under the mighty hand of God, that He may exalt you at the proper time, casting all your anxiety on Him, because He cares for you. Be of sober spirit, be on the alert. Your adversary, the devil, prowls around like a roaring lion, seeking someone to devour."

The challenge through the Church age is that false teachers and false teaching arise in *every* generation. They secretly introduce new heresies and repackage old heresies to lead churchgoers astray. In their defense, many seminaries and parachurch organizations were developed with good intent and offered many important contributions to help believers serve the Lord. The challenge to continued success is the supervision and management of these organizations by the local church, which itself comes with baggage of poorly trained people, biases of inherited traditions, and false or unbalanced teaching that crept in and was never addressed or eradicated.

At the time that John Whitcomb joined the faculty of Grace Theological Seminary, the foundation was still being laid by godly men from strong local churches who were passionate for accurate interpretation and application of God's Word (Chapter 12). But the tension between being recognized as an institute of higher education, continually garnering financial support, attracting students, and recruiting academically qualified faculty to cover the full curriculum while still remaining under the authority and accountability of local churches distributed around the country had already begun.

### The Early Writings of John C. Whitcomb

John Whitcomb, as a young professor, was *not* interested in academic advancement; he was interested in being a missionary to China.

However, after reading *Therefore Stand* by Wilbur Smith and recognizing his God-given abilities in scholarship, he became motivated to address some of the major attacks on the accuracy and inerrancy of the Bible.

Among the benefits of seminaries in the past was the availability of libraries and other intellectually astute faculty that provided resources to study the writings of previous authors and to articulate arguments supporting a better understanding or application of Scriptures in new articles and books. The fact that these resources are now typically available online at a fraction of previous costs allows members of the local church to have these same resources at their fingertips and in their own home.

Whitcomb's publishing efforts began with his honors project from Princeton University (a biography of the American evangelist Dwight L. Moody), followed by his required theses for a Master of Divinity degree, his Master of Theology program, and then his dissertation for a Doctor of Theology at Grace. Independent of his academic requirements was his first editorial effort for the 1951 Grace yearbook and writing brief commentaries on the Old Testament books of Ezra, Nehemiah, and Esther for the Wycliffe Bible Commentary.[6] These academic efforts served two purposes: to complete the requirements for graduation and to provide a clear defense of the historical authenticity and accuracy of the Bible (and the Grace Brethren churches) for the encouragement of believers in general.

John Whitcomb authored four major documents during his seminary training. The Grace Yearbook (May 1951); "The Temple of Jerusalem in the Light of History, Archaeology and Prophecy" (Master of Theology thesis, May 1953); "Darius the Mede" (May 1954); and "The Genesis Flood: An Investigation of its Geographical Extent, Geologic Effects, and Chronological Settings" (Doctor of Theology dissertation, May 1957). Three of the four were published, with the final one eventually impacting the world through a co-authored book with Henry Morris entitled *The Genesis Flood*.

**Ground-level Research During the "Flying Seminar"**

Research in theology is generally within the Scriptures and libraries. Research in ancient history must include the Bible, the work of secular

---

6. Charles F. Pfeiffer and Everett F. Harrison, eds., *The Wycliffe Bible Commentary* (Chicago, IL: Moody Press, 1962), 1525 pages.

history, and archeology (including seeing and examining the historical sites and artifacts in person). John Whitcomb took advantage of a program through the Winona Lake School of Theology's Flying Seminar designed to transport biblical scholars to the Holy Land for lectures by leading experts at key geographical sites. The purpose for John Whitcomb was twofold: to complete graduate studies in seminary and to better prepare lectures from the Old Testament.

In July and August 1952, Whitcomb joined the Flying Seminar in the Bible Lands along with 85 students, pastors, professors, and college presidents from the United States and Canada. The seminar was under the direction of four professors: Dr. Edward J. Young of Westminster Seminary; Dr. Carl F.H. Henry of Fuller Seminary; Dr. Arnold Schultz of Northern Baptist Seminary; and Dr. John Huffman, the tour director. Before leaving on this trip, the students were required to submit two written examinations and two term papers to professors, based upon over 4,000 pages of reading in the fields of archaeology, the Old Testament, philosophy, and Church history. This work, in addition to lecture notes taken during the trip, provided ten hours of credit toward a master's degree in theology.

The five-week Flying Seminary tour included four-day visits in England, France, Italy, Greece, and Egypt; a two-day visit in Switzerland; and ten days in Lebanon, Syria, the Hashemite Kingdom of Jordan, and the new state of Israel. To document this trip, John Whitcomb kept a detailed notebook and took over 1,300 photographs of the places visited, including Amman, Jericho, the Dead Sea, Bethany, Hebron, Bethlehem, Jacob's Well, Nablus, Samaria, Old and New Jerusalem, Tel Aviv, Haifa, Nazareth, Cana, Tiberius, and Capernaum.

In Jerusalem, he specifically visited the Mount of Olives and the Temple Mount. Other historical sites that he visited included the Gihon Spring, Hezekiah's Tunnel, the Pool of Siloam, the Greek Orthodox Colony, the Via Dolorosa, the Church of the Holy Sepulcher, Gordon's Calvary, the Tombs of the Kings, the Palestine Archaeological Museum, the Dominican Ecole Biblique, and the American School of Oriental Research. But the academic highlight was the Temple Mount, the site of the Temple of Jerusalem.

John Whitcomb focused on the Temple Mount because it represented the center of worship and theocratic authority in the past, and it is highlighted as the center of worship in the prophetic future. Thus, the Temple of Jerusalem, standing on the top of Mount Moriah, represented the most important historical site in biblical history.

## Seven Wonders of the Ancient World

People love to debate the relative ranking of people, places, and things based on a continually changing spectrum of criteria. The Seven Wonders of the Ancient World represent a famous ranking of man-made structures. The ancient Greeks ranked the seven wonders as: (1) the Great Pyramid at Giza, Egypt; (2) the Hanging Gardens of Babylon; (3) the Statue of Zeus at Olympia, Greece; (4) the Temple of Artemis at Ephesus; (5) the Mausoleum at Halicarnassus; (6) the Colossus of Rhodes; and (7) the Lighthouse of Alexandria, Egypt. Obviously, the ancient Greeks did not know about the Great Wall of China and perhaps some other notable man-made wonders, but they did know about the Temple at Jerusalem, and it was not on their list. The only temple that was included was the Temple of Artemis at Ephesus, and in size and economic importance, it was clearly a "wonder."

*Temple of Artemis*

There were at least three successive temples of Artemis that together stood for over a millennium. Nobody knows when the first temple was built, although it was attributed to the Amazons. A flood destroyed the first temple in the 7th century B.C. The second temple was built about 550 B.C., which is the one that became one of the Seven Wonders of the Ancient World. It was over 375 feet long and 150 feet wide,[7] making it longer than a football field, including the end zones. It was more than four times larger than the Parthenon in Athens, Greece, and more then 20 times larger than Solomon's Temple (1 Kings 6:2).[8] It had a spectacular design, being the first Greek-style temple built of marble, and it set the standard from which all future temples were measured. The temple was an architectural masterpiece and also an art gallery. It was filled with sculptures and artwork of the greatest artists of the time,

---

7. This review is based on the following online articles, http://en.wikipedia.org/wiki/Temple_of_Artemis, accessed January 2–13, 1913.
8. The Temple of Artemis was at least 375 feet long by 150 feet wide, which equals 56,250 square feet. Solomon's temple was 60 cubits (90 feet) long by 20 cubits (30 feet) wide, which equals 2,700 square feet.

including a striking cult statue of Artemis (also called Diana). There was so much wealth that the temple also served as an international bank. In 356 B.C., the year Alexander the Great was born, the temple was burned to the ground by a madman named Herostratus, who wanted his name to be remembered forever. The local spin on the fact that Artemis failed to save her temple was that she was busy assisting in the birth of Alexander the Great in Macedonia.

A third temple was built by the citizens of Ephesus, who rejected any outside help, including financial support by Alexander the Great. The third temple was even greater than the second temple in size and grandeur, stretching over 450 feet long and 225 feet wide. This was the temple of Paul's time, and it survived until A.D. 262 when Gothic tribes from Germany destroyed it.

## Temple of Jerusalem

The Temple in Jerusalem was a place of great splendor, but it was not as great in size or economic impact as the Temple of Artemis at Ephesus. However, Solomon's Temple was infinitely greater because it was dedicated to the one true God and because the Shekinah Glory of the Almighty God filled the Holy of Holies (1 Kings 8:10–12). Tragically, because of disobedience and unbelief, God's glory finally departed from the Temple (Ezekiel 10:3–4, 18–20, 11:22–23) just before the Babylonians destroyed it in 586 B.C.

The Temple of Jerusalem has been built, destroyed, rebuilt, remodeled, and destroyed again. The significance of the Temple to the Jews cannot be overstated, while its significance to Christians is limited to history and prophecy. But unlike other temples, the Temple of Jerusalem will again be rebuilt, according to the words of God through the prophet Haggai to Zerubbabel, " 'The latter glory of this house will be greater than the former,' says the LORD of hosts, 'and in this place I will give peace,' declares the LORD of hosts" (Haggai 2:9; NASB 1995). The prophecy was given during the building of the second temple structure, but since it paled in comparison to Solomon's Temple, there must yet be a greater temple in the future.

A major portion of Old Testament prophecy, especially after the destruction of Solomon's Temple, is dedicated to details of a new temple. This is often called Ezekiel's Temple, based on the blueprint-type details give in Ezekiel chapters 40–46. Ezekiel's Temple must still be in the future because the temple built by Zerubbabel was the wrong size and design to fulfill the prophecy given by Ezekiel at the time Solomon's Temple was destroyed (compare Ezra 6:3 to Ezekiel 41:13). Appreciating the certainty of the prophecies of the Old Testament that have not yet been fulfilled, especially related to a future Kingdom of Christ on earth after the Second Coming, requires some attention to the design and purpose of the Temple of Jerusalem.

## "The Temple of Jerusalem in the Light of History, Archaeology, and Prophecy" — May 1953

Jack offered a complete thesis on the Temple of Jerusalem to the faculty of Grace Theological Seminary as a part of the requirement for the degree of Master of Theology. The intention of the careful and thorough document went beyond obtaining a diploma. It was to serve as the foundation of a new book linking history and prophecy from a premillennial viewpoint.

The final thesis was 120 pages long with a bibliography of 59 books, articles, and related references; 97 Scripture references; and 41 illustrations, many of them hand drawn. The purpose was not to address questions of the existence or history of a temple *per se*, but rather to provide a critical review of the features of the Temple Mount based on a personal examination, reports of historians, and analyses of archaeologists.

John Whitcomb noted in the introduction to his thesis:

> If any fact of Old Testament prophecy is clear, it is this: Jerusalem shall be the center of Christ's reign upon the earth during the thousand glorious years which shall follow His return from heaven at the Second coming.[9] For many peoples shall go and say, Come ye, and let us go up to the mountain of Jehovah, to the house of the God of Jacob; and He will

---

9. The time span of a "thousand years," or Millennium, comes from Revelation 20, which occurs chronologically between the Second Coming of Christ (Revelation 19:11–21; cf. Zechariah 14:1–9; Matthew 24:29–31, 25:31–34; etc.) and the New Heavens and New Earth and New Jerusalem (Revelation 21:1-22:5), and has no temple (Revelation 21:22). The Millennium is the only place in the timeline of biblical history or prophecy for a revived Kingdom of Israel with a king of the line of David (i.e., Jesus) in the land of Israel (cf. Jeremiah 33:14–26), serving in a temple fitting the size and functional description of Ezekiel's temple (Ezekiel 40–44).

teach us of His ways, and we will walk in His paths: for out of Zion shall go forth the law, and the word of Jehovah from Jerusalem (Isaiah 2:3).[10]

The trip through the land of Israel in the summer of 1952, just a few years after it again became a nation, provided a poignant perspective on the people of Israel. He writes that he was "amazed at the optimism and zeal of this new nation, in its struggle for growth and security in the midst of hostile powers." Furthermore, he confessed his conviction that "No Christian can look upon these events with disinterest, for they point with unmistakable clearness to the soon return of our blessed Lord for His Church."[11] But in light of biblical prophecy, "for Israel, these events point to the soon coming of her Great Tribulation and national conversion, when 'it shall come to pass that in all the land, saith the Lord, two parts therein shall be cut off and die; but the third shall be left therein. And I will bring the third part into fire and will refine them as silver is refined, and will try them as gold is tried. They shall call upon My Name, and I will hear them: I will say, It is my people; and they shall say, Jehovah is my God' (Zechariah 13:8–9)."

From the perspective of the Old Testament, there is no other spot that reflects the history and destiny of Israel as the site of the Temple of Jerusalem on Mount Moriah. It is central in the history of Abraham (i.e., his encounter with the King of Salem [Jerusalem] in Genesis 14:18–20; cf. Psalm 110:4; Hebrews 5:5–10, 7:1–7), Isaac (Genesis 22:2), David (1 Chronicles 21:15–28), and Solomon (2 Chronicles 3:1), who built the first Temple. From the time of Solomon forward, the Temple of Jerusalem remained the center of national identity and worship. Furthermore, in spite of repeated desecrations and destructions since the time of Solomon, the Temple has always retained its identity in the sight of the Bible writers and in the sight of Jews to the present day. It is the location and purpose of the building that make it the Temple, not the individual bricks and mortar of the moment.

John Whitcomb decided his thesis would include a historical and prophetic chapter, then proceed through a study of the ancient outer walls, following them around from the Northwest Angle in a clockwise

---

10. From page 3 of "The Temple of Jerusalem in the Light of History, Archaeology and Prophecy," John C. Whitcomb's Master of Theology thesis.
11. Ibid., 4.

direction. The various gates and points of interest would be treated more in detail, especially when they provided clues as to the appearance of the Temple in the time of Christ and possibly in the time of Solomon. The study would finish with the Western Wall, also known to Jews as the Wailing Wall.

The first chapter of the thesis was titled "The Temple in History and Prophecy." The chapter focused on ancient documents and histories rather than archeological findings, including a number of interesting facts. Sadly, the historical details of the building and appearance of Solomon's Temple are lost in time (destroyed in 586 b.c.), but complementary information on the expansion, beautification, and appearance of Herod's modification of the Second Temple, built under the leadership of Zerubbabel after the 70-year Babylonian captivity, remain. Whitcomb summarized the history of the construction project from several historical sources.

> [I]n the year 20 b.c., 1000 wagons were prepared for hauling stones, 10,000 skilled workmen were chosen, and 1000 priests were instructed in building crafts, in order that they themselves might erect the Holy House. "So Herod took away the old foundations, and laid others, and erected the temple upon them . . . the temple itself was built by the priests in a year and six months" (Josephus, Antiquities, XV,11:3,6).
>
> Although the Holy House was completed in eighteen months, it took many years to finish the outer courts, porches, and connecting structures. Long after Herod's death, while the Lord Jesus Christ was teaching in the Temple on one occasion, Jesus remarked that the Temple had already been under construction for forty-six years (John 2:20).[12]

The appearance of the temple was inspiring, as noted in Mark 13:1 and Luke 21:5, as the people around Jesus commented on the great stones and wonderful beauty. The impressions of the historian Flavius Josephus were also quoted in Whitcomb's thesis:

> Now the outer face of the temple in its front wanted nothing that was likely to surprise either men's mind or their

---

12. Ibid., 16.

eyes; for it was covered all over with plates of gold of great weight, and, at the first rising of the sun, reflected back a very fiery splendor, and make those who forced themselves to look upon in, to turn their eyes away, just as they would have done at the sun's own rays. But this temple appeared to strangers, when they were coming to it at a distance, like a mountain covered with snow; for as to those parts of it that were not gilt, they were exceeding white.[13]

But while the people surrounding Jesus in the days before His crucifixion were focusing on the Temple's size and beauty, Jesus foresaw its complete destruction. Jesus said, "As for these things which you are looking at, the days will come in which there will not be left one stone upon another which will not be torn down" (Luke 21:6). Ironically, Whitcomb notes, "Herod's magnificent Temple was not completed until the time of procurator Albinus (A.D. 62-64) just a few years before its final destruction under Titus in A.D. 70!"

From the destruction of Herod's temple in A.D. 70 until the present, the Jews have been banished from the holy site. Jerusalem and the site of the Most Holy Place of the Temple have largely been controlled by Arabs and Muslims who also see the site as second only to Mecca in importance. The Temple area is now the Muslim "Noble Sanctuary," or Haram esh-Sharif, and the Dome of the Rock building now stands directly over the Sakhrah Stone, thought to be the site of the Jewish temples, the altars, and of so many important events in Old Testament history.

*Chapters II to VI*

Chapters II to VI provide a step-by-step tour of the Temple Mount, beginning with (Chapter II) the Sakhrah Stone, (Chapter III) the Northeast Angle and the Golden Gate, (Chapter IV) the Southeast Angle and Solomon's Stables, (Chapter V), the Southern Wall and the Southwest Angle, and (Chapter VI) the Western and the Northern Walls. Whitcomb noted that one of the main purposes of the thesis was "to present a survey of the results of archaeological excavations and researches around the Temple (now known as the Haram esh-Sharif),

---

13. Ibid., 17, quoting Flavius Josephus (A.D. 37–95), Wars of the Jews, V, 5:6.

as they have shed light upon the age of the Temple and the size and shape of the Temple in the times of Solomon and Herod." The personal examination of the Temple Mount and key excavation sites was used to provide perspective and clarity on the work of previous investigators, including Sir Charles Warren, who conducted the principal excavation from 1867 to 1870. Detailed archeological discussion came from Sir Charles Warren's two volumes, *Underground Jerusalem*[14] and *The Recovery of Jerusalem*.[15]

*Conclusions About the Temple*

The Temple of Jerusalem is a God-designed, man-made building in the city that God designated as the center of worship for the Jewish people in the past and the nations of the world in the future. The study of history and archeology support and further clarify statements in the Bible, adding complementary perspectives and insights. Several such points were highlighted.

There have not been three or four <u>different</u> temples. There has been, and is, <u>one Temple</u>. This temple has seen the arrival and departure of Jehovah's Shekinah Glory; the preaching and the persecution of the apostles; the destroying armies of Babylonians and Romans; the desecrations of the Antiochus, a Pompey, and a Hadrian; and it has seen the conquest and occupations of Crusaders and Mohammedans.

Archaeology has revealed to us the astounding fact that through these three millenniums of time, there are certain features of the Temple structure that remain until the present day. The Sakhrah Stone is the original foundation of Solomon's altar of burnt-offerings; and parts of the outer retaining walls are the work of Solomon's builders. Such discoveries have revealed much to us concerning the significance of the Temple of Jerusalem.[16]

14. Ibid., 7, referencing Charles Warren, *Underground Jerusalem* (London: Richard Bentley & Sons, 1876).
15. Ibid., 7, referencing Captain Wilson and Captain Warren, *The Recovery of Jerusalem: A Narrative of Exploration and Discovery in the City and the Holy Land* (New York: Appleton Co., 1871).
16. Ibid., 104.

And with respect to currently unfulfilled prophecies concerning the Temple of Jerusalem, Whitcomb concluded,

> Perhaps the most interesting feature of this Temple for the Bible student, however, is the role it shall play in the future, as revealed by <u>Biblical prophecy</u>. It is astonishing to turn the pages of our Old and New Testaments and discover how much information is given concerning the Temple. Information concerning its past is abundant; indeed, but its future likewise is unveiled by the sure light of prophecy. In this light, we see the Temple of the future once again in the hands of the Jews, immediately following the Rapture of the Church. The old Jewish sacrifices will be reinstated, probably through permission of the world ruler of that time. But within three and a half years these sacrifices shall be stopped by force, and this world ruler will set himself up in the Jewish Temple as a god to be worshipped. For three and a half more years, the Jewish people shall experience a time, known as the Great Tribulation, of suffering and persecution unparalleled in their tragic history. This period will be cut short by the glorious appearance of Jesus Christ from Heaven, rejected indeed by Israel since Calvary, but then to be acknowledged and received by the remnant nation as their long-awaited Lord and Messiah. Through the famous Golden Gate, or a gate that shall be located on the same foundations, this Christ, the returning Shekinah Glory of Ezekiel's vision, shall enter in triumph, never again to depart from His people. The Temple, according to Ezekiel, will then be rebuilt, and perhaps moved to a more central and commanding position in the midst of all the tribes of Israel to be settled in their Promised Land in final fulfillment of God's promise to Abraham.

The last paragraph summarized the impact of the thesis on the author:

> Such a study of Jerusalem's Temple, including a personal examination of its walls and connected buildings, has served to stimulate the writer's appreciation for the written Word of God. For even its numerous historical references to the

Temple have been verified and substantiated by the archae-ologist's spade, even so, its prophetic utterances shall be ver-ified before our eyes as the God of Israel, yes the God of this Temple, shall perhaps in our generation fulfill the promises spoken long ago through His apostles and prophets. May our hearts be prepared for these glorious future events by a glad submission to the One whose glory shall one day return to this Temple, even Jesus Christ, the Savior of the World!

## Publishing the Temple Thesis as a Book

Despite the fact that the thesis was original work and brought new perspectives to light, multiple attempts to publish the work failed. The manuscript was given to and reviewed by a number of friends and Bible teachers of the time, who voiced support of the author but lacked enthusiasm for the document. Apparently the publishers, including Jack Whitcomb's friend Bill Eerdmans, believed that most Christians really do not care about the details of the Temple of Jerusalem since it is not relevant to the Church or everyday life, and thus such a book would be an economic failure. It remains unpublished.

## Defending Daniel — A Master of Theology Thesis

One of John Whitcomb's favorite Old Testament books is the Book of Daniel. This book may have been especially fascinating to him be-cause of the prophecies that predict four sequential world kingdoms that dominated the people of Israel, the promised land, and Jerusalem for more than 600 years into the future. The visions and descriptions of a statue, of four beasts, and of future kings and battles perfectly char-acterizing the kingdom of Babylon, the Persians, the Greeks, and the Romans, including their kings, battles, and intrigue, must have been of particular interest to ancient Middle Eastern historians such as John Whitcomb! And the accuracy of the prophecies in such detail screams of the wisdom and power of God Almighty, who both knows the fu-ture and makes it come to pass as part of His eternal plan.[17]

Atheists and willful agnostics must explain away such clear evi-dence of an all-powerful, all-knowing, and personal God to maintain

---

17. The predetermined plan for the universe before creation and the fact that it will be ac-complished by a sovereign God is referred to as His divine Decree. See Isaiah 14:26–27, 44:24–28, 48:3; Ephesians 1:4, 11, and others.

their world and life views. Thus, critics wasted no time or energy attacking this book as being a fraud, suggesting that it had to have been written ~400 years *after* the Daniel in the biblical story was dead.[18] It was too accurate to have been written by a supposed prophet (excluding the possibility of Divine inspiration!). The book was supposedly contrived in such a way as to make the text "appear" to be prophetic even though the events were far in the rearview mirror of the "real" authors, who they believed wrote the Book of Daniel *after* 170 B.C. when the key events had already transpired. An example of such a critic is Farrell Till, who recently wrote:

> Critical readers, of course, will recognize that stories like the casting of Daniel into a lions' den and Shadrach, Meshach, and Abednego into a fiery furnace were just fanciful tales that originated in a time when people superstitiously believed that gods routinely intervened in their lives.[19]

The dating of the book of Daniel after 170 B.C. is linked to the Maccabees, who linked their struggle against Antiochus Epiphanes, whom believing Jews of the time identified as one of the Kings of the North in Daniel 11:21–35 (the despicable person). The secular history leading up to and surrounding the Maccabean revolt against the Greeks perfectly follows the prophecy of Daniel, and key events of the time are celebrated by Jews around the world each December as Hanukkah.

### Hanukkah and the Prophecies of Daniel

*Hanukkah*, which is Hebrew for "dedication," is the Festival of Lights that is celebrated by Jews in early December. The celebration marks the end of Greek rule in 165 B.C. and a short period of independence until 63 B.C., when the Roman general Pompey captured Palestine and began Roman rule.

The history of Hanukkah begins with Alexander the Great, who conquered the Medo-Persian empire by defeating Darius III in the

---

18. For example, in the article on Daniel on Wikipedia (https://en.wikipedia.org/wiki/Daniel_(biblical_figure, accessed January 3, 2020), the authors state, "The consensus of modern scholars is that Daniel never existed, and the book is a cryptic allusion to the reign of the 2nd century BCE Greek king Antiochus IV Epiphanes."
19. Farrell Till, "Darius the Mede: An Actual Historical Character?" *The Skeptical Review Online*, http://www.theskepticalreview.com/jftdanieldariusthemede.html.pdf, accessed October 23, 2016.

Battle of Gaugamela in 331 B.C. This change in world power was clearly prophesied in the Book of Daniel:

> In the first year of **Darius the Mede**, I arose to be an encouragement and a protection for him. And now I will tell you the truth. Behold, three more kings are going to arise in Persia. Then a fourth will gain far more riches than all of them; as soon as he becomes strong through his riches, he will arouse the whole empire against the realm of Greece. And a **mighty king will arise**, and he will rule with great authority and do as he pleases. But as soon as he has arisen, his kingdom will be broken up and parceled out toward the **four** points of the compass, though not to his own descendants, nor according to his authority which he wielded, for his sovereignty will be uprooted and given to others besides them (Daniel 11:1–4; NASB 1995; emphasis added).

In exact fulfillment of prophecy, three Persian kings[20] followed Cyrus (who was king at the time of Darius the Mede). Then the "fourth king," Xerxes, conquered Greece. Xerxes' son allowed Nehemiah to rebuild the walls of Jerusalem, establishing a Jewish country under Persian rule.[21] However, the Persian Empire was later destroyed by a "mighty king," Alexander the Great. When Alexander died, his kingdom was divided among his four generals, and two of their kingdoms overlapped Palestine: Egypt (Kings of the South) and Syria (Kings of the North). Daniel 11:5–20 continues with incredible details of the conflicts, including the relationship between rulers, their successors, and who would win which battle.[22]

The prophecies continue in Daniel 11:20–34, focusing on "a despicable person" (v. 21) who would seize the northern kingdom by intrigue, and whose identity is recognized by all as Antiochus IV Epiphanes.

---

20. The three kings were Cambyses, Smerdis, and Darius I Hystaspes, followed by Xerxes, who "arouse[d] the whole empire against the realm of Greece."
21. See the Book of Nehemiah in the Old Testament.
22. See John C. Whitcomb, *Daniel — Everyman's Bible Commentary* (Winona Lake, IN: Moody Publishers, BMH Books, 1985), 176 pages. He quotes Walter K. Price, who noted that, for the most part, "attempts to expound Daniel 11:5–20 have been notoriously tedious. A confounding array of unfamiliar names, dates, battles, and political intrigues challenge every endeavor to relate Daniel's prophecy to its fulfillment in the historical events of the third century B.C." (p. 149).

Antiochus Epiphanes sought to force Greek language and culture throughout his kingdom.[23] He forbid the Jews from worshiping Yahweh/Jehovah with a penalty of death and killed the Jewish high priest. In 165 B.C., he set up an altar to Zeus Olympios in the Temple of Jerusalem and initiated sacrifices at the feet of an idol in the image of himself. This was clearly seen as the "abomination of desolations" that was prophesied in Daniel 11:31.

Judas Maccabeus was a God-fearing Jew who organized a guerrilla war against Antiochus that grew into an army. The Maccabees were apparently inspired by the prophecies in Daniel 11, such as:

> Forces from him will arise, desecrate the sanctuary fortress, and do away with the regular sacrifice. And they will set up the abomination of desolation. By smooth words he will turn to godlessness those who act wickedly toward the covenant, **but the people who know their God will display strength and take action. Those who have insight among the people will give understanding to the many**; yet they will fall by sword and by flame, by captivity and by plunder for many days (Daniel 11:31–33; NASB 1995; emphasis added).

The Maccabees repeatedly defeated the generals Antiochus sent to suppress the uprising and eventually conquered Judaea. In December 164 B.C., they were able to tear down the altar of Zeus and re-consecrate the Temple. Tradition states that when they lit the menorah, which is the candelabrum with seven branches, they only had one vial of oil, enough for one day. However, the lamp remained lit for eight days! This was interpreted as miraculous confirmation of God's blessing in rededicating the Temple. Since then, the Jews celebrate Hanukkah and the Festival of Lights each December.

## Higher Criticism of the Book of Daniel

Those who deny that the Bible is authoritative, inspired, and inerrant in all matters on which it speaks cannot accept the fact that Daniel wrote the Book of Daniel four centuries before Antiochus IV Epiphanes, including the details of the history between the fall of Babylon

---

23. The process of infusing Greek culture, religion, and language into foreign nations by the Greeks is called Hellenization.

and the Maccabees. As noted above, critics argue that it was authored at the time of the Maccabees to inspire the revolt, claiming that their cause was of God.[24]

Two major arguments were made against the historicity of the book of Daniel as presented in the Bible. The first is the account of Belshazzar (Daniel 5:1–30; Daniel 7:1; and Daniel 8:1), since he was *not* the last ruler of the Babylonian empire and there were no secular histories or inscriptions of his existence known. The second was Darius the Mede, who, like Belshazzar, was not a king of Persia and was not mentioned by secular historians of the past. These appeared to be unsolvable problems since all ancient historians and many cuneiform documents agree that last king of the Neo-Babylonian empire was Nabonidus, not Belshazzar, and the new king of the Medo-Persian empire was Cyrus, not Darius.

## Belshazzar

The first shock to the errantists (those who believe the Bible is filled with errors) was the discovery in 1854 of four clay cylinders excavated from Ur with identical inscriptions.[25] These Nabonidus Cylinders contained Nabonidus' prayer to the moon god for "Belshazzar, the eldest son — my offspring." In 1882, more information about Belshazzar emerged in the translation of another ancient cuneiform text called the Nabonidus Chronicle. Many more archeological findings in the 20th century confirm and extend the historical certainty of Belshazzar — all of them being remarkably consistent with the text and nuances described in the Book of Daniel. Thus, Nabonidus was the last king of the Babylonian Empire, but he seldom visited Babylon, leaving his son Belshazzar as a regional king or co-regent. This also explains why Belshazzar gave Daniel authority as the *third ruler* in the kingdom rather than the second, since Belshazzar himself was *second* in command.

## Darius the Mede

To date, no cuneiform writings have ever been found that mention Darius the Mede, and there is no ancient historical record of anyone by

24. See *Book of Daniel*, from Wikipedia, https://en.wikipedia.org/wiki/Book_of_Daniel, updated December 22, 2018, accessed December 30, 2018.
25. See Keaton Halley, "Belshazzar: The second most powerful man in Babylon," *Creation*, 37(3):12–15, July 2015. Available online at https://creation.com/archaeology-belshazzar, accessed December 30, 2018.

this name. Furthermore, there were numerous arguments about potential confusion of the supposed second century B.C. authors of pseudo-Daniel with other ancient kings named Darius who were Persian — not Median. John Whitcomb decided to consider all the evidence in light of a careful review of the Book of Daniel, all available archeological and ancient historical evidences, and analysis of the arguments of other authors.

His interest in this topic began in 1951 and culminated in a Master of Theology thesis, where he argued that he identified Darius the Mede through ancient archeological records and used this document as partial fulfillment of the requirements for graduation in May 1954. He went on to transform the thesis into a book, based on additional research and multiple trips to the Oriental Institute of the University of Chicago (about a 2-hour drive from Winona Lake), where he made use of the files of the Assyrian Dictionary and other resources. He also consulted many Old Testament scholars and historians to critically review the manuscript. The book was finally published as *Darius the Mede* by Wm. B. Eerdmans Publishing Company in February 1959.

## Identification of Darius the Mede

The findings, submitted first as a Master of Theology thesis, was finally published as *Darius the Mede,* a short book of only 84 pages. Yet, it proved to be one of the most important scholarly efforts on the historicity of the Book of Daniel in the 20th century. It is a highly technical book and deals with places and people that are unfamiliar to the vast majority of Christians, including devoted students of the Bible. However, more than 60 years later, it stands as the best answer to critics of the inerrancy of the Bible and the authenticity of the Book of Daniel.

The thesis is that Darius the Mede is a man named Gubaru, as found in ancient cuneiform tablets. The key was a famous clay tablet called the Nabonidus Chronicle, a historical record describing the reign of Nabonidus (556–539 B.C.), the rise of the Persian king Cyrus the Great, and the demise of the Babylonian Empire.[26] Mistranslation

---

26. The URL includes a brief introduction and an updated translation of the text by A.K. Grayson, with some changes from previous translations "based on more recent research," that follow the arguments of Prof. Whitcomb. "ABC 7 (Nabonidus Chronicle)," https://www.livius.org/sources/content/mesopotamian-chronicles-content/abc-7-nabonidus-chronicle/, accessed August 31, 2021.

of the Nabonidus Chronicle[27] in 1882 and afterward indicated that Gobryas[28] (or Ugbaru), the Governor of Gutium who conquered Babylon for Cyrus the Great but died three weeks later, was also commissioned by Cyrus to appoint governors or district officers in Babylon. Since Gobryas died shortly after the fall of Babylon, Whitcomb argued that he *could not* have been the king over Daniel as outlined in Daniel 5:31, chapter 6 (including Daniel in the lions' den), and 11:1. However, his careful analysis of the cuneiform indicates that the name of the person appointed by Cyrus to appoint district officers appeared slightly different in the cuneiform text than Gobryas and should have been translated as Gubaru. With this clue, all of the pieces could be put together to demonstrate that Gubaru was none other than Darius the Mede and that the information in the Book of Daniel *had to* originate at the time of the Neo-Babylonian and Medo-Persian Empires, since key pieces of information were unavailable to ancient historians but revealed by modern archeology — including ancient copies of the Book of Daniel among the Dead Sea Scrolls that were discovered in 1946–1956. All of the opposing, compromising, or inadequate theories and objections to the authenticity of the Book of Daniel being written by a Jewish captive named Daniel at the time of the Babylonian captivity of the Jews were addressed, flaws in facts or logic were exposed, and the objective facts confirming inerrancy of the Scriptures were placed in proper perspective.

The book is divided into seven chapters:

I. The biblical data concerning Darius the Mede
II. The cuneiform source material concerning Gubaru the Governor of Babylon

27. The text of the Nabonidus Chronicle translation by Theophilus Pinches in 1882, A. Leo Oppenheim, and others. In Oppenheim (*Ancient Near Eastern Texts Relating to the Old Testament*, Princeton, 1950), under *Seventeenth year*, line 13 reads, "The sixteenth day, Gobryas [litt: Ugbaru], the governor of Gutium, and the army of Cyrus entered Babylon without battle." Line 21 reads, "Gobryas, his governor, installed subgovernors in Babylon." The translation of the name in line 21 was challenged by Prof. Whitcomb. The following URL (https://www.mesopotamiangods.com/the-nabonidus-chronicle-cyrus-takes-babylon/, accessed August 29, 2012) reflects the Oppenheim translation that was linked to another URL that was also used by the author (http://fontes.lstc.edu/~rklein/Documents/chronnab.htm) but is currently unreachable (August 2021).

28. "Gobryas [litt: Ugbaru], the governor of Gutium" is the name given to the Assyrian leader under Cyrus the Great who orchestrated the capture of Babylon in the ancient story called Xenophone's *Cyropaedia* (written about 370 b.c.). Section IV, 6:1–9 and VII, 5:7–34. These sources are reproduced in Appendix IV of Whitcomb's *Darius the Mede*.

In addition, the book has four appendices, including an outstanding historical sketch of the Medes and Persians down to 520 B.C.

Darius the Mede fit the following profile. He was born in the year 601 or 600 B.C., since he was about 62 years old in the autumn of 539 B.C. when he was made "king over the kingdom of the Chaldeans" (Daniel 9:1; NASB 1995) after the death of Belshazzar (Daniel 5:31). His father's name was Ahasuerus and was a Mede, not Persian (Daniel 9:1). Although he had the same name as Darius I (Darius the Great), who later became *king of Persia* (521–486 B.C.; cf. Nehemiah 12:22) and who was the father of the Persian king Xerxes,[29] Darius the Mede and Darius I king of Persia were clearly not the same person.

Although Darius the Mede is called "king," the term could also be governor since he had administrative authority over Babylon and the surrounding area, which was a small component of the Medo-Persian Empire under Cyrus the Great. Darius the Mede is also distinct from Gobryas, who captured Babylon and then died; from Cyrus the Great; from Cambyses (successor to Cyrus); or from any other ancient person, except for "Gubaru," who is now recognized from many historical and archeological sources and perfectly fits the descriptions given in the Book of Daniel.

## Continued Debate about Darius the Mede

Arguments against the inerrancy of Scriptures, the authenticity of the Book of Daniel, and the identity of Darius the Mede continue. However, it is no longer the weight of evidence and sound logic, it is the presupposition that the biblical account is untrue and filled with errors — because the *consequences* of the alternative view must be rejected by

---

29. Xerxes (ruled from 486 B.C. to 380 B.C.) is called Ahasuerus in the Bible; cf. Ezra 4:5–6 and the Book of Esther. This Ahasuerus is not to be confused with Darius the Mede's father!

the unregenerate mind. The consequence of accepting that the Bible is God's inerrant Word in all matters in which it speaks includes the facts that God is taking account of the actions of our lives, our decisions as to accepting Jesus Christ as our Savior, and the punishment of eternal hell for those who reject Christ and the gospel. So the fight is really about whether or not we are responsible to God for carefully reading and believing all the Scriptures,[30] interpreting them in a literal, historical sense and seeking to apply the truths to our lives.

The evidence of the competing world and life views is illustrated in the persistence of public resources such as Wikipedia[31] that states:

> The Book of Daniel is not regarded by scholars as a reliable guide to history. The broad consensus is that Daniel never existed, and that the author appears to have taken the name from a legendary hero of the distant past mentioned in the Book of Ezekiel. . . . Daniel 5 and Daniel 6 belong to the folktales making up the first half of the book.

Notably, the Wikipedia article is based on a 1935 document by H.H. Rowley, who quotes the original *mistranslation* of the Nabonidus Chronicle by Theophilus Pinches in 1882 but not the correct (and verified) translation by Sidney Smith in 1924[32] that distinguish Gubaru and Gobryas, or the more recent translation by A.K. Grayson[33] with the same distinction. The authors of the Wikipedia page completely ignored Whitcomb's *Darius the Mede* and therefore did not need to

---

30. See Jesus' comments to the men in Luke 24:25–27 (NASB 1995; emphasis added), "And He said to them, 'O foolish men and slow of heart to believe in all that the prophets have spoken! Was it not necessary for the Christ to suffer these things and to enter into His glory?' Then beginning with Moses and with **all the prophets**, He explained to them the things concerning Himself in all the Scriptures." Also see 2 Timothy 3:16–17.

31. From "Darius the Mede," Wikipedia, https://en.wikipedia.org/wiki/Darius_the_Mede, last edited on October 29, 2018, accessed December 31, 2018. Note that the primary reference for the article is H.H. Rowley's 1935 study, *Darius the Mede and the Four World Empires of Darius the Mede* (Cardiff: University of Wales Press Board, 1935), which demonstrated that Darius the Mede cannot be identified with any king.

32. Pinches TG, TSBA, VII (1882), 139ff, and Sidney Smith, *Babylonian Historical Texts Relating to the Capture and Downfall of Babylon* (London: Methuen & Co., 1924). Reference cited in John C. Whitcomb, *Darius the Mede* (Grand Rapids, MI: Wm. B. Eerdmans Publishing Co., 1959), 84.

33. See https://www.livius.org/sources/content/mesopotamian-chronicles-content/abc-7-nabonidus-chronicle/, accessed August 29, 2021.

respond to the compelling arguments on the identity of Darius the Mede nor Whitcomb's clear refutation of the arguments of Rowley.

Likewise, the errantist blogger Farrell Till went to great lengths to show that Darius the Mede could not be Cyrus the Great but side-stepped Whitcomb's work with one question.[34] Till writes:

> Let us first consider the case for the Gubaru equation. Whitcomb suggests that "there is one person in history, and only one who fits all the Biblical data concerning Darius the Mede. He is never mentioned by the Greek historians, but appears in various sixth century B.C. cuneiform texts under the name of Gubaru." [Whit.DMede, 10-16].
>
> Can Whitcomb now show us that this chronicle identified Gubaru as 'Darius the Mede'?
>
> No, there is no supporting evidence here, just assertions. If Whitcomb has any evidence that Gubaru was 'Darius the Mede,' why didn't he cite it?
>
> Inerrantists just don't want to admit that he could have been only a fictional character who never existed.

Any reader of Whitcomb's *Darius the Mede* will see an abundance of evidence that Gubaru *was* Darius the Mede, although there is no ancient cuneiform tablet that says, "Gubaru is Darius the Mede." And if there were, would it convince Till and other "errantists" that the Bible is inerrant?[35] The issue is no longer the evidence, as the old rhyme goes, because "a man convinced against his will is of the same opinion still!" But this also goes for those who know God and trust Him that His Word is true.

---

34. Farrell Till, "Darius the Mede: An Actual Historical Character?" *The Skeptical Review Online*, http://www.theskepticalreview.com/jftdanieldariusthemede.html.pdf, accessed October 23, 2016.

35. Other authors, such as Clyde E. Fant and Mitchell G. Reddish in *Lost Treasures of the Bible: Understanding the Bible through Archaeological Artifacts in World Museums* (William B. Eerdmans Publishing Company, Grand Rapids, Michigan/Cambridge, U.K., 2008), cover details of the Nabonidus Chronicle but completely ignore the discussion of Gubaru — while later indicating that the book of Daniel was written 400 years after the fall of Babylon. Others, such as William H. Shea, continue that Darius the Mede is Gobryas in the Nabonidus Chronicle, unaware of the mistranslation and apparently unaware of Whitcomb's book. (See William H. Shea, *Journal of the Adventist Theological Society*, 7/1 [Spring 1996], 1–20. PDF transcript available at https://digitalcommons.andrews.edu/cgi/viewcontent.cgi?article=1390&context=jats.)

The effort by John Whitcomb to examine all of the biblical and extra-biblical evidence and solve a 2,500-year-old mystery was driven by the conviction that the Bible is inerrant on every topic it touches — not just inerrant in its message or teachings — also known as "limited inerrancy."[36] Accurate biblical exegesis and commitment to applying what it says under the authority of God is critical to opposing the greatest threat to Christianity, which is false teaching and deceptive heresies. The outstanding scholarship that culminated in publishing *Darius the Mede* serves to confirm and strengthen the confidence of believers. In contrast, every objection imaginable has been thrown at the Book of Daniel, especially a late date of writing, to avoid the conclusion that Daniel's prophecy was a supernatural act of God. But it was.

## Other Publications

### Bible Charts

In addition to *Darius the Mede*, Professor Whitcomb began creating, and then publishing, a series of Bible charts (see Chapter 11, August 13, 1946). These now include "Chart of the Period from the Creation to Abraham," "Chart of Old Testament Patriarchs and Judges," "Chart of Old Testament Kings and Prophets," "Babylonian Captivity," "Chart of the Period Between the Testaments," "New Testament Chronological Chart," "Chronology of the Crucifixion and the Last Week," "Christ's 2nd Coming," "Chart of the Five Worlds," and "Chart of the Thousand-Year Reign."[37] Furthermore, they have been reproduced and used in numerous other publications such as study Bibles and lecture series.

### Commentary on Ezra, Nehemiah, and Esther

Professor Alva J. McClain, president of Grace Theological Seminary, also had a personal and professional interest in the success of young Dr. Whitcomb. He began inviting him to provide technical review, critique, and edits on commentaries and publications related to ancient Middle Eastern history that were sent to McClain. Whitcomb, as a young faculty member, proved his aptitude and diligence in completing these tasks. As a result of his work, and support from the senior

---

36. For further discussion, see http://defendinginerrancy.com/a-seismic-shift-in-the-inerrancy-debate/.

37. Available at http://www.whitcombministries.org/charts.html.

faculty at Grace, Whitcomb was asked to write short commentaries on the books of Ezra, Nehemiah, and Esther for Moody Press. This was published as part of *The Wycliffe Bible Commentary*,[38] establishing Whitcomb as an expert in this part of the Old Testament.

Thus, by 1960, John Whitcomb was being recognized as an expert in ancient Middle Eastern history and in synchronization of ancient historical records and archeological discoveries with the biblical record.

---

38. John C. Whitcomb, "Ezra," "Nehemiah," and "Esther," in *The Wycliffe Bible Commentary: A Phrase by Phrase Commentary of the Bible*. Charles F. Pfeiffer and Everett F. Harrison, eds. (Chicago, IL: Moody Publishers, 1962), 1534 pages.

# Chapter 16

# Edisene

"It is not good that the man should be alone" (Genesis 2:18; KJV)
August 1951–1970

## The Bachelor

The year 1951 was pivotal for John Whitcomb. At 27 years of age, he faced multiple life-altering decisions. Up until now, life's pathways appeared clear and obvious; he followed the guidance of his physical and spiritual fathers — and Uncle Sam. In June of 1951, he completed his Master of Divinity training at Grace Theological Seminary (Grace), receiving the training required to be a missionary.

Jack had one life goal — to serve the Lord as a missionary in China. He had no other plans. But the evils of communism closed the doors to the land of the Forbidden City,[1] and the hopes to return to China ended.

In June of 1951, Dr. McClain, recognizing that China was not an option, offered Jack a faculty position at Grace and an opportunity to continue his education toward a doctorate. Being paid to study and teach was a welcomed change, although the salary was minimal.

Jack reassessed his status, his position, his future, and his plans. He was living in a small student's apartment, using a bicycle for transportation, and serving in multiple ministries from morning to night, seven days a week. His closest friend from Princeton and classmate at Grace, John Rea, was married, and he and his wife Elaine were expecting their first child. His fellow student and street evangelist friend, Sib Edmiston, was also married with a fine wife and beautiful family

---

1. The Forbidden City was the Chinese imperial palace for 500 years. It is in the center of Beijing, China, and is used here as a metaphor for all of China.

of three children and more on the way. Furthermore, his father and mother chose retirement in Lima, Peru — too far away for holiday visits. Jack, in the likeness of his *spiritual father*, Donald Fullerton, was alone.

Jack's *theological father*, Alva J. McClain, advised Jack on more than scholastics. McClain strongly encouraged Jack to consider becoming a permanent academic faculty member, getting married, and establishing a home. While Jack's diligent study and theological training equipped him for an academic career, major concerns remained in his mind about establishing a Christian home.

Jack was raised in a godless home. Many times, I can remember my father expressing memories of the sadness and pain he felt as a child as he watched the empty lifestyle, parties, guests, social behavior, and goals of his military career parents. Being raised, to a large extent, by servants rather than his own mom, also left concerns that he lacked good examples of parenting. He continued to have feelings of inadequacy and disqualification for various leadership roles in the Christian community and Christian home, in spite of the miracles of salvation and sanctification. Regardless of the opinions of others, Jack felt a major void, especially after visiting godly and loving Christian homes where his new friends and colleagues were born and raised.

McClain addressed this issue by assigning Jack to study under the nurturing of a mature Christian couple, Bill and Ruth Short. They established a weekly meeting to guide and encourage him in areas of practical Christian living and personal walk with the Lord — in addition to his academic studies. Bill and Ruth provided advice and examples on how to seek a Christian wife, how to establish a Christian home, and how to lead a Christian family. The plan worked perfectly, as Bill and Ruth played important roles in guiding future aspects of Jack's complete Christian life.

Just to be certain of this advice, Jack consulted his lifelong bachelor-mentor, Donald Fullerton, about this idea of marriage and a family. Fullerton offered his complete advice in a single verse, "It is not good that the man should be alone" (Genesis 2:18; KJV).

## "Something Happened"

On August 28, 1951, Jack moved to a new apartment at 105 14th Street, Winona Lake, Indiana. In addition to moving, he reserved time to finish some tasks at the seminary before going to an evening service. The National Fellowship of Grace Brethren Churches was in town for their annual conference. The agenda for the evening featured a Sunday school pageant — not a top pick for a bachelor and budding theologian. Jack attended anyway, in part because he had previously volunteered to be an usher.

Collecting an offering is typically an uneventful exercise. Jack, after working his way to the back of the auditorium, recognized Willie Edmiston, the wife of his friend and classmate, Sib Edmiston. Next to her sat a tall, blonde-haired young lady — and she caught Jack's eye. The girl was Willie's sister, Edisene Hanson, who went by the nickname Senie. Senie noticed Jack as well, confiding to her sister, "I don't know what happened, but when that usher took the plate, SOMETHING HAPPENED!"

Edisene spent the summer of 1951 in Winona Lake on a special mission. In July, the Hanson family, who lived in Long Beach, California, recognized that Willie, now in Winona Lake, Indiana, had her hands full with a husband who was active in seminary and street evangelism, three rambunctious young children, and a fourth child on the way. The California Hansons decided to send Willie a blessing for the summer. They secretly arranged to send Edisene, the youngest of four siblings, on a trip east.

Edisene boarded an eastbound train from Long Beach, California, to Warsaw, Indiana — the town immediately adjacent to Winona Lake. Following family tradition, Senie walked from the train station, luggage in hand, up to the front door of the Edmiston house, rang the doorbell, and surprised (shocked) her sister Willie by arriving without warning. Willie desperately needed her domestic help and deeply appreciated her family's "care package." The summer was uneventful for Edisene until late August, when the dog days were waning and the new school year was imminent.

Just before returning to California, Senie, in an evening Bible conference service, suddenly felt a special connection with a young man after passing an offering bucket to this complete stranger. Immediately following the service, Willie introduced Senie to Jack. He clearly felt something too, abandoning the evening's plans in exchange for a conversation with this young woman. Jack documented the event that night in his diary: *"Talked with Mrs. Edmiston's sister (Edisene) a while after the service."*

The next day, there was a knock at the Edmistons' front door. It was Jack Whitcomb. He came to ask permission from Sib if he could take Senie to the Bible conference meeting that night. Senie had reservations, voicing concerns to Willie that Jack's hair was messy and his pants were not pressed. Willie reassured Senie that these superficial issues could easily be fixed, but that beneath the poor grooming existed a very fine man.

The request from Jack to accompany Senie to the evening service was approved. Jack would pick her up at 7:00 p.m. Jack recorded the details of his first date: *"I met Edisene at the Edmistons, and we heard Rev. John Aeby preach at the evening service on Home Missions. Afterwards, we went to Bethany Camp, where the BYF [Brethren Youth Fellowship] talent was presented, and Ralph Colburn showed color slides. Got home by 11:00."* An unusually late-night outing for Jack!

On Thursday, August 30, Jack swung by the Edmistons' again — this time in the early afternoon. The "reason" was to meet some of the people from the Long Beach Grace Brethren churches (as well as Senie). Jack spent the rest of the day with Senie, including showing her his pride and joy — his seminary office and theological library. That evening, they attended an alumni banquet together at the historic Winona Hotel. However, the hotel was not air conditioned, and it was *"very hot."* Jack, Edisene, and Willie slipped out the back door together and walked to the Bethany youth camp to watch the Brethren youth perform their skits. Overall, it was a good second date, as Jack *"got home at midnight."* The next day, Edisene boarded a train back to southern California.

There are two types of diaries. One serves as an outlet for internal thoughts, fears, hopes, frustrations, love, and passion. The other is an organized record of the day's events. The Whitcomb diaries are the latter type, so it is unclear what Jack was thinking. But the meeting was more than a historical event. Willie Edmiston still remembers that John Rea, Jack's friend and classmate from Princeton, was "shocked" at the time to see Jack with a beautiful young woman. To him, they looked like a perfect couple.

## Young Edisene

Edisene was providentially destined to become Jack's first wife. She was the youngest of four girls born to Albert Fred Hanson and Blanche Hester (Tahash) Hanson. She was born on February 11, 1930, the birthday of Thomas Edison,[2] who invented the light bulb. Her father named her Edisene in honor of the Wizard of Menlo Park. She joined three older sisters — Winifred (Winnie), Willetta (Willie), and Alberta (Bertie) — in a small wooden house in sunny Long Beach, California.

Edisene's parents were poor Midwesterners who moved to Long Beach from a small town in rural Iowa, just like many of their friends and neighbors who now populated the west coast. Bert grew up as a Danish[3] farm boy who worked with the Long Beach police department as a radio dispatcher after moving to California. At night, Bert tinkered with electronic things in the garage and broadcast as an amateur, or "ham" radio operator, using the call letters W6HHU. Immediately after the March 10, 1933, earthquake that left Long Beach in rubble, Bert coordinated the city's emergency services from his house. The city honored Bert with an official certificate, and he was featured in *Popular Mechanics* in a special article called "Neighbors on the Air."

Blanche was a strong, kind woman of German ancestry. Blanche accepted the Lord Jesus Christ as her Savior when she was nine years of age at a revival meeting in Tama, Iowa, but was never discipled or taught the Bible systematically while growing up. Blanche decided she must raise their children in a "Christian" home, reading the Bible to them and taking them to the local church whenever the doors were open. They began attending an outstanding, Bible-believing church within their neighborhood, the First Brethren Church of Long Beach, pastored by Louis S. Bauman. The Hanson family came to know the Lord as their personal Savior, and several of them dedicated their lives to His service. Blanche became a Sunday school and women's Bible study teacher, faithfully serving non-stop for 31 years.

Edisene Marjorie Hanson was born on February 11, 1930. Her next-older sister and close, lifelong friend was Alberta Hanson, known

---

2. Thomas Edison was born on February 11, 1847, in Milan Ohio, and died October 18, 1931. He was considered one of the greatest inventors of his generation.

3. The family changed the spelling of their name from Hansen to Hanson, a common Swedish surname, likely to be accepted into a Swedish community in the New World as "family."

as "Bertie."[4] The next oldest was Willetta, who married a neighborhood boy and member of the Grace Brethren Church, Sib Edmiston.

As kids, Senie and Bertie joined all of the school sports teams (field hockey, volleyball, soccer, softball) and social clubs and organized neighborhood sport and social activities with a group of local kids that they called "The Gang." Senie proved to be an excellent athlete, and as a tall (eventually reaching 5'7"), blonde, blue-eyed girl with Danish-German roots, she could compete in sports with any of the local boys. On the social-service side, whenever there was an election among her peers, she would immediately be voted in as "secretary" — the highest office that could be held, in those times, by a girl. The only question was, who would serve under her as "president"?

After high school, both Senie and Bertie attended the Bible Institute of Los Angeles (BIOLA), where they finished degrees in Bible. Senie continued her education at Long Beach Community College (LBCC) and the University of California Santa Barbara (UCSB), majoring in nutrition and home economics. It was during the summer break of 1951 that Edisene traveled to Winona Lake, Indiana, to help her sister Willie — and there she met John C. Whitcomb Jr.

## Long-distance Dating

At the end of the summer, Senie returned to California and school, and Jack continued his usual routine of study, teaching, and service. However, Senie remained at the forefront of Jack's mind. Although she was six years younger, she was pretty, smart, fun, educated, a dedicated Christian, and a Grace Brethren girl. On September 4, 1951, Jack discovered that he was in possession of Sib Edmiston's fountain pen — and what an opportunity. He noted in his diary, "Took Sib's fountain pen to Mrs. Edmiston, & got Edisene's address." Jack likely probed a little on whether Willie thought Senie liked him too. During the next two days, he studied *Youth's Courtship Problems* by Alfred Murray[5] and then wrote his first letter to Miss Hanson.

Senie's return to Long Beach forced her and Jack to date by mail. Her sister Bertie remembers that every Wednesday, a letter would arrive addressed to "Miss Edisene Hanson." Edisene's mother, Blanche,

---

4. Personal communication, February 2015.

5. Alfred Murray, *Youth's Courtship Problems* (Grand Rapids, MI: Zondervan Publishing House, 1940). A well-known Christian book on friendship, courtship, and marriage.

was impressed by the reliable timing of the letters and perfect handwriting on the envelope. The letters themselves have since disappeared, and the precious words are lost. But the contents certainly impressed Senie and nourished the blossoming relationship.

## Planning for the Future

On Friday, September 21, 1951, Jack received his first letter from Senie. It must have been wonderful, as he clearly received a very positive response to his initial letter. Sunday afternoon, after thought and prayer, he sat down and penned his response. Although Jack wrote many letters, this type was different and dangerous for a gentle young man who possessed deep and strong emotions — including a yearning to love and be loved. It may also have been challenging because he was never a ladies' man, nor someone who played upon the emotions of young women for attention or personal pleasure. He had no clever phrases, and each word must be selected to convey respect, to express growing interest in the intended recipient, to foster future communications, and yet to guard his heart from someone who might not be interested or capable of giving and receiving true love over a lifetime. But he also knew that "The steps of a *good* man are ordered by the LORD" (Psalm 37:23; KJV), and "something happened" in his heart too that he knew was right.

It appears that things moved quickly behind the scenes. Jack visited with Sib and Willie Edmiston on multiple occasions during the fall of 1951. Willie, as a matchmaker, relayed positive character assessments and quality reports — in both directions. But to the casual observer, the budding relationship remained hidden.

Jack felt comfortable in confiding his feelings and intentions to Bill and Ruth Short. In late October, Bill passed a special book to Jack — *A Virtuous Woman* by Oscar Lowry. Jack took the book, which he "*read through quickly.*"

Whit, Jack's dad, officially retired from the Army and made arrangements to live in Lima, Peru. However, before leaving Washington, D.C., Whit took the opportunity to make a short trip to Winona Lake with his wife to see their son, whom he called "the professor," and to visit the school. On November 19, 1951, during his parents' visit, Jack unveiled a picture of Edisene for his mother and father. They apparently underestimated the importance of this young lady, since Jack's mother, Salome, never mentioned it in her letters to Jack in the coming months.

Jack also sought dating and marital advice from Donald Fullerton and Alva J. McClain, while correspondence with his dad remained rather technical — e.g., "Should I buy a car?" "How much should I pay?" "How do I choose the best car for me?" "Do I need life insurance?"

Senie displayed strong interest in moving the relationship forward and invited Jack to come to California to meet her parents — definitely a good sign. However, transcontinental travel was not so easy in 1951 since there were no interstate highways.[6] The fastest connections were by train, although regular airplane flights between Los Angeles and Chicago were on the horizon. By the beginning of December, it was clear that the Christmas trip would be postponed. After receiving a box of candy from Edisene on December 10, Jack sent his regrets to her with a box of stationery for Christmas — and also a portrait of himself, as requested!

## Nana

The first mention of Edisene in Jack's diary in 1952 was on January 11, after he received a letter and portrait of Edisene and some color slides. Jack had an open invitation to California, but he also had a "once in a lifetime" opportunity to participate in a "Flying Seminar" — an eight-week trip to Europe, Israel, and Egypt guided by an outstanding faculty to teach the significance of major historical sites while standing on them! The timing and cost of doing everything would be challenging.

On February 14, Jack attended a prayer meeting. He "requested prayer for my family, having received a letter today from Mother in St. Petersburg [Florida] telling of Nana having had a heart attack." His mother was with her, while Nana, his paternal grandmother, was being treated in an oxygen tent.

On Saturday, February 16, he spent the morning studying *Early Persecutions of the Church* by Canfield in his apartment and the afternoon in his seminary office, reading world history focusing on the Glorious Revolution,[7] the American Revolution, and French Revolution.

---

6. The Interstate System was the work of President Dwight D. Eisenhower, who signed the Federal-Aid Highway Act of 1956 to initiate building the system.
7. The Glorious Revolution of 1688 was the overthrow of King James II of England by the Dutch under William III, Prince of Orange, with help by the British parliament. The revolution ended Catholic power, the idea of the divine right of kings, and development of the Bill of Rights.

When he finally got home, he found a note instructing him to call his mother in St Petersburg. Nana had died. The funeral would be near Washington, D.C., where she would be buried in Arlington National Cemetery next to her husband, Col. Clement Colfax Whitcomb.

The following Tuesday, after classes, he boarded the 7:30 p.m. train headed to Washington, D.C. He settled into his Pullman,[8] read *The Protestant Dilemma* by Carl F. Henry, and drifted off to sleep.

Jack's parents arrived from Florida at around 3:00 p.m. the next day, giving Jack nearly a full day to study world history alone in the Statler Hotel in Washington, D.C. He joined his mom and dad at 6:30 p.m. for supper and talked for some time before returning to his hotel.

The next day, Thursday, February 21, Jack purchased a new hat and gloves and then went to Arlington Cemetery. At 10:00, a hearse led a short line of cars to a plot next to the grave of Col. C.C. Whitcomb, where Nana's ashes were placed. An Episcopal chaplain led a brief service, attended by about 15 old friends.

After the service, Jack's mother and dad bought him a new overcoat to go with his hat and gloves, and a suitcase, which would be useful in the coming months — if the travel plans worked out. His parents took him to the train station for a brief supper before catching the 6:15 p.m. train back to Winona Lake. At supper, Jack revealed his portrait of Edisene and spoke of his intentions to visit her in California.

Whit settled Nana's estate. In her last will and testament, Nana bequeathed *everything* to Jack. The total amounted to $16,997.04. Whit recommended that Jack use $3,000 for the Flying Seminar and trip to the Holy Land, *plus* a trip to California! The rest would be put into stocks. Jack agreed and asked his father to pick the stocks and set up the financial transactions. He would coordinate a possible road trip west with the Edmistons, who were planning to visit southern California that summer.

## Marriage Advice from an Old Bachelor

The chasm between long-distance correspondence with someone you knew for three days and marriage can be great. Although Jack possessed deep emotional feelings, wanting to love and be loved, he

---

8. A Pullman referred to an upscale railway car that had sleeping compartments.

guarded his actions and interactions with careful intent. The short time with Edisene, however, sparked a new type and depth of interest in relationships and marriage, and it appeared to be of God.

Jack confided in Donald Fullerton and asked for advice — especially since the personal connections with Edisene grew stronger with every letter, with every glance at her portrait, and every conversation with her sister Willie and brother-in-law Sib. On May 25, 1952, the first round of advice came from Mr. F., arriving in the form of a letter with two key paragraphs.

> Now that is great news about the young lady of California. Her qualifications sound 'wunderbar.' If she be the Lord's choice for you, may He incline your hearts toward each other and in his time unite them into one. "He that findeth a wife, findeth a good thing." Of course after living for years on Graham crackers, dried apples, tins of sardines and an occasional raw carrot and an apple or banana, it is needless to remind you "it is not good every man should be alone." Only make sure the helpmate for you is of the Lord's making. The Lord Jesus prosper your trip to California and give you both his wisdom in the matter. I haven't given up hope for you and shall remember this in prayer.

Fullerton added — possibly in response to an idea of a combined honeymoon/missionary trip,

> A honeymoon to Mexico, protected and chaperoned constantly by an old man and several college students would be unique and unforgettable.

The signal was clear — advance toward California with intent and confidence. And the faint "positive" response to a group honeymoon in Mexico indicated subtle advice to keep "other options" open.

## A Trip to California

The 1952 spring semester at Grace wound to an end with exams, grading of papers, and graduation, all completed by Monday, May 26. At 6:30 the next morning, Jack arrived at the Edmistons' house to have breakfast and pack the car for the long and winding roads linking

Winona Lake, Indiana, with Long Beach, California. The Edmiston family (two adults and four children) and hitchhiker Jack rolled onto the first of many connecting streets and roadways by 7:30 a.m. For an academically focused young man who grew up without siblings, this trip must have been both challenging and educational!

The travel plan for the small company working their way west included visiting multiple places and people involved in various churches and missions. The trip took eight days, including a stop in Leavenworth, Kansas, where Jack nearly died two decades earlier. He took pictures of the "Beehive," one of several old boyhood homes across the globe. In the old town of Taos, New Mexico,[9] the car overheated from engine problems, requiring three days to fix. Fortunately, the Edmistons had friends who were church planters and who worked with the Pueblo Indians in this rural part of northeastern New Mexico. Jack and Sib visited the evangelistic and church planting efforts of their friends in the area, and they were invited to speak at several of the small churches on Sunday. On the way to one church, the missionaries loaded "23 [people] into the station wagon before reaching the church." They continued on the famous Route 66 through the night until the car tire blew out in Grants, New Mexico, a tiny town known locally as "The Uranium Capital of the World." They stopped again in Desert View, Arizona, to see the Grand Canyon and in Boulder City, Nevada, to see the Hoover Dam. They finally reached Long Beach, California, at 3:00 p.m. on June 5, 1952.

They immediately went to the Hanson home, but Edisene was not there. So they met with Mr. and Mrs. Hanson and moved on to Sib's mother's house, where Jack was given Sib's old room for the rest of the visit. Jack, wanting assurance that he would be back in Winona Lake in time for the Flying Seminar, made arrangements for a return trip to Indiana by train. The visit lasted three weeks.

## Jack Meets the Hanson Family

The evening of June 5, 1951, was beautiful. It included a special dinner at the Hansons' home, with Jack as the special guest. Throughout the evening, Jack remained affable, good-hearted, and dignified.

---

9. Taos is known for the ancient multistory adobe complexes built by the Pueblo Indians and inhabited for centuries. The pueblo was built between A.D. 1000 and 1450 and is considered to be one of the oldest continuously inhabited communities in the United States.

## Edisene

The Hanson "girls" concocted some special plans for Jack — just in case his intentions for Senie included some long-term plans.[10] Jack's formal and proper demeanor needed "fix'n" before Edisene would take him!

First, the Hanson girls decided that Jack must address Senie by her "real" name, "Edisene Marjorie Martha Mary Magdalene Gasoline Kerosene Marline Hanson." Second, he must demonstrate proper etiquette at the supper table at all times. The challenge would include multiple pranks and sabotage. Jack's place setting included a "dribble glass," a drinking glass possessing holes in the intricate design that allowed water to leak onto the shirt of the unsuspecting target when they attempted to drink. There was the "whoopee cushion," the pneumatic plate tipper, and anything else the sisters could imagine. Jack, who learned versatility and adaptability in the Battle of the Bulge, navigated the potential disasters with good humor and dignity. The Hanson family exceeded his expectations, and Jack passed his little tests — which exceeded their expectations.

Next, it was the men's time. The women arose to clear the supper table and clean the dishes. Jack and the other men joined Mr. Hanson as they piled into the garage to watch a boxing match on a television set.

Finally, with the dishes cleaned and the boxing match over, Jack got some time with Edisene. She was under the pressure of time and appeared somewhat distracted. Edisene was finishing a college degree, and she needed to ace a U.S. history exam scheduled for the next morning. Fortunately, Jack was an ace in history and willingly spent the evening reviewing notes and significant historical events with Edisene.

Edisene took her U.S. history exam the next morning — and passed. Sib and Jack picked her up from LBCC at 11:00 a.m. and had lunch. They sang some songs around the piano. Then Sib and Jack took Edisene to the bank where she worked in the afternoons. After work, they ate supper at the Hansons', then Jack showed his color slides of Peru. Edisene was sleepy after her exam and work and went to bed.

Edisene's plans for Saturday did not include Jack. So, Jack ran some errands and wandered over to the Hanson house to talk with Alberta and Mrs. Hanson in their backyard. After supper, Jack, Senie, Bertie,

---

10. Personal communication from Alberta Hanson and Willetta Edmiston, who continued to relish the details of the evening, over 60 years later.

Sib, and Willie drove up to a Spanish section of Los Angeles to visit the Spanish church *La Resurrección* where a friend, Dr. Morales, preached.

## Courtship

On Sunday, June 8, Jack finally got some time alone with Edisene. They attended the Second Brethren Church of Long Beach, where Jack taught the young married class with a technical lesson on Jewish festivals from Leviticus 23. It was the first time that Senie heard the rookie seminary professor teach.

After a more stirring lesson by pastor George Peek on Jacob and Esau, Senie introduced Jack to her friends, including her roommate from BIOLA where Senie previously obtained a degree in Bible. Jack and Senie then drove to the Municipal Auditorium to attend a second church service. Afterward, when Jack and Senie were finally alone, he framed their potential futures together from a divine perspective: *"Edisene & I had prayer together, concerning God's will for our lives."* After lunch, they drove to the seashore for some relaxation and conversation and then headed home for a quick supper before the evening church services. They chose to visit BIOLA, in downtown Los Angeles, to hear Dr. Louis T. Talbot preach.[11] After the service, Jack and Senie went out for ice cream! It was an outstanding day.

Senie was busy finishing school and working at the bank. So, Jack used his time on the West Coast to meet pastors and missionaries, to visit their works, and to prepare for his own teaching and preaching opportunities. Sib, who was from the area, was anxious to introduce the new Grace Theological Seminary professor to the Southern California Grace Brethren pastors. On Monday morning, Sib took Jack to a ministerial meeting at the First Brethren Church, where Jack met numerous Grace Brethren pastors and leaders. After a morning of reports, they moved to the Wilton Hotel for lunch then addressed the issue of the day: Should a divorced Christian hold an official church office? After eating supper with the Hansons, Jack and Senie drove over to the house of Edisene's oldest sister, Winnie, for refreshments with her and her husband, George Kramer.

---

11. Dr. Talbot, the new president of BIOLA, argued for development of a formal school of theology within BIOLA, and his plan had just been approved. The new school was established that year, and the program would eventually become Talbot Theological Seminary.

# Edisene

The next two days Jack spent shopping, mostly for books. His first stop was Acres of Books, where he found some old treasures, paying $30.00 for the stack. These he shipped to Winona Lake. Since he still had time, he went to a department store and selected a nice brown summer suit costing him $71.00. He also noticed a jewelry store and slipped in to learn something about engagements rings. He returned to the Hansons' for supper and spent the evening with Senie. They got out a map and selected some fun and useful destinations to visit together while Jack was in Southern California and Senie was out of school and away from work.

June 12 was Edisene's graduation from Long Beach City College with an Associate of Art degree. The ceremony lasted the entire morning. Senie had Jack, the amateur photographer, take pictures of her with three of her girlfriends. Edisene then informed him that she promised to spend the rest of the day, the evening, and the next day with her friends, and they left.

Jack finally met Edisene again at church, as she attended his Sunday school class at the Second Grace Brethren Church. They again attended two Sunday morning services, hearing George Peak preach on Isaac, then traveled to hear Charles Fuller speak at the Long Beach Municipal Auditorium in Long Beach. Fuller's messages were nationally syndicated to over 650 radio stations on the ABC Radio Network as *The Old Fashioned Revival Hour*. Fuller had also started Fuller seminary five years earlier, which was led by his son Dan Fuller. They also recruited Wilbur M. Smith — author of *Therefore Stand*, one of the most influential books in Jack's early Christian life. Although Donald Fullerton (and Jack) had serious concerns about Fuller Seminary's neo-evangelical approach, Jack's old Princeton friend Lenox Palin enrolled at Fuller Seminary as a student. After the service, Jack and Senie spoke at length with Mr. Fuller then headed out together for the afternoon.

Jack and Senie walked together along the breakwater of the Pacific Ocean. They drove to San Pedro, where they viewed the harbor through a telescope. They visited a glass roadside chapel and visited some of Senie's friends. The afternoon began slipping away, and they rushed back to the South Gate Brethren Church, getting there just in time for Jack to preach on Isaiah 53.

Monday was a great day. Edisene picked Jack up at 8:15 a.m., and they traveled together up the California coast to Los Angeles, San Bernardino, and Santa Barbara. They had a wonderful picnic by a stream and visited an old mission with a personal tour led by a monk.

The next few days included similar adventures with trips east to Redlands and the dessert, a trip to Tijuana, Mexico, with the Edmistons, a visit to the Mount Palomar Observatory, a day at the Los Angeles County museum, and a series of sightseeing hot spots. Several evenings included visits to special ice cream shops or making homemade ice cream in the backyard of the Hansons' home.

## Planning the Wedding Engagement

Tuesday, June 24, proved to be another watershed day in Jack's life. He wrote in his diary that, after supper, he and Senie *"went over to American Ave, & played a game of miniature golf. We discussed plans for our engagement next Christmas, when Edisene comes East for a visit. She took me home afterwards."*

Over the next few days, Edisene worked at the bank, limiting the time together to the evenings with Jack and other family members. Jack visited Lenox Palin twice, meeting his wife and seeing his six-month-old baby boy. They had long talks discussing their plans for the future and discussed some issues concerning the fledgling Fuller Seminary.

Sunday, June 29, the date of Jack's departure for Indiana, arrived quickly. Jack and Senie drove to the Hollywood Presbyterian Church to worship with 2,000 other believers. Jack recorded the highlights of the afternoon: *"We drove 25 miles north to Mount Wilson Observatory. We read Emily Post on Engagement & Weddings together, & discussed plans for Christmas vacation. We had to hurry to get to the Santa Fe [railroad] Station by 5:45. Got my ticket for $68.00, called the Hansons, checked my large suitcase & said goodbye to Edisene."* The train left at 6:15.

## More Advice from Fullerton

The trip to Long Beach had been wonderful. Jack sent an update on his visit with Edisene to Donald Fullerton, who responded with more sound advice.

> Of course I am delighted over what you write about Edisene. Hope you do not have to wait too long before being

united in the wondrous marital union ordained of God. If you both are confident it is our Lord's will for your lives, and truly love each other, do not delay any longer than absolutely necessary.

May our God, lead you both very definitely into His perfect will for you, in His own time. I shall rejoice when the wedding bells ring, but regret that the event must take place all the way across the continent. Remember, "It is not good for the man to be alone." God said it and I am a witness to the truth of it. Also, whoever finds a wife from the Lord, finds a good thing. The Lord Jesus bless you abundantly!

Give my heartiest greetings to Edisene and tell her I look forward to meeting her someday, here or in the Glory.

The rest of the summer was consumed with the Flying Seminar to the Holy Land. However, Senie was not far from Jack's mind. When the group stopped in Paris, Jack went shopping and found some beautiful French lace, which he purchased. He sent these to Senie, who used it to make her own wedding dress.

Jack returned from the Middle East late on the night of Sunday, August 31, 1952. The next morning, after unpacking, he went to the home of Sib and Willie Edmiston to show them some souvenirs and get an update on Senie. They decided to make a wire recording of the events and spent the following evening talking into a microphone for about 30 minutes. On Thursday, the seminary faculty had their first official meeting of the fall semester at Grace Theological Seminary, and the school year began.

Jack remained rather quiet about his hopes and plans for the future with Edisene.

On November 21, 1952, Jack received a letter from Donald Fullerton with the following paragraph:

Was glad to hear of the safe arrival of Linda Jay but you have not mentioned anything recently about your California "Joy." How is she and how are you progressing with the Lassie? If you are sure she is the right one I hope you will redeem the time bringing up at every opportunity to hasten the consummation of the Blessed Union. "He that findeth a wife findeth a good thing, and obtaineth favor with the Lord" Ps 18:22. Of course I'm only speaking theoretically. But "God said it, I believe it." However I do know, "It is not good that a man should be alone" the Lord give you wisdom in this matter also.

The words of encouragement from Mr. Fullerton to progress toward marriage only endorsed Jack's plans. Jack had already made arrangements for Edisene to fly to the closest airport, Chicago, Illinois, in December 1952.

## The Diamond

On December 19, Senie boarded a TWA Constellation, a propeller-driven, four-engine airliner, to take the red-eye flight 702 from Los Angeles International Airport to Midway Airport in Chicago. At the same time, Jack finalized the plans to meet Senie in Chicago driving in from the east.

At noon, Jack received his paycheck from GTS, withdrew $250.00 from the bank, and left Winona Lake for Chicago at 1:30 p.m. by car. The traffic was heavy and confusing, and he missed Lake Shore Drive, requiring him to go through "70 blocks of town traffic." He finally arrived at Martin's Jewelers in time to buy a diamond set for $306.00.

Arising at 5:15 the next morning, Jack left the room he had rented at Moody Bible Institute to meet Edisene at the airport. A delay in the flight allowed him to get a haircut and breakfast.

The plane landed at 9:15, and immediately after meeting Senie, he sent a telegram to her family to confirm a safe arrival and sped north to Moody Bible Institute for a pre-arranged tour of the school and visit to radio station WMBI. By noon, it was pouring rain, so the couple returned to their car and sat and talked. At 2:20 p.m., Jack pulled a box out of his pocket. The box contained the diamond ring — and Edisene accepted the engagement ring. Miss Hanson officially agreed to become Mrs. Whitcomb.

The ring did not fit. So, the couple returned to Martin's Jewelers for an adjustment. After a Chicago dinner, they drove to Winona Lake, arriving at the Edmistons' by 7:30 p.m. Willie and Sib celebrated the engagement with Jack and Senie. The Hanson girls immediately started planning the wedding, targeted for June 1953 in southern California.

Senie stayed in Winona Lake until January 3, 1953. Jack introduced her to faculty and friends and showed her his office, books, and photo albums. He gave her Nana's engagement ring, dated 1891. A priority was introducing Edisene to Bill and Ruth Short, which lasted about two hours. They received some books on marriage and read the Scriptures together. The couple also sent numerous letters to their parents, family, friends, and others, including Mr. Fullerton, about the engagement. Then they asked Alva J. McClain to consider officiating the wedding.

The short stay was frenetic but highlighted by the great social opportunities for Jack and Senie to visit as a couple with Johnnie and Elaine Rea, Herb and Ruth Bess, Homer and Bev Kent, and even Sib and Willie. It was exciting — and represented the foundation of a true "Whitcomb family."

Jack also began realizing that minimalistic apartment living, bicycle transportation, and bachelor necessities must end. Wednesday, December 31, 1952, for example, included a 40-mile trip east to Fort Wayne, Indiana, to shop. New necessities included formal china dishes, silverware, dining room furniture, a hope chest, a matching bedroom suite, and window-shopping for more! Jack also bought a tie for himself.

January 3, 1953, came quickly. Jack picked Edisene up from the Edmistons' at 5:30 a.m. to catch United Airlines flight 631 from Chicago to Los Angeles. A winter storm of snow and ice made the trip treacherous, as cars ahead of them and behind them slid off the road and into the ditch. Planning to leave early paid off, as Miss Hanson arrived in time to catch her flight, leaving the Midwest for the next six months and returning as Mrs. Whitcomb.

**Preparing for a Future Home**

Edisene arrived safely in sunny southern California and began the dual task of a full-time college student at the UCSB, majoring in physical education and nutrition, and preparing for the wedding.

At the same time, Jack resumed his full teaching load and worked diligently on his thesis on *Darius the Mede* (see Chapter 15). He kept a steady flow of letters heading west and planned the accommodations for a wife and home. Jack quickly discovered that the cost of living for a man and wife was many times greater than the cost of a frugal bachelor!

Jack located an apartment of the size and features needed for him and his new bride. He signed a lease on February 2, 1953, for $50.00 per month. Next he bought a Frigidaire° electric range from the Reas for $125, which was used as a trade-in for a new stove. The Reas also loaned him two tables, three chairs, two lamps, and a rug, and Elaine gave instructions on finding good used furniture. He ordered a 9-cubic-foot Frigidaire° refrigerator. He took his shares of the Eastman Kodak Company from Nana's will and took them to the First National Bank of Warsaw as collateral for a $1,000 loan to buy more things in Fort Wayne, Indiana, including a complete bedroom suite from Wolf and Dessauer for about $400.00.

The trip to Fort Wayne was synchronized with a grueling speaking tour. After shopping, he drove 17 miles north to the town of Garrett, Indiana, a whistle-stop for a train heading east for a flurry of meetings in northern Maryland and eastern Pennsylvania — including an Easter morning sunrise service in a cemetery in Hagerstown, Maryland. He returned by train to Garrett, arriving at 4:00 a.m., drove home to his new apartment in Winona Lake by dawn, and collapsed.

Sadly, Jack did not recover well and felt worse throughout the week, skipping chapel on Thursday and staying home with flu-like symptoms on Friday and Saturday. On Sunday, he discovered that he was covered with red spots, called the doctor to make a house call, and was diagnosed with measles.

On Monday, Dr. Homer Kent Sr. stopped by Jack's apartment with his mail. Kent noted that "everyone laughed" in chapel when it was announced young professor Whitcomb had the measles! The next day, Kent returned with more mail and updated Jack on the chapel announcements. Kent told the student body that he was reading all of Jack's mail to him, "except for pink letters from California"! That information apparently "brought a great response from the students." Upon Jack's recovery, he assured the student body that *no one* except him read any pink letters.[12]

**Planning the Wedding and Honeymoon**

Donald Fullerton received Jack's announcement to be married with great joy. However, he remained concerned about the idea of a group

---

12. Of note, the author of this biography, with full access to thousands of letters and documents, has never seen any pink letters or others between his parents during their courtship.

missions trip to Mexico for a "honeymoon" and included the following advice in his letter of February 2, 1953.

> Now, beloved son may I offer a suggestion. You probably know all I can say. But just in case you may not, just a word. Very keen Christian physicians have told me that the first two weeks of married life may either wreck the future blessings of the marriage or establish it as a most joyous union in our Lord, 'till death us do part.' Lack of consideration of either for the other, especially in connecting with the marital union may have disastrous results.

Jack took this advice to heart. He discussed the options with John and Elaine Rea, and Elaine loaned Jack some pamphlets on a beautiful resort near Banff, Alberta, Canada, on Lake Louise. This idea trumped Mexico, and Senie happily agreed.

The bulk of the wedding plans traditionally rest on the bride, and Jack decided to drive to California as soon as the spring semester was over to help finalize the plans in person. He remained in Winona Lake for commencement, where his friend and future brother-in-law, Sib Edmiston, graduated *cum laude*. However, he skipped the opportunity to drive west again with a family with multiple children, packed his car, and drove west by himself.

Jack's second 2,300-mile trip west to Long Beach in his new Plymouth took only five days. The trip included stopping in Waterloo, Iowa, to preach on Sunday and a detour to visit Meteor Crater Museum just off Route 66 near Winslow, Arizona. He arrived on the morning of May 22, 1953 — and this time, Senie was waiting for him! He was amazed to see all of the wedding gifts that were pouring in, and they talked until midnight.

The days leading up to the wedding were a whirlwind of activities. The tailors measured Jack for a white jacket and black trousers. The baker took the wedding cake order. Department of Health officials took blood for testing prior to granting a marriage license, which required a trip to the courthouse in downtown Long Beach. They met many friends and family members — carefully recording and organizing gifts and coordinating thank you cards. Jack's parents arrived and checked in to the famous Statler Hotel in Los Angeles.[13] Jack entertained them and attended the Bible conference in Long Beach, featuring Dr. McClain, in the evenings.

Jack received a letter from Donald Fullerton stating that he would not be able to attend the wedding. However, he offered a blessing and a perspective.

> What a responsibility is yours! As Christ is the savior of his body in the church so the husband must protect, shelter, provide in loving devotion even until death for the needs of his wife. A husband is privileged to manifest on earth this amazing aspect of the Lord of glory.
>
> Ponder this amazing passage with your beloved, Jack. Doubtless you have already! May you each be enabled by the Holy Spirit so that you may reveal Christ in the way he has purposed in his holy ordinance of marriage.

In the final days leading to their union, the couple also carefully planned their honeymoon. They drove to Laguna Beach to make reservations for the 7–9 of June. They also mapped out the trip to Canada, with plans to end up in Winona Lake by June 29.

On Friday, June 5, Jack drove Edisene to the Statler Hotel for a luncheon with his mother and dad. They returned to Long Beach to pick up the wedding outfits, with a total cost of $47.65. They also bought additional cups, nuts, and mints for the reception. At 7:30, Dr. McClain gave his last lecture on Daniel's 70 Weeks. Afterwards, they had the wedding rehearsal. Following the rehearsal, a group of "hobos" (who closely resembled Senie's friends) kidnapped the bride-to-be and took her to Ranchos. Sib, Bertie, and Jack followed and joined the final festival for single friends and returned to Long Beach by midnight.

## The Wedding

The wedding took place on Sunday afternoon, June 7, 1953, at 4:00 p.m. As with many weddings involving hundreds of hours of planning, the ceremony took just 30 minutes. Over 450 people attended,

---

13. The Statler Hotel was a huge (1,275 rooms) grand hotel and the crown jewel of the Hilton hotel empire. It hosted movie stars, presidents, kings, and a pope, as well as many famous events. It opened in 1952 and was demolished in 2013.

and Alva J. McClain presided. A long reception line, pictures, and a wedding-car parade followed the ceremony. The couple returned to the Hanson home to open packages and say goodbye, and they rushed off to Laguna Beach, arriving by 10:00 p.m.

## The Honeymoon

John and Edisene Whitcomb stayed in Laguna Beach until Wednesday, June 10. They met a moving company, who estimated it would cost nearly $200.00 to ship the gifts to Indiana. They returned the next day to help with packing and then drove to the Jergins Trust Building to attend the trial of Dr. Fischer,[14] former pastor of the Calvary Baptist Church in North Long Beach. At 4:30 p.m., they returned to the Hanson house, finished packing, and started their trip to Canada.

The trip included a stop in Santa Barbara to visit the University of California and Senie's old dorm room. They took a leisurely drive up the California coast on Route 1 along the coast to San Francisco and across the Bay Bridge to visit friends at the Berkeley Baptist Divinity School. They drove farther north to Seattle, where Jack showed Senie his old house on Harvard Street and took a picture of the old Steward School where he had studied. After a short ferry ride to the beautiful San Juan islands and Victoria B.C., they headed east through Washington state, visiting Grand Coulee Dam on the Columbia River, and then north into Canada. They saw bears, deer, and a moose, finally arriving in Banff at 5:00. It was June 22, Jack's 29th birthday.

The resort was beautiful. They took full advantage, visiting the "Museum of Stuffed Animals," taking a 3,000-foot ride on a chairlift overlooking the mountains and lakes below. Jack took Edisene golfing, but Jack was distracted — losing the three balls that he bought, plus two others that Senie found for him by the 12th hole.

---

14. The trial focused on a 47-year-old Baptist minister, Harlan Fischer, who was on trial in Long Beach Superior Court on charges of "contributing to the delinquency" of a 14-year-old blonde schoolgirl, whom he said "had a crush" on him. Previously, he had been arrested twice and jailed once (for 22 days of a 180-day sentence) on charges of molesting the same girl. He had been fired from his Redondo Beach high school teaching job, where she was his student, and dismissed from the Calvary Baptist Church of Long Beach, where she attended church — although he pleaded complete innocence. After dismissal from the church, he took a substantial number of church members with him to start the Fellowship Baptist Church. Harlan Fischer was found guilty on Thursday, June 18, 1953. From the *Long Beach Independent* newspaper, June 17 and 19, 1953.

So they left, and Senie made her famous tamales in their cabin for supper.[15]

On June 26, they packed their things and took off for Winona Lake. It poured rain, and the trip took longer than they expected. After passing through Calgary, Alberta, Canada, and Bismarck, South Dakota, they went east through Fargo, North Dakota, around Minneapolis, and through northern Illinois. Unfortunately, Jack was caught speeding through Plainfield, Illinois, outside of Chicago and arrested. He paid the $20.00 ticket, was released from the police station, and finished the trip to Winona Lake, arriving at 10:30 p.m.

## Married Life

Married life comes with both joy and sorrow. The good things for Jack and Senie came quickly and in abundance. Donald Fullerton visited the Whitcombs shortly after their return to Winona Lake as newlyweds, and he sent this follow-up note to Edisene on September 3, 1953:

> How good it was to be with you and Jack! And how good of you both to take us into your apartment and make us so comfortable! Our Lord has blessed you both, wonderfully in giving you each other, and then in adding all these other things He knows your need. But He has done all this for you because you have both placed our Savior first in your heart's affection. May He continue to enrich and bless your married life as it is kept for His glory.

Jack and Senie immediately joined into the social life of Grace Theological Seminary faculty couples in Winona Lake. This included dropping by each other's homes for dinner, dessert, games, color slides, and cooperative events. Edisene proved to be a wonderful partner as Jack shared and received the love and acceptance that he yearned for in his childhood. His personality also appeared to blossom as he began integrating into the social activities of the church and community as well as the academic organizations. He included Senie in as many events as possible and celebrated the anniversary of their wedding each month

---

15. As a child, I remember helping my mom make tamales. They may have been the supper special at least once a week. They were not wrapped in corn husk, and they had some resemblance to enchiladas, but they tasted fantastic to me. My dad always complimented them too — perhaps remembering them as the feature meal of their honeymoon.

with a special dinner at the Wagon Wheel Restaurant between Winona Lake and Warsaw[16] or with a short 20-mile drive to the Pagoda Inn[17] near the south shore of Lake Wawasee. On December 20, 1953, John and Edisene also celebrated the first anniversary of their engagement — at the Pagoda Inn.

On September 7, John took Edisene's transcript from BIOLA, LBCC, and UCSB to the Dean, Dr. Homer Kent Sr. He determined that she had almost enough credits to graduate, so Edisene entered Grace College, taking Bible doctrine, Spanish, and American literature for the next two semesters. In addition, the administration asked her to help with the collegian women's physical education program as an instructor. Senie joined the church choir. She also actively participated in the Brethren Women's Missionary Council (WMC) to support domestic and foreign missionaries and the seminary wives fellowship.

John Whitcomb's service commitments shifted from street evangelism to administrative, with meetings on church and denominational issues, seminary events, faculty and student meetings, itinerant speaking, and other tasks that continued days, nights, and weekends. In addition to his seminary classes, he taught courses in world history and in philosophy at Grace College. He also continued to edit the yearbook, and he ran the Grace Alumni organization that maintained addresses and mailing lists, monthly alumni newsletters, news bulletins, personal letters to regional representatives, and an Alumni Bible Conference. Senie helped with coordinating the mailings, addressing envelopes and stuffing them with letters and information — including pleas for financial help for the school.

*Pregnancy #1*

In December 1953, Edisene began feeling tired and sick to her stomach. On December 17, 1953, she visited Dr. Murphy for side pain, and

---

16. The Wagon Wheel Restaurant was the fine dining center of the area in the 1950s known for its grand buffet. In the summer of 1956, they began offering a summer theater program that grew into an outstanding theater-in-the-round that continues today, even though the restaurant itself has been replaced by a hotel.

17. The Pagoda Inn, owned and run by Foo and Faye Fong was considered one of the best Chinese restaurants in the area. The Pagoda Inn was well known for their enormous handmade egg rolls. Dr. Whitcomb typically noted in his diary after a visit, "I had a delicious Chinese dinner." It was probably his favorite restaurant, as he continued to take his family there for any special event or other excuse for many years. See https://digital.library.in.gov/Record/ISL_p16066coll7-2806.

further testing revealed that she was pregnant. John accompanied his young wife to see Dr. Murphy on January 7, 1954, for her first official prenatal exam.

Anticipating one's first child touches every area of life — hopes, dreams, fears, future plans, lifestyles, finances, and career choices. Many couples who discover they are pregnant guard the news until after the first trimester, when the most dangerous time of miscarriage passes, and the little tummy bump and facial glow announces the coming child.

Edisene continued with her classes and social activities as planned. On March 2, 1954, John took Edisene to see Dr. Murphy for her regular exam. The doctor appeared a little concerned and ordered Edisene to go to McDonald Hospital for some blood work. No problems were reported.

Senie had another checkup on March 24 while John was teaching. As soon as he heard about the doctor's growing concerns, he called the doctor's office for a report. The doctor instructed him to come down to his office the following evening. At the office, Dr. Murphy explained that Senie's blood pressure was high and albumin levels were rising in her urine test. These were ominous signs of toxemia,[18] and the doctor recommended that Senie stay in bed and not go to school. John arranged for her course work to be delivered to their house.

Edisene's condition worsened over the next week, and John called Dr. Murphy to alert him of her condition. He made a house call the next morning, taking her blood pressure and obtaining urine and blood for further testing.

April 2, 1954, was a trying day. First thing in the morning, John was called into Dr. Hoyt's office to address multiple complaints from his students about the Old Testament class. He came home to find that Dr. Murphy had been there earlier to take more blood samples from Senie. At 1:30, the doctor returned. Her blood pressure was still rising,

---

18. Toxemia of pregnancy is now called preeclampsia. Preeclampsia is a multisystemic disorder characterized by new onset of hypertension (i.e., systolic blood pressure ≥ 140 mmHg and/or diastolic blood pressure ≥ 90 mmHg) and proteinuria (> 300 mg/24 h) arising after 20 weeks of gestation in a previously normotensive woman. In addition, women often have swelling in the feet, legs, and hands, and can have dysfunction and/ or failure of multiple internal organs that can be fatal. The disorder is called eclampsia if seizures develop.

her NPN was 168,[19] and her urine had 4+ protein (the highest level), suggesting that her kidneys were shutting down. Her situation was becoming critical, such that it was necessary to interrupt the pregnancy at once.[20] John quickly packed some things and rushed Senie to McDonald Hospital, insisting on a private room, #203, for his wife.

The doctors ordered intravenous fluids with 10% glucose, and a private nurse was provided. An additional doctor was consulted, and they decided to postpone emergency surgery and break the amniotic sac to induce labor. After 24 hours of slow progress, the doctors began inducing labor with intramuscular shots of pituitrin.[21] After an additional five hours of labor and three shots of pituitrin, the pregnancy ended and Senie's symptoms of toxemia rapidly began returning to normal.

Many couples, including my wife and I, have experienced miscarriages. It is a horrible thing for the father, even though the developing baby is obscure and the child theoretical. For the mother, it is personal, as they experience the loss of another human being that is developing within them. The comfort, support, and expressions of love from close Christian friends and family, especially those who have also lost a child, remains invaluable as the pain, lost dreams, suspended love, physical trauma, and awkward social situations dominate the experience of the grieving mother. But times were different in previous generations, where the previously expecting mother was to continue on with her activities as if nothing happened and as if she was never pregnant. Fortunately

19. NPN stands for non-protein nitrogen in the blood. This is an older test that has been replaced by blood urea nitrogen (BUN) that more accurately reflects renal function. The normal NPN concentration in blood is 20–40 mg/dL, and a level of 168 is approximately a BUN of 100, indicating renal failure.

20. The exact cause of preeclampsia is still not known. What is known is that the blood vessels in the placenta do not develop properly, leading to progressively reduced blood flow to the baby, with all of the danger signals of the lack of oxygen (ischemia) flooding into the mother, causing the mother's blood vessels to leak and leading to maternal organ dysfunction and organ failure. The only known treatment is to remove the placenta from the uterus. There is still no other effective treatment. In the 1950s, the preterm baby could not be saved.

21. Pituitrin is the extract of the posterior pituitary gland obtained from cattle, which contained oxytocin, a 9 amino acid peptide hormone that induces uterine contractions. The extract also contains vasopressin (also known as antidiuretic hormone, ADH) and other small polypeptides with biologic activity that can worsen hypertension and kidney function. Oxytocin became the first polypeptide hormone ever to be synthesized and became commercially available in the late 1950s as pitocin.

for Edisene, the strong support from her husband and community, and reflections on God's sovereignty and blessings, were invaluable.

John wrote the following note to Edisene's parents shortly after she returned to their apartment from the hospital:

> Everyone here agrees with us that we have had much to be thankful for, and we know that you will feel that way too. It has been a source of great comfort to us to entrust these matters to the Lord, who does all things well, and in his perfect accord with His great plan for our lives. Neither Senie nor I have been able to get anxious or discouraged or even disappointed, for that reason. We have experienced so many Blessings from our Lord already, that we hardly know how to be thankful enough to Him. Senie's complete recovery, and our future prospects for a family are not the least of these!

Edisene, who became my mother a mere 22 months later, eventually shared some of the details with my three siblings and me from time to time. She was pregnant with twin girls that died before birth. Therefore, we have older sisters who live in heaven with Jesus, and someday we will all meet them.

After a week of recovery, with the support of her husband and several close friends, Edisene returned to her life as a student and wife. She graduated from Grace College with her bachelor's degree on May 31, 1954, with her parents, who made a special trip from California for the occasion, proudly looking on. The event was also attended by Donald Fullerton, who received an honorary Doctor of Divinity degree from Grace Theological Seminary at the same time.

*Pastor Whitcomb*

On June 9, 1954, John Whitcomb was asked to spend two months in Leon, Iowa, as an interim pastor. Accepting the challenge, Edisene quickly packed their needed belongings, and on June 16, they left for Iowa.

Being a pastor demands different skills and temperaments than being an academic professor. Furthermore, the church was in turmoil as different factions fought for control of the church assets and of choosing the future direction, affiliations, and pastor. Shortly after arriving, he was called to the hospital to visit a 16-year-old girl who had just shot herself. He invited her to attend services at the church. On his first Sunday, none of the youth showed up at the Brethren Youth Fellowship, so he called a meeting of the men of the church to address this issue. Between church services, John and Edisene made numerous visits to parishioners' homes for hours at a time, typically ending in a meal of chicken or beef — and highlighted by ice cream, once the secret of Pastor Whitcomb's love of this dessert leaked out.

On July 12, a church member, Don Gitterger, committed suicide. This is a disaster for everyone. Providing appropriate and sensitive spiritual and emotional support to friends and family is challenging for any pastor — especially an inexperienced interim pastor.

On Wednesday, July 22, George Ronk filed a lawsuit against the church, giving ten days to reply.[22] The next Sunday, John Whitcomb taught a Sunday school lesson on Acts 6, "The first church trouble," and tried to apply it to the current situation. The morning sermon followed with a lesson on "What Does the Bible Teach About the Resurrection Body?" This was followed by an emergency meeting to decide on a response to the lawsuit (which lasted for months) and where to meet if the church doors were padlocked the following Sunday. At the evening service, a Mrs. Manchester stood and delivered a strong warning speech against the remaining church members and walked out.

In addition to the church responsibilities and ongoing drama, John found time to finish reading several books and prepare a series of lectures for the coming seminary semester. He also cared for Edisene, who was having digestive problems and was found to have an enlarged gall bladder, requiring a special diet.

The pastoral experience ended on August 16. John and Edisene rushed back to Winona Lake, Indiana, completing the 500-mile drive in one day. John Whitcomb was now convinced of his divine called to teach at the seminary and provide itinerant preaching rather than serving as a pastor in a local church.

## Home Sweet Home

Home would definitely be located in Winona Lake, Indiana. John and Edisene Whitcomb found a house for sale at 305 Kelly Street and

---

22. It appears that this reflected the recent split in the Brethren Church, with some members favoring taking the church with the old order, and others pushing for the new. The issue of who "owns" the church can be complicated and dicey.

purchased it with a 20-year loan for $25,600 with monthly mortgage payments of $79.00. They also bought a new blue 1954 Plymouth sedan that Senie named "Blue Beetle." The house needed significant renovations requiring time and energy from the man of the house. The new homeowners also purchased multiple appliances, and John built an office in the basement next to an old coal chute and storage bin. The house also came with a large yard, requiring mowing, and beautiful maple trees, requiring leaf raking multiple times each autumn. The couple also discovered a drainage problem during a heavy rainstorm, leading to the creation of a small lake in the side yard and water seepage into the basement.

Autumn 1954 included a full teaching load for John and full-time seminary classes for Edisene, including Archeology, Zechariah, Romans, and Evidences and Apologetics. They also continued a frenetic schedule of services, trips, events, and visitation. Edisene continued with the WMC; church choir; knitting shawls, blankets, and sweaters for friends and family; household chores; and outreach opportunities. She used her art skills to help make posters, fliers, and charts for her husband and decorations for various social events for the ladies — especially the growing number of joyous baby showers as the young faculty members started families.

Edisene's sister Alberta moved to Winona Lake in January 1955 to advance her own Christian education training at Grace Seminary and to support her sister. Edisene continued her education and began teaching art and physical education at Grace College.

Edisene became pregnant again and, on December 7, 1955, delivered a healthy baby boy named David Clement Whitcomb. On August 14, 1957, she had a second son, Donald Albert Whitcomb (named to honor Donald Fullerton and Albert Hanson). Her first daughter, Constance Salome Whitcomb (Salome was Dr. Whitcomb's mother's name), was born on October 14, 1958, and a final child, Robert Edward Whitcomb, was born on August 24, 1960. It was a happy family as Edisene's time and efforts transitioned to motherhood, homemaking, and helping her husband complete his doctorate and continue teaching, preaching, and co-authoring *The Genesis Flood* (with Dr. Henry Morris). And just like God made Eve for Adam, he fashioned Edisene for John to be a partner and helpmate for him. He finally became a complete person.

# Epilogue

Sadly, the toxemia of pregnancy that took the life of Edisene's twin girls also triggered an autoimmune disease that resulted in her death about 15 years later. So, she is now with her oldest daughters while John Whitcomb and her younger children continue on.

I remember Edisene as an incredible mom — loving, caring, creative, and fun. I still see her snuggling with her kids in the evenings as she reads children's stories with us on the sofa and as my dad sat across the room in an easy chair grading piles of term papers. I can feel the warm summer days in Indiana, lying on a blanket in the side yard, gazing at the puffy white clouds, as she helped us imagine what the shapes could represent. I remember picnics at home and trips to Pike Lake for swimming and frisbee with the Kents and other friends. I can smell her cooking her favorite dishes — including Long Beach enchiladas and her famous tamales. I can feel her placing a cold cloth on my head when I was sick and hear her roaring with laughter at my dad's silly jokes. She displayed unwavering love for my father, kept us from disturbing him from his important work, and supported him in everything he did.

But I also remember her frustrations. The autoimmune disease that killed her, primary biliary cholangitis (PBC),[23] was never diagnosed until I was in medical school, 15 years after she died. She suffered from increasing fatigue; early exhaustion; and ratcheting obesity with each pregnancy, leading to morbid obesity. My dad took her to numerous doctors and clinics for help — but the only clear abnormality that emerged was progressive liver cirrhosis. Multiple exploratory surgical operations, the diagnostic tool of choice before the invention of the CT scan, revealed the complications of cirrhosis, but no answers to the cause of the disease. Instead, she began suffering gastrointestinal bleeding,[24] jaundice, and horrible itching to the point that her skin was scratched raw.

---

23. PBC is a complex autoimmune disease with inflammation of the bile ducts of the liver, leading to liver injury. The disease was previously called primary biliary cirrhosis, but the name was changed since liver cirrhosis is a late feature.

24. One of the common complications of liver cirrhosis is the blockage of blood flow to the liver from the intestines via the portal vein, resulting in portal hypertensions. For the blood to return to the heart, it must bypass the liver through small veins that eventually become huge internal varicose veins. The network of veins radiating from the umbilicus across the internal abdomen to bypass the liver is called a caput medusa, which Edisene had been diagnosed with. Blood returning along the stomach and esophagus results in esophageal varices that are typically the source of gastrointestinal bleeding in patients with liver cirrhosis.

# A Good and Faithful Servant

Upon visitation to her hospital bed or convalescent center, I remember that some of the doctors or nurses pulled me aside in private and asked me about her alcoholism — since they never saw such terrible liver cirrhosis in an non-alcoholic before. I assured them that, to my knowledge, she *never* had a sip of alcohol in her life, and I can still see the looks of disbelief and dismissal to my answers in the faces of the health care professionals. Perhaps those early childhood experiences fueled my own passion to conquer another disease that has been inaccurately linked solely to alcoholism but that is actually a complex genetic disorder — chronic pancreatitis.

By November 1969, the progressive liver disease dragged Edisene into a coma. I remember that, for some reason, prayer meetings began coalescing to pray for her, petitioning the Almighty God to raise her up and bring her home to her family for one last Christmas. Although I was raised in a Christian community and had attended numerous prayer meetings, this was an extraordinary movement that extended beyond our local church to the national fellowship of churches, to the missionaries, and to others. People pleaded for God's mercy — which I thought was peculiar since the doctors all said that hepatic coma came just before death, and nobody recovers.

The doctors and nurses were shocked, and everyone else was amazed, when Edisene suddenly woke up! Not only did she awaken, but she began sitting, walking, eating, and regaining strength. She progressed to the point that she was released from the hospital and came home for Christmas — just as God's people had requested. It was a miracle.[25]

Over the next six months, her symptoms returned, and her health again deteriorated. The doctors transferred Edisene to a specialty ward at Cook County Hospital in Chicago, Illinois, in hopes of helping her. After a couple of weeks, my father took us there to visit her. The old massive building appeared dark and creepy. Lime-green hospital paint covered the walls, black linoleum tile covered the floors, and wobbly carts with bottles and linens cluttered the hallways. The air felt dense with odors of rubbing alcohol, old bandages, and chicken soup. My siblings and I received special permission to visit our mom in her

---

25. See Alberta Hanson, "Miracle of Prayer," *Brethren Missionary Herald*, April 17, 1970, p. 14, 22.

room. Rather than being in a ward, she had a small, semi-private room without windows, painted in lemon-mustard yellow, and shared with another woman whose presence was obscured by cloth partitions. The ivory-white painted iron bed frame and firm mattress appeared uncomfortable. Two glass bottles with some type of fluid hung on either side of the bed on thin poles, with plastic tubing tracking down to my mother's arms.

She turned and looked at us as my father woke her from her sleep to present her children to her, nicely organized by age and height. Her face beamed, and we talked as best we could, of trivial things. Then, succumbing to waves of sleep, she gazed at us and said, "My beautiful, wonderful children. I will miss you." Then she relaxed, allowed her head to sink deeply into her pillow, closed her eyes, and drifted into sleep. A few days later, on June 28, 1970, at the age of 40 years, she died.

## Seminary Life, Edisene, and Early Family

**4.1.** Freshman class of 1948. Jack Whitcomb and Johnny Rea are back center.

**4.2** Students packed into the rented lecture hall to hear the founder of Grace Theological Seminary, Alva J. McClain, teach theology. (From *The History of Grace Theological Seminary, 1931–1951*, edited by John Whitcomb, p. 111.)

**4.3** McClain Hall under construction, November, 1950 (Ibid., 37).

**4.4** Seminary class taking an examination circa 1949. Jack Whitcomb is in the third row on the left.

**4.5** Jack Whitcomb, Howard Vulgamore, and Johnny Rea (standing) were all over 6'2" tall — and fellow student Johnny Fusco complained about being too short. So, his classmates agree to stretch him to a similar physical height.

**4.6** During seminary, Jack Whitcomb used a bicycle or walked, as he did not own a car.

**4.7** Jack rented the second-floor room at this house near the school for easy commuting on bicycle or foot.

**4.8** Jack's parents welcoming him to Peru in July 1950 where they retired. The family is seen here at Machu Picchu. They were happy that Jack's Princeton education would be used by a professor in a reputable seminary rather than as a missionary in China.

**4.9** Jack with jungle missionary Chris Sheldon and local pastor Federico Munoz near Huancayo, Peru. The three men had great discussions about the people of Peru and unmet needs. This was a highlight of the trip.

**4.10** Jack was fascinated by the indigenous people of Peru, including a boy at Casma Pass and a native in traditional dress.

# Flying Seminar to the Holy Land, Summer 1952

**4.11** Jerusalem seen from the Mount of Olives, August 1952. Just beyond the trees is the Kidron Valley. The Temple Mount stretches across the middle of the picture with the Dome of the Rock in the center.

**4.12** Temple area. (Left) Gold-covered Dome of the Rock at the sight of the Temples and the Holy of Holies. (Right) Guide standing at the western base of the Temple Mount, known to the Jews as the "Wailing Wall." Dr. Whitcomb's MDiv thesis would be on the history of this site and archeological evidences (Chapter 15).

**4.13** A picture taken by Jack Whitcomb of his guide from the top of a pyramid in Gizeh, Egypt.

**4.14** This was one of my father's favorite pictures of himself, sitting on top of a camel named "Princess" in Gizeh, Egypt (near Cairo), with the pyramids in the background, August 5, 1952.

**4.15** John Whitcomb with the Moabite Stone, Paris, France, 1952. This stone, from the ninth century B.C., commemorates the victory of the Moabite king Mesha over the Israelite king and his armies. The same history is found in 2 Kings chapter 3 of the Bible, providing extrabiblical evidence of the historical accuracy of the text. A similar ancient stone would be critical to Whitcomb's ThM thesis, Darius the Mede (Chapter 15).

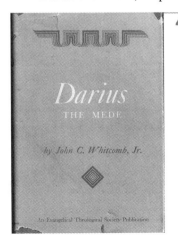

**4.16** John Whitcomb's interest in demonstrating the Bible's historical accuracy focused on Darius the Mede. The key to solving the mystery of who this man was in history was an ancient cuneiform stone record called the Nabonidus Chronicle (Chapter 15). Whitcomb's ThM thesis on the topic was completed in 1954, but the book was not published until 1959. The evidence from this ancient cuneiform record is ignored by secular scholars since it does not fit the narrative that the book of Daniel was written by confused Jews centuries after the supposed historical events.

439

# Edisene pictures and marriage

**4.17** Edisene Hanson at age 22 years. This is a copy of the portrait that Jack insisted on having after meeting her in August 1951.

240th day — 125 days follow

I took the new apartment at 105 14th St, & made a #10.00 deposit. Went over the to the new bldg. to assemble chairs for an hour (making a total of 6) with Charles Koontz. Went back to my office after lunch, and had a long talk with John Harper, about the chronology of kings of Israel & Judah. Borrowed Johnny's car to move books into my office. Attended the evening service, which was a Sunday School pageant. Talked with Mrs. Edmiston's sister (Edisene) a while after the service.

241st day — 124 days follow

At 9:00, I heard Lewis Sperry Chafer on the Second Coming. Went to the Auditorium to hear Dr. Mayes on the Evidences for the Resurrection. Went up to the bldg. for awhile, & then down to invite Edisene to the service tonight. She was at Bethany Camp, so I told the Edmistons that I would be by for her at 7:00 P.M. Heard Vance Havner on Separation at 11:30. Rested after lunch, & spent 3 hrs. at my office studying Joshua & making a chronology (1497 - 1161). At 7:00, I met Edisene at the Edmistons, & we heard Rev. John Aely preach at the evening service on Home Missions. Afterwards, we went to Bethany Camp, where BYF talent was presented, & Ralph Colburn

**4.18** Diary entries highlighting Jack Whitcomb's first encounter with Edisene Hanson, his future wife.

**4.19** John Whitcomb meets the family. Senie's sisters Willie (left) and Winnie (back right) with their families and Bertie (far right). Her parents are on the left in the back.

**4.20** Valentine's Day, 1953.

**4.21** Wedding picture, June 6, 1953.

## Married Life

**4.22** Mrs. Whitcomb on her honeymoon at Lake Louise, Alberta, Canada.

**4.23** Mr. Whitcomb golfing on his honeymoon. The sport never caught on with his wife!

**4.24** Newlyweds, Edisene (Senie) and John (Jack) Whitcomb.

**4.25** Jack and Senie shared the experience of pastoring a church in Leon, Iowa, in the summer of 1954. The experience confirmed the calling to be a professor and lecturer.

**4.26** Edisene as a college instructor, 1955. In contrast to the prevailing cultural ideas of the role of a wife, John Whitcomb believed that Senie should utilize her education in nutrition and physical education to teach, which was Edisene's passion. She also enjoyed organizing service events, entertaining, and outreach. This was a perfect complement to Jack.

**4.27** (Left) John Whitcomb establishes a family (with Senie and the author) and a home with a house at 305 Kelly Street, 1956. (Right) Three generations of Whitcombs with David, John Jr., and Col. John Whitcomb.

**4.28** The Whitcomb family in fall 1960. David, Senie, Bob, John, Connie, and Don.

**4.29** Senie standing with Dr. Alva J. McClain and his wife, Josephine, summer 1959.

**4.30** Prof. John Whitcomb with the author, age 2.

# Section 5

# The Genesis Flood

# Chapter 17

# Cornelius

"We must move with the TRUTH"
July 1955

My father loved to talk about his four fathers: Whit (biological), Donald Fullerton (spiritual), Alva J. McClain (theological), and Henry Morris (scientific). However, he sometimes spoke of a "fifth" father, Cornelius Van Til. Van Til taught him a biblical way to defend the Bible, a concept that John Whitcomb embraced — influencing his thinking and his teaching for the rest of his life.[1]

Cornelius Van Til earned a place in church history by articulating and championing a biblical approach to defending the Scriptures, known as "presuppositional apologetics." Born on May 3, 1895, in Grootegast, Holland, to a Christian Dutch dairy farmer, he immigrated to the United States with his family at 10 years of age, settling in Highland, Indiana.[2] His family connected to the Dutch immigrant community of the midwestern United States and to Dutch Reformed theology. He quickly learned English and excelled in school, becoming the first in his family to receive a higher education. After high school, he attended Calvin College in Grand Rapids, Michigan, and started graduate work at Calvin Seminary. Then, after a year, he transferred to Princeton Theological Seminary. He completed a Th.M. in 1925 and earned a Ph.D. in philosophy in 1927. He returned to Michigan to become the pastor of a Christian Reformed Church in Spring Lake.

---

1. See addendum at the end of this chapter.
2. Adapted from John M. Frame, *Cornelius Van Til: An Analysis of His Thought* (Phillipsburg, NJ: Presbyterian and Reformed Publishing, 1995). Of note, John Frame was also a Princeton graduate and PEF member.

## A Good and Faithful Servant

Van Til made good friends and strong impressions both at Calvin College and Princeton Seminary. He took a leave of absence from his church during the academic year of 1928–1929 to teach an apologetics course at Princeton Seminary. The administration was so impressed with him that they immediately offered a permanent position as Chair of the Apologetics Department. He refused, as Princeton Seminary languished in a sea of turmoil over orthodoxy and Presbyterian denominational policies driven by the General Assembly. That summer, J. Gresham Machen resigned from Princeton Seminary, along with Robert D. Wilson[3] and Oswald T. Allis, to start Westminster Theological Seminary, 45 miles southwest of Princeton in Philadelphia, Pennsylvania. Van Til returned to Spring Lake to continue as pastor, but with the persuasive efforts of Machen, he moved east, becoming a founding member of the faculty of Westminster Theological Seminary in the fall of 1929. He remained there as a professor of apologetics until his retirement in 1972.

The premise of Van Til's teaching was that humans' *a priori*[4] reasoning is inherently contaminated by their sin nature, and all reason must start from God's revelation of truth, the Scriptures. Thus, the Scriptures are essential and sufficient for spiritual enlightenment,[5] for coming to know who God is, why He created us, why He redeemed us, and His plan for the ages. Inductive[6] and analytical reasoning by men should therefore be seen as a part of the process of interpreting God's universe. Van Til also recognized the necessity of critically appraising unbiblical human philosophies and warning believers of the dangers of mixing Divine revelation and rationalisms. These topics dominated his writings, making him both famous and infamous.

---

3. Robert D. Wilson was the father of Christy Wilson and taught classes with Donald Fullerton at PEF meetings while Dr. Whitcomb was a student and for a few years afterward. See Chapters 7, 11, and 14.
4. *A priori* knowledge is independent of experience and serves as the criterion for analyzing and evaluating experience.
5. Spiritual enlightenment is having a knowledge and understanding of truth through the work of the Holy Spirit acting in the hearts and minds of regenerate believers who are in a right relationship with Him.
6. Inductive reasoning is logic that uses specific examples to understand or define general principles. As a Bible study method, an inductive approach follows the steps of *observation* (what does it say?), *interpretation* (what does it mean?), and *application* (what does it mean for my life?). Deductive reasoning is logic that goes from general principles to specific inference. For deductive reasoning to be sound, the premise must be correct.

## Winona Lake School of Theology, July 1955

Throughout the mid-20th century, Winona Lake, Indiana, flourished as a hub of Christian activity. Among the many programs and conferences was the Winona Lake School of Theology, an organization that took advantage of the resort-town and conference centers in the summers, inviting top preachers and theologians to Winona Lake to offer short courses on the Bible and theology. The school was not affiliated with Grace Seminary, but it complemented the faculty and curriculum on many occasions.

In July of 1955, John Whitcomb was in the midst of writing his doctoral dissertation at Grace Seminary on the Genesis Flood (1953 to 1957). Taking a correct approach to defending the Bible's version of history against secular theories and Christian rationalism was critical. Whitcomb became familiar with some of Van Til's writings, including *Common Grace*[7] and *Witness Bearing*,[8] which raised a number of questions in Whitcomb's mind. He wrote to Van Til with some specific questions about his approach but never received a reply.

In the summer of 1955, Cornelius Van Til, Th.M., Ph.D., came to the Winona Lake School of Theology to teach a course entitled Christian Apologetics. Whitcomb decided to audit these summer classes.

The short course was intense and compressed. It commenced on July 12, 1955, and continued through July 27, beginning each day at 7:00 a.m. During the course, Van Til analyzed details of church history and the impact on the orthodoxy of groups that resorted to rational arguments and philosophies, while abandoning the principle of the Scriptures defining the truth. My father remembers that Van Til's teaching "was quite complex but thoroughly biblical."

The timing of the course coincided with the publication of Van Til's initial work defining his distinctive approach to apologetics, *The Defense of the Faith*.[9] This work included a systematic review of the history of Greek and European philosophers, theologians, reformers, and heretics. His writings also included a heavy dose of the Dutch

7. Presbyterian and Reformed Publishing Co., Philadelphia, 1947.
8. "Common Grace and Witnessbearing" first appeared in the *Torch and Trumpet*, December 1954–January 1955, and was later published as a separate booklet by L.J. Grotenhuis, Phillipsburg, NJ. It became chapter 5 of later editions of *Common Grace*.
9. Cornelius Van Til, *The Defense of the Faith* (Phillipsburg, NJ: Presbyterian and Reformed, 1955), 299 pages.

Reformed traditions and detailed critiques of Karl Barth and David Hume. But the critical accomplishment was demonstrating the futility of attempting to prove anything from the Bible to unbelievers by rational and logical arguments based on human philosophies.

As a teacher, Van Til was intense but engaging. My father also remembered Van Til as being confrontational but not offensive and that he left him with the impression that he believed the Bible because it was self-authenticating. His vocabulary included many technical and philosophical terms, challenging the average student. At times he was very humorous. But if a student dozed off during the early morning class, he would lob a piece of chalk at them to startle him back to attention. Whitcomb remained intensely engaged, taking copious notes in a little 3 x 6-inch lined notebook. Here are some important statements from Van Til's lectures in his little notebook:

- You cannot overthrow either election or free will because you cannot understand it. You cannot surrender to rationalism.
- Unless we presuppose God, there is no proof for anything, no relationship between facts and logic.
- Christians believe the Bible is divinely inspired and self-authenticating. There is no use for external evidences to confirm its truthfulness.
- Van Til has been accused of discrediting Christianity in university circles because his students refuse to appeal to logic.
- True apologetics underlie New Testament preaching and teaching even as true systematic theology does.
- The meaning of words comes from defined systems. Sin changes the connotations of words. All schools of philosophy, science, and psychology argue against the Creator-creature distinction because of Adamic sin. They cannot accept creation *ex nihilo*. They are out to demolish God and Christianity.
- We must not be afraid of these confusing movements. We must move with the TRUTH! (Van Til's concluding remark)

Whitcomb decided to invite Van Til over to his house for an informal interview and further discussion. At 4:00 p.m. on July 20, 1955, he escorted Dr. Van Til from the theology school's library to his home for an hour-long chat. As a former Presbyterian and a Princeton graduate,

Whitcomb began the discussion with an analysis of the Orthodox Presbyterian Church, Westminster Seminary, and then proceeded to the theory of evolution. The benefits of that interview were enormous.

By the end of the course, Whitcomb became convinced that Van Til's approach to apologetics arose from sound biblical principles and interpretations. Dr. Van Til provided John with an autographed copy of his new book, *The Defense of the Faith*, and bid him Godspeed.

John's mind was made up. He had grasped the fundamental concepts and their implications, and he would apply them in his future teaching and writings. Furthermore, for his doctoral dissertation, there would be no apology or rationalistic arguments for believing the Genesis account — he would start on the foundation of "God says. . . ." There was no need for cleverly devised academic or rational arguments; he would allow the Bible to defend itself, since "The word of God is living and active and sharper than any two-edged sword. . . ."[10] If minds and hearts were to be changed, it would be through the power of the Scriptures and the work of the Holy Spirit.

Upon reflection of that encounter nearly 60 years after the class ended, my father credits Van Til as being God's instrument on how to approach arguments made against the Bible. He noted that this approach was no different from the approach used by Drs. McClain, Hoyt, and Kent Sr. at Grace Theological Seminary in teaching the Bible.

## Whitcomb Becomes an Advocate of Presuppositional Apologetics

Van Til's approach provided an effective way to address unbelievers and critics without being trapped in their paradigm of rationalistic thinking based on their own ideas and perceptions of reality. The influence of Van Til on Professor Whitcomb's teachings and approach to apologetics is widely recognized,[11] especially with the application of presuppositional principles to the greatest modern argument against the Bible — the theory of evolution.

Although the foundation of Grace Seminary's curriculum and the approach of its founders to the teaching of Scripture was "presuppositional," no one had ever justified this approach, contrasted it to rationalistic approaches, or discussed the appropriate use of extra-biblical

---

10. Hebrews 4:12.
11. John M. Frame, *Cornelius Van Til: An Analysis of His Thought* (Phillipsburg, NJ: Presbyterian and Reformed Publishing, 1995), 394.

evidences within discussions and debates. A clear understanding and articulation of these perspectives was critical, as great men of the faith were systematically failing to defend the faith by depending on extra-biblical evidences.[12] Whitcomb studied Van Til's arguments from the perspective of Scriptures and became the expert and champion of this approach at Grace Seminary — making many complex arguments of Van Til simple and understandable to the faculty and students.

Van Til's arguments and writings are very complex and challenging, even to graduate students.[13] The biblical arguments for the presuppositional approach to apologetics needed to be extracted, organized, expanded, and illustrated. Dr. Whitcomb therefore developed a new course at Grace Seminary called CHRISTIAN EVIDENCES AND APOLOGETICS. Over a rather short time, Whitcomb also convinced the faculty of the importance and implications of this approach, which became the *de facto* position of Grace Seminary. The course became a requirement for all seminarians.

In the introduction to this graduate course, outlined in the syllabus,[14] Whitcomb included an important discussion on the reason why intellectual arguments are powerless to convert the unbeliever. In the discussion, entitled "Christian Apologetics, Human Depravity and Satan," he noted the traditional approach which many theologians and church leaders had taken to evangelism or proselytizing unbelievers.

> In our efforts to make the Bible and Christianity attractive and acceptable to men we find ourselves immediately confronted with two stupendous obstacles: man's fallen nature and the Satanic forces which surround him. Though these facts should come as no great surprise to one who is even superficially acquainted with Biblical Christianity, it is astonishing to me how few of the better-known evangelical works on Christian apologetics today give them serious consideration. One is almost led to believe, when reading such books, that what we really need to win intellectuals to Christ

---

12. See Chapter 7 for the example of B.B. Warfield and the resulting demise of Princeton Seminary as an effective defender of the faith.
13. See, for example, John M. Frame, *Cornelius Van Til: An Analysis of His Thought* (Phillipsburg, NJ: Presbyterian and Reformed Publishing, 1995).
14. John C. Whitcomb, "Syllabus for Christian Evidences and Apologetics," unpublished.

(in addition to the Gospel) is an arsenal of carefully developed arguments against the various false religious and philosophical systems we may confront today and/or an impressive array of evidences from, say, archaeology and history, that the Bible and Christianity are true. If this were really so, one might be forgiven for wondering why Christianity has not long since made a clean sweep of the religious world, since it is uniquely possessed of infallible proofs of its claims (cf. Acts 1:3, 26:26).

He then goes on to explain the primary problem of trying to convince a man against his will — man's fallen nature.

But if we are willing to be truly honest with the Biblical perspectives on this question, we must admit that we have too often been guilty of building our systems of apologetics upon other foundations than the one set forth in Scripture. Instead of giving us the impression that men are eagerly waiting for proof that Christianity is true, we find the Bible exposing men's hearts as sealed shut against any and all finite pressures for conversion. The basic problem of the non-Christian is not merely academic and intellectual. It is moral and spiritual. The Bible indicates that all unbelievers (including so-called honest doubters) are enemies of God, under divine judgment because of their deliberate distortion of all reality to fit into their own spiritual frame of reference. There is not the slightest desire in that natural man to seek Him, find Him, and acknowledge Him for who He is. "The wicked, in the haughtiness of his countenance, does not seek Him. All his thoughts are, 'There is no God' " (Psa. 10:4). In another location, the Holy Spirit informs us by the pen of David, that God "looked down from heaven upon the sons of men, to see if there are any who understand, who seek after God" (Psa. 14:2). But what did he discover? A significant minority of God-seekers? Consider his answer! "They have all turned aside; together they have become corrupt; there is no one who does good, not even one" (also quoted in Romans 3:10–12).

Not only does the unbeliever not seek and practice truth, he consistently suppresses whatever truth he does receive: "For the wrath of God is revealed from heaven against all ungodliness and unrighteousness of men, who suppress the truth in righteousness. . . . They are without excuse" (Rom. 1:18–20). In fact, the Scriptures makes it clear that fallen men, so far from being open to arguments about God's claims upon them are in a state of enmity against Him. "The mind set on the flesh is hostile toward God; for it does not subject itself to the law of God, for it is not even able to do so" (Rom. 8:7). "While we were enemies, we were reconciled to God through the death of His Son" (Rom. 5:10).

Whitcomb's argument continues with the limits of rational arguments alone with unbelievers.

Christian apologetics has been traditionally concerned with giving rational answers to the challenges of unbelievers concerning God's special revelation of Scripture. But what kind of minds are we appealing to? To what extent have sin and spiritual rebellion against God affected man's rational capacity? Ponder these statements: "You were dead in your trespasses and sins, in which you formerly walked according to the course of this world . . . indulging in the desires of the flesh and of the mind, and were by nature children of wrath, even as the rest" (Eph. 2:1–3). "The Gentiles . . . walk in the futility of their mind, being darkened in their understanding, excluded from the life of God, because of the ignorance that is in them, because of the hardness of their heart" (Ephesians 4:17–18).

But is the human "mind" capable of detaching itself from the so-called "heart" and of drawing its own conclusions about God independent of the downward direction of the fallen nature? The answer is no. Mark our Lord's explanation of the unbreakable relationship between the mind and heart: "out of the heart comes evil thoughts" (Matthew 15:19; cf. Mark 7:31). He later asked his disciples: "why do doubts arise in your hearts?" (Luke 24:38). The scripture offers us no hope of bringing about a fundamental change in man's thinking about God apart from a profound change in his "heart", the moral/spiritual center of his personal being. This is a basic reality that no Christian apologist can afford to ignore.

If this problem were not great enough, Whitcomb added comments on the confounding effect of satanic forces in the world. He continues:

> In addition to the obstacle of the human heart/mind being in opposition to the truth of God, there is the obstacle of Satan, "the god of this world" (2 Corinthians 4:4), and his demonic forces. When I speak to an unbeliever about Christ, there are two or more persons, all but one of whom are invisible. The apostle Paul spoke of this astonishing fact several times. He explained that "our struggle is not against flesh and blood, but against the rulers, against powers, against the world forces of this darkness, against the spiritual forces of wickedness in heavenly places" (Ephesians 6:12). He knew that Christians "formerly walked according to . . . the prince of the power of the air, of that spirit that is now working in the sons of disobedience" (Ephesians 2:2). He fully recognized that "if our gospel is veiled, it is veiled to those who are perishing, in whose case the god of this world has blinded the minds of the unbeliever, that they might not see the light of the gospel of the glory of Christ, who is the image of God" (2 Corinthians 4:4). In the parable of the sower, our Lord also spoke of this obstacle to the reception of His Word when he identified the birds that devoured the seed: "when anyone hears the word of the kingdom, and does not understand it, the evil one comes and snatches away what has been sown in his heart. This is the one on whom seed was sown beside the road" (Matthew 13:19).
>
> A system of Christian apologetics that underestimates the power of Satan in the minds of the unbeliever may not exactly be guilty of reviling angelic majesties as Jude warns us (Jude 8). But by ignoring to some extent the enormity of Satan's power, it is to that same extent unable to follow Michael's example and to say affectively: "The Lord rebuke you"

(Jude 9; cf. Zechariah 3:2). What we desperately need today is an apologetic with power!

This clear presentation of the impossible task of arguing unbelievers into God's kingdom with extra-biblical evidences typified Whitcomb's clarity and teaching approach on the subject. It was clear, organized, heavily referenced in Bible texts, and compelling. However, the fact that Whitcomb proceeded to invest the better part of the 1950s in researching and writing *The Genesis Flood* indicates that he believed that careful scholarship and rational arguments DID play an essential role in Christianity in other important ways (see below).

## Revisiting *Therefore Stand*

If Van Til was correct, then was Whitcomb's dedication to conservative Christian scholarship and commitment answering the objections of the critics based on the call to action in Wilbur Smith's book *Therefore Stand* wrong? Did Paul take the wrong approach to defending the faith in Athens? What exactly happened on Mars Hill outside of Athens as described in Acts 17? Whitcomb needed to reconsider Wilber Smith's arguments in more detail. He did so through a careful study of Acts 17, framed within the greater context of Scripture.

The premise of Wilbur Smith's "semi-rationalistic" approach to apologetics articulated in *Therefore Stand* came from Acts 17:22–31 (NASB 1995; emphasis added). Here, Paul presents the following message to the Athenians on Mars Hill:

> So Paul stood in the midst of the Areopagus and said, "Men of Athens, I observe that you are very religious in all respects. For while I was passing through and examining the objects of your worship, I also found an altar with this inscription, 'TO AN UNKNOWN GOD.' Therefore what you worship in ignorance, this I proclaim to you. The **God who made the world** and all things in it, since He is Lord of heaven and earth, does not dwell in temples made with hands; nor is He served by human hands, as though He needed anything, since He Himself gives to all people life and breath and all things; and He made from one man every nation of mankind to live on all the face of the earth, having determined

their appointed times and the boundaries of their habitation, that they would seek God, if perhaps they might grope for Him and find Him, though He is not far from each one of us; for in Him we live and move and exist, as even some of your own poets have said, 'For we also are His children.' Being then the children of God, we ought not to think that the Divine Nature is like gold or silver or stone, an image formed by the art and thought of man. Therefore having overlooked the times of ignorance, God is now declaring to men that all people everywhere should repent, because He has fixed a day in which **He will judge the world** in righteousness through a Man whom He has appointed, having furnished proof to all men by **raising Him from the dead.**"

It has been observed that Paul did not give any direct reference to the Holy Scriptures in this message, but he did quote two Greek poets. Does this mean that he argued on the basis of rationalistic human reasoning?

Whitcomb's critical analysis of the events on Mars Hill clarified Paul's historic debate with the Athenians.[15] He first points out the greater context, including Acts 17:16–18 (NASB 1995; emphasis added):

Now while Paul was waiting for them at Athens, his spirit was being provoked within him as he was observing the city full of idols. So *he was reasoning in the synagogue with the Jews and the God-fearing Gentiles, and in the market place every day* with those who happened to be present. And also some of the Epicurean and Stoic philosophers were conversing with him. Some were saying, "What would this idle babbler wish to say?" Others, "He seems to be a proclaimer of strange deities," — because *he was preaching Jesus and the resurrection.*

Then he clarifies Paul's comments within the context of this background,

It is very important to recognize that before the Mars Hill confrontation began, Paul has already been "preaching Jesus and the resurrection" day after day in the marketplace

---

15. Dr. John C. Whitcomb, Syllabus for CHRISTIAN EVIDENCES AND APOLOGETICS (Winona Lake, IN: Grace Theological Seminary), 21–22.

of Athens (Acts 17:18). Thus, his Mars Hill address was not presented in a total vacuum. These Greek thinkers wanted to know <u>more</u> about "this new doctrine" (Acts 17:19–20).

Furthermore, so far from proving the existence of the God of Christianity, Paul simply and authoritatively declared Him to these men (verse 23). He <u>declared</u> this God to be the creator and the Lord of the world and of mankind (verses 24–26). He <u>declared</u> the nearness and thus accessibility of God to mankind (verses 27–28), and the utter ignorance of idolatry (verses 29–30). And, finally he <u>announced</u> that this great God will someday judge all men through that resurrected man whom Paul had previously named as Jesus (verse 18, 31); and, therefore, He "is now <u>declaring</u> to men that all everywhere should repent" (verse 30).

Whitcomb argued that Paul could not have demonstrated any of these assertions to the Athenians on a scientific, historical, or logical basis, even if he had five to ten years. He simply declared what God had said. In this debate, the "common ground" was that man was made in the image and likeness of God through creation. But, most important, Paul was true to the biblical message and method throughout. While he did quote two statements from Greek poets and pointed out that the Athenians recognized that there was an unknown "god," the comments were a model of effective communication, not a model of semi-rationalistic apologetics.

Thus, the discussion on Mars Hill represented a summary of extended teaching from the Scriptures. And the message delivered was, in fact, the gospel. Paul elsewhere summarized these truths:

> Now I make known to you, brethren, the gospel which I preached to you, which also you received, in which also you stand, by which also you are saved, if you hold fast the word which I preached to you, unless you believed in vain. For I delivered to you as of first importance what I also received, that Christ died for our sins according to the Scriptures, and that He was buried, and that He was raised on the third day according to the Scriptures (1 Corinthians 15:1–4; NASB 1995).

Finally, Whitcomb noted how the Holy Spirit used the message, as delivered by Paul in Athens.

> Luke[16] records, "*34But some men joined him and believed, among whom also were Dionysius the Areopagite and a woman named Damaris and others with them*" (Acts 17:34). The fact that some believed and others rejected the message reflects the effect of preaching the Gospel in every city, in the midst of ridicule and persecution; "*When the Gentiles heard this, they began rejoicing and glorifying the word of the Lord; and as many as had been appointed to eternal life believed*" (Acts 13:48).

Thus, Whitcomb concludes, God's method for evangelism is for Christians to clearly present the gospel to unbelievers so that God might lead the elect to believe the message and be saved.

**In What Way are Extra-biblical Evidences Important?**

Whitcomb clearly saw that in terms of the gospel, the focus must be on presenting Christ's life, death, and Resurrection according to Scriptures (e.g., see 1 Corinthians 15:1–4). Appealing to extra-biblical evidences and philosophical arguments fail.

However, he also realized that extra-biblical evidences, seen through the eyes of biblical thinking, were also critical for world and life views and for refuting false doctrines and false arguments that could confuse new or immature believers and render them useless. This point was made in confirming the theory of evolution. Whitcomb wrote:[17]

> In exposing and refuting the Satanic theory of organic evolution, our purpose cannot be to bring men to God or even to establish the faith of those who are already Christians. Only the Spirit of God through the written Word can do that. Instead, our purpose is to rethink the natural sciences in terms of a Biblical worldview, and thus by reinterpreting in detail God's universe and the laws He has established in it, in the light of His special revelation in Scripture, we are

---

16. Luke is the author of the Book of Acts.
17. John C. Whitcomb, Syllabus for CHRISTIAN EVIDENCES AND APOLOGETICS (Winona Lake, IN: Grace Theological Seminary), 71.

fulfilling our God-given responsibility to subdue the earth (Genesis 1:28), and to appreciate the wonders of His ways (Job 38–41).

Thus, Whitcomb argued that there IS value in extra-biblical evidences of God's work, especially for *believers*. He notes,[18]

> For the <u>believer</u>, they can provide a certain degree of intellectual satisfaction, deeper appreciation for the marvels and complexity of God's universe, and helpful background materials for this study of various aspects of Biblical revelation. For the <u>unbeliever</u> they can be used to arouse interest and hold attention (something like a sign-miracle during the period of the Gospels and the Book of Acts), carefully and skillfully handled by the Christian <u>in conjunction with the true Gospel witness</u>.

He goes on to note that Christian evidences can neither create, sustain, nor increase true faith in God, because "faith comes from hearing, and hearing by the Word of Christ" (Romans 10:17; NASB 1995).

## The Preeminent Role of the "Whole Council of God" in the Life of Christians

If, in fact, it is only the gospel through the work of the Holy Spirit that can lead to saving faith in Jesus Christ, then why, some may ask, does more extensive study and debate matter? The answer is *that an effective Christian life* is dependent on the study of *all* Scripture, distinguishing truth from lies and acting on the truth.

Several additional examples of instructions of the Apostle Paul to Timothy illustrate this point.

> You, however, continue in the things you have learned and become convinced of, knowing from whom you have learned them, and that from childhood you have known the sacred writings which are able to give you the wisdom that leads to salvation through faith which is in Christ Jesus. **All Scripture is inspired by God and profitable for teaching, for reproof, for correction, for training in righteousness; so that the man of God may be**

---

18. John C. Whitcomb, Syllabus for CHRISTIAN EVIDENCES AND APOLOGETICS (Winona Lake, IN: Grace Theological Seminary), 32.

**adequate, equipped for every good work** (2 Timothy 3:14–17; NASB 1995; emphasis added).

The first bolded statement indicates that truths from the whole of Scripture can "lead to salvation through faith which is in Christ Jesus." Indeed, the exposure of Jack Whitcomb to the *biblical* teaching of James McCallie in high school and Donald Fullerton and others in college, with the invisible work of the Holy Spirit, "led to" hearing the "Word of Christ" (Romans 10:17).

The second bolded statement points to the effectiveness of Scripture in making the "man of God" adequate and equipped for every good work. This includes teaching truth and refuting error for true Christians *within the church*. This is exactly what Paul warned the Ephesian elders of in Acts 20:27–32 (NASB 1995; emphasis added), where Timothy would later be sent by Paul:

> For I did not shrink from declaring to you **the whole purpose of God**. Be on guard for yourselves and for all the flock, among which the Holy Spirit has made you overseers, to shepherd the church of God which He purchased with His own blood. I know that after my departure **savage wolves will come in among you, not sparing the flock; and from among your own selves men will arise, speaking perverse things, to draw away the disciples after them.** Therefore be on the alert, remembering that night and day for a period of three years I did not cease to admonish each one with tears. And now **I commend you to God and to the word of His grace**, which is able to build you up and to give you the inheritance among all those who are sanctified.

The danger would arise from within the church, from among the *elders*. The remedy was a reliance on God and His Word — teaching the "whole purpose of God."[19]

---

19. The great outcome of this near disaster in Ephesus was determined by the clear teaching of the Scriptures to the laymen by Timothy and others, recorded in Revelation 2:1–3, "To the angel of the church in Ephesus write: The One who holds the seven stars in His right hand, the One who walks among the seven golden lampstands, says this: 'I know your deeds and your toil and perseverance, and that you cannot tolerate evil men, and you put to the test those who call themselves apostles, and they are not, and you found them to be false; and you have perseverance and have endured for My name's sake, and have not grown weary.' "

A Good and Faithful Servant

Paul also warned the Corinthians of the origin, nature, and effects of false teaching though crafty arguments — and the need for correcting error (including church discipline) based on the Scriptures and the knowledge of God and His ways:

> For though we walk in the flesh, we do not war according to the flesh, for the weapons of our warfare are not of the flesh, but divinely powerful for the destruction of fortresses. We are destroying speculations and every lofty thing raised up against the knowledge of God, and we are taking every thought captive to the obedience of Christ, and we are ready to punish all disobedience, whenever your obedience is complete (2 Corinthians 10:3-6; NASB 1995).

Paul warned Timothy about the character of well-educated false teachers, the importance of Scripture in understanding the truth, and how understanding the truth is the solution to exposing the errors of false teaching.

> But realize this, that in the last days difficult times will come. For men will be lovers of self, lovers of money, boastful, arrogant, revilers, disobedient to parents, ungrateful, unholy, unloving, irreconcilable, malicious gossips, without self-control, brutal, haters of good, treacherous, reckless, conceited, lovers of pleasure rather than lovers of God, holding to a form of godliness, although they have denied its power; Avoid such men as these. For among them are those who enter into households and captivate weak women weighed down with sins, led on by various impulses, **always learning and never able to come to the knowledge of the truth.** Just as Jannes and Jambres opposed Moses, so these men also oppose the truth, men of depraved mind, rejected in regard to the faith. But they will not make further progress; **for their folly will be obvious to all**, just as Jannes's and Jambres's folly was also. . . . All Scripture is inspired by God and profitable for teaching, for reproof, for correction, for training in righteousness; so that the man of God may be adequate, equipped for every good work (2 Timothy 3:1–9, 16; NASB 1995; emphasis added).

Timothy was instructed by Paul to "preach the word; be ready in season and out of season; reprove, rebuke, exhort, with great patience and instruction. For the time will come when they will not endure sound doctrine; but wanting to have their ears tickled, they will accumulate for themselves teachers in accordance to their own desires" (2 Timothy 4:2–3; NASB 1995).

Thus, the greatest battle of Christians is generally not with non-believers outside the church, but with false teachers within the church. The primary defense is knowing the Scriptures and refusing to accept distortions of truths within the Word or distortion of evidences seen throughout the universe. The beginning and end of every argument must be based on a correct interpretation and application of the Scriptures.

## An Illustration from the Battle of the Bulge

David Jeremiah told me that one of the things he admired most about my father was that he had fundamental understanding of very difficult and complicated concepts that were intellectually far above almost everybody else. However, he was then able to take the same truths and make them applicable and exciting to the people.

How did John Whitcomb present the complex arguments of presuppositional approaches to apologetics to the average person? In this case, he drew from his own experiences in 1944 and the Battle of the Bulge.[20]

> During the 1944 Ardennes campaign in Belgium, better known as the Battle of the Bulge, the writer [John Whitcomb] served as a "fire direction computer" in a US field artillery battalion. It was his job to sit with two other men in a basement behind the front lines and to telephone directions to the artillerymen who handled the twelve 105mm guns.
>
> The really dangerous job was entrusted to the forward observer, usually a lieutenant. He had to position himself in a high place near enough to the front lines to see enemy tanks approaching.
>
> When the tanks came into view, a potential crisis emerged. He could either panic or he could follow strict instructions. If he panicked and fled to the rear, the tanks would proceed unchallenged, and the battle might be lost,

---

20. From http://www.whitcombministries.org/uploads/1/3/8/9/13891775/priorities_paper_the_conversion_of_an_evolutionist.pdf, accessed January 10, 2019.

including the forward observer. Or, he might rush toward the tanks and start firing on them himself. That would also prove disastrous to him, and to his military unit.

There was, however, a third alternative. That would be to "sanctify" the field artillery in his heart![21] In other words, he could follow instructions and phone the "fire direction center," giving them the number, size, location and apparent speed and direction of movement of the enemy tanks, confessing thereby his inability to handle them in his own strength, and the ability of the field artillery to do the job which he could not do.

It hardly seems necessary to explain that once the artillery had located these tanks, they were in desperate danger. As dozens of armor-piercing shells whistled over the head of the forward observer and penetrated the tanks one by one, exploding inside, he was giving his greatest apologetic to the challenge that confronted him.

As God's "forward observers" in Satan's world of demons and fallen men, Christians must learn to call upon their Lord. No other system has ever really worked nor ever shall.

What, then, is the "answer" that each of us must be prepared to give to everyone who asks us to give an account for the hope that is in us?[22] The answer must be basically God's Word, not our own word. God's thoughts are vastly higher than our thoughts (Isaiah 55:9), and His words penetrate far deeper into men's hearts than our words.

In every sincere soul-winning effort, the believer soon discovers that his own words are dead, inactive and dull.

But — "the Word of God is quick, and powerful, and sharper than any two-edged sword, piercing even to the dividing asunder of soul and spirit, and of the joints and

---

21. From 1 Peter 3:14–16: "But even if you should suffer for the sake of righteousness, you are blessed. AND DO NOT FEAR THEIR INTIMIDATION, AND DO NOT BE TROUBLED, but sanctify Christ as Lord in your hearts, always being ready to make a defense to everyone who asks you to give an account for the hope that is in you, yet with gentleness and reverence; and keep a good conscience so that in the thing in which you are slandered, those who revile your good behavior in Christ will be put to shame" (NASB 1995).
22. From 1 Peter 3:14–16 quoted in the previous footnote.

marrow, and is a discerner of the thoughts and intents of the heart" (Hebrews 4:12).

It was Christ the Lord Who set the apologetic example for all believers when He thrice defeated Satan with accurate, appropriate quotations from the Word of God, and with the formula - "It is written" (Matthew 4:1–11). In His great confrontation with unbelieving Pharisees in John 8:12–59, our Lord appealed constantly to basic spiritual realities, such as the witness of His Father (John 8:14, 26, 28, 29, 38, 42, 49, 54), rather than to sign-miracles. It is noteworthy that "as he spoke these words, many believed on him" (vs. 30).

Do modern Christians sometimes feel that they have, because of archaeological, historical, scientific, and other discoveries that shed light on the Scriptures, a superior apologetic to that of our Lord and His apostles and of the early church?

If so, they have not really sanctified the Lord God in their hearts and their answers to lost men can bring neither conviction nor conversion in the biblical sense of those terms. God's work must be done in God's way if it is to receive God's approval (cf 1 Corinthians 3:10–15).[23]

## Conclusion

Cornelius Van Til played a critical role in the development of Whitcomb's thinking about apologetics. The answer to every question must start and end with the Scriptures. Jesus Himself articulated this fact in a few words of prayer to His Father, "Sanctify them in the truth; Your word is truth" (John 17:17; NASB 1995).

The "extra-biblical evidences" for the existence and works of God are overwhelmingly obvious to God's people (cf. Psalms 19:1–6, as natural revelation), but the *meaning* of these "evidences" remain invisible to the eyes of the spiritually blind.

The process of an unbeliever becoming a believer is through "hearing the Word of Christ." It is not through extra-biblical evidences. But a fascination with the creation, or even the effects of the Genesis Flood, can be used by the Holy Spirit, within the context of all of Scripture, to lead a person to the point of salvation.

---

23. Interview of David Jeremiah by the author on May 21, 2019.

# A Good and Faithful Servant

Appropriate and biblically based apologetics serve a major role in clarifying and correcting *false teaching* related to God's Word and His works. False teaching, the primary weapon of the devil, is destructive to believers and to the Church of Jesus Christ. The argument for apologetics cannot be that "extra-biblical evidences support the Scriptures as true." The argument is "All Scriptures are true, and false teaching must be exposed as error through careful biblical scholarship and clear presentation of the facts." It is exposure to truth that enlightens the mind and reveals the errors. The goal is "taking every thought captive to the obedience of Christ," and to accurately teach all Scriptures so that "the man of God may be adequate, equipped for every good work."

John Whitcomb used his God-given teaching gifts to help evangelists preach the pure gospel and provide teachers and pastors with a biblical approach to detecting and exposing false doctrine through knowledge and application of the truth. Many aspects of his work have rippled through Bible-believing churches, bringing stability, growth, and effectiveness. This is exactly what Christ intended by special gifts to His Church.

> And He gave some as apostles, and some as prophets, and some as evangelists, and some as pastors and **teachers**, for the equipping of the saints for the work of service, to the building up of the body of Christ; until we all attain to the unity of the faith, and of the knowledge of the Son of God, to a mature man, to the measure of the stature which belongs to the fullness of Christ. As a result, **we are no longer to be children, tossed here and there by waves and carried about by every wind of doctrine, by the trickery of men, by craftiness in deceitful scheming;** but speaking the truth in love, **we are to grow up in all aspects into Him who is the head, even Christ**, from whom the whole body, being fitted and held together by what every joint supplies, according to the proper working of each individual part, causes the growth of the body for the building up of itself in love (Ephesians 4:11–16 NASB 1995; emphasis added).

In the realm of apologetics, John Whitcomb's life verse, 2 Timothy 2:2, resonates: "The things which you have heard from me in the presence of many witnesses, entrust these to faithful men who will be able to teach others also." Whitcomb took what he heard from Van Til, digested it, clarified it, simplified it so that it could be understood, and entrusted it to *many* faithful men, who continue to teach others throughout the world.

## Addendum

I asked my father to write brief summaries of whom he considered his "fathers," which was sent to me on June 3, 2016 (see Chapter 1). In 2017, linked to reviewing this chapter, he sent me the following note.

### Cornelius Van Til

The last of my so called "theological fathers" was Cornelius Van Til. In the providence of God, Dr. Van Til came to the Winona Lake School of Theology, to teach a course on Christian Apologetics. July 12–27, 1955. This course of intense study, for which I have many pages of notes, was God's means to alert me as never before, to the importance of Presuppositional Apologetics. His teaching was quite complex but thoroughly biblical. As explained by John M. Frame, in his book *Cornelius Van Til: An Analysis of His Thought.* As Dr. Frame expressed, "Now Van Til was — and still is, through his writings — the leader of a movement in theology, philosophy, and apologetics. I write as a committed member of that movement. I am not ashamed at its existence. I honestly wish that everyone would be converted to Van Til's basic principles, for such conversion is to nothing other than consistent Christianity. Were everyone a Van Tillian at heart, our society would be vastly transformed, and that for the better." (10–11). In his book, Dr. Frame concludes "Van Til's influence has been felt beyond his basic Reformed constituency. Some dispensational theologians have been attracted to his ideas. John C. Whitcomb taught Van Tillian apologetics for many years at Grace Theological Seminary." (394–395).

# Chapter 18

# Henry

"Perhaps Today!"
1918–2006

Lewis and Clark, Wilbur and Orville Wright, Watson and Crick, Whitcomb and Morris — these are but a few examples of two-person teams who will forever be remembered for the extraordinary things they accomplished together.

Through collaboration on *The Genesis Flood*, the Whitcomb-Morris team accomplished something that had eluded other godly and well-meaning Christians in the 100 years following Darwin's publication of the *Origin of Species*. Together they transcended common opinion and theory by applying hermeneutic rigor and scientific principles to demonstrate the perspicuity[1] of Scripture on creation and the global Flood. Amazingly, this achievement was not the primary goal of Whitcomb or Morris's life or career. In both cases, the number one goal of these brilliant scholars was to serve the Most High God and to evangelize the world with the gospel of Jesus Christ.

John Whitcomb held Henry Morris in the highest level of respect. He not only counted Henry Morris as a great Christian friend and

---

1. Perspicuity is a word that is derived from a Latin word meaning "to see through." The doctrine of the perspicuity of Scripture states that those things which are necessary to be known, believed, and observed are so clearly propounded and opened in some place of Scripture or other that not only the learned, but the unlearned, in a due use of the ordinary means, may attain unto a sufficient understanding of them. Dr. Whitcomb demonstrated that this principle was applied to the creation and the Flood. When all Scripture was systematically considered, it was internally consistent and unequivocal in its meaning.

470

outstanding scholar, but also as one of his "four fathers." In this instance, Henry Morris served as John Whitcomb's *scientific* father.

Henry Morris also held John Whitcomb in the highest level of respect. Morris wrote, "He is not only an outstanding scholar, but a gracious Christian gentleman and, in my judgment (shared by hosts of others), just about the finest Bible teacher one could ever hear."[2]

These two men came from very different backgrounds and only met each other face-to-face twice before the final phase of publishing *The Genesis Flood*. They were different in their general interests, fields of study, and spheres of influence. But they both loved God's Word and focused their lives on evangelism. They each recognized the stumbling blocks to faith that were generated by the theory of natural evolution. They were both convinced that, especially for young Christians, any doubts and concerns about the Scriptures that were generated by godless philosophies and theories would be overcome through clear presentation of the Bible and scientific evidences.

## Young Henry M. Morris

Henry M. Morris Jr. (known as H.M.) had a difficult and unhappy childhood. The details are now documented in a thoughtful biography written by his youngest daughter Rebecca.[3]

H.M.'s father, Henry Sr., and mother, Ida, were high school sweethearts who were secretly married and started a family. Each had a godly Christian mother, but fathers and other family members with no interest in Christianity. Henry Sr. enlisted in the U.S. Army during World War I and was stationed at Camp Bowie near Dallas, where H.M. was born.

One of the chaplains at Camp Bowie was the internationally acclaimed evangelist, pastor, educator, and author, R.A. Torrey.[4] One day,

---

2. Henry M. Morris, *History of Modern Creationism*, Second edition (Santee, CA: Institute for Creation Research, 1993), 164.
3. Rebecca Morris Barber, *Henry M. Morris: Father of Modern Creationism* (Dallas, TX: Institute for Creation Research, 2017).
4. Reuben Archer (R.A.) Torrey (1856–1928) was one of the best-known evangelists and teachers of the early 20th century. Educated at Yale, he joined Dwight L. Moody and helped found Moody Bible Institute, and then the Bible Institute of Los Angeles. His evangelical crusades covered the English-speaking world. He published 40 books, pastored several churches, and served as a chaplain at Camp Chickamauga during the Spanish-American War and at Camp Bowie and Camp Kearny during World War I.

Torrey stopped by the Morris's house and met Ida and her little baby, H.M. He took the baby in his arms, prayed over him, and dedicated him to the service of the Lord. This act made a lasting impression on the young mother, who decided to raise him as a Christian. Providentially, Dr. Torrey's prayer was answered.

After WWI, H.M.'s parents returned to their family's home in El Paso, Texas. Henry Sr. sought financial success and social standing through various businesses, but alcohol, gambling, and a secular lifestyle led to family dysfunction and economic failure. The Great Depression added to the hardships. The family lived in a series of bungalows, and H.M. and his siblings periodically fell into the care of his paternal grandmother, known as Mamie.

Mamie faithfully taught H.M. and his siblings about the love of Jesus, the gospel, and the Scriptures. One day, in response to Mamie's careful Bible teaching, H.M. accepted the Lord as his Savior and began sharing his faith with other kids.

Grade school was easy for the brilliant young H.M., and he quickly rose to the top of his class. His love for the Lord and determination to witness to his friends resulted in a reputation of being a "goody-goody." He recalled, "A combination of moral rectitude and academic superiority tends to give one the position of 'teacher's pet' and such a reputation, of course, is quite deadly, guaranteed to generate a high degree of peer-group unpopularity."[5] Furthermore, H.M.'s family situation and a lack of friends left him as an independent, introverted, introspective, and lonely little boy.

During high school, the depression economy and family dysfunction resulted in H.M. being sent to live near Houston with some extended family on his mother's side. Despite his home front challenges, H.M. continued to excel in school. He was especially gifted in writing, including publishing a poem about baseball in the local newspaper.

## Rice University

H.M. wanted to pursue journalism. However, he chose Rice University, one of the elite schools of the South *without* a journalism school but with strengths in engineering. This decision was apparently influenced

---

5. Quoted in Rebecca Morris Barber, *Henry M. Morris: Father of Modern Creationism* (Dallas, TX: Institute for Creation Research, 2017), 33.

by one of the most attractive girls in H.M.'s high school choosing Rice and the fact that he was offered a full-ride scholarship. H.M. picked civil engineering as his major.

Although the quality of math, engineering, and scientific education at Rice University was outstanding, it was steeped in secular humanistic philosophies, including the theory of evolution. H.M. focused on his academic studies, noting that during that time, he was a "nominal evolutionist as well as a nominal Christian."[6] Providentially, he got a part-time job in a civil engineering laboratory where he met key people, became familiar with research equipment, and learned about applied sciences.

As graduation approached, he took the Civil Service examination and obtained a top score. A degree from Rice University and objective evidence that he was top talent paved the way to become Junior Engineer in the U.S. Civil Service. He accepted a position with the International Boundary Commission back in El Paso, Texas.

Once he was established in El Paso, H.M. returned to Houston to propose to Mary Louise Beach. They married on January 24, 1940.

## A Bible-believing Church and the Gideons

Upon returning to El Paso, H.M. returned to his childhood church — the First Baptist Church of El Paso. An old friend encouraged him to attend the Baptist Training Union, and he began reading and studying the Bible regularly. He became increasingly aware that the Word of God was *reality* rather than *theory*.

H.M. joined other laymen in a group called the Gideons, an organization focused on providing the Word of God to every person in the nation. H.M. remained active in the Gideons as a worker and speaker for many years to come.

Two series of Bible messages had profound impacts on H.M. The first was by a pastor on the Book of Revelation. H.M. recognized that hope of the believers was the resurrection of believers who died and the rapture of those who remained alive on the earth, both to forever be with their Lord.[7] He understood that Christ's return was imminent and that it could be *today*. He placed a plaque in his office that only said, "**Perhaps Today!**" but it said everything. Thereafter, his life was

6. Ibid., 58.
7. 1 Thessalonians 4:13–18.

driven by the urgent recognition that time was short and that the good news of the gospel must be delivered to everyone possible before it was too late. He kept the plaque in a prominent place in his office for the rest of his life.

Dr. Irwin Moon came to El Paso in 1941 to deliver a series entitled "Sermons from Science." Lectures highlighted the biblical account of a global Flood and theories of the nature and effects of a water canopy above the antediluvian world. Having endured four years of collegiate indoctrination in evolutionary theory, H.M. had many unanswered questions. This series of messages triggered his critical thinking of the evidence of the Flood around him. While he did not know how to reconcile the Genesis account of creation with science, he accepted the fact that the Bible is truth and that, even though he could not yet see the answers, they must be there![8]

**The Science of Rushing Water**

As the new guy on the job for the Texas Highway Department, H.M. quickly got his feet wet in the Rio Grande River. His job included drafting and developing specification for 11 Rio Grande River bridges, as well as dams on both the Rio Grande River and Devil's River. Within this project, he worked on hydraulic structures, flumes, canals, gauging stations, and monitoring plans. Working with both theoretical and experimental experts, H.M. helped on numerous studies targeting backwater curves, hydraulic designs for canals, gates, desilting basins, and the effects of dams on rivers.

H.M. studied the principles behind the observations and developed a number of new and effective computational techniques to provide engineers mechanistic support for the projects and reports. He authored a detailed technical document titled "Report on the Rio Grande Water Conservation Investigation." This report served as a lever to open doors and a foundation on which to develop the academic discipline of Hydraulic Engineering.

**WWII**

As the USA entered WWII, every young man was called to do his part. H.M. determined to enlist in the Civil Engineering Corps of the Navy

---

8. Rebecca Morris Barber, *Henry M. Morris: Father of Modern Creationism* (Dallas, TX: Institute for Creation Research, 2017), 71.

rather than to be drafted. He called upon one of his professors at Rice University for a letter of reference as to his qualifications as an engineer. Professor R.B. Ryon wrote that letter, noting that H.M. was "one of the best men we have had: an excellent student, clear and original thinker, and had a fine personality."[9] Professor Ryon also reached out to H.M., asking him to come back to Rice for a visit. H.M. accepted the offer, and after the visit, Ryon offered him a position as Instructor in Civil Engineering, specifically to train Naval ROTC and Navy V-12 students for the government. The Navy granted a waiver from active military duty, allowing H.M. to serve as a Navy Instructor at Rice University while remaining a civilian.[10]

*Teaching Seabees*

H.M. was assigned to teach all types of engineering to young men assigned to the United States Naval Construction Battalions, better known as the Seabees (from C.B.). The assignments from Professor Ryon must have appeared overwhelming to anyone who was just 23 years old and equipped with only an undergraduate education and a little field work. However, H.M. proved to be up to the task.

Professor Ryon took the approach of being an administrative supervisor rather than a micromanager, giving H.M. as much freedom in course development, organization, and student assessment as he could handle without help. The spectrum of education expected by the Navy included all aspects of engineering, science, mathematics, management, and war training programs — forcing H.M. to both educate himself and learn to develop and manage a training program of higher education while "under fire."

The experience at Rice University was life changing. H.M. embraced the academic challenges, gained creative administrative experience, and honed his mind to address the gods of the ivory towers with rigorous arguments and truths. These qualities qualified him for the future task of building and managing new academic departments

---

9. Quoted in Rebecca Morris Barber, *Henry M. Morris: Father of Modern Creationism* (Dallas, TX: Institute for Creation Research, 2017), 82.
10. During WWII, many universities became training centers for officers (ROTC) and technicians, including Virginia Polytechnic Institution (Now Virginia Tech), where John Whitcomb was trained — see Chapter 8.

in secular universities, where he would serve as chair, and building the Institute for Creation Research[11] a few decades later.

## "That *You* Might Believe"

The dark underside of humanism and atheism that H.M. saw as a student at Rice University became more obvious as an instructor. He noted an almost universal disbelief in the scientific or historical accuracy of the Bible. He realized that most students graduated with indifference to Christianity, being steeped in modernistic and atheistic philosophies and beliefs. The university library provided no solutions to the Bible and science, as the tenants of natural evolution permeated nearly every page of every book and journal articles. However, H.M. grew increasingly convinced that these arguments for natural evolution were fundamentally wrong.

Morris later wrote,

> Every time I would look at an insect or a tree or any living organism and then try to imagine how such a thing could ever be produced by mutations and natural selection, it seemed so absurdly impossible that the very idea almost made me angry! In fact, it was these evolutionary books that eventually helped convince me that evolutionism was completely unscientific.[12]

The Southern Baptist literature and local Christian bookstores were no better than the academic library at Rice University. The available Christian books and commentaries tended to accept the theories of evolution as a scientific fact, weaving the natural evolution story into the first chapters of Genesis using the day-age or gap theories to somehow find harmony. Eventually, H.M. discovered a small bookstore operated

---

11. The Institute for Creation Research (ICR) was founded by Henry Morris in 1970 and is located in Southern California at Christian Heritage College (now San Diego Christian College). ICR was designed to conduct scientific research within the realms of origins and earth history and then to educate the public both formally and informally through graduate and professional training programs, conferences, and seminars. They also produce books, magazines, and media presentations. In 2007, they relocated to Dallas, Texas. See http://www.icr.org/who-we-are.
12. Quoted in Rebecca Morris Barber, *Henry M. Morris: Father of Modern Creationism* (Dallas, TX: Institute for Creation Research, 2017), 52–93.

by a Plymouth Brethren businessman that offered outstanding, but often rigorous, works that were characterized by solid biblical exegesis. Within this treasure trove were books on biblical creationism from the early 20th century by Harry Rimmer, Carle Schwarze, Arthur I. Brown, and George McCready Price. None of them were qualified scientists except Carle Schwarze, who was a retired civil engineering professor. Although the scientific arguments were weak and decades out of date, the biblical arguments in these books were sound and some of the scientific explanations plausible. The book by Price entitled *The Modern Flood Theory of Geology*[13] was especially helpful in recognizing that it was the Flood in Genesis that offered insights into the origin of geological strata and continental geography, indicating that these features could be formed quickly rather than requiring millions and millions of years of gradual formation. H.M. also noted that these authors tended toward the gap theory — but they did not need to do so. He wrote:

> . . . the more I studied both science and Scripture, the more certain it became that such compromises were impossible. The Bible taught unequivocally that all things were made in six literal days only a few thousand years ago, and that was that![14]

H.M. recognized that a clear, up-to-date book was needed to help college students who were wrestling with the issues surrounding the Bible and science. With only a B.S. degree, he realized that in the area of hydrodynamics and flood geology, he might be one of the most qualified voices among Bible-believing evangelical Christians.[15] H.M. then

---

13. George McCready Price, *The Modern Flood Theory of Geology* (Fleming H. Revell Company, 1935), 118 pages.
14. Rebecca Morris Barber, *Henry M. Morris: Father of Modern Creationism* (Dallas, TX: Institute for Creation Research, 2017), 94, quoting an unpublished manuscript by Henry Morris dated 1997.
15. I was struck by the fact that Henry Morris saw the need for a messenger of truth regarding the Bible and science at this time and place and embraced it. In a similar way, John Whitcomb, after reading *Therefore Stand*, knew that he was to defend the Scriptures against false doctrines, and he dedicated himself to that task. The calling of these men in their youth reminds me of Isaiah the prophet (Isaiah 6:8), "Then I heard the voice of the Lord, saying, 'Whom shall I send, and who will go for Us?' Then I said, 'Here am I. Send me!'"

began writing down his arguments, resulting in a short book entitled *That You Might Believe.*[16]

The manuscript was completed in the summer of 1944 and sent to several trusted Christian leaders for review and comment. The reviewers gave encouraging comments and recommendations, with Stacey Woods of InterVarsity Christian Fellowship (IVF) recommending the book to Good News Publishing. Although Good News Publishing focused on printing gospel tracts, they agreed to publish *That You Might Believe* as their first book — provided that Henry Morris would purchase 500 copies in advance.

W.S. Mosher, a wealthy Christian friend of H.M. through the Gideons, agreed to underwrite the book, provided that the 500 copies were given away to IVF students and others who promised to read it. In 1946, the first edition rolled off the press and distribution began.

*That You Might Believe* contained seven chapters with a focus on science and the Bible.

The book was thoughtfully and skillfully written. It proved to be a powerful personal testimony, and a number of people came to accept Jesus Christ as their Lord and Savior through the book. Even more individuals, who were already Christians, were strengthened in their faith. However, the book fell short as a serious defense of the faith on at least two accounts:

(1) *Lack of accurate hermeneutics:* H.M. gave a strong testimony on what he believed, and this witness has some value. However, the real issue is the demonstration of exactly what the Bible says, what it does not say — and what the text means and what *it cannot mean*. Since the Bible is a unique, God-inspired text, the apologetic can, and must, be presuppositional.

(2) *Lack of scientific rigor:* H.M. provided a strong witness of what he believed to be the correct interpretation of the scientific evidence based on the Flood narrative on Genesis, but he based his proof on the analysis of Price and rejected the position of the vast majority of scientists because they rejected the Bible. Although H.M. may have been right, the scientific arguments must be based on first principles of scientific reason, defining

16. Henry M. Morris, *That You Might Believe*, First edition (Good News Publishers, 1946), 156 pages.

observable phenomenon based on math, physics, and known mechanistic principles when possible, and strong statistical associations or other evidences (e.g., quantum physics, epidemiology, chemistry, etc.) based on reproducible observations in relevant models. He also failed to provide accurate scientific critiques of the failure of the theory of evolution to meet any standards of scientific rigor based on the testing of theories using scientific methods and models.

The nature of the arguments for the biblical account and scientific evidences would require the formal and systematic approach that would eventually be provided in *The Genesis Flood*.

Some examples from *That You Might Believe* are highlighted here:

*Chapter 1:* "That Ye Might Believe" — set the tone of the book by acknowledging that the 1940s was a time of confusion and uncertainty in many areas of politics and science, but especially so in religion. By page 3, H.M. pointed out that God has not left us in a dilemma without providing something of true certainty and understanding. The truth he was referring to is the Rock of Ages, the Lord Jesus Christ. H.M. testified to his absolute faith in Jesus Christ. He further stated that his belief in God was not a faith without reason and fact, despite the charges of religious critics — especially in "intellectual" circles. He finished the first chapter by stating that the book was intended for college students, who were by nature both critical and inquisitive; to strengthen the faith of Christians; and convince others that Christianity is supported by historical and scientific facts.

*Chapter 2:* "Modern Science and the Bible" — provided a list of statements from the Bible about the universe that could not have been known in ancient times. For example, in the most ancient of all books within the Bible, Job stated that God "hung the earth on nothing." The prophet Isaiah stated that God sits above the sphere that is the earth (Isaiah 40:22). David and Solomon both described the water cycle in Psalms and Ecclesiastes, describing the process of water moving from the sea, to thunderclouds, to rain, to the earth, and back to the sea. Other examples of biblical accuracy prior to modern science were given, except for creation and the Genesis Flood (reserved for Chapters 3 and 4). The chapter concluded with a plea for the reader to refrain from accepting the judgment of most academic authorities, but to consider the facts themselves, with assurance that if this was done fairly, the reader would come to a point of accepting Christ and the Bible.

*Chapter 3:* "The Theory of Evolution" — began by acknowledging that over the preceding century, nearly all scientists accept the theory of evolution, that nearly all colleges and universities teach it as fact, and most churches and seminaries revised their theology to accommodate this worldview. H.M. pointed out that creation of the world and evolution of living beings was not witnessed and that not one example of genuine evolution had ever been observed. Thus, "in view of the rather shaky scientific grounds on which the theory stands, it seems hazardous to deliberately reject what God has revealed in the Bible about the origin of life in favor of an unproven hypothesis" (page 27). He then outlined why the Bible (read in a natural, literal, historical way) can only mean that God created the world in six 24-hour days. With respect to theistic evolution, H.M. stated, "If God actually did create the universe, including all living creatures, by the method of evolution, He certainly picked the most inefficient and cruel and downright asinine method of doing it that it is possible to imagine" (page 30). H.M. went on to cite many of the arguments against evolution that others had pointed out, based primarily on the fact that all creatures and systems demand intelligent design, and that there is no known or imaginable mechanism by which things could have come into existence by random chance.

H.M. then pointed out some facts about himself and his approach that likely served as a major point of criticism of the book and that apparently provided strong motivation to join with John Whitcomb to write *The Genesis Flood.* On page 32, H.M. wrote,

> I am not a biologist, nor a geologist, nor an authority on evolutionary theory, nor, for that matter, a theologian. But being an engineer, I am interested in all fields of science; and being a Christian and having experienced something of the power of the Bible in my own life, I have become especially interested in those few realms of science which, it is claimed, have discredited the Scriptures. It is not necessary to be a specialist in these fields to get some understanding of the facts involved nor to understand the interpretation of

these facts that have gone into the building of the theory of evolution. I have read fairly extensively on the subject and believe I am conversant with the general features at least of all proofs that have thus far been advanced. And to an engineer, accustomed to basing his work on sound mathematics and practical experiences, with logical inductive reasoning where necessary, these "proofs" must appear woefully weak.

The problem with this statement was that the entire premise of the arguments within *That You Might Believe* is on what H.M., who admitted that he was an expert in neither science nor the Bible, personally believes. The self-affirming argument that the author is "logical" is considered, among academics, to be the lowest level of evidence.

Personal opinions, hypotheses, and conclusions of "experts" *does* have some value. We often face situations or phenomena that are not well defined, complex, where the underlying mechanisms are unknown and where many explanations are possible. The experts are individuals who have studied the phenomena for many years in systematic ways or who have experience dealing with similar situations. Although they cannot define the mechanisms determining the behavior or outcome of the thing, they can provide evidence of what the mechanism is *not*. Therefore, personal opinions of true experts can provide valuable insights in framing the thing for current and future considerations. In contrast, the value of an expert in one field who is giving "expert opinion" on another is typically of minimum value (e.g., the opinion of an actor, athlete, or singer, speaking on science, international politics, or other domains which they have not studied or mastered).

One of my mentors at Duke University would point this out to me, as I had a lot of ideas that I wanted to share as a trainee. He emphasized, "You need to *earn* the right to speculate in public." Therefore, I focused on providing scientific evidence in peer-reviewed scientific literature, then waited until I was asked to speculate on an area of my expertise.

Following the "expert opinion" politics, it was rather easy for an academic, a scientist, or a theologian to dismiss the entire work as the figment of the imagination of a college instructor with a bachelor's degree who thinks he is a lot smarter than he actually is. But the targets for criticism became worse in Chapter 4.

*Chapter 4:* "Modern Science and the Flood" — was a critical chapter in supporting a biblical view, but it also undermined H.M.'s goals for the book. Many interesting examples are given about fossils, strata, landmasses, coal seams, and other observations that support a global Flood and that refute the uniformitarian approach of the theory of evolution popular in 1946.[17] However, H.M. undermined his own "expert opinion" arguments on pages 60–61,

> There are few geologists, even today, who hold to some form of the flood theory. Probably the outstanding of these is George M. Price, who is probably as conversant with the whole subject of historical geology as anyone living. Because of his views, he has been subjected to a great deal of criticism and ridicule by orthodox geologists, but his wealth of accumulated facts and his incontrovertible logic have never been answered. Much of the material in this chapter is taken from his works.

Here, H.M. added to the previous statements made in Chapter 3 that he himself is not a geologist or an educated scientist (i.e., no Ph.D.) but relies on the materials of Price (who is not a scientist either, whose arguments have been rejected by "real" geologists,[18] and who is also at odds with most theologians).

George McCready Price[19] was a Seventh-day Adventist (SDA) author, teacher, and speaker who became the most notable advocate for six days of creation and a global Flood in the early 20th century. His educational background included a college degree at Battle Creek College and a one-year teacher-training course at the Provincial Normal School of New Brunswick with an emphasis on natural sciences. An exceptionally intelligent man, he authored numerous books on creation science, and his views influenced the arguments of William Jennings Bryan

---

17. Noting that the theory of evolution continues to evolve, especially to one that now embraces catastrophism — except a catastrophe caused by a global Flood.

18. Price's views were summarily dismissed during the Scopes "Monkey" trial by Clarence Darrow, who attacked Bryan for mentioning Price "because he is the only human being in the world so far as you know that signs his name as a geologist that believes like you do . . . every scientist in this country knows [he] is a mountebank and a pretender and not a geologist at all." https://en.wikipedia.org/wiki/George_McCready_Price.

19. George McCready Price was born on August 26, 1870, and died on January 24, 1963.

against evolution in the 1925 Scopes Trial.[20] Unfortunately, H.M. fell into the same trap as Bryan in appealing to Price as an authority on the matter of geology rather than doing his own research and reporting his independent findings and their implications.

Theologians criticized Price for being an SDA, with the assumption that his views on a six-day creation came from the authoritative doctrines of Ellen G. White, one of the founders of the SDA. White and the SDA point to a literal six days of creation with a seventh day of rest as the primary argument for worshiping on the "seventh" day.[21] Most evangelicals reject the claim that Ellen White had divine authority to speak truth, endangering the group to be a "cult."[22] Thus, Price was never accepted as orthodox by mainstream protestant denominations, as they assumed his interpretations of the Bible were biased. However, Price's writings clearly had a major influence on H.M., as attested to in *That You Might Believe*. This was noted by H.M.'s detractors, claiming later that *The Genesis Flood* was a rehash of Price's rejected ideas.[23]

In retrospect, many of the issues surrounding the theory of evolution that Price and other six-day creationists and global Flood proponents raised were legitimate, but the context and arguments were often inadequate. Graduate education, such as earning a Ph.D., is not just receiving a diploma and license to pontificate; it represents mastery of a scientific or engineering discipline through rigorous course work and

---

20. See https://en.wikipedia.org/wiki/George_McCready_Price.

21. There is no biblical prohibition for worshiping on Saturday (e.g., Colossians 2:16), nor is there an ordinance (i.e., command) in the New Testament to worship on Sunday. The SDA are correct in saying that Sunday is not the Sabbath, which is Saturday. By tradition, Christians worship together on Sunday as the Lord's Day to celebrate the Resurrection of Jesus from the dead. The concern that protestants and evangelicals have with SDA worshiping on Saturday is the SDA doctrines upon which the practice is based.

22. The term *cult* means different things depending on the context. For evangelical Christians, a cult is any group that deviates from the orthodox teachings of the historic Christian faith being derived from the Bible. A cult may include an individual or group of people who claim to be sent by God with special insights or to lead the "one true religion." A list of characteristics of a cult is given in *Christianity Today*, "What Is a Cult?" by Don Veinot in the July/August 2001 issue. Examples include all-knowing leadership and Scriptures get an added twist.

23. For example, see https://en.wikipedia.org/wiki/George_McCready_Price and Michael Hawley's blog on "Henry Morris' Deception" at https://michaellhawley.com/henry-morris-deception.

systematic reading. It also includes the process of critically researching and analyzing a phenomenon, generating hypotheses and testing them through research projects, critically analyzing the data from the framework of previous work in the field, proposing and defending new theses, and generating a dissertation. The dissertation must withstand the critical analysis of experts in the field, must demonstrate that the insights add new information and knowledge to the field, and that these new ideas can be successfully defended against criticisms. In short, college teaches people how to memorize facts and apply information to the task at hand. Graduate school teaches smart people how to think critically in unexplored areas and defend their new knowledge against the harshest critics.

## Positive Effects of *That You Might Believe*

*That You Might Believe* did have a strong impact among many college students. After donating most of the initial printing to friends and IVF chapters throughout the United States, the demand for additional copies resulted in a second printing. Copies made their way to Princeton University as well, likely through IVF. And a copy made its way to John Whitcomb. On Wednesday, February 26, 1947, Whitcomb entered a brief note in his diary:

> *At the room I read "That You Might Believe" by Morris.*

There was no additional comment on what he thought nor another mention of the book in his diary or among his papers. Little did he know that his life would be linked forever to that of Henry Morris in God's eternal plan.

## "Higher" Education

WWII ended shortly after the Americans dropped atomic bombs on the Japanese cities of Hiroshima and Nagasaki on August 6 and 9, 1945. Over the next year, the U.S. military moved to mothball its machines, muster out millions of men, and minimize training programs. Such was the fate of the Naval program at Rice, and H.M. needed a new job.

H.M. realized that he enjoyed teaching and was an effective teacher. He also realized that he needed graduate training in order to give an effective defense of his faith in God.[24] His friend and supervisor, Professor Ryon, supported H.M.'s career goals but recognized that there was no real opportunity at Rice University in his newly embraced area of science.

Dr. Ryon suggested some graduate schools for H.M. to advance his career, as the entry-level jobs in the private sector would be flooded with veterans who had engineering experience. H.M. investigated multiple universities that specialized in hydraulic engineering, and doors opened for a master's degree at the University of Minnesota. In 1946, he packed his car and headed north.

H.M. discussed his desire for full-time Christian service with Dr. A.I. Brown, looking for some advice and leads. To his surprise, Dr. Brown advised H.M. to continue beyond his master's program and get his Ph.D., as he would be far more effective in the long run. Indeed, Brown noted, with the proper credentials, H.M. might just be the one whom God would use to meet the need for a Christian scientist with expertise in Flood geology.

The University of Minnesota accepted Morris into their Ph.D. program, where he majored in hydraulics and minored in geology. In addition to his own studies, he became a graduate teaching assistant and taught fluid mechanics, hydrology, applied hydraulics, structural analysis, and other subjects. He conducted his graduate research at the St. Anthony Falls Hydraulics Laboratory to study the hydraulics of culverts (especially the flow of water over rough surfaces, such as the corrugated metal culvert pipes). The math and principals behind these studies resulted in a new understanding of the enhanced capacity of turbulent flowing water to carry large amounts of sediment that would settle out in calmer states. He published several landmark papers and a dissertation entitled "A New Concept of Flow in Rough Conduits." This was the perfect academic setting to gain international attention as a scientist and academic engineer and to be the first to

---

24. "Defending the Bible" is the realm of "apologetics," as discussed in Chapter 17. A key Scripture is 1 Peter 3:14–16, "But even if you should suffer for the sake of righteousness, you are blessed. AND DO NOT FEAR THEIR INTIMIDATION, AND DO NOT BE TROUBLED, but sanctify Christ as Lord in your hearts, always being ready to make a defense to everyone who asks you to give an account for the hope that is in you, yet with gentleness and reverence; and keep a good conscience so that in the thing in which you are slandered, those who revile your good behavior in Christ will be put to shame."

truly understand the *mechanism* of geological formation caused by a universal Flood.

While a graduate student, H.M. also pursued his goal to combine the disciplines of hydraulics and geology because he believed that this was the best way to understand the doctrine of creation and the impact of the Flood in Genesis 6–9. He capitalized on an outstanding library, copying key articles and building a reference library.

As he continued his education, H.M. recognized many of the shortcomings of his initial book and in 1947 wrote an updated and expanded version called *The Biblical Evidences for a Recent Creation and Worldwide Deluge*. He sent draft copies to some of the leading Bible apologists for advice and endorsement, and he received thoughtful and critical reviews. Wilbur Smith, from Moody Bible Institute, noted that some parts seemed to be "theories suspended in air" and that these areas need to be supported with vast amounts of research. Dr. Arthur I. Brown, a Bible scholar and conference speaker who often recommended *That You Might Believe* at his conferences, recommended that H.M. should study further before placing his ideas before the public or else afterwards he would regret it. Dr. Oliver Buswell from the National Bible Institute in New York wrote a scathing review, noting the lack of footnotes and references to previous works.

H.M. decided to continue working on the replacement for *That You Might Believe* as a true scientific analysis of the Flood and drafted the first three chapters of a new book, *The Creation and Destruction of the World*, in about 225 pages. He sent the initial draft to Alton Everest, president of the American Christian Association (ACA), who read and returned it. According to Morris, "He didn't agree with it, he couldn't refute it, so he preferred to ignore it."[25] But with the demands of graduate school, the arrival of multiple children, and continued Christian outreach, the chapters drifted further and further back on the "to do" list.

Dr. Morris finished his Ph.D. in 1950. He wanted to go into full-time Christian work, perhaps working as a foreign missionary in countries such as Afghanistan to start a civil engineering department in the proposed new Afghan Institute of Technology. This strongly Muslim country was open to American engineers but closed to

---

25. Henry M. Morris, *History of Modern Creationism*, Second edition (Institute for Creation Research, 1993), 167.

Christian missionaries. But just as the Morris family committed to this new adventure, the door closed, and H.M. began looking for a new job once again.

## Dr. Henry Morris as a Professor and Chair

After graduation, Dr. Morris needed to find a job. After exploring several possibilities, he decided to move south and accepted a job in Louisiana. In June 1951, he drove his family to Lafayette, Louisiana, to become the founding Head of the Civil Engineering Department at the University of Southwestern Louisiana. The position provided many opportunities to organize and develop an academic program, including developing the curriculum, recruiting teachers, and developing a faculty. His mandate from the university was to establish a high-quality program that would receive official accreditation. This goal was finally achieved in 1955.

In addition to his work at the university, Dr. Morris became increasingly active with the Gideons, traveling and speaking throughout the state. He also worked to build and grow a strong Bible-believing church and raise a family. In addition, he completed one new chapter in his book on creation and the Flood.

## Morris Meets Whitcomb

Whitcomb and Morris met in person for the first time in Winona Lake, Indiana, on September 3, 1953. Morris had traveled to Winona Lake to attend a meeting of the American Scientific Affiliation, an organization of Christians with graduate-level science degrees who were primarily theistic evolutionists.[26] Morris presented a paper at the meeting entitled "Biblical Evidences for a Recent Creation and Universal Deluge." The presentation received a cool reception, although it fascinated Whitcomb.

Whitcomb noted in his diary,

> *At 9:00 I heard Dr. Henry Morris present a paper on the Deluge Theory of Geology before the ASA. He was criticized by*

---

26. For a discussion of the ASA in the 20th century, see Henry M. Morris, *History of Modern Creationism*, Second edition, Chapter IV, "Creationist Associations before the Centennial," pages 147–161. Published by the Institute for Creation Research (1993), 444 pages.

*several. Two other papers were read on physics and geology. Afterwards, I spoke briefly to Dr. Morris.*

On September 16, 1953, shortly after returning to Louisiana, Dr. Morris wrote to a friend bemoaning the fact that it was now six years since he began his "complete Biblical and Geological exposition based on the literal interpretation of the Genesis record of creation and the Flood."[27] He now intended to devote special effort, setting aside other things as much as possible, to continue this great work.

Less than a week later, John Whitcomb sent a letter to Morris, dated September 20, 1953, stating,

> I greatly appreciated your paper on "recent Creation and Universal Deluge" which you read at the A.S.A. convention. I feel that your conclusions are scripturally valid, and therefore must be sustained by a fair examination of geological evidence in time to come. My only regret is that so few trained Christian men of science are willing to let God's Word have the final say on these questions. May God richly bless you in your ministry for His glory.

The two men began exchanging correspondence, with John Whitcomb noting that he planned to write his doctoral dissertation on the Genesis Flood, and Morris noted that he was attempting to write a book on the subject.

After an exchange of letters, H.M. suggested to Whitcomb,

> Perhaps we can be of mutual help to each other from time to time.

---

27. Rebecca Morris Barber, *Henry M. Morris: Father of Modern Creationism* (Dallas, TX: Institute for Creation Research, 2017), 132.

# Chapter 19

# Th.D.

"Christians can no longer believe Creation AND evolution;
it is now Creation OR evolution"

1949–1957

John Whitcomb decided to write his doctoral dissertation on the Genesis Flood. To understand the circumstances surrounding the writing of his dissertation as a major part of earning his Doctor of Theology (Th.D.), we need to rewind the time clock to the initial years of John Whitcomb's training at Grace Theological Seminary. The focus is on the interpretation of Scriptures.

John Whitcomb entered Grace in the fall of 1948 with the vision of being a missionary to China. But by the spring of 1951, it was clear that the road for missionaries to China was closed. Prof. Herman Hoyt, the academic dean, encouraged John to continue his education at Grace, working toward a Master of Theology degree. He also discussed a possible graduate teaching position to help him support himself going forward.

On May 16, 1951, Dr. Hoyt officially offered Whitcomb the opportunity to teach World History, History of Hebrew People, Total Systems, History of US, and Bible Survey in the collegiate division at $5.00 an hour (12 hours per week). But a few days later, Robert D. Culver, Th.M., Professor of Old Testament, resigned from the seminary faculty, leaving a sudden opening. In response, Dr. Hoyt and Dr. McClain each approached Whitcomb with a new offer to become a seminary faculty member rather than only a college instructor with the opportunity to teach Culver's courses to the new M.Div. students starting in the fall.

## The Gap Theory at Grace

All Grace Theological Seminary professors held the gap theory as a way to harmonize the Bible and the theory of evolution. The gap theory supposed that long ages existed between Genesis 1:1 and Genesis 1:2 in order to make Genesis compatible with the evolutionists' timetable and to explain the existence of the fossils of dinosaurs and remnants of strange creatures deep inside the earth's crust. This teaching appeared to be one of consensus within the evangelical world rather than one of conviction, and it was not without controversy.

When John Whitcomb entered Grace as a new student, he was taught the gap theory in the Christian Evidences and Apologetics course under Professor Bauman. On April 26, 1949, for example, Bauman gave a lecture outlining the theory of evolution,[1] and on April 28, he discussed the six days of creation — both within the framework of the gap theory. Two lectures represented the full extent of the teaching on these topics. Whitcomb remembers the class discussions where a small subset of students critically questioned this interpretation by insisting, ". . . but the biblical text clearly says . . . !" After class, Whitcomb had two sequential discussions with various students on the issues of a literal six days of creation.

There were a number of students at Grace who opposed the gap theory. Ed Miller, a senior seminary student who became a missionary to Brazil, also held to a six-day creation view. During the chapel service on May 3, 1949, he presented his "Critical Monograph"[2] in which he formally argued *against* the gap theory to the students and faculty. The next day, John Whitcomb sent a copy of *That You Might Believe* by Henry Morris to his mother.

## Student Becomes Teacher

The teaching assignments that McClain and Hoyt gave John Whitcomb in May 1951 placed him in the center of the creation

---

1. In preparation for this class, Whitcomb purchased *Modern Science and the Christian Faith* and read the chapter on geology. The book was based on a collection of essays over a period of six years at the Christian Students Science Symposium and sponsored by the American Scientific Association. It is unclear if the volume was helpful, but the members of the ASA were primarily theistic evolutionists. See Members of the American Scientific Association, *Modern Science and the Christian Faith* (Wheaton, IL: Van Kampen Press, 1948), 289 pages.
2. "A Critical Monograph" was the name used for the formal thesis required for a Master of Divinity degree at Grace Theological Seminary.

controversy. He would start his new job by teaching Hebrew Exegesis and Old Testament Historical Books in the fall of 1951, followed by The Pentateuch and Evidences and Apologetics in the spring semester of 1952. Dr. McClain also offered John Whitcomb $80 per month in financial support during the summer of 1951 to study and prepare his teaching materials. Whitcomb accepted the offer.

The summer months of June, July, and August of 1951 were used to focus on preparing the assigned seminary courses, but also were used to lay the groundwork for many of Whitcomb's later professional accomplishments. The most common diary entry was, *"studied Hebrew grammar."* In addition, he read numerous books, continued his outreach ministries, and participated in the summer offerings of the Winona Lake School of Theology.

Highlights of the summer included a compelling lecture by Wilbur M. Smith, author of *Therefore Stand*,[3] on "The Present Struggle for the Word of God." Whitcomb requested an interview with Wilber Smith and was granted a meeting on the afternoon of July 20, 1951. Whitcomb used the time to discuss his past, present, and future plans, and receive advice from this admired author. This was a critical introduction, as Smith and Whitcomb developed a life-long friendship. Whitcomb also attended messages by Harry Rimmer[4] and other teachers and preachers, including Billy Graham.[5]

To prepare for the Old Testament Historical Books courses, Whitcomb worked out the details of his Old Testament chronological charts on the *Kings of Israel and Judah* (see Chapter 15). But the highlight of the summer came in late August when he met his future wife, Edisene Hanson (Chapter 16).

---

3. Wilbur M. Smith, *Therefore Stand: A Plea for a Vigorous Apologetic in the Present Crisis of Evangelical Christianity* (Boston, MA: W. A. Wilde Co., 1945), 614.

4. Harry Rimmer (1890–1952) was an early earth creationist, a famous lecturer, amateur scientist, archaeologist, author, pastor, crusader, debater, fundamentalist, soul winner, and "one of America's most thrilling speakers" (http://www.creationdays.dk/Harry%20Rimmer/0.php, accessed January 20, 2020). He established *Science Research Bureau* in Los Angeles, California, to prove the veracity of the Bible through studies of biology, paleontology, and anthropology. He wrote many books, including *Modern Science and the Genesis Record* (Eerdmans, 1937) and *The Theory of Evolution and the Facts of Science* (Eerdmans, 1944).

5. On July 10, 1951, Whitcomb wrote in his diary, *"At 3:45 I went to the Billy Sunday Tabernacle to get a good seat to hear Billy Graham. Read Carnell on Apologetics. It poured rain outside, and finally at 8:30, Billy Graham brought a sensational message on the judgment to fall on America for its sins, & the Communist threat. There were many decisions."*

Although Whitcomb's pathway forward was unclear after the road to China closed, he would definitely concentrate on his scholarly activities and join "The Present Struggle for the Word of God," as highlighted earlier by Wilber Smith. Teaching at a graduate seminary level was the next step.

## Challenges in Teaching

In the fall of 1951, John C. Whitcomb Jr. began teaching a graduate-level course on the historical books of the Old Testament (beginning with Genesis) and Hebrew Exegesis (the science of exact interpretation and/or critical explanation of a text). In addition, he continued to read and prepare to teach The Pentateuch (the first five books of the Bible, starting with Genesis) and Apologetics (including the issue of evolution) for the spring semester of 1952.

A common surprise and challenge of moving from student to teacher is the sudden realization that the teacher is expected to know the answers to all the tough questions — with supporting evidences. Fortunately, Whitcomb gained valuable experience and insight into students' questions and perspectives by grading term papers and written exams for Dr. McClain. He also received valuable feedback and perspective on many key and specific issues during dinner-time discussions with his theological father at the McClains' dining room table.

Whitcomb's perspective on a primary goal of a seminary education was likely influenced by Wilbur Smith's book *Therefore Stand: A Plea for a Vigorous Apologetic in This Critical Hour of the Christian Faith* that he read in August 1946. Now he had the opportunity to teach and inspire the up-and-coming generation of seminary students to meet the needs for outstanding scholarship and decisive thinking. He also recognized the high standards of scholarship demanded of students at Princeton and expected nothing less for men of God being trained in a seminary. Whitcomb's experiences and perspectives resulted in some specific challenges and successes as a new faculty member.

The goal of a course within a seminary curriculum and the specific information that students are expected to master in each course presents at least four basic challenges to the teacher during course preparation.

*1. Goals of seminary training*. Whitcomb's goal in choosing Grace was to be trained for missionary work in China. But his gifts and inspiration were to deliver "a vigorous apologetic in this critical hour of the Christian faith." He recognized that God preserved his life in WWII for a reason and that his training at Princeton prepared him for challenging tasks ahead. What he may not have fully appreciated, at the time, was that *he was uniquely gifted by God* to meet specific theological and apologetic challenges and that the other students did not have the same gifts, goals, and purpose. In contrast to the two types of training that Whitcomb sought, the primary goals and needs of the average seminarian is good solid training to be pastors, learning the basics of how to study and teach God's Word to lay people, how to identify and respond to error, and how to apply these tools to the ministry that God was giving *them*. Only a few would be elite scholars.

*2. Educational goals of a specific class.* A good graduate school course provides a rigorous framework for the topic being taught along with examples of how to utilize information in practical ways. A course cannot cover all the details of the discipline nor all of the possible applications. Balancing principles, examples, and information is challenging, and this skill is best learned by experience.

Whitcomb's enthusiasm for the topics being taught and the desire to fully equip his students to defend the faith proved, at first, to be too much information at too high a level at too fast a pace for the average seminary student. As a result, students complained to the administration about the pace, volume, and difficulty of Whitcomb's classes. On December 21, 1951, after the first semester of O.T. History ended, the class presented their professor with a "special" Christmas gift reflecting their perspective on their new instructor. *The gift was a whip!*[6] Fortunately, with the guidance and counsel of McClain and others, Whitcomb got the message that his classes were too demanding and tests too hard (with constant reminders from Dr. Hoyt over several years).[7]

---

6. Whitcomb diary, December 21, 1951: *"Gave an exam on the Reformation, and in O.T a lecture on Hezekiah vs Sennacherib. – The Class presented me with a whip for Christmas."*
7. The initial experience of Professor Whitcomb in teaching appears to be a common challenge of new instructors at the graduate level. As a new graduate student at the Ohio State University, I noted that the younger instructors taught the upper level classes and the more senior professors teach the introductory courses. A senior professor told me that younger instructors are full of new knowledge, having successfully passed their qualifying examinations, defended their thesis, and launched into the details of an important new area. These teachers want the new students to learn *everything* in their basic courses. The older professors recognize the importance of the basic principles

With experience and feedback, he became one of the most effective and beloved Bible teachers of his generation.

*3. Perspectives and priorities of individual teachers.* Each teacher brings their own perspectives on what is correct, what is important, and what should be emphasized to the classroom. Of the four courses that John Whitcomb was assigned to teach, the class on Apologetics received the most attention and restructuring. Although the general topics remained the same as when Whitcomb was taught in the spring of 1949 by Dr. Bauman, the approach to apologetics would markedly change (i.e., a presuppositional approach — see Chapter 17), and the entire second half of the course would be replaced by the teaching of a six-day creation and a global Flood, with a systematic refutation of the theory of evolution (discussed below).

*4. Knowledge base of the teacher.* Teaching is an outstanding learning experience for the teacher. Students seldom recognize that the teacher must study harder than any of the students because they cannot "guess" at test questions — they must study to deeply understand and defend the right answers and to know the errors leading to wrong answers. Written assignments are especially useful because this exercise tests the student's ability to think and argue issues. In grading these tests, the young teacher learns through their students' perspectives and insights, especially when the student has an unusual, complementary background or area of expertise.

After teaching a tough course for several years, a good teacher is typically well equipped to discuss the toughest issues with anyone. John Whitcomb had the dual experience of sitting in the seat of a student and then standing behind the lectern as the official teacher to lead open discussions on the first nine chapters of Genesis, from historical, grammatical, theological, and apologetic perspectives. These exercises in teaching and debating the specifics proved to be an outstanding background for John Whitcomb's eventual doctoral dissertation on the Genesis Flood.[8]

---

and some useful examples. They leave out the extraneous details that young teachers find fascinating. The details *are* important — but first, a basic understanding of the principles and context is needed. Thus, the most experienced teachers typically teach the introductory courses.

8. John C. Whitcomb Jr., *The Genesis Flood: An Investigation of Its Geographical Extent, Geologic Effects and Chronological Setting* (Th.D. dissertation, Grace Theological Seminary, May 1957), 452 pages.

## Teaching on Genesis and Evolution

Each of the courses assigned to John Whitcomb worked in a complementary fashion to prepare for the writing of his thesis on Noah's Flood, and eventually the book that he coauthored with Henry Morris, *The Genesis Flood*. The principles and skills of Hebrew Exegesis unlocked the meaning of the words of Scripture penned in the Book of Genesis and other passages. The historical and theological issues were included in the O.T. Historical Books course and The Pentateuch. The course on Christian Evidences and Apologetics built on the foundation of a deep understanding of what the text actually says and builds on the framework of history, philosophy, theology, and the natural sciences.

Designing the course on Apologetics would be the biggest teaching challenge. Whitcomb had the advantage of being a student during discussions surrounding the gap theory and Noah's Flood at Grace just three years earlier. He understood all the basic arguments for the various theories of the timing of creation and the fossils within geological strata — with a working knowledge of the fields of geology and paleontology from courses at Princeton University. Now, as a teacher, he believed that he could modify and develop the course to a significant degree — while remaining orthodox and embracing the clear teaching of the Holy Scriptures.

Having been *taught* the gap theory as a way of harmonizing the Bible and the theory of evolution in seminary is one thing, but taking a stance to *oppose* the gap theory in front of a class of seminary students who were previously taught the gap theory *and* evolution was another. Furthermore, what he understood to be the clear Genesis account and his interpretation of various geological and scientific evidences[9] would require teaching against the position held by *all* of the other Grace Theological Seminary professors and most of the Christian world. But

---

9. It appears that Whitcomb never tried to defend the gap theory. Teaching Genesis and Hebrew Exegesis first helped establish that the Scriptures were unambiguous in describing creation and the Flood. He was clearly aware of the historical controversies on creation and the Flood and studied Rehwinkel in the fall of 1951 in preparation for the Apologetics class (Alfred M. Rehwinkel, *The Flood in the Light of the Bible, Geology, and Archaeology* [Saint Louis, MO: Concordia Publishing House, 1951], 372 pages). Furthermore, in his diary account of his class on The Pentateuch for February 6, 1952, he stated that he discussed the Flood account (Genesis 7 and 8) using Rehwinkel and the Babylonian Deluge account — i.e., a recent global Flood perspective.

if the Sacred Text was clear and unequivocal, then the interpretation of extra-biblical evidences, as framed and presented by evolutionists and the gap theory, must somehow be wrong. Whitcomb, previously captivated and energized by Wilbur Smith's book *Therefore Stand*, believed that now was the time to use his God-given abilities — to STAND.

Whitcomb chose to divide the course on Christian Evidences and Apologetics into two sections: Apologetics proper and Evolution. The teaching outline for the second half of spring semester 1952 was as follows:

| | |
|---|---|
| April 15, 1952 | Introductory lecture on Evolution |
| April 22, 1952 | Proofs from Geology and Geographical distribution of animals |
| April 23, 1952 | Lamark, Darwin and De Vries hypotheses of species[10] |
| April 24, 1952 | Mendel's law and genetics |
| April 25, 1952 | Ape-man and the "Missing Link" |
| April 29, 1952 | Conclusion of Evolution and begin the Flood: Physical conditions before the Flood |
| April 30, 1952 | Noah's Ark: its size and capacity |
| May 1, 1952 | The cosmic changes involved in the Flood: Climate, earthquakes, fissures |
| May 6, 1952 | The Mammoth as an evidence for the Flood |
| May 8, 1952 | Flood Traditions (included reading the Babylonian account) |
| May 13, 1952 | Discussion on the date of the Flood |

The Apologetics course was taught without apology, using the literal-historical-grammatical interpretation method, but Whitcomb did not understand the importance of a presuppositional perspective until 1955. However, this strong fundamental, biblical approach was apparently a breath of fresh air to many Bible-believing students and was well received by the students in general.[11]

---

10. Note that the neo-Darwinism/synthetic theory of evolution came *after The Genesis Flood* was published.

11. Henry Morris reported that "Whitcomb began teaching strict creationist position in his classes and found an excellent response from his students. Previously, the Grace faculty, including its distinguished president, Dr. Alva J. McClain, had been teaching

Whitcomb would not teach Genesis and Apologetics again until the fall of 1953, and efforts to develop his ideas was put on the back burner. In the fall of 1952, four *new* courses were added to his teaching schedule. These included Psalms and the O.T. Poetic Books in the seminary and World History and Spanish in the college. He also focused on his Master of Theology thesis (see Chapter 15 on *Darius the Mede*), which he finished in April 1953.

As he was completing his master's thesis, Whitcomb determined to continue in his education to earn a doctorate. On January 26, 1953, he met with Dr. Hoyt about receiving eight hours of credit toward a Th.D. for research courses related to his area of interest. Dr. McClain then met him on February 23 with some ideas on writing his dissertation within the area of theology. But Whitcomb had other ideas.

On May 15, 1953, John C. Whitcomb received his Th.M. degree and headed west for his wedding (Chapter 16). Alva J. McClain also traveled to California to conduct the wedding ceremony. McClain took advantage of the trip to conduct a Bible conference, including a special lecture on June 4, 1953, on the gap theory! Whitcomb heard the lecture, packing some of the contents in the back of his mind. The forefront of his mind remained occupied with the wedding, the honeymoon, and setting up a new home in Winona Lake, Indiana.

*Doctoral Dissertation to Focus on Genesis and Evolution*

In mid-August 1953, Whitcomb set aside his books from the spring semester and dusted off his earlier notes and references to focus his efforts on the Book of Genesis and other relevant documents, beginning with Leupold.[12] These efforts further solidified his convictions on the early earth from a biblical perspective, derived from deep study and careful hermeneutics.

The idea to write a dissertation on the Flood described in Genesis had been growing for many years. Whitcomb documented

---

the gap theory, but Whitcomb was able to help many of them see the scriptural validity of recent creation." Henry M. Morris, *History of Modern Creationism*, second edition (Santee, CA: Institute for Creation Research, 1993), 165.

12. Herbert C. Leupold, *Exposition of Genesis: Volumes 1 and 2* (Baker Book House and others). Originally published in 1942, this classic commentary has gone through multiple printings.

his long-standing interest in the preface of his doctoral dissertation, completed in May 1957:

> Since the year 1942, when I was first introduced to the fascinating subjects of geology and paleontology at Princeton University, I have been deeply interested in the relationship between the Book of Genesis and the modern scientific theories concerning the history of the earth and its inhabitants. This interest has been greatly intensified during the six years of teaching graduate courses in Genesis and Christian Apologetics at Grace Theological Seminary. In these courses, without exception, a careful study of the Biblical account of Creation and the Flood has produced a desire on the part of teacher and students alike to investigate more carefully the possibilities for reconciling the record of Scriptures with a record of the rocks.

*American Scientific Association Meeting at*
*Grace Theological Seminary*

Grace Seminary hosted the annual meeting of the American Scientific Affiliation (ASA) in Winona Lake just before the 1953 fall semester. This was a great opportunity for Whitcomb, who had been updating and strengthening his class on Christian Evidences and Apologetics to enhance the second half of the course, now dedicated to issues of creation and the Flood, with the perspectives of Christian scientists. The conference lasted from September 1 to September 3, 1953.

The ASA was formed in 1941 by Dr. Irwin Moon, the speaker who triggered Henry Morris's interest in critically evaluating geology from the perspective of the Genesis Flood (Chapter 18), and F. Alton Everest, who was a Christian teaching electoral engineering at Oregon State College.[13] The purpose was to integrate and organize the efforts of many individuals desiring to correlate the facts of science and the Holy Scripture, to promote and encourage the study of the relationship between the facts of science and the Holy Scriptures, and to promote the dissemination of the results of such studies. The organization grew

---

13. From American Scientific Affiliation (http://www.asa3.org/ASA/PSCF/) and Henry M. Morris, *History of Modern Creationism*, Second edition (Santee, CA: Institute for Creation Research, 1993), 147–162.

rapidly, attracting scientists, preferably with an M.S. or Ph.D., to join and participate in writing papers and participating in conferences. However, the leaders of the association were becoming progressively opposed to conservative interpretation of the Scriptures and to recent creation and a global Flood, and in favor of theistic evolution.

John Whitcomb eagerly attended the ASA conference at Grace in the fall of 1953. A summary of his diary notes highlighted the speakers and key perspectives — with a providential encounter on September 3.

> September 1, 1953. *The conference started at 9:30 AM. Heard Drs. Everest, Bauman, McClain, Tinkle[14] and Mixter give reports, followed by scientific papers Henry Weaver, Jr and M.T. Brackbill. At 1:30 Dr. Mixter read a paper on Evolutionary Literature in the 1950's.*
>
> September 2, 1953. The usefulness of some of the lectures from the first day must have been less than anticipated since, rather than listening to more lectures, Whitcomb spent the morning in his office preparing notes for his classes. He visited the ASA meeting again to pick up copies of the ASA Journal and to read Kulp's attack on the deluge theory of geology.
>
> September 3, 1952. *At 9:00 I heard Dr. Henry Morris present a paper on the Deluge Theory of Geology before the ASA. He was criticized by several. Two other papers were read on physics and geology. Afterwards I spoke briefly to Dr. Morris. . . . Attended the afternoon session at which Mr. Sinclair read a paper on genetics which refuted evolution.*

The next day, Whitcomb finished reading Tinkle's paper on biology (presented on September 1) and then returned to his classes. He gained a deeper understanding of the arguments for a global Flood and the surprising antagonism against this view by a number of Christian scientists and science hobbyists.

Following the ASA conference, Whitcomb had a little over a week to fine-tune his classes, meet with faculty, and welcome new students. He

---

14. William Tinkle, Ph.D., was a zoologist, geneticist, and mathematician who was active in the ASA and became a founding member of the Creation Research Society in 1963, serving as secretary.

corresponded with several authors, including a letter to Henry M. Morris, Ph.D., asking him to forward a copy of his presentation to the ASA. Morris's response of September 22, 1953, stated:

> It is very encouraging to have found that there are a number of other very capable Christian scholars who believe that the Scriptural evidence requires acceptance of a literal, six-day creation and a subsequent universal Deluge, regardless of ephemeral geological theories. . . .
>
> I have been trying to write a book of my own for some time, setting forth a scientific and Scriptural exposition of the geologic data, harmonizing the latter with the basic facts of a recent, genuine Creation, and universal aqueous cataclysm. I hope to find time to get this work finished this year, but there are so many other things continually pressing on one's time. I would surely appreciate your prayers about this.

It would be eight years before these chapters were finally published, after being completely rewritten and integrated with Whitcomb's doctoral dissertation.

*Teaching and Learning During the Fall of 1953*

Classes started in mid-September, and Whitcomb began teaching a revamped and extensive course on Genesis and a complementary class of Christian Evidences and Apologetics. A summary of the class schedule and focused study (in addition to his other courses and responsibilities) noted in Whitcomb's diary follows:

> September 21, 1953 (Monday) *"In [Old Testament] class we finished Genesis 1 and started on 2:1–4. In Evidences class we glanced through more pages in the text, by Keyser."*[15]
>
> September 22, 1953 *"In OT class we discussed the last part of Chapter 2 and 3:1,2. I showed the class my book by*

---

15. Leander S. Keyser, *A System of Christian Evidence*, Tenth edition (Burlington, IA: The Lutheran Literary Board, 1950). Note that this was prior to Whitcomb accepting a presuppositional approach to apologetics advanced by Cornelius Van Til, outlined in Chapter 17.

*Marsh*[16] *on* Evolution, Creation and Science. *Discussed the star-light problem with John Strom.*

September 26, 1953 *"Studied Marsh on Evolution."*

September 30, 1953 *"In OT class we began a discussion on the Flood and its universality."*

October 1, 1953 *"In OT class we finished the discussion on the Flood, and I read from the Gilgamesh Epic."*

October 3, 1953 (Saturday) *"Got an article in the Saturday Evening Post at the library on Carbon 14."*

October 4, 1953 (Sunday) *"We went to have dinner with Homer and Beverley* [Kent Jr]. *I discussed the Flood Geology Theory with Homer."*

October 6, 1953 *"Did some reading in Marsh's volume on Evolution."*

October 7, 1953 *"Read more on evolution."*

October 9, 1953 *"Studied my evolution book"*

October 10, 1953 *"Wrote to Dr. Irvin A. Wills at John Brown Univ."*[17]

October 12, 1953 *"In OT we discussed Gen 16, 17 and I handed out mimeographed papers by* **Morris on Recent Creation and Universal Deluge.** *"*

October 24, 1953 *"We got several books at the Herald this morning including Clark, the New Diluvialism."*[18]

November 2, 1953  *"Read Ramm."*[19] (Ramm's book argued

---

16. Frank Lewis Marsh, *Evolution, Creation and Science* (Silver Spring, MD: Review and Herald Publishing Association, 1947), 381 pages.

17. Dr. Irvin A. Wills was a dominant figure in John Brown University history. He had a B.S. from Wheaton College and a master's and doctorate degrees from the State University of Iowa. He was a professor of biology from 1935–1974 and sponsor of the Science Club for several decades (see https://www.jbu.edu/giving/endowed/list/?id=11221).

18. Harold W. Clark, *The New Diluvialism* (Angwin, CA: Science Publications, 1946), 222 pages. Harold W. Clark was a Seventh-day Adventist science teacher. Clark's book laid out his theory of ecological zonation in opposition to Price. According to Clark, the regular order to the fossil record could be explained on the basis of changes in elevation as the Flood waters rose and buried successive ecosystems.

19. Bernard Ramm, *The Christian View of Science and Scripture* (Grand Rapids, MI: Eerdmans Publishing Company, 1954). Ramm was a leading neo-evangelical who was Professor of Religion at Baylor University until 1957 when he studied for a year under Karl Barth. In 1958, he moved to American Baptist Seminary of the West at Covina, California, where he was Professor of Systematic Theology. Whitcomb's diary tracks his focused study of this book through November 6, 1953, and multiple times afterword.

that the Genesis Flood was local — although "appeared" to be universal and "appeared" to wipe out the human race, but it really didn't. He supported progressive creationism, also known as theistic evolution. This book was rejected by conservative biblical scholars and embraced by liberal scholars — but never adequately answered until the publishing of *The Genesis Flood* in 1961. Note references to this book below.)

November 5, 1953 *"Studied Marsh on Evolution."* [20]

November 14, 1953 (Saturday) *"Went to the office and worked on my evolution notes until 5:30 PM. Mrs. Male had finished mimeographing the Deluge articles of Henry Morris (200 copies)."*

November 16, 1953 *"In evolution class we discussed definitions and the Christian view of baramin."* [21]

November 28, 1953 *"Wednesday — evolution class. Refuted the 'Similarity of Adult Organisms' view."*

December 7, 1953 *"In apologetics class we discussed vestigial organs and geology."*

December 8, 1953 *"I studied my evolution material on Proof from Geography for tomorrow."*

December 9, 1953 *"In Apologetics class we discussed the difficulties of the geology view. I studied awhile at school before coming home. Read Handrich on coal formations."* [22]

December 14, 1953 (Monday) *"Apologetics on Geology 'proof.'"*

December 16, 1953 *"Concluded our discussion on the Proof from geography."*

---

Chapter 2 of Prof. Whitcomb's dissertation focused on a point-by-point refutation of Ramm's book.

20. Byron C. Marsh, *After Its Kind*, Second edition (Minneapolis, MN: Augsburg Publishing Company, 1952).

21. "Baramin" is from the Hebrew בָּרָא (*bārāʾ*, "he created") + מִין (*mîʾn*, "kind"), coined by Frank Lewis Marsh in 1941. It defines a set of organisms descended from some originally created species based on the biblical doctrine of special creation. Animals reproduced "after their kind."

22. Theodore L Handrich, *The Creation: Facts, Theories and Faith* (Chicago, IL: Moody Press, 1953).

## Th.D.

*Christmas break*
**1954**
January 4, 1954 *"Evolution class — discussed Darwin &*
*Lamarck's explanation of evolution."*
January 11, 1954 *"Discussed missing links in evidences class."*
January 21, 1954 *"At 1:00 I gave Evidences Final. Dr. Hoyt*
*spoke to me about some student criticisms . . ."* [emphasis
added].

The fall semester had been a whirlwind since Whitcomb also taught other seminary, college, and Sunday school classes, and he preached and traveled — plus the ongoing graduate work and a new wife. The pace and intensity of this schedule remains hard to imagine! Nobody can continue this pace indefinitely.

### Time Under the Juniper Tree

Although the fall semester ended on January 22, John Whitcomb needed to spend all day on Saturday, January 23, 1954, grading papers from multiple courses. In the evening, he began reading Young[23] on Daniel 1 in preparation to teach The Book of Daniel. Sunday included teaching a class at church on Christ's temptation and then traveling to the Mexican migrant worker's camp near South Whitley, Indiana, to teach an adult Bible class to 12–15 Mexicans in Spanish. He was accompanied by his wife, who was now pregnant and feeling sick. As soon as possible, he wrapped up the outreach efforts and headed back to Winona Lake.

On Monday morning, he was back in the office to finish grading final exams from the last semester, gearing up for the new class in Daniel, as well as teaching philosophy in the college and everything else. It was too much!

As the young husband, future father, student, preacher, and teacher tried to focus on Daniel, he became overwhelmed and deeply discouraged. The volume of teaching and the continued criticism from his students to the dean that his courses were "too hard" was taking its toll.

---

23. Edward J. Young, *The Prophecy of Daniel: A Commentary* (Grand Rapids, MI: Wm. B. Eerdmans Publishing Company, 1947), 330 pages. Edward Young was one of the Westminster Seminary scholars who approached the Book of Daniel from an amillennial perspective.

That evening, John and Senie attended the evening service of the Grace Bible Conference and heard a message by Ivan French on Elijah under the juniper tree.[24] It was an excellent and timely message for John to hear.

Whitcomb spent the next few days attending the Bible Conference and listening to talks and testimonies. The conference ended on Thursday evening, with Friday, January 29, 1954, dedicated as the "Annual Day of Prayer."

The Day of Prayer included a time of personal testimony. John Whitcomb stood and spoke of his discouragement the previous Monday and the blessing of French's message. Afterwards, Dr. Hoyt asked Whitcomb about what happened. Dr. Hoyt contacted Dr. McClain, and McClain in turn spoke to Whitcomb about the Daniel and Philosophy courses that he was expected to teach. McClain listened with interest and concern.

That night, Senie picked John up at the school and surprised him by taking him out for a steak dinner at the Eskimo Inn. When they got home, Dr. Hoyt called him and suggested that he turn over the Daniel course to Homer Kent Jr., and Whitcomb (gladly) agreed. He would also give up teaching the college courses on World History and Philosophy — *after* the spring 1954 semester.

John Whitcomb continued to teach Old Testament Historical Books in the seminary and World History and Philosophy courses

---

24. The juniper tree story is from 1 Kings 19 about Elijah after the confrontation with the prophets of Baal on Mount Carmel where he called down fire from heaven to burn the sacrifice, which had been soaked in water, and then killed 450 prophets of Baal and 400 prophets of the Asherah (1 Kings 18). The juniper tree is about God's care and provision when His servants reach the end of their reserves — and collapse. 1 Kings 19 (NASB 1995) begins, "Now Ahab told Jezebel all that Elijah had done, and how he had killed all the prophets with the sword. Then Jezebel sent a messenger to Elijah, saying, 'So may the gods do to me and even more, if I do not make your life as the life of one of them by tomorrow about this time.' And he was afraid and arose and ran for his life and came to Beersheba, which belongs to Judah, and left his servant there. But he himself went a day's journey into the wilderness, and came and sat down under a juniper tree; and he requested for himself that he might die, and said, 'It is enough; now, O LORD, take my life, for I am not better than my fathers.' He lay down and slept under a juniper tree; and behold, there was an angel touching him, and he said to him, 'Arise, eat.' Then he looked and behold, there was at his head a bread cake baked on hot stones, and a jar of water. So he ate and drank and lay down again. The angel of the LORD came again a second time and touched him and said, 'Arise, eat, because the journey is too great for you.' So he arose and ate and drank, and went in the strength of that food forty days and forty nights to Horeb, the mountain of God."

in the college. He also continued his own course work and research, with an update on his dissertation proposal. But in addition to the ongoing professional challenges, his wife, Senie, was becoming progressively ill.

In late March, Whitcomb presented his doctoral dissertation plans to Dr. Hoyt. The proposal generated some concerns since a literal interpretation of Genesis, without a gap, was not the position of the other faculty members in the seminary. A few days later, Dr. Hoyt called John back into his office to relay to him various *additional* complaints from the students about the rigor of his Old Testament class. He decided to go home for lunch — and found Dr. Murphy making a house call to tend to Senie. The situation with his wife was critical. It would lead to the loss of their first unborn children, twin girls (see Chapter 16).

*Return to the Flood*

Whitcomb's graduate work on creation, evolution, and the Flood had remained on the back burner since completion of the fall 1953 semester. On May 31, 1954, Senie graduated from Grace College, and Donald Fullerton received his Doctor of Divinity degree from Grace Seminary. The summer included a two-month trip to Iowa to serve as an interim pastor (see Chapter 16).

Finally, on August 9, 1954, while completing his tenure as an interim pastor, Whitcomb returned to his graduate studies and class preparation linked to creation and evolution. He noted in his diary, *"Spent several hours on my evolution notes on the 'proof' from anthropology."* Notes about this study were entered into his diary almost daily, such as *"studied Nelson and Marsh on genetics and mutations," "received a letter from Bernard Ramm,"* and *"finished my evolution notes on genetics, geographical distributions and the seven negatives of special creation."*

On August 16, 1954, he left Iowa and drove 500 miles east to Winona Lake, arriving home late in the evening.

## Establishing a Home and Career

The return to Winona Lake marked the beginning of the future. Jack and Senie bought at house at 315 Kelly Street (which needed cleaning, painting, and minor renovations) and moved into it on August 30. On August 31, they bought a new, blue 1954 Plymouth. After getting settled, the couple held an "open house," which was attended by over 60 friends and well-wishers.

Whitcomb's position at the seminary was also becoming established. His college teaching was now limited to Philosophy — no more World History. Furthermore, his core seminary courses were familiar and only required updating rather than developing from scratch or completely rewriting. He also began planning a greater role in faculty activities as it became clear that his long-term ministry would be at Grace.

For his Christian Evidences and Apologetics course, he further developed the class syllabus and expanded his library of key books and manuscripts. He developed a number of contacts and discussed his views with various Christian leaders who came through Grace (below). On October 27, 1954, for example, he met with the Reverend Jeremiah, president of Cedarville Baptist College in Cedarville, Ohio, and father of a future doctoral student of Dr. Whitcomb's, David Jeremiah.[25] However, on December 31, 1954, Dr. Hoyt *AGAIN* swung by his office to ask him to take it easy on the Old Testament assignments!

## Beginning a Doctoral Dissertation

By January 1955, John Whitcomb had outlined the key elements of his doctoral dissertation and was ready to move forward. On January 11, 1955, he set up a meeting with Dr. Hoyt to discuss the gap theory — which Whitcomb was about to attack. However, as in the previous year, little progress was made during the hectic spring semester. The summer would be reserved for graduate work.

After the famous "Scopes Monkey Trial" in 1925, the majority of the evangelical world conceded to the opinions of atheist scientists and hypothesized about possible ways to integrate the Bible narrative of Genesis (and the rest of the Bible) with the uniformitarianism framework and timeline pushed by the 19th-century evolutionists Lyell, Darwin, and others. Growing criticisms of the theory of evolution arose from the SDA, led by George McCready Price, by scientists and scholars within the Lutheran Church Missouri Synod, and other isolated voices from other denominations.

Whitcomb and other conservative Christians had recently been shocked and alarmed by Bernard Ramm's 1954 book, *The Christian*

---

25. David Jeremiah is the senior pastor of Shadow Mountain Community Church in El Cajon, California. He is also the founder of Turning Point Radio and Television Ministries.

*View of Science and Scripture.* Ramm's view supported the evolution timetable while suggesting that Noah *thought* the Flood was global (which lasted a year), but it wasn't, and that Noah *thought* that all mankind was destroyed, but they weren't. In other words, the narratives of creation and the Flood given in the Bible were false. Worse yet, the book was enthusiastically supported by many Christian leaders, schools of higher education, and religious groups. No high quality, substantive, and scholarly rebuttal to this view was forthcoming, so Whitcomb took on the challenge of focusing much of his thesis on specific issues raised in this volume.

On July 4, 1955, Whitcomb started his thesis work in earnest. He was invited to write a series of articles for the Grace Brethren periodical, *Brethren Missionary Herald* (*Herald*), on the Flood, which would correspond to much of his thesis work. He sought to understand the positions and rationale of many of the 20th century thought and opinion leaders for his dissertation. He typed a questionnaire on creation and the Flood and sent it to the leading authors and authorities to learn how they were dealing with these current controversies. These responses would be integral to Chapter VII, *Flood Geology in the Twentieth Century.*

He spent several (partial) days writing a letter to Dr. Bernard Ramm on his book. Among other things, Ramm had referred to belief in a six-day, literal creation story and a worldwide Flood to explain the fossil record as the "naive-literal view." This letter represented a follow-up of a letter to, and response from, Ramm during the previous summer.

Thesis writing took a brief hiatus from July 12–26, 1955, to take Dr. Van Til's course at Winona Lake School of Theology (Chapter 17). And the timing could not have been better. He would not waste time trying to prove the Bible; he would start with the Bible and test the ideas and hypotheses of mortal man against the divine framework of creation and a global Flood.

By July 30, 1955, Whitcomb finished his first *Herald* article on Noah's Flood and submitted it for publication.

Throughout August and September, he critically reviewed major books and articles on topics related to creation and the Flood. As he finished his critique, he wrote detailed letters to the authors to address specific issues and clarify or defend their perspectives. He also began receiving letters in response to his questionnaire and began making plans to correspond with or interview as many leaders as possible.

On September 8, he submitted his second installment on the Genesis Flood to the *Herald*.

By early fall 1955, Whitcomb finished Part III of the dissertation, *The Chronological Setting of the Flood*, including Chapter IX, "The Genealogies of Genesis 5 and 11," and Chapter X, "A Chronological Setting for Adam and Noah."

## The Insurmountable Problem

While Whitcomb was making headway on the biblical, hermeneutical, exegetical, and historical issues, he found himself struggling to critically assess some of the scientific hypotheses and the implications of some of the issues that were being debated. He therefore reached out to one of the few men he believed was a devoted, Bible-believing Christian; a respected scientist in the area of geology, hydrodynamics, and floods; and an articulate writer. On September 16, 1955, he wrote the following letter.

> Dr. Henry M. Morris
> 512 Taft St.
> Lafayette, Louisiana.
>
> Dear Dr. Morris:
>
> Perhaps you will recall our correspondence of two years ago concerning your article on "The Biblical Evidence for a Recent Creation and Universal Deluge". Since then I have done much studying and thinking on these problems, especially in connection with my forthcoming (1957?) doctoral dissertation on Creation and the Flood, and I am more convinced than ever that a biblical catastrophism is the correct solution to the so-called evidence for vast geological ages.
>
> In your letter of December 5, 1953, you mentioned that you were working on a book which would deal with some of these problems. I am wondering if you have made further progress, and if so, whether I could somehow share in the fruits of your investigations. On the other hand, I have

some very interesting documents that might be of great help to you. If you would be interested in seeing these, I shall be happy to send them. Under separate cover I am mailing some notes that you might like to glance thorough in your spare moments.

May the Lord richly bless you as you continue to serve him.

Sincerely,
John C. Whitcomb Jr.

Within two weeks, Morris replied with a few recommended books and questions of what Whitcomb meant with the statement in his September 16 letter, "I have some very interesting documents that might be of great help to you." Whitcomb responded on October 8, 1955, with a three-page, single-spaced, narrow-margin outpouring of progress in his analysis of the major Christian leaders' positions and their view of strength and weaknesses of other experts' theories. The following excerpt outlined Whitcomb's concerns, beginning about halfway through the long letter.

My purpose in burdening you with all of these results of my questionnaire (and I could, of course, go on and on) is to show that evangelicals are confused, very confused, on these basic matters. And Dr. Ramm is not an exception to this statement.

The letter continues, describing many of the negative views published by Christian periodicals on Ramm's book, such as a Prof. Kuschke of Westminster Seminary, who labeled it as "a desperately bad book." Whitcomb also noted Ramm's book had "aroused the wrath of many, including [a lists of Christian leaders] . . . I have talked personally to all of these this summer except Witmer, Lindsell, Unger and Allis. But it is going to take more than wrath to undo the frightening effects of this book." He continues,

Even if I had no other reason for wishing to write a dissertation on Creation and the Flood, Dr. Ramm's book would be sufficient incentive for me. To me, his book is final proof of the logical absurdities to which one is driven as an evangelical by following uniformitarian geology. So now we are told that the Flood was not only geographically local, but also anthropologically local! If the book serves no other purpose, it will at least show us the alternatives. **But here is my problem**. The minute I open my mouth about the geological effects of the Flood, or put my thoughts into print (see enclosed sample), I am told that I have no right to say anything, because I do not have a Ph.D. in geology![26] So you see, I must depend upon those who have received the training in such fields, as you yourself have, and quote from their works. Note, for example, how Ramm ridicules Price for his lack of 'scientific' training (footnote, p. 181). Where are the Ph.D.'s in geology today who take Genesis 6–9 seriously? [emphasis added]

Whitcomb goes on to detail specific observations and questions about several topics and ask for help in obtaining various references, etc. He concludes the letter with:

> May our Lord richly reward you for our faithful service to Him in these trying days, and give you ample strength to carry on the important work He has committed in your hands.

*Morris Responds*

On October 8, Whitcomb received a letter from Morris acknowledging that he received and enjoyed the letter and agreed with Whitcomb's assessment of Ramm's book. He noted that Stacy Woods, general secretary of Inter-Varsity Christian Fellowship, and the IVCF leaders were "greatly disturbed by Ramm's book, and are taking a strong stand against it" (see Chapter 14 and gracious letter from Woods). He concluded by noting that "Your remark about 'closed-shop' geology is all

---

26. Note that Whitcomb had a strong undergraduate education in geology and paleontology from Princeton and rigorous engineering training from Virginia Polytechnical Institution between 1942 and 1944. This gave him the foundation and background to study and understand the writing and arguments of authors and experts in these fields. He did not, however, conduct independent research studies, publish peer-reviewed papers in geology, or obtain the academic credentials that are typically required to be taken seriously by competitors or detractors.

too true," as he went on to describe how one young Christian trainee was forced to hide his belief in the Genesis Flood to get his Ph.D. and to obtain a faculty position. Morris also sent Whitcomb his manuscript, *in progress,* on the scientific aspects of a global Flood.

On November 1, 1955, Whitcomb sent another long letter to Morris in which he endorsed, but also critiqued, Morris's work.

> Dear Dr. Morris:
>
> I am indeed grateful for your willingness to send me your manuscript on "The creation and Destruction of the World." When it arrived Saturday morning I was amazed at its size. And since I have been reading it, I have been amazed at the wealth of information you have gathered and the great skill with which you have presented it. I think you have done a tremendous piece of work — a <u>magnum opus</u> — which will prove to be of encouragement to those who dare to take Genesis seriously, and a scholarly challenge to those Christians who do not seem prepared to do so as yet. I might say at this point (for what it is worth) that I hope you will not feel rushed to get this work into print. By that I mean to say, I hope you will take the time to <u>multiply</u> references, important quotations, illustrations, arguments, and bibliographical material to such an extent that your book will prove to be a textbook or reference work rather than a semi-popular work [emphasis added].

The rest of the letter was a series of editorial comments, typos, etc. It also included this recommendation,

> Before leaving Chap. 3, may I suggest that the confidence of your readers would be encouraged if you omitted the following remark on p. 6 — "the writer makes no claims of being a geologist or having much technical knowledge of geology." In addition to the fact that "new deists" will use this statement to their advantage, it is, I feel, an overstatement of the case. Anyone who reads Chapters 2–6 of our proposed book will certainly be justified in thinking that you write with some technical knowledge, and that you have some knowledge

of geology from the practical standpoint, even though your Ph.D. is not in geology as such. In other words, let the burden of proof rest upon the "uniformitarians" to show that you have no right to speak on such matters. How much, actually, does any "geologist" really <u>know</u> about his subject, apart from what he hears and reads?

Whitcomb added one more important suggestion,

> Finally, in Chapter 2, pp 122 and following, you present some of the "theistic proofs" to support the Christian position, "to which all straight-thinking people would literally be driven by the inescapable facts and logic of the situation" (p. 133). In discussing this subject in my Apologetics class this fall, I received tremendous help from Dr. Cornelius Van Til's new book, <u>The Defense of the Faith</u>. ... he shows the right and wrong methods of reaching intellectuals with the Truth, and reveals some of the basic weaknesses of the "theistic proofs" in accomplishing this task.

After this brief but intense interaction, Whitcomb returned to his teaching, family, and dissertation while Morris moved to Virginia to serve as chairman of the Department of Civil Engineering. They would finally reactivate their long-distance collaboration in January of 1957.

The Whitcomb diaries of the fall of 1955 are filled with notes on his reading, writing, correspondence with various Christian leaders (e.g., excerpts of letters with Henry Morris, above), and completing of installments 4 and 5 of his series on the Genesis Flood for the *Herald*. He again taught Christian Evidences and Apologetics. He also made two trips to Grand Rapids, Michigan, in early November and December linked to Calvin Theological Seminary and conferences of the Evangelical Theological Society and American Scientific Affiliation, where he interviewed key leaders in the fields of theology and the sciences.

## Child #1

Of personal interests, on December 7, 1955, John Whitcomb's wife gave birth to their first child, the author of his biography. Since none of the faculty and students at Grace Seminary smoked cigars, young Professor Whitcomb handed out Hershey's' chocolate bars.

Th.D.

## 1956

The entire year of 1956 was consumed with graduate teaching and graduate research. He took several trips to the Chicago area to use the library of Northwestern University and to interview various faculty members at Wheaton College on science and evolution. He finished his series of articles for the *Herald* in May and took his qualifying exam in Greek. During the summer, he finished his primary research and focused on writing the dissertation. He also took advantage of Christian leaders visiting Winona Lake during the summer and the School of Theology, including visiting with Cornelius Van Til and Wilber Smith, and listening to internationally acclaimed speakers, including Dr. Martin Lloyd Jones and Billy Graham, preach at the Tabernacle. After finishing a draft of the first three chapters, he made copies and sent them to a number of Christian leaders for comments.

By August 7, John was again exhausted. He wrote an unusually brief entry for the day in his diary, *"Became tired of working on my thesis. Read up on Antarctica in the National Geographic."* The next day's entry was *"Cut grass & relaxed."* He did nothing more for two weeks — except an occasional game of chess with Sib.

*ASA Meeting in Wheaton, Illinois*

On Thursday, August 23, John Whitcomb got back in the saddle, leaving Winona Lake by car for Wheaton, Illinois, with his wife and son to attend the morning session of the ASA. Controversy was brewing as members of the ASA were preparing chapters for a book to coincide with the upcoming centennial of the publication of Darwin's theory of evolution.[27] Whitcomb interviewed Dr. John Klotz;[28] Dr. Russell L. Mixter (zoology professor at Wheaton College and theistic evolutionist and editor of the proposed centennial book); R. Laird Harris, Ph.D. (Old Testament scholar, Covenant Theological Seminary); Dr. G. Douglas Young (founding president of Jerusalem University College);

---

27. The American Scientific Affiliation's efforts resulted in the book *Evolution and Christian Thought Today*, edited by Russell Mixter (Grand Rapids, MI: Wm. B. Eerdmans Publishing Company, 1959), 224 pages.
28. Dr. John W. Klotz was from a generation of Missouri Synod Lutheran professors and theologians. He went on to earn a Ph.D. in genetics from the University of Pittsburgh and post-docs at Washington University, St. Louis, Missouri, and the University of Minnesota in Minneapolis. He was a founding member of the Creation Research Society.

and Dr. William Tinkle. He would meet these men again! After the meeting, the Whitcombs returned home.

*Fall Semester 1956*

The resumption of classes and the responsibilities of a husband and father slowed progress on the dissertation research. The weekly pattern at Grace Seminary was to have classes Tuesday through Friday, with professors traveling and teaching at Brethren churches on the weekend and Mondays off. This schedule resulted in a pattern of diary entries on Mondays such as *"worked on my thesis most of the day,"* with little progress on other days. However, chapter after chapter was slowly completed.

## 1957

The new year came with acceleration of work on the dissertation. Whitcomb's survey of the thoughts and opinions of the Christian leaders of the day on creation and the Deluge, the series of articles in the *Herald*, and the intense correspondence and personal interviews with many leaders was getting outside attention. Dr. Howard Vos of Moody Press approached Whitcomb about possibly publishing a book on the Genesis Flood, with the condition that it was about 300 pages and that the chapters dealing with the scientific aspects of the Flood were carefully checked or written by a Ph.D. in science. On January 25, Whitcomb wrote to Henry Morris asking for help and suggesting a personal meeting, perhaps the following summer.

By February 7, 1957, the first draft was done and soon delivered to Herman Hoyt, Th.D., John Whitcomb's advisor. From that point on, there were enormous efforts to revise and finalize the dissertation based on the feedback of many.

One week later, Dr. Hoyt called Whitcomb back into his office. There was good news and bad news. The bad news was continued complaints from students that his grading of exams in his Daniel class was too critical. The good news was that he would be promoted to full professor with a $500 raise to $4,100 (a year). The dissertation was looking good!

By now, two problems were evident. First, the dissertation was over 450 pages in length — too long for Moody. Secondly, Whitcomb related a recurring problem to Henry Morris in an April 19, 1957, letter:

You will be interested to see a letter I received recently form John C. Sinclair of the A.S.A. whom I questioned on the Flood. He says in part: "I believe the flood was a local fresh-water inundation. I hope to write a paper on this when I get a chance. **I assume you are not trained in science**, and yet you have come to a conclusion which is at odds with the best scientific data we have at present. This puzzles me. Do you believe that your interpretation of scripture is accurate enough to justify taking such a stand — knowing that if you turn out to be mistaken your conclusion will be another discredit to Evangelical Christianity?" [emphasis added].

After years of study of the Scriptures and the various arguments, Whitcomb was 100% convinced of what the Bible said, and that was that!

May 6, 1957, marked a happy day. Whitcomb's diary entry read: "[James] *Boyer photostated my last thesis diagram. Finished the Table of Contents and list of tables. Hamilton processed the dissertation and I took it to Heckman Bindery in N. Manchester."* The dissertation was done!

*Introduction and Outline of Whitcomb's Dissertation*

**The Genesis Flood: An Investigation of its Geographical Extent, Geologic Effects and Chronological Setting.** John C. Whitcomb Jr., May 1957. 452 pages.

*Excerpts from the Preface*

One fruit of this investigation has been the conclusion that a person's view of the Creation Week will be determined in large measure by his view of the Flood. If the Flood was geographically universal, then uniformitarianism, with its immense geological ages, cannot be a valid interpretive key for the fossiliferous strata. And if uniformitarianism, as it is commonly understood today, is invalid, then it is unnecessary to press "geological ages" into the Creation Week in one way or another.

Another fruit of study has been the rewarding conviction that the proper place to begin an investigation of the history of our planet is not in a geology laboratory, or even in the open field, but rather in the Word of God. In the very nature of the case, men of science must begin their study of the earth with certain basic philosophical presuppositions which were not obtained by scientific method. History itself bears ample witness to this fact. Consequently, unless a man's starting point is the infallible Word of God, it cannot be expected that he will succeed in unraveling the mysteries of the world in which he lives.

All of this, of course, is not to say that the Bible is a sufficient textbook of geology and paleontology in itself. No Christian scholar would dream of making such an assertion, nor is that the issue of the present hour. The real issue, it seems to me, that faces contemporary evangelical science, is whether or not the Word of God is to be permitted to exercise its rightful prerogative of establishing the basic framework within which scientific investigation must be carried on. May the Christian anthropologist accept it as a basic starting point, on the basis of the authoritative statements of Scripture, that man was not involved from lower forms of life but rather was created directly by God; and then, from this point, go on in his studies? May the Christian geologist and paleontologist pursue his investigations of the earth's crust with the confident assurance that the Scriptures are to be trusted when they state repeatedly that in the days of Noah God sent a year-long universal Deluge to destroy all land life except that which was in the Ark? Or must the Scriptures be pressed, somehow, into the changing molds of modern thought concerning the early history of the earth and its inhabitants? That, to me, is the supreme question which must be answered by the Christian man of science today.

Since I am persuaded that an ultimately fruitful study of geology and paleontology, insofar as it seeks to understand the <u>history</u> of the earth rather than its present status, must be carried on within the framework of revealed truth, I make no apology for building my entire case upon exegetical and hermeneutical considerations. And if the case is lost, it will have to be lost on the battleground of the Hebrew and Greek text of Scriptures, not on the steep and slippery heights of mountains which were never endowed with the ability of telling men about the history of the earth as Moses and the prophets were.

An overview of the dissertation is provided by the Table of Contents.

---

29. A mode of argumentation that seeks to establish a contention by deriving an absurdity from its denial, thus arguing that a thesis must be accepted because its rejection would be untenable (from Internet Encyclopedia of Philosophy, IEP, https://www.iep.utm. edu/reductio/, accessed January 21, 2020).

## Graduation Day!

After nearly a decade of graduate work, John C. Whitcomb Jr. became Dr. John C. Whitcomb Jr., Th.D. The day was May 29, 1957. Whitcomb noted in his diary,

> "GOT my **_Th.D Degree_** – had a party at home. Folks gave $50."

# Chapter 20

# The Genesis of *The Genesis Flood*

"The Battle Between the Whales and the Elephants"
1957–1961

## Changing a Dissertation into a Book

Immediately upon receiving a bound copy of the dissertation on May 11, 1957, Dr. Whitcomb mailed his personal copy of "The Genesis Flood" dissertation to Moody Press, care of Dr. Howard Vos. After a two-month review, Dr. Vos phoned him from Evanston, Illinois, to tell him that **Moody Press would publish "The Genesis Flood"** *if* it were reduced to **300 pages**.

Whitcomb cleared his calendar and, beginning July 15, spent nearly every day on "Flood revisions." This effort continued through early September.

## Child #2

On August 14, 1957, Edisene complained of cramps, so they drove to the hospital in Columbia City, about 15 miles east of Winona Lake. At 11:45 a.m., Senie gave birth to a strong little boy. They named him Donald in honor of Donald Fullerton.

*Eerdmans*

The next day, August 15, John Whitcomb swung by the bookstore and ran into his old friend Bill Eerdmans, who came into town as a book salesman. The two former soldiers discussed old times and the Genesis Flood. Bill offered to have the dissertation reviewed by the editors of Eerdmans Publishing company in Grand Rapids. Two days later, Mr.

Wm. B. Eerdmans (Bill's dad and president of Eerdmans Publishing) gave Dr. Whitcomb a personal call as well. However, on September 24, Dr. Whitcomb learned that the Flood book was rejected. Three months later, they did agree to publish *Darius the Mede*.

*Back to Moody*

By September 2, 1957, Whitcomb had completely rewritten the first seven chapters of *The Genesis Flood* for Moody. He made multiple copies of this "work in progress" and sent them to a number of scholars and critical reviewers for their comments. One of the scholars who received a copy of the manuscript and a detailed letter was Henry Morris.

Henry Morris replied on October 7 with a three-page, single-space, narrow-margin response. Within it he noted the many small corrections, insights, and suggestions, but also included this proposal:

> I had thought at one time to suggest that perhaps you and I might work together on a dual-authorship volume, you dealing with the Scriptural exegesis and theological implications, and I with the scientific problems. However, with the heavy demands on time and energies experienced by me in recent years, it has seemed impracticable to suggest such a thing, as much as I would like to do it. This might be a possibility for some time in the future, however, if you want to consider it.

John Whitcomb responded within a week with another long letter, including a plea to Morris to help him publish *The Genesis Flood*.

> Dear Brother Morris:
> You will be interested to learn that the first time Dr. Howard Vos of Moody Press suggested that I should submit my dissertation to them for review (about a year ago) we discussed the possibility of having a Christian man of science like yourself write the chapters pertaining to geology and paleontology. I was always favorable to the idea, but remembering your oft-repeated expression of discouragement concerning the lack of time for writing, I never dared make any such suggestion to you. But in recent days I have come to the conclusion that I must say something to you about this. . . .

**Here is my proposition:** will you prayerfully consider undertaking the task of writing one or more chapters for this volume? This has not been an easy decision for me to reach, but one that will honor the Lord in the long run, I am convinced: I will gladly wait for another year or so for you to prepare this material, if you feel led to do so. The more I think about it, the more convinced I am that I would only be doing harm to the cause of biblical truth by rushing a manuscript into print that has weak arguments at crucial points. . . .

Henry Morris responded on October 26, 1957, that he would be "highly honored by such a suggestion, since I think you have done a splendid and thorough job as it stands." But he raised a note of concern in another aspect of Whitcomb's letter, requesting detailed treatment of key issues with heavy references that would lead a pivotal decision. Morris noted, "Its size would thereby become larger by considerable than the publisher appears to desire." Furthermore:

I'm afraid that, to present a geological case that would have a chance of more than a very limited acceptance, a mass of documentation would be necessary on a very wide range of geological subjects — all presented from a new perspective different from that of Price, Clark, etc., but incorporating the major features of their evidences. This obviously is no mean task, and would certainly involve a larger volume than Moody is evidently contemplating, as well as quite a bit of time in its preparation.

Whitcomb responded on November 16, 1958, noting that he was gradually recognizing that if the book "is a faithful setting forth of the Biblical teaching of the Flood and its implications for modern science, the Lord may see fit to use it for His glory in years to come." He would wait another year to see Morris's proposed chapters. He also emphasized,

I want to have this to be a strictly equal enterprise if we go into it together. It would not be Whitcomb on The Genesis Flood with some of the chapters contributed by Morris.

A few days later, Whitcomb sent another letter affirming his conviction that writing a joint book was the right thing to do. He included a draft outline of his perspectives, one that that would closely resemble the final table of contents.

## 1958

Whitcomb and Morris would continue to correspond, but Whitcomb felt that his contribution was essentially done. He awaited Morris's chapters and further suggestions. In the meantime, the vast majority of extra-curricular time and effort went into re-writing *Darius the Mede* for publication by Eerdmans.

On July 11, Dr. Whitcomb received a long-awaited package from Dr. Morris. It was a draft chapter for the new book. He responded,

> August 12, 1958.
> Dear Dr. Morris:
>
> I was very happy to receive your manuscript yesterday, and read it with much interest. I think you have done an excellent piece of work, and I am anticipating the other chapter with great enthusiasm. Please let me assure you that I am not in any great rush to get the volume into print. If it takes you another year to do a good and thorough piece of work, it is well worth waiting for. My only concern would be that my chapters would not add materially to the quality of your book and that you could do a better job than I on the subjects I dealt with in my chapters. For my own part, however, I would consider it a great privilege to be associated with you in the production of a volume of this type, and would be willing to wait until you have completed your chapters. . . .
>
> Your manuscript convinced me of the importance of having a scientific background before writing on scientific subjects! My own efforts in dealing with uniformitarianism certainly reveals the folly of a Biblical scholar trying to come to grips with the geologists! Sort of like **the battle between whales and elephants**. The only corrections I made (in red pencil) were typographical and sentence structure ones. . . .
> Why not divide your later material into at least three chapters? One on the geological implications of Scripture with

suggested divisions of pre- and post-diluvian formations from the actual Flood deposits. Another on the geological disciplines other than historical geology. And still another on a refutation of arguments against flood geology. This would give you ample room for each discussion and yet not make your chapters top-heavy. The trend in books today is more and more toward smaller chapters, I believe.

The remainder of the year was tied up with a trip to Puerto Rico for the foreign mission society where there was a Bible institute; teaching; finalizing *Darius the Mede*; and starting to write chapters for Wycliff Bible Commentary on Ezra, Nehemiah, and Esther.

## Child #3

Jack and Senie welcomed their *first daughter*, Constance Salome Whitcomb, into the world on October 14.

## 1959

On January 25, 1959, Dr. Whitcomb wrote back to Dr Morris, assuring him that he was still "in the land of the living"! He noted that Morris had made tremendous progress and that "your manuscript was a source of great joy to me, as I read page after page of excellent material, thoroughly documented." Indeed, Dr. Morris made so much progress that the idea was floated to publish the book in 1959! This letter contained numerous suggestions and recommendations on how to handle some of the material from Dr. Whitcomb's dissertation on Flood geology in the 20th century, which was shortened and modified while developing a detailed, annotated bibliography, etc.

The letters began flowing rapidly between the two men, with many suggestions as each worked on the other's chapters, working to integrate all of the data and arguments into a cohesive volume — regardless of the eventual length or technical detail that both agreed was needed.

Henry Morris remembers working through some of the most difficult sections. He later wrote,[1]

> Time and again, after encountering a difficult geological (or other) problem, I would pray about it, and then a reasonable

---

1. H.M. Morris, *History of Modern Creationism*, Second edition (Santee, CA: Institute For Creation Research, 1993), 172–173.

solution would somehow quickly come into my mind or hand, and the manuscript gradually took shape. I had to add another lengthy chapter on the problems of Biblical geology and all three of my chapters went through two complete rewrites before I got them into final form. The same was true of Whitcomb's chapters.

When Dr. Whitcomb heard that Dr. Morris would be in Pittsburgh for a meeting during the week of June 15, 1959, he decided to rearrange his own schedule so that the two could have their first face-to-face meeting since September 1953.

*Pittsburgh Meeting*

My father told me on several occasions how useful the Pittsburgh meeting was where the two authors met face-to-face and hammered out the essence of the final manuscript. The record of the meeting from Dr. Whitcomb's diary is summarized.

> Sunday, June 14, 1959. *"Arrived at 4:45 AM by train and proceeded to the Webster Hall Hotel. Henry Morris came at 8:00. Discussed ASA meeting and reviewed letters of people who read Morris' manuscript. Walked several blocks for lunch after making corrects in his MS. Slept several hours, and my manuscript arrived by special delivery. . . . We then began going through my chapters & looked over Rushdoony's revised Introduction."*

> Monday, June 15, 1959. *"We spent the morning going through the rest of my chapters and making some large revisions. Morris will have his secretary retype the entire manuscript after his geology corrections are received. Went to the Cathedral of Learning tower. . . . Took 7:00 limousine to airport and plane to N.Y."*

He changed airplanes and headed on to Puerto Rico on behalf of the Brethren foreign missions.

Rousas Rushdoony was an Orthodox Presbyterian pastor in California. He was highly enthusiastic about *The Genesis Flood* and was asked to write the introduction, as noted in Dr. Whitcomb's notes above. He was also a friend of Charles Craig, a Princeton alumnus with a background in geology and related sciences who ran a small independent publishing company called Presbyterian and Reformed Publishing Company. After returning from Puerto Rico, Dr. Whitcomb found letters waiting for him from Rushdoony and Vos.[2] Rushdoony, hearing that Moody was unlikely to publish a larger book, independently contacted Charles Craig and urged him to consider offering Moody Press to print 1,000 copies of a complete, 400+ page manuscript for the first printing. Vos was surprised and made no promises since he had still not seen a copy of the manuscript. Dr. Whitcomb received a letter from Vos in August, suggesting that Moody was still interested in the book.

In the meantime, Dr. Morris's secretary was retyping the entire manuscript while Whitcomb returned to writing his commentary on Ezra, Nehemiah, and Esther; teaching; preaching; and caring for his family. It appeared that the book would be done by October. However, the continued editing, dribbling in of comments and reviews from various readers, and expansion of appendices pushed the volume's completion into the next year.

## 1960

On January 19, 1960, Whitcomb noted in his diary, *"Finally finished Appendix II for the Flood book."* January 23, *"Worked most of the day revising my chapter II on the American Indians and the Flood."* January 28, *"Henry Morris sent his photo illustrations for the book."*

Apparently, Moody was having second thoughts since the six-day creation and global Flood was controversial and in contrast to other books that Moody was publishing,[3] which would likely diminish the strength of their endorsement and vigor of their promotion. However, on February 6, 1960, Whitcomb noted in his diary, *"Letter from Vos finally came, accepting* The Genesis Flood *for publication and enclosing contract. I wrote to Morris, encouraging him to have Craig do the Publishing."*

Three days later, Whitcomb wrote in his diary, *"Phoned Henry Morris and he wants Craig to publish for us. Phoned Vos and asked him*

---

2. Letter from John Whitcomb to Henry Morris, June 25, 1959.
3. H.M. Morris, *History of Modern Creationism*, Second edition (Santee, CA: Institute For Creation Research, 1993), 173.

*to send us the MS. Phoned Craig to tell him we want him to publish The Genesis Flood.*" On February 16, the original copy of *The Genesis Flood* manuscript arrived from Moody.

Whitcomb re-reviewed the entire manuscript for punctuation errors. He also received copies from other reviewers with marginal notes that were each addressed. On March 7, he received more corrections from Morris. They also needed a preface and asked one to be written by Dr. McCampbell.

On March 25, more revised pages came from Morris. Finally, on March 31, 1960, Dr Whitcomb noted in his diary, *"Made final corrections in the Flood MS (except Appendix II) and mailed it to Craig in the evening!"*

In early April, Dr. Whitcomb received a long letter from Mr. Craig telling of a probable three-month delay in publishing *The Genesis Flood*. It would not come out until 1961. Dr. Whitcomb responded by sending the last addition, Appendix II, to Mr. Craig. Now it was time to wait.

*Summer of 1960*

Dr. Whitcomb's schedule kept him very busy in May and June, including a trip to New Jersey and New York, and a trip to California for the Grace Brethren's California-Arizona District Conference.

On a personal note, many fond memories also came to me in reviewing the daily diary entries about family events in the late 1950s and early 1960s. These typically included comments on painting rooms in the house (*"the boys got into the white paint"*), errands into town (*"I took David with me"*), organizing a new office (*"David helped me put books on the shelf"*), or, my favorite, *"Took the boys to Pike Lake to swim and took pictures."* He also spent time taking his wife, sister-in-law, and other ladies to Fort Wayne, Indiana, 35 miles east of Winona Lake for shopping. He did not follow the shoppers, carrying their purses, bags, or pushing a shopping cart, but rather would sit in the car in silence, reading or grading papers. His only reward was to stop at a favorite Chinese restaurant for dinner or at least a dairy for ice cream!

On June 12, Dr. Whitcomb received galley proofs of *The Genesis Flood*. The next six weeks were spent with detailed review. The daily diary entries often only said, *"galley proofs."*

*Visit of the Henry Morris Family to Winona Lake*

It is important for academic professors, such as Henry Morris, Ph.D., to attend professional society meetings and conferences to hear the latest research results, to ask questions, and to meet other faculty and students in strategic side meetings. It is where national and international business and positioning is done.

Dr. Henry Morris needed to attend a Civil Engineering Conference at the University of Michigan in July 1960, so he decided to drive, with his family, and swing by Winona Lake for a visit. The families enjoyed a Fourth of July picnic together, as well as other vacation events. Drs. Whitcomb and Morris used much of the time to review the galley proofs and make corrections. Dr. Morris went on to his conference, returning on July 13 for further discussions on the book, which included Charles Craig, who came in for the meetings.

Dr. Whitcomb continued to review every detail. On July 27, 1960, he happily wrote in his diary, *"Sent off final (!!) corrections to Craig and Morris, air mail, special delivery."*

## Child #4

On August 24, 1960, Dr. Whitcomb and his wife had their final child. He wrote, *"The nurse phoned at 7:00 to tell me that the water broke at 6:15 and Senie was in labor. At 9:25 she went to the delivery room and Robert Edward Whitcomb was born at 9:46, 21 ½ inches, 10 lbs 11 oz!!"*

## 1961

The year 1961 was a great year. The manuscript for *The Genesis Flood* was in the hands of the publisher. Drs. Whitcomb and Morris waited with great anticipation to have a copy of the completed book in their hands and to see the response of key scholars, scientists, and Christian leaders when copies were placed in their hands.

*Arrival of the First Copies of the First Printing*

On Saturday, February 11, John Whitcomb celebrated the 31st birthday of his wife Edisene (Senie). The family and friends enjoyed a turkey dinner and watched Senie open presents. Then a letter came in the mail from Mr. Craig saying that *The Genesis Flood* printing was *complete* and the books were shipped to his distribution office.

The long-awaited and eagerly anticipated day for Dr. Whitcomb was Monday, February 20, 1961. He noted in his diary, *"While at school, Senie phoned to say that* The Genesis Flood *had arrived! I went home at once, & found my 25 copies, some bent and soiled because the box had been ripped open a little. Walked to the bookstore with the boys to get jet packs, & mailed copies out to loved ones & friends in the afternoon."* The long journey to the initial goal was done. Now the authors waited to see the response of the readers.

*Visit to Blacksburg, Virginia*

Both Dr. Whitcomb and Dr. Morris had very busy professional lives outside of the grind of being authors. The previous summer, Henry Morris brought his family to Winona Lake to visit the Whitcombs while on his way to a conference in Ann Arbor, Michigan. In May 1961, Whitcomb had a conference in eastern Virginia and decided to take his family with him, swinging down through Virginia in their new Ford station wagon to visit the Morris family.

The Whitcomb family left early on April 29, arriving at the Morrises' home about 8:00 p.m. The next morning was Sunday, and John Whitcomb joined Henry Morris at 7:00 a.m., where Dr. Whitcomb spoke at Gideon's Breakfast. Dr. Whitcomb then joined Dr. Morris to hear him teach Sunday school at a Southern Baptist church, then Morris joined Whitcomb to hear him teach a class at the Lusters Gate Community Church on his new favorite topic, "The Flood & The Final Judgment." Whitcomb then preached on Colossians 3:1–3 to an overflow crowd including some Intervarsity Fellowship students from Virginia Polytechnical Institute (VPI, now Virginia Tech). That evening, about 20 people came to the Morris home for a Bible study and prayer. Although Whitcomb heard Morris give a scientific lecture in Winona Lake in 1953, this was the first time either one had heard the other speak on the Bible!

The following day, Monday, Dr. Whitcomb followed Dr. Morris to VPI and attended his 9:00 lecture on Hydraulics of Flow in Open Channels. About 20 students in the post-grad division were present. Whitcomb noted in his diary:

*Visited my old dorm, Lane Hall ('43-44) and at 11:00 I lectured to the class on Costal Hydraulics ('Wave pressures and*

The Genesis of *The Genesis Flood*

*Forces') on 'The Biblical Flood — Its Historicity and Signifi-
cance' About 20 attended. Senie and I drove to Roanoke to visit
Bible bookstore and do sightseeing. It poured rain. At 6:30 I
spoke to VPI IVF group of 10 students on II Tim 3:16. Discussed for ½ hour.*

The next morning, the Whitcombs packed up to get an early start to
the conference in Tennessee.

Unfortunately, I remember the visit to Blacksburg very well. On
the night that we arrived in Blacksburg, the Whitcomb children were
in the front yard of the Morris home with Morris children and some
neighborhood kids. There was some pushing and shoving of the visitors, eventually resulting in a fist fight between an older kid and a
younger kid who was only 5 years old (me). Although I won the fight
(as I remember), it brought great embarrassment to my dad and mom.
Only recently, while reviewing Dad's diaries and letters, did I know
what he was doing there.

*Extensive Feedback on the Arguments*

With publication and distribution of *The Genesis Flood*, both Drs.
Whitcomb and Morris began receiving letters and other feedback
from those who read the book — and most of them were very good. A
number of book reviews also began emerging that were a mix of strong
positive or negative, with little in the middle.

The Evangelical Theological Society (ETS) met at Grace Seminary
on May 12–13. About 35 scholars attended from 14 schools. Dr. Whitcomb was elected the Chairman of the Midwest District. The plans for a
joint ETS-ASA meeting in Goshen, Indiana, on June 24–25 was noted.

Prior to the ETS-ASA meeting, Dr. William J. Tinkle, who was
now retired, drove the 20 miles on old country roads from his home
in North Manchester, Indiana, to Winona Lake to speak at length
with Dr. Whitcomb.[4] Dr. Tinkle was "thrilled" with *The Genesis Flood*.
But he was deeply concerned about the trends in the ASA. Dr. Tinkle
was perplexed how so many young earth creationists could "just drift
along." He noted that those scientists in the ASA who read *The Genesis
Flood* and accepted its arguments must agree that the ASA, who had

4. John Whitcomb, letter to Henry Morris, May 28, 1961.

just published *Evolution and Christian Thought Today* edited by Russell Mixter, was radically wrong in its approach. Tinkle had already written to nearly a dozen creationists to explore the possibility of a new association, perhaps informal in nature.

## ETS-ASA Meeting in Goshen, Indiana

Early evidence of the growing impact of *The Genesis Flood* on the Christian world emerged at the ETS-ASA joint meeting at Goshen College on June 24–25.[5] A number of papers were presented by different scientists, as usual. Dr. Whitcomb was very impressed by a scientist named Duane Gish with a Ph.D. in biochemistry from the University of California, Berkeley, in 1953, and recommended that Morris reach out to him.[6]

On June 15, the second day of the conference, two papers with a "good Biblical emphasis" were presented by Dr. G. Douglas Young and Dr. James Bales. Following the presentations, the chairman asked for comments from Dr. Edwin Y. Monsma[7] and Dr. Whitcomb. Monsma pointed out the importance of accepting the biblically revealed framework of historical sequences, the six days of creation, and the impact of the Edenic curse and of the Flood. He then gave a strong endorsement of *The Genesis Flood*. Dr. Whitcomb highlighted the privilege of having God's truth available to us and trying to prove that man came from animals, or prove the uniformitarian approach to geology, is fruitless because God tells us these are false ideas. Thus, for Christian scientists, such as ETS-ASA members, discussions aimed at supporting these false ideas are "off limits."

This sparked a strong rebuttal by Dr. G. Douglas Young, who rejected the idea that some areas of science are "off limits" to Christians. Whitcomb stood by his statement and emphasized, again, that this was *not* to imply that Christian men of science should not investigate such

---

5. Summarized from the John Whitcomb diary entries of June 14–15, 1961, and a letter from John Whitcomb to Henry Morris on June 19, 1961.
6. Duane Gish, Ph.D. (1921–2013), would become a founding member of the Creation Research Society and eventually vice president of the Institute for Creation Research (ICR). He became famous for formal Creation-Evolution debates with prominent evolutionary biologists, usually held on university campuses.
7. Edwin Y. Monsma, Ph.D. (1894–1972), earned his Ph.D. from Michigan State and was a professor and chairman of the Department of Biology at Calvin College from 1954 to 1961.

areas, but rather that they should not study them with the attitude that these false theories might be <u>true</u>. This was followed by a panel discussion that clearly defined the dividing lines of theistic evolutionist and biblical creationist.

The second speaker of the afternoon session, Dr. Ralph D. Lowell, who was a professor of biology from North Park College, Chicago, outlined a number of reasons why the theory of evolution is unproven and encouraged everyone present (about 80 men) to study *The Genesis Flood*! After quoting several sections, he stated that he was surprised to find that one of the co-authors was *at the meeting*! He then asked Dr. Whitcomb to raise his hand and identify himself.

Following Lowell, others stood to repeat arguments or quote sections directly from the new book, and several key members of the ASA rose to endorse it (to John Whitcomb's shock). The result was that many pro-theistic evolutionists began to backtrack (and least publicly). Dr. Mixter, who was in attendance, remained completely silent, leaving the ASA president, Dr. Frank Cassel, to defend his position from Drs. Tinkle, Gish, Laird Harris, and others.

Drs. Tinkle and Harris, for example, forced Cassel to list the various types of evolutionary theory and then to state which one *he* held! He became completely confused, finally admitting that he did not believe in the evolution of man.

That evening during the group banquet, Dr. Cassel, in his remarks, publicly invited the ETS to help the ASA strengthen their doctrinal statement. This was especially important since the association was already losing members following the publication of the ASA-authored book celebrating a century of Darwinism and uniformitarian theories that Mixter had edited.

### After the ETS-ASA Meeting

By the end of the meeting, Dr. Whitcomb was also greatly encouraged by multiple words of appreciation and invitations from scientists, Bible teachers, and faculty at various colleges, universities, and churches, asking him to come and speak. Others faculty members and teachers told him that they were so impressed by the book that it was now required reading for all their students, who also raved about it.

# A Good and Faithful Servant

The direction and ineffectiveness of the ASA as pro-evolution was also exposed. Drs. Tinkle, Gish, Monsma, and Laird Harris, who were in attendance at the ETS-ASA meeting, along with Drs. Walter Lambert, John Grebe, Wilbert Ruscha, John Klotz, and Henry Morris banded together and, by 1963, had started the new and effective Creation Research Society.[8] Throughout the United States and the world, many other associations and societies were formed that were dedicated to the study of the physical world from the perspective of a six-day creation and a global Flood.

The tide had turned.

Dr. Whitcomb was especially encouraged by the very positive comments of Wilber Smith, who had so greatly challenged him with *Therefore Stand*; his four adopted fathers, Morris, Van Til, McClain, and Fullerton; and his biological father, Whit, who wrote these words to his son, "Renewed congratulations on a tremendous job so excellently done."

John Whitcomb knew that God had made him, saved him, preserved him through WWII, and molded him through multiple circumstances. His intellectual gifts, personality, physical endurance, experiences, and circumstances, in retrospect, were the perfect preparation for this task. But these gifts were also joined together with a will, passion, dedication, and perseverance in every sphere and every opportunity, to do all that he could for the glory of God.

There may be a parallel to this story linked to the words of Mordecai to Esther at a time of Jewish crisis in Babylon, "For if you remain silent at this time, relief and deliverance will arise for the Jews from another place. . . . And who knows whether you have not attained royalty for such a time as this?" (Esther 4:14; NASB 1995). John Whitcomb, in the 20th century, did not remain silent. He clearly and exactly spoke the Word of God — which went out and *did not return empty*, accomplishing what God desired and succeeding in the matter for which it was sent.[9]

John Whitcomb never wanted positions of power. He, like a good soldier, wanted to please his commander and his adopted fathers. And

---

8. H.M. Morris, *History of Modern Creationism*, Second edition (Santee, CA: Institute For Creation Research, 1993), 200.
9. See Isaiah 55:11.

he did receive words of true praise from all of them. But there is one more accolade that John Whitcomb is no longer waiting for. It is from his Heavenly Father, who will say:

> "Well done, good and faithful servant . . .
> enter thou into the joy of thy lord." [10]

## Postscript

John Whitcomb was actively involved in reviewing and editing this volume of his biography over a period of more than 10 years. A draft copy of the entire work was presented to him by the author in mid-January 2020. On the night of February 4, 2020, he handed his final edited copy of Chapter 16, "Edisene," to his son Donald, who had built a small apartment in the basement of his house where Prof. Whitcomb and his second wife, Norma, could live with family support. He told Don, "I am now finished," and went to bed. That night, he passed on to finally meet his Lord — February 5, 2020. He was 95 years old.

---

10. From Matthew 25:23.

## JCW Joins Faculty at Grace

**5.1** Donald Fullerton (center) visits Grace Seminary in 1951. Two of his favorite PEF students, Jack Whitcomb (left) and Johnny Rea (right) are completing their M.Div. degrees and will be joining the faculty. Fullerton would invite both of these young protégés to join the PEF council.

**5.2** John Whitcomb as a new faculty member at his desk in 1953 (left) and 1954 (right). Note the rapidly growing library in the background!

**5.3** Dr. Whitcomb (right, standing) teaching his Evidences and Apologetics class. This was the launching pad for his career and international notoriety (1954).

**5.4** Senie encouraged the Whitcombs to be active in social settings with the faculty along with other faculty and their wives outside of the classroom and office. From left, Edisene Whitcomb, John Whitcomb, Wendell Kent, Beverly Kent, Homer Kent Jr. (faculty), Homer Kent Sr. (faculty), and Alice Kent (1954).

**5.5** John Whitcomb receiving his Th.D. from Drs. Herman Hoyt and Alva J. McClain in May 1957. (Below) Title page of his 452-page dissertation.

THE GENESIS FLOOD:
AN INVESTIGATION OF ITS GEOGRAPHICAL EXTENT,
GEOLOGIC EFFECTS, AND CHRONOLOGICAL SETTING

BY

John C. Whitcomb, Jr.

Submitted in partial fulfillment of the requirements
for the degree of Doctor of Theology in
Grace Theological Seminary
May 1957

**5.6**  Dr. John C. Whitcomb (left) after completing his Th.D., seen here with other young faculty including Homer Kent Jr. (back), John Stoll (front center), and John Rea (right).

**5.7**  John Whitcomb standing in his office with his books and files. He has a figure of a Chinese man pulling a rickshaw on the filing cabinet as a reminder of the people of China.

**5.8** JCW in 1952 teaching about his personal observations and experiences in the Holy Land during his visit with the Flying Seminar.

Reverend & Mrs. John C. Whitcomb, Jr.
106 Thirteenth Street   Winona Lake, Indiana

Sept. 20, 1953

Dear Dr. Morris,

I greatly appreciated your paper on a Recent Creation and Universal Deluge which you read at the A.S.A. convention. I feel that your conclusions are scripturally valid, and therefore must be sustained by a fair examination of geologic evidence in time to come. My only regret is that so few trained Christian men of science are willing to let God's Word have the final say on these questions.

Your paper was most timely for me, because this fall we are beginning our two-year (4 hrs a week) cycle in O.T. studies here at Grace Seminary, and have already entered into a study of Genesis. I have adopted your views, as well as those of Rehwinkle, Nelson, and Price, and am presenting them to my class as preferable alternatives to the gap-theory and the day-age theory.

Many students have become interested in this matter as a result, and would like to have your mimeographed notes to study. Could you tell me how much 50 copies would cost? If you do not have that many, could I obtain your permission to mimeograph duplicates of the copy you gave me? I shall appreciate an answer at your earliest convenience.

May God richly bless you in your ministry for His glory.

Sincerely in Christ,
John C. Whitcomb, Jr.
Associate Prof. of O.T.
Grace Theological Seminary

**5.9** Copy of John Whitcomb's letter to Dr. Henry Morris in September 1953, initiating correspondence that would culminate in *The Genesis Flood* book (from Rebecca Morris Barber).

# Henry Morris

**5.10** Henry Morris at an engineering conference on the campus of the University of Pittsburgh in July 1959. John Whitcomb joined him to review the manuscript for *The Genesis Flood*. This was only the second time the two co-authors met in person.

**5.11** The Morris family visits Winona Lake in July 1960. Back row: Henry Morris and wife Mary Louise. Front row: Andy, Rebecca, Mary, and John.

**5.12** Henry Morris, John Whitcomb, and Charles H. Craig from Presbyterian & Reformed Publishing Company, who took the risk to publish a highly technical and controversial book, *The Genesis Flood.*

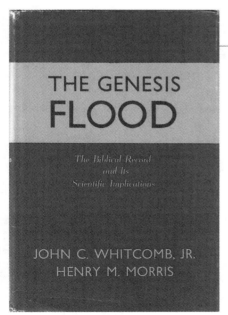

**5.13** *The Genesis Flood* is finally published in 1961.

**5.14** Henry Morris and John Whitcomb at a conference in Lansing, MI, in May 1966.

**5.15** Whitcomb and Morris reminiscing on the writing of *The Genesis Flood* and the impact on their lives and the lives of millions (April 1984).

**5.16** John Whitcomb, John Morris, and Henry Morris at the Institute for Creation Research, November 10, 1995. Copyright © Institute for Creation Research, used with permission.

**5.17** One of the last meetings between John Whitcomb and Henry Morris in Southern California in January 2003. Copyright © Institute for Creation Research, used with permission.

**5.18** John Whitcomb is seen with his grandson, John C. Whitcomb III. Dr. Whitcomb loved clever jokes and uninhibited laughter (summer 2019).

**5.19** The final meeting of the author with his father, January 18, 2020. My dad was shocked to receive a completed draft of Volume 1 and worked on the final edits until the night he died, February 5, 2020. His constant admonition to me was, "This cannot be about me, but about what Christ has done for me and through me."

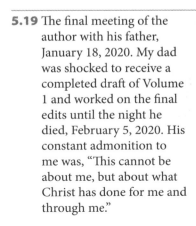

# OTHER BOOKS IN THE
# HENRY MORRIS
## SIGNATURE COLLECTION

978-1-68344-175-5

978-1-68344-161-8

978-1-68344-160-1

978-1-68344-197-7

978-1-68344-214-1

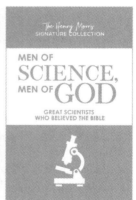

978-1-68344-237-0

# THE COMPLETE HENRY MORRIS STUDY BIBLE

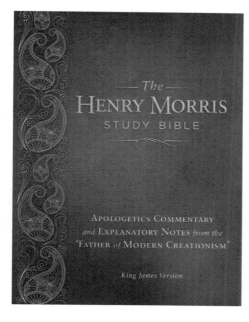